ANDREW ROGERS RHYTHMS OF LIFE

Silvia Langen

ANDREW ROGERS
RHYTHMS OF LIFE

A Global Land Art Project

PRESTEL
Munich · London · New York

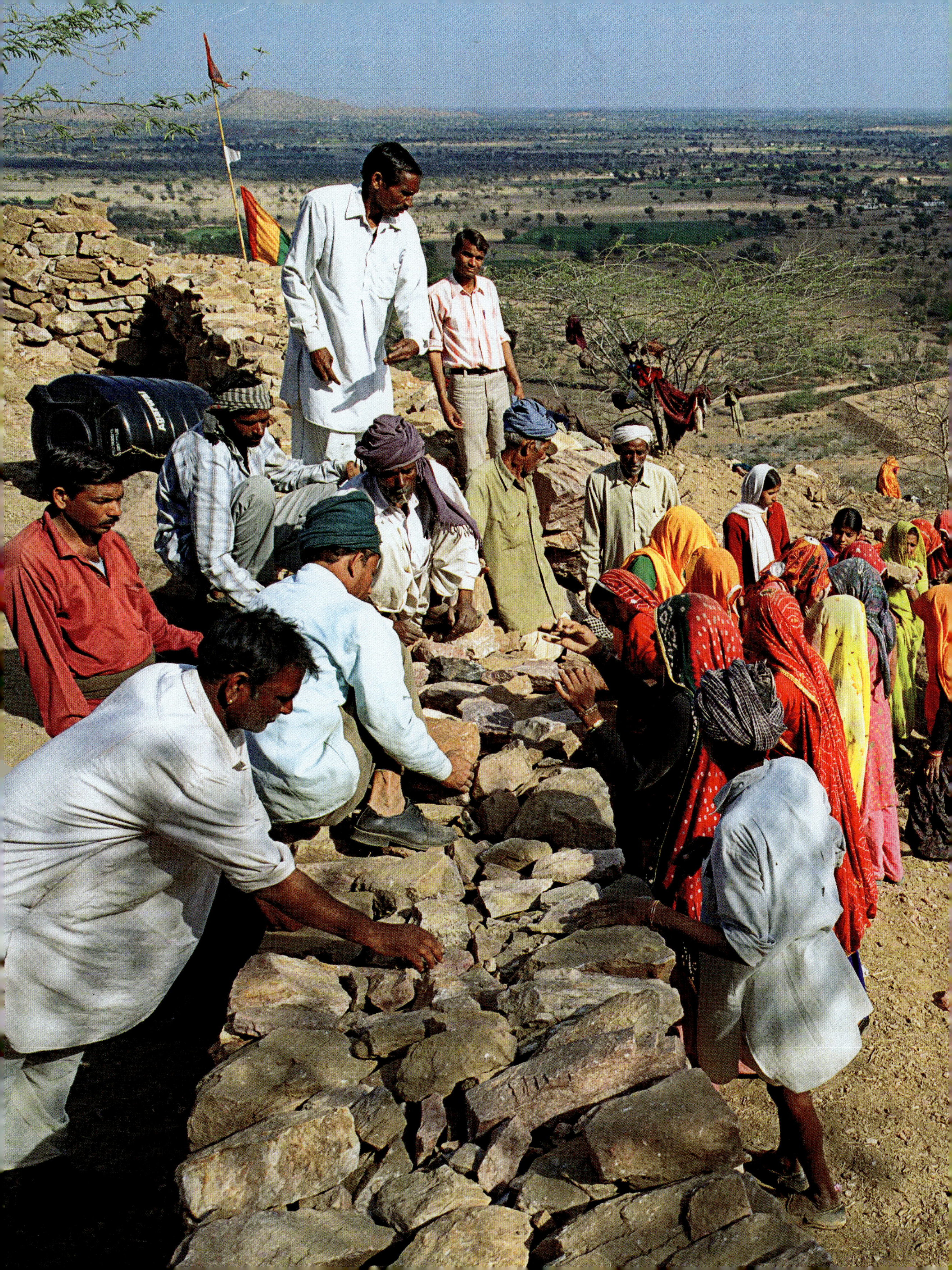

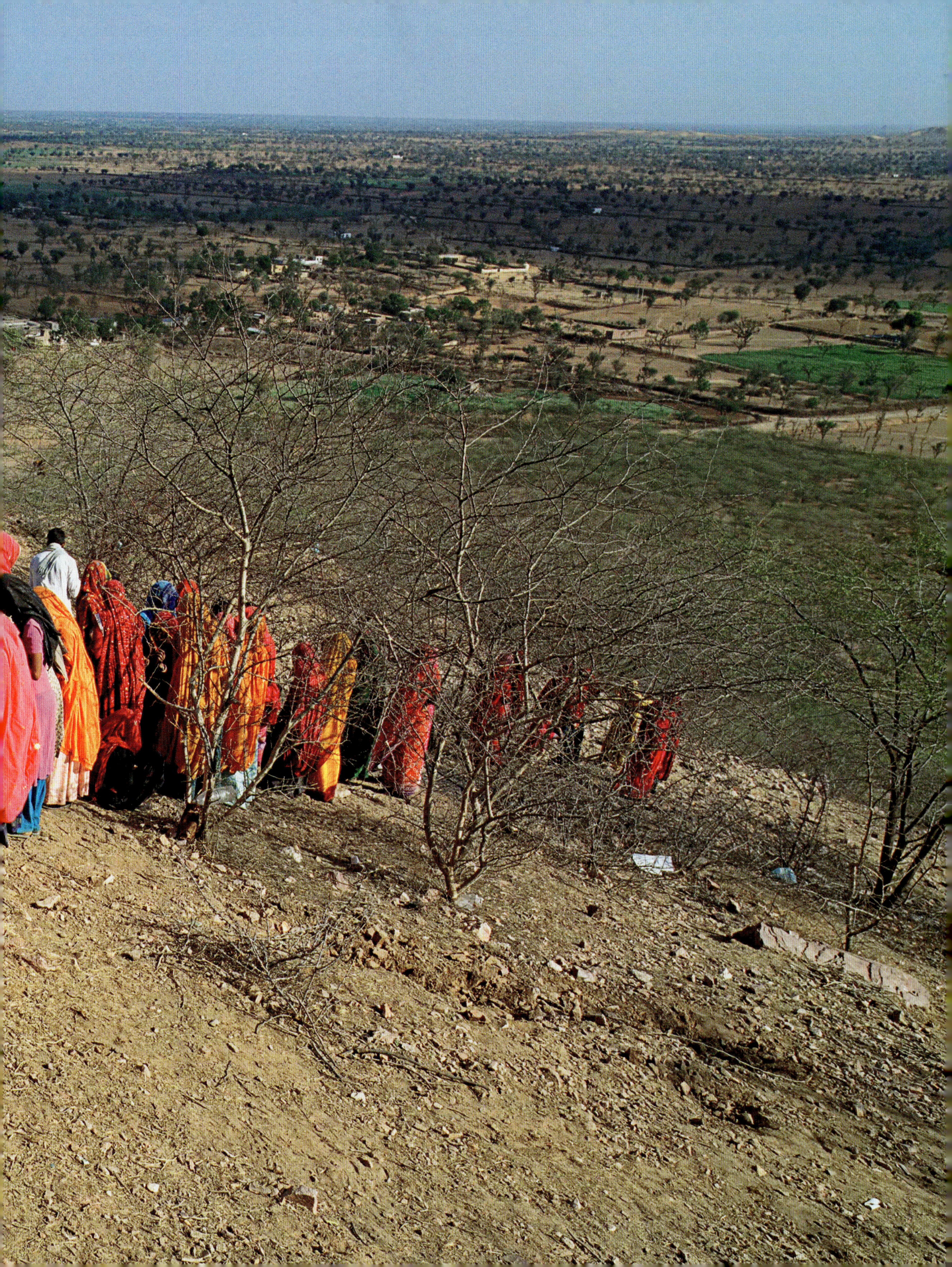

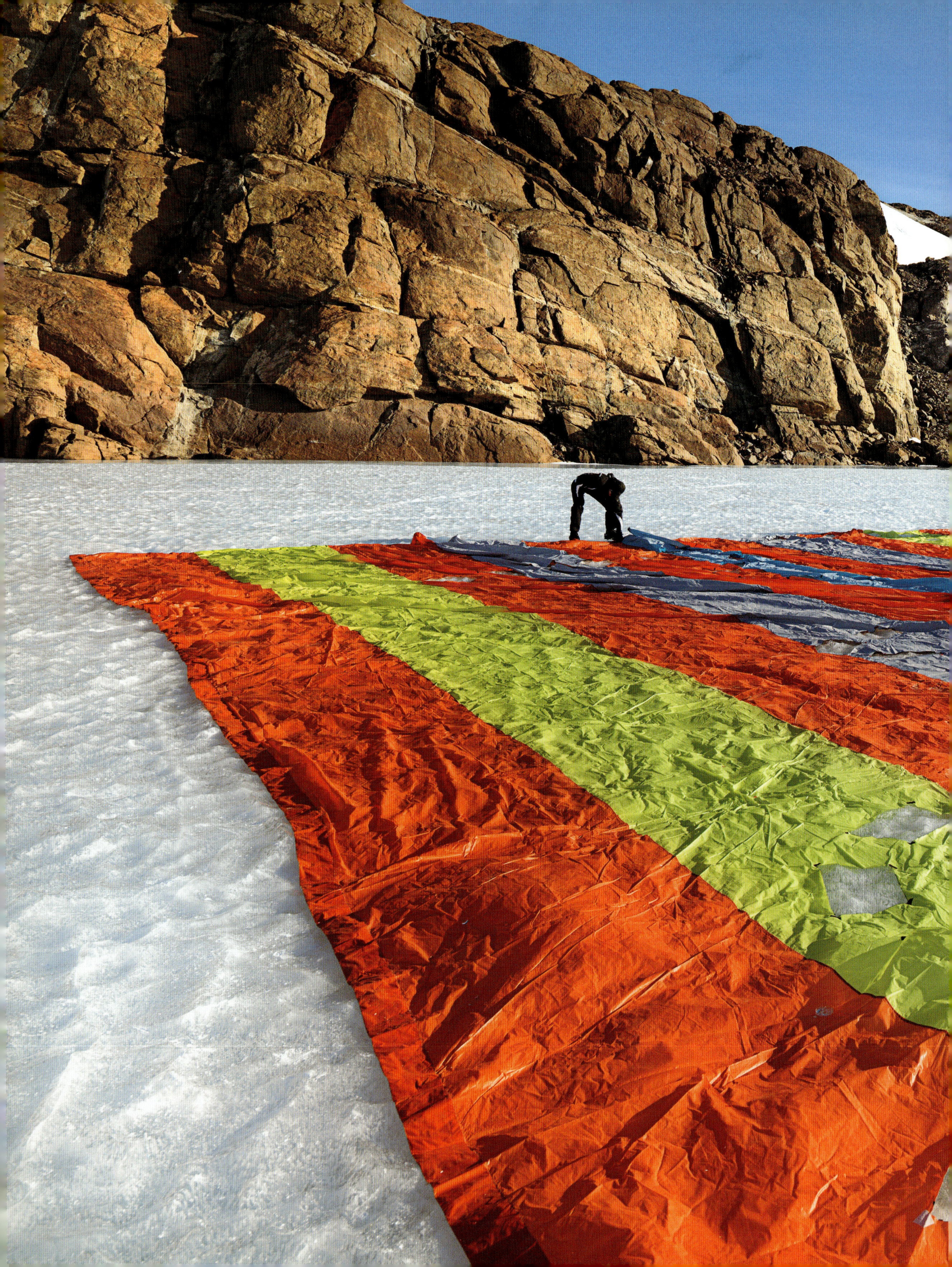

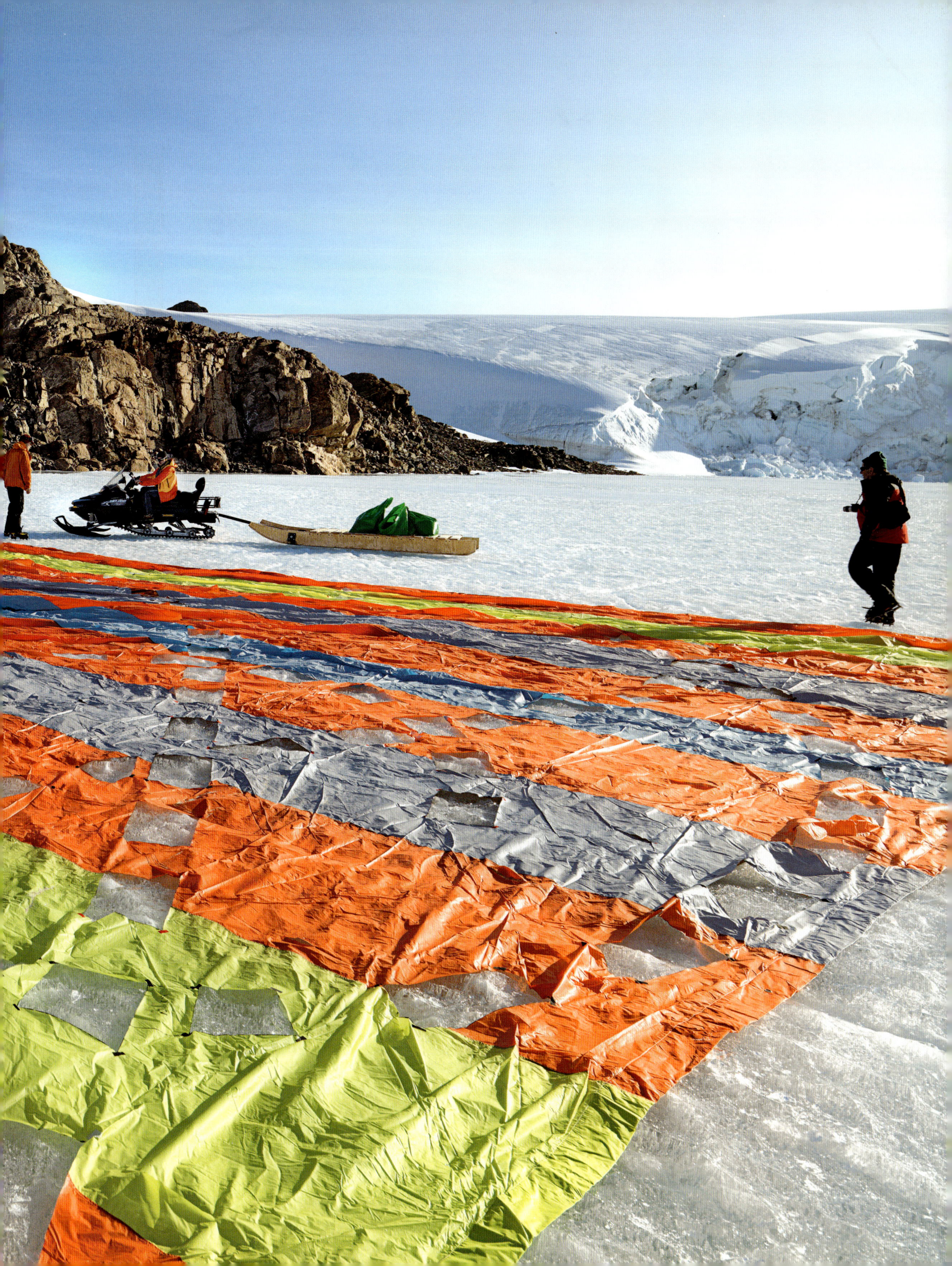

CONTENTS

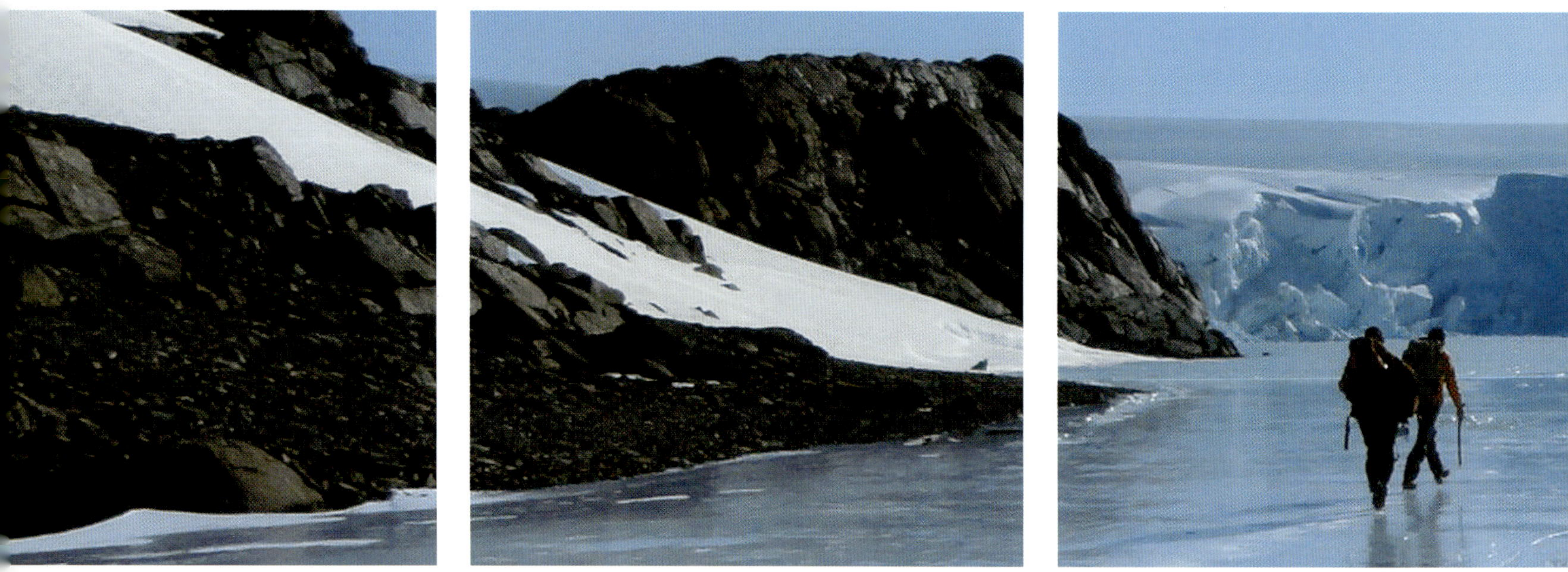

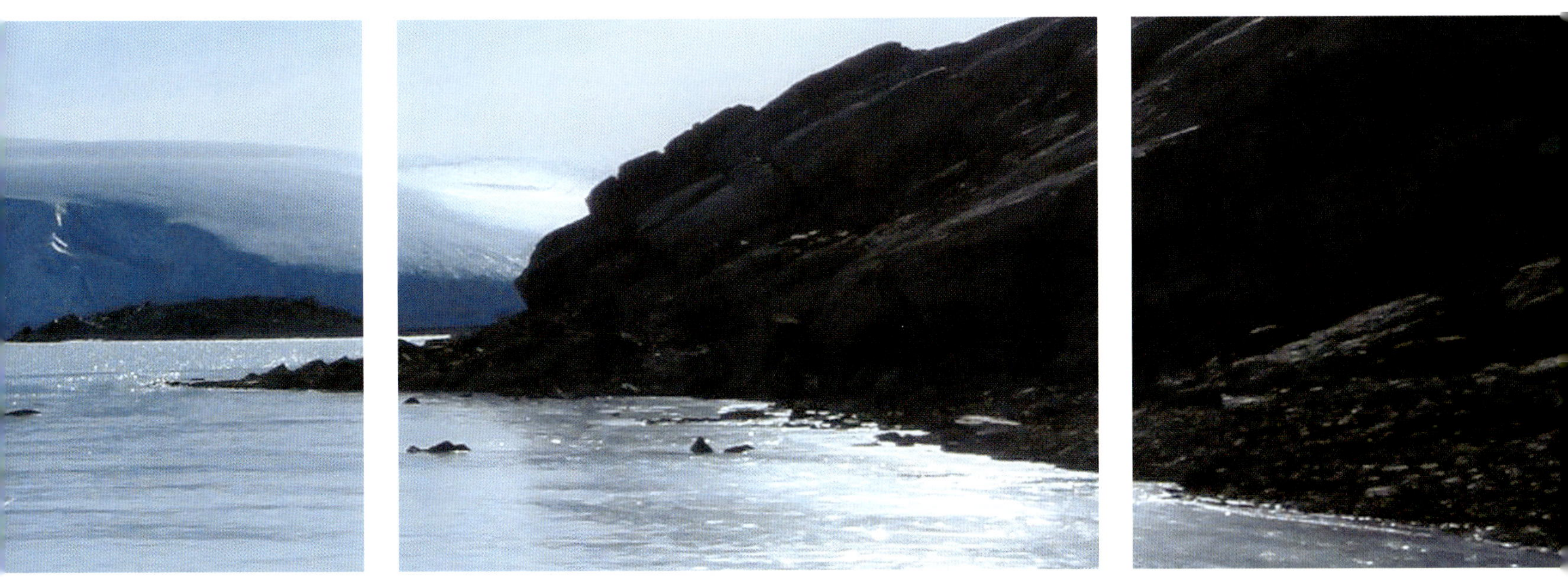

PROJECTS

1. ARAVA DESERT, ISRAEL
2. ATACAMA DESERT, CHILE
3. ALTIPLANO, BOLIVIA
4. KURUNEGALA, SRI LANKA
5. GEELONG, AUSTRALIA
6. AKUREYRI, ICELAND
7. GOBI DESERT, CHINA
8. RAJASTHAN, INDIA
9. POKHARA AND JOMSOM, NEPAL
10. SPIŠSKÝ HRAD AND THE HIGH TATRAS, SLOVAKIA
11. MOJAVE DESERT, UNITED STATES
12. CHYULU HILLS, KENYA
13. DAKSHIN GANGOTRI GLACIER, ANTARCTICA
14. CAPPADOCIA, TURKEY
15. NAMIB DESERT, NAMIBIA
16. UTAH, USA
17. IBIZA, SPAIN

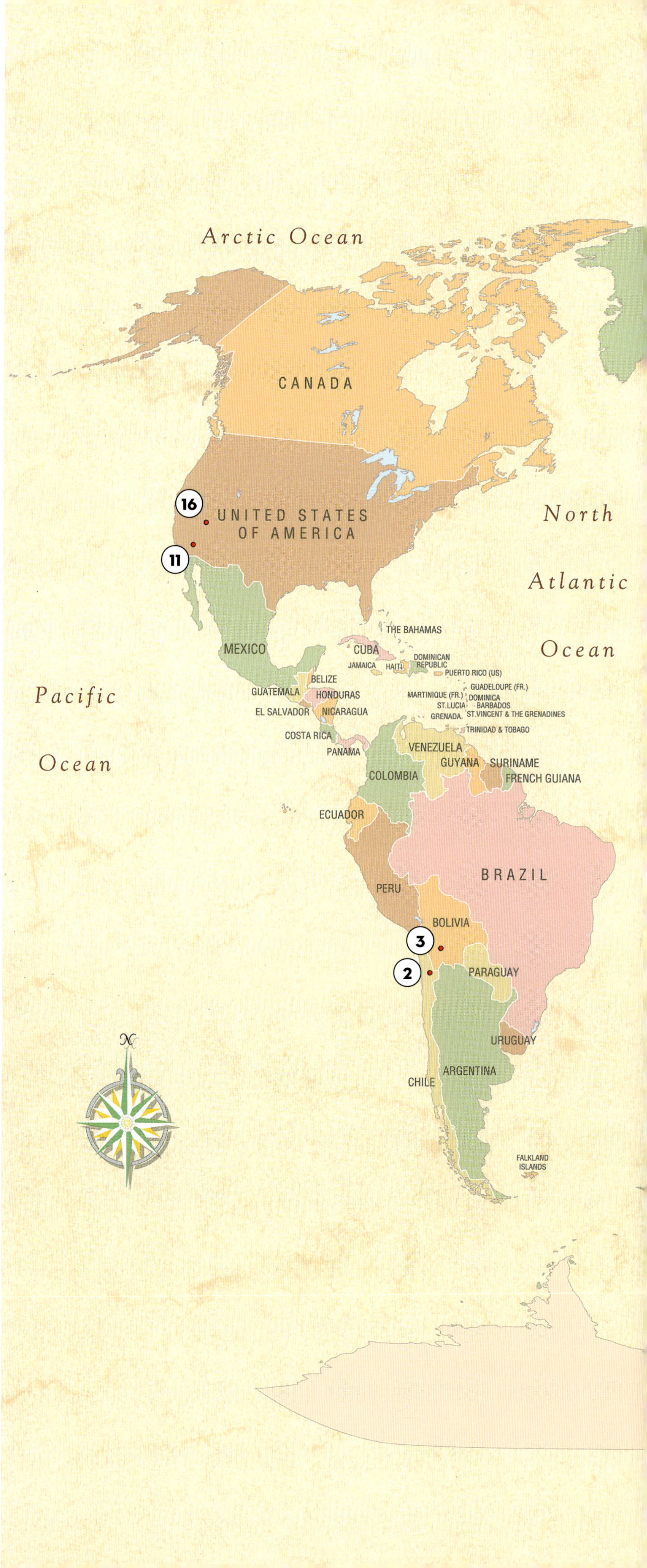

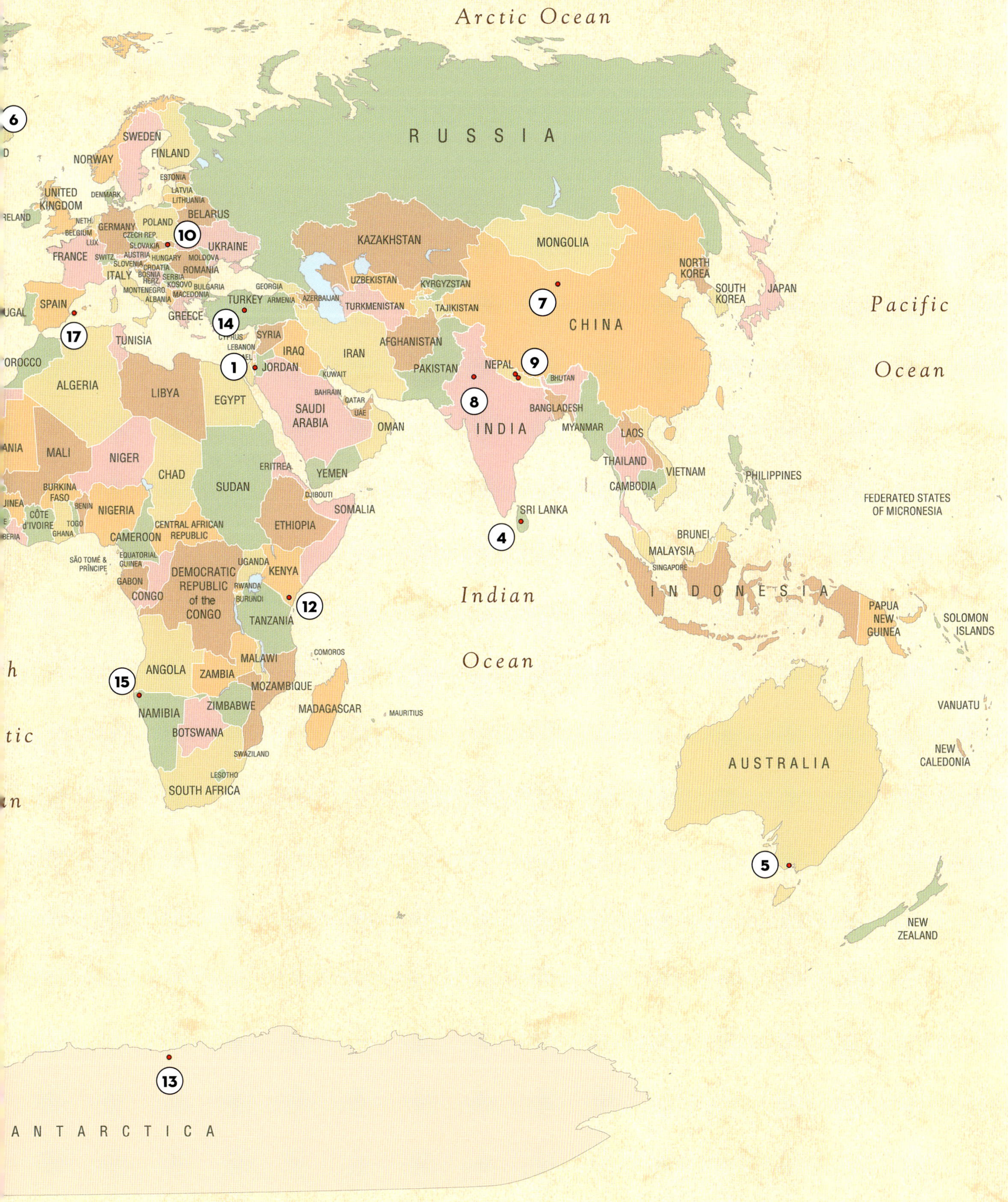
Arctic Ocean
RUSSIA
Pacific Ocean
Indian Ocean
ANTARCTICA
AUSTRALIA
CHINA
INDIA
INDONESIA
SWEDEN
FINLAND
NORWAY
ESTONIA
LATVIA
LITHUANIA
UNITED KINGDOM
DENMARK
BELARUS
POLAND
GERMANY
NETH.
BELGIUM
LUX.
CZECH REP.
SLOVAKIA
UKRAINE
FRANCE
SWITZ.
AUSTRIA
HUNGARY
MOLDOVA
SLOVENIA
CROATIA
ROMANIA
ITALY
BOSNIA HERZ.
SERBIA
KOSOVO
BULGARIA
MONTENEGRO
MACEDONIA
ALBANIA
GREECE
SPAIN
TURKEY
GEORGIA
ARMENIA
AZERBAIJAN
CYPRUS
LEBANON
SYRIA
IRAQ
IRAN
JORDAN
KUWAIT
BAHRAIN
QATAR
UAE
SAUDI ARABIA
OMAN
YEMEN
KAZAKHSTAN
UZBEKISTAN
KYRGYZSTAN
TURKMENISTAN
TAJIKISTAN
AFGHANISTAN
PAKISTAN
NEPAL
BHUTAN
BANGLADESH
MYANMAR
LAOS
THAILAND
VIETNAM
CAMBODIA
SRI LANKA
MONGOLIA
NORTH KOREA
SOUTH KOREA
JAPAN
PHILIPPINES
BRUNEI
MALAYSIA
SINGAPORE
PAPUA NEW GUINEA
SOLOMON ISLANDS
FEDERATED STATES OF MICRONESIA
VANUATU
NEW CALEDONIA
NEW ZEALAND
TUNISIA
ALGERIA
LIBYA
EGYPT
MALI
NIGER
CHAD
SUDAN
ERITREA
DJIBOUTI
ETHIOPIA
SOMALIA
BURKINA FASO
BENIN
NIGERIA
CÔTE d'IVOIRE
TOGO
GHANA
CAMEROON
CENTRAL AFRICAN REPUBLIC
SÃO TOMÉ & PRÍNCIPE
EQUATORIAL GUINEA
GABON
CONGO
DEMOCRATIC REPUBLIC of the CONGO
UGANDA
KENYA
RWANDA
BURUNDI
TANZANIA
COMOROS
ANGOLA
ZAMBIA
MALAWI
MOZAMBIQUE
MADAGASCAR
MAURITIUS
NAMIBIA
ZIMBABWE
BOTSWANA
SWAZILAND
LESOTHO
SOUTH AFRICA
1
4
5
6
7
8
9
10
12
13
14
15
17

RHYTHMS OF LIFE

THE LARGEST LAND ART PROJECT IN THE WORLD

Since the 1980s, more and more spectacular land art projects are being created far away from big cities and for the first time outside of the United States and Europe. Although these art landscapes can normally only be reached with great effort, the synthesis of nature and art obviously fascinates a great many people—artists, visitors, and local residents alike. In the truest sense of the word, working in an open landscape gives artists space to freely think, experiment, and work in new, greater dimensions. They are in a direct and permanent dialogue with the environment, which is itself a work of art whose infinite facets are constantly reinvented in harmony with the time of day and the seasons as well as with the weather. Ideally, art and nature not only enhance each other but ultimately merge to become a new and unique gesamtkunstwerk.

The internationally renowned Australian sculptor Andrew Rogers has succeeded in doing this with *Rhythms of Life*. Since 1999, he has produced fifty-one land art sculptures in sixteen countries, across all seven continents; these stone structures are thematically interrelated. *Rhythms of Life* is Andrew Rogers's life work. The largest contemporary project of its kind in the world, Rogers has introduced a new dimension into land art—the global work of art.

GEOGLYPHS AS GLOBAL ARTWORK

They are archetypal symbols of civilization in the most extreme topographies—be it the Gobi Desert, the South American Altiplano, the African steppe, or the glacial ice of Antarctica—where the artist makes a mark in the truest sense of the word: he builds them into the open landscape as geoglyphs, gigantic drawings and structures from local rock. Andrew Rogers goes to the limits of what is possible with respect to their dimensions. His sculptures are deliberately arranged in such large proportions so that they are clearly recognizable on satellite images from space. With *Rhythms of Life* Andrew Rogers frames his personal artistic answer to the big questions of our society, which is faced with enormous challenges: globalization with the threat of the loss of collective memory and independent cultural identities, with climate change, new technologies, and increasing commercialization.

THE TOPOGRAPHICAL CONTEXT

Like Michael Heizer and Robert Smithson, protagonists of the first generation of land art artists in the 1960s, Rogers consciously anchors art in the landscape in a lasting way. Land art only explains itself in a topographical context. Andrew Rogers also wants to provoke, to challenge viewers to reflect on the past in reference to the present and the future and to act responsibly and oriented toward positive values. He therefore creates highly aesthetic sites that invite one to contemplate. "It is about the importance of the perspective that we are caretakers and have responsibilities to those around us and to those who will follow," Rogers explains. "We receive the environmental consequences created by our predecessors. In turn we leave a consequence for our descendants. The present will be reflected in the future. If we have regard for our earth, what should be the criteria we live by?"

As an Australian who himself lives in a country in which nature is omnipresent, working with and in nature is a matter of course. Surrounded by the whole gamut of highly diverse, gigantic, and above all often virgin landscape backdrops of a continent, he feels intimately familiar and connected with all kinds of topographies. Like his bronze sculptures, his land art is therefore time and again an expression of his own fascination with the diversity of nature and the place of the individual in relation to it. In this respect, Andrew Rogers's approach is very similar to that of European land art artists such as Andy Goldsworthy and Jacek Tylicki. In the early 1970s they developed a new land art orientation that no longer focused on sociocritical messages but concentrated completely on nature and its aesthetic. Existing structures in nature are identified and placed in an artistic context, an extreme example of which is the British land art artist Andy Goldsworthy, who brings together impermanent natural materials such as leaves or branches to produce ephemeral, fragile installations.

OF ROCKS

Andrew Rogers also works with natural materials. However, he concentrates on massive material, rock in all of its manifestations—from gravel and boulders to large columns of stone that he in part processes. For him, rocks and earth are the fundamental components of the geography of our world. Rocks are also intrinsic to the entire history of humankind. They were of major importance from the beginning of human civilization, be it as caves as the first dwellings or bifaces used as hunting weapons and tools. People continue to have a special relationship with stones to this very day.

Fascinated by the natural sciences, in his creative work Andrew Rogers often references forms and structures that, like the Fibonacci sequence, describe growth as a recurring underlying pattern in nature.

THE LEITMOTIF *RHYTHMS OF LIFE*

With titles such as *Becoming, Growth, Balance*, or *Gaia, Mother Earth*, and *Living*, Rogers concentrated on the creative in his early bronze sculptures—on growth and decay, on matter, on the universe's system of order. It is not for nothing that the selection of his leitmotif *Rhythms of Life* for his land art makes reference to the title of a bronze sculpture, produced in 1996, in which he celebrated the play of forces: a calligraphic zigzag ribbon winds around an ascending line, on which in turn a sphere appears to balance. Rogers describes this dynamic structure as "embodying the changing rhythms of life. These rhythms are reflected in the juxtaposition of shape and line echoing the unpredictable journey through life." They are forces that can also be felt in music and elicit something like an inner resonance or vibration of the soul in the listener or viewer. This formalist composition of the various elements became his personal signature and the thematic bracket for all of his land art projects within his global mega-project. The *Rhythms of Life* sculpture can therefore be found as an independent built stone drawing in each of his individual land art projects around the globe.

ART TO NATURE

As is the case with Andy Goldsworthy, for Andrew Rogers there is no endpoint or point of culmination, no finished product in his art. On the contrary: he consciously accepts the deterioration of the work of art, the return of art to nature; it is predetermined. In the same way that life is defined by birth and death, art is also ultimately meant to be impermanent. Andrew Rogers therefore makes no claim to eternity or even longevity with his installations and structures made of stone found in the immediate environment. The artworks are meant to deliberately enter the life cycle of nature. They weather, deteriorate, and disintegrate. This process of development is an inherent part of his land art. Yet unlike Goldsworthy, whose art is rendered visible in the instant of impermanence and in the end leaves behind no traces whatsoever in nature, Andrew Rogers arranges his geoglyphs in nature in such a way that although still ephemeral, they will not disappear for centuries and consequently will lay a long trail of memory and contemplation.

LOCAL PEOPLE

What is completely new in land art is Andrew Rogers's inclusion of local people in the conception and construction of his installations. It is not enough for him to develop art in reference to a specific topography; rather, art, nature, and individuals need one another and also have taken on their respective roles in his artistic work on equal footing. Thus he clearly goes further than his prominent predecessors Smithson and Heizer, who were content with the formal local integration of their works made of earth, or nature artists such as Andy Goldsworthy, who place their focus on the impermanence of the artworks. Andrew Rogers extends the context of the work of art through factors such as history; the environment that influences the rhythm of the lives both of local people and around the world; and the meaning of myths that are passed down over generations and give people their cultural identity.

"We define our existence from the interplay of space and time. Nowadays we live in a world where technology is constantly advancing but human nature is not. That is why the old values from the past are so valuable for us today. Our roots are in ancient civilizations and cultures whose legacy we still carry around with us today. That is why I want to connect the old and the new." In his land art, Rogers unites art, history, archaeology, religion, and culture as a complex unit—the foundations of our civilization. By rendering them visible he wants to sensitize viewers, challenging them to participate in developing ethical principles and moral responsibility for a future oriented toward sustainability. His choice of topographies for his installations therefore has special meaning. He finds them for the most part in remote regions where urbanization has not yet occurred, where people still live according to tradition and in close touch with nature. The artist's central concern is developing an awareness and appreciation of precisely these things: "I believe that history and culture are something essential for people," Rogers emphasizes time after time.

It is therefore part of his concept that wherever possible he involves the local population in the project from the very beginning. Collectively they seek symbols in their myths, in archives, or local museums that are important for their cultural identity. These include numerous universal archetypes that can be understood the world over: a lion with two bodies as a symbol for strength, or a palm tree as a tree of life. Rogers sees them as "optimistic symbols of life and regeneration—expressive and suggestive of human striving and introspection." Yet these also stand for the worldwide intercultural dialogue beyond time and space. For weeks at a time, together with the village community he layers stone upon stone, going to the limits of what is possible with the material and the dimension of his installations. It is a gigantic undertaking until the enormous artworks are completed, often with groups of hundreds of people who assist the artist and only speak the local dialect. A network of communication must be set up with the aid of interpreters; workers have to be organized, sophisticated logistics drawn up, and technical problems have to be solved with the simplest of means. Sometimes it is only construction vehicles, sometimes the Chinese army, other times it is Bolivian farmers or African nomads who form a long human chain for the purpose of bringing stones to the construction site and piling them up according to Andrew Rogers's concepts. At the same time, Rogers places the utmost importance on men and women's being equal, and even paid and treated above the customary level. For it is precisely this social component, working collectively with a total of 7,500 individuals, but also celebrating together according to local traditions and identifying oneself with the works of art as a collective goal that are important factors in his artistic concept.

DRAWINGS ON EARTH

He understands his art as "art created by many people for many people." Rogers's geoglyphs were inspired by one of the earliest forms of land art: the Nazca Lines near the Andes in Peru, huge images that were carved into the earth with sharp sticks around 800 BC. Archaeologists have interpreted these images as relics of a prehistoric civilization that was rich in mythology and rituals. They could have been sacred sites along pilgrimage routes. Rogers takes up the idea and makes his own marks in nearly untouched landscapes to connect himself with prehistoric or at least still primordial civilizations that venerate the earth as the most supreme deity, as Mother Earth, a goddess who created everything that is alive. However, unlike the Nazca Lines Rogers does not carve his symbolic motifs into the ground but constructs them in enormous dimensions as stone walls that are meters high. As such, these built images are best recognized from a bird's-eye view—be it from an elevated standpoint in the surroundings or high up in the clouds from a hot-air balloon. Rogers also wanted his geoglyphs to be visible from space. For the first time in the history of contemporary art, an artist had high-resolution satellite images taken from an altitude of between 440 and 770 kilometers (275 and 480 miles) for the purpose of making his land art understandable for viewers as a global work of art.

"I WANT PEOPLE TO TOUCH THE WALLS"

He seeks the interaction of visitors to the sites and above all the local inhabitants. He wants them to be able to experience his installations with all of their senses. "I want people to touch the walls, to run around, to hide in them, to climb them. Our sense of touch can teach us a lot about the relativity of our bodies to the space or objects that surround them. It also helps us understand form and scale. It helps us sense the magnitude of the vista we are in at the time and assists us to understand that spatial experiences affect feelings and thoughts. Tactile qualities affirm our sense of the world and our three-dimensional selves."

THROUGH TIME AND SPACE

BY ANDREW ROGERS

These connected drawings on the surface of the earth refer to the physical building blocks of history and civilization while addressing the interconnection of humanity throughout time and space.

A unique intent of this undertaking is to have these drawings on the earth photographed by specifically commissioned satellites from a distance of between 440 and 770 kilometers (275 and 480 miles) above the earth, revealing the structures as specks in space and moments in time—reminders that we are part of the environment, not in control of it.

The *Rhythms of Life* land art structures establish consecrated space. The structures denote the separation from the ordinary and provide contemplative settings.

It is a group of structures in time that weave together our conduct and thoughts with the environment. The process of building structures establishes communal distinctions and linkages. These structures enlarge a limited definition of "ruins" by taking the ruins into the domain of speculation. The ruins have been initiated with ceremonies and act as catalysts for reflection within their special space. There is blurring of the physical and conceptual boundaries between structure and environment, and exploring the search for heritage.

This is an open-ended conversation, which everyone is invited to be part of.

THE *RHYTHMS OF LIFE* SCULPTURE

Rhythms of Life is a dynamic structure in space that embodies the changing rhythms of life. These rhythms are reflected in the juxtaposition of shape and line echoing the unpredictable journey through life.

Rhythms of Life is an exploration of our state of reality as we interact with what is around us. The rhythms of our life oscillate as do our emotions as we move through a series of points punctuating time and space. These connected points comprise a line representing the individual's journey and the essence of life.

Rhythms of Life is a reflection of our society, our dreams, and our aspirations. It is a reflection of our interaction with people and the interdependency with the environment around us, including the states of change we pass through and the challenges that confront us. It is the interplay between the two certainties in life: birth and death.

To express oneself is a timeless need; this sculpture is a manifestation of this need. It is a melding of intelligence and imagination, a reflection of an ability to put concepts into form. It is an expression of the heart, not just the application of a skill. These ideas manifest in the bronze sculptural composition *Rhythms of Life*.

It is this form and its encompassing philosophy from which the *Rhythms of Life* geoglyphs are derived.

GEOGLYPHS

Geoglyphs constructed in desert and altiplano landscapes, on sheer rock monoliths and gentle slopes, comprise the *Rhythms of Life*. They are metaphors for the eternal cycle of life, growth, and all the attendant emotions that color human existence. They are optimistic symbols of life and regeneration—expressive and suggestive of human striving and introspection.

Spectacular views are found distant from the city and, with an unfettered outlook, create in us the reverence that natural scenery and vastness of space can generate. The sublime is expressed where the dome of the sky meets the pristine surface of the earth. It is in this terrain that the spiritual calls.

Creating earth art in the form of contemporary geoglyphs is to reach back in history and to civilizations past. They are giant metaphors linked to the prehistoric traffic routes of ancient inhabitants and, as such, borrow from the ancients to devise new forms. But their messages are greater than their forms. Derived from beliefs, rock carvings, and paintings, and related to my sculptures, they invoke what was awesome and wondrous to the hunter and to our predecessors.

The scale of the geoglyphs is imposing, even in their massive desert and altiplano landscapes, under great expanses of sky. Geoglyphs can alter the space and light around them in ways that cause heightened awareness. The geoglyphs provide a spatial experience that enhances the colors of sunrise and sunset and articulates the silence of the land; they are a fulcrum for contemplation. Set in this theater of nature as they are, the geoglyphs reflect the absolute freedom to create art in this environment.

Geoglyphs suffer the wild vagaries of time, kissed by the hot sun and lashed by storms. Geoglyphs correlate with their surrounding environments. They are made of rocks and the earth, which are basic components of the geography of our world but are also intrinsic to the history of civilizations both old and new.

This is what intrigues me. Rocks for me are about the present focus of our being. Rocks bring me together with the earth and being part of nature. They are the components that allow the use of imagination to create. Stone is enjoyable—it is part of Mother Earth. The earth that geoglyphs are laid down upon is also part of their structure and a dimension of the form. The structures closely follow the contours of the ground upon which they rest.

If people encounter them, they should walk through and climb on these geoglyphs. The tactile sense we all possess helps us to discover the relativity of our bodies to the space or objects that surround them. It also helps us understand form and scale. It helps us sense the magnitude of the vista we are in at the time, and assists us to understand those spatial experiences that affect feelings and thoughts. Tactile qualities affirm our sense of the world and our three-dimensional selves. Forms that help us to achieve this knowledge are perceived with an immediacy that is more effective than intellectual explanation.

To touch is to absorb emotionally, with our heart and mind, the significance of the geoglyph. There is special enjoyment creating large-scale forms that are eventually a minute element within the grandeur of nature—preferably sited outdoors so they can interact with space, varying light, and topography. No matter how large the form, it is just a speck in space. There is a message inculcated in the form—the reaction to this message is what is important. The eye leads, the mind follows. Creation of the form is one element, but the creation of the idea and experience derived from the form are central.

Time and movement are integral to life and geoglyphs—time to travel to exotic locations and to traverse around the geoglyphs, comprehend them, and the impressions received—time for the mental journey of our mind's eye.

The *Rhythms of Life* geoglyph's meaning is not absolute, but is contingent upon personal history and memory—and reaching back into the distant past—and on individual projections into the future. How geoglyphs are received depends on individual perception.

Physical and mental approaches to the geoglyphs provide an opening to how the past is encountered. They extend the continuity of history and project into the future that which may become future history. They are a contemporary symbol for contemplation about

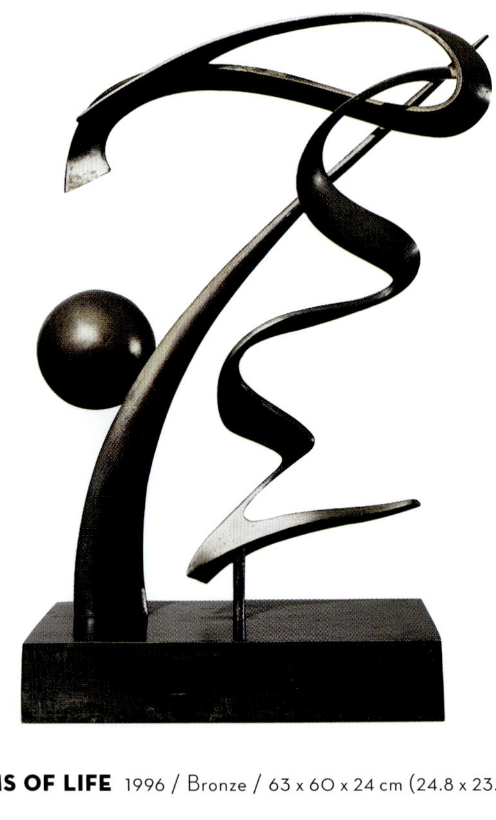

RHYTHMS OF LIFE 1996 / Bronze / 63 x 60 x 24 cm (24.8 x 23.5 x 9.5 in.)

past society and its possible meaning. Geoglyphs are about time and the depth of our heritage.

Geoglyphs are about imagination and ideas—not simply about physical structures. They encompass feelings and dreams. It is taking the ordinary and making it extraordinary. Random stones lying on the earth's surface are rearranged into an inimitable form.

THE PROCESS AND EXPERIENCE

The act of creating geoglyphs is a huge logistical exercise that has found an artist struggling with teams of up to 1,000 indigenous people, having to communicate complex instructions in a foreign language, and moving thousands of tons of rocks in all types of physical conditions: dust storms; desert heat; at high altitudes, panting with less-than-normal oxygen; and in freezing temperatures with snow falling. Such exercises, redolent with persistence and fortitude, are only undertaken in the service of the imagination. The final form will only come into being and resonate at a particular moment—a moment that has taken years of effort to arrive.

Integral to the creation of the geoglyphs is the process of creation, the experience of working closely with many people and coming to a common understanding of that which was an abstract concept to many minds. It is the smile of recognition and pride that lights up a face in response to a positive comment about the skill or quality of the work. It is the invitation offered to come home, and the request to have photographs taken together, or the request to come and inspect a finished section of work. It is the cacophony of many voices.

It is a demonstration of what a focused, harmonious, whole community effort can achieve in the movement and placement of thousands of tons of rocks.

It is the color of many a traditional dress. It is the notion of the geoglyph's belonging to the community that helped create it, theirs for an eternity of future generations to experience. It is knowing that you have engaged with people and enriched their life experience. It is the diversity of rich and vibrant cultures, yet the sameness of the human spirit. It is the demonstration of the tenet of humans' capabilities that within all communities of people there is a normal distribution of ability and intelligence, and the fact that some people just lack opportunity. Here destiny is a matter of chance, not a matter of choice.

Dedication of some sites has meant participating in exotic sacrificial rituals and Pachamama ceremonies celebrating Mother Earth, which brings to mind the antecedents of the monotheistic religions. These monotheistic religions have derived from such ancient traditions as those I experience. Sacrifice was part of ancient religion, and harvest festivals are still celebrated.

It is the feeling of solitude at the end of the day when one sits upon the structure and thinks. It is the noise of the silence of the land.

Finally, it is the excitement and anticipation of climbing into a strange and often primitive flying machine, an air balloon, or an ancient Russian helicopter—preferably with no doors. Then it is lifting off into the sky and buffeting winds to see the marvel of the crisp new form revealed below.

THE CELEBRATION OF LIFE

Fecundity and the Rhythms of Life: The Earth and Its Fullness and Intimacy

This first Celebration of Life, with three of the largest sculptures in the world—stone geoglyphs in the Arava Desert, Israel, upon which forty-two pregnant women stood on September 19 and 20, 2003.

Pregnant bodies in the ancient desert landscape framed by distant mountains. A landscape of wonderfully taut and curved flesh signed with the *linea nigra* insignia of future birth. Attended by a gynecologist, ambulance, security, and provided with accommodation, shade, chemical toilets, water, and transportation—a major logistical feat.

Celebration of birth and life is a dramatic contrast to the turmoil in the world. Beautiful pregnant women with all that this means for the human future: unspoiled, unblemished children coming into our world. Hope.

This was not a commercial happening. Participants, some of whom traveled up to five hours to attend, were not paid. It was about an idea and the joy of participation. To be in 40° C (104° F) temperatures in the sandy, windy, dry desert, contrasting with so many palpably physical, vibrant, expectant women about to give birth in a few weeks, was a wonder-filled, inspiring experience that I cherish.

The Celebration of Life in Iceland: 3° C (37° F), threatening to snow, clouded skies; densely grassed slopes dotted with a pattern of volcanic boulders and beautifully distended bodies. Bodies turning, standing still, sitting in unison on the command of the photographer—perched above a fjord that opens to the Atlantic Ocean, not far distant from the Arctic Circle. A surreal scene etched in my memory, it was an affirmation that if you dare to dream, anything is possible.

The body is a landscape and the body temporarily is an integral part of the earth's unspoiled natural landscape. The human form is not just an object, but also an envelope for our values. Human forms highlight that that we are just a transitory, minor participant within the forces of nature—a small part of the earth's existence. Humans are a foil to highlight the vista and its vastness.

Human figures emphasize contrasts and harmony, and our simply being…

TO LIFE
ARAVA DESERT, ISRAEL

Andrew Rogers could not have suspected that a passing remark made in the Israeli desert in 1998 would turn into a visionary global art project. At the time, the internationally renowned sculptor was working in Haifa for several weeks at the Technion (Israel Institute of Technology) as an artist in residence. As Rogers is always curious about his surroundings, the chairman of the Arava Regional Council offered to show him the faraway Arava Desert. While talking with Rogers about the living conditions of the people in this inhospitable environment, he suddenly paused and asked the artist: "Why don't you create a work of art for these people here, something really big?"
"This was the initial catalyst for my first work, *To Life*," recalled Rogers. It was not long before he began drawing up plans for the giant symbol made of ancient, water-smoothed boulders in the middle of the desert sand. It would be the start of his global project, *Rhythms of Life*, with fifty-one land art installations in sixteen countries, a mammoth project that would engross him for the next two decades.
Rogers laid down the criteria for all of the subsequent installations with his concept for *To Life*: his land art installations were to be located in a vast, open landscape. They had to make exclusive use of existing building material such as stones and sand; they had to fit in with the terrain; and they had to correspond in size with the landscape setting. They had to be a clearly defined form so that they would be legible from great distances. In particular they had to have clarity from above so they could be captured by earth observation sensors, which provided satellite images underscoring the global nature of the project. It was obvious to him from the very beginning: this was to be more than l'art pour l'art. Rather, it was to render visible a distinct message—the cultural legacy of civilization as the most important component of its existence. For this reason, only those sites that had a complex history or a special topography were to be addressed. From the outset, Rogers wanted to touch people, to include them in the genesis of his projects and prompt them to reflect on themselves and their interconnectedness with the world.

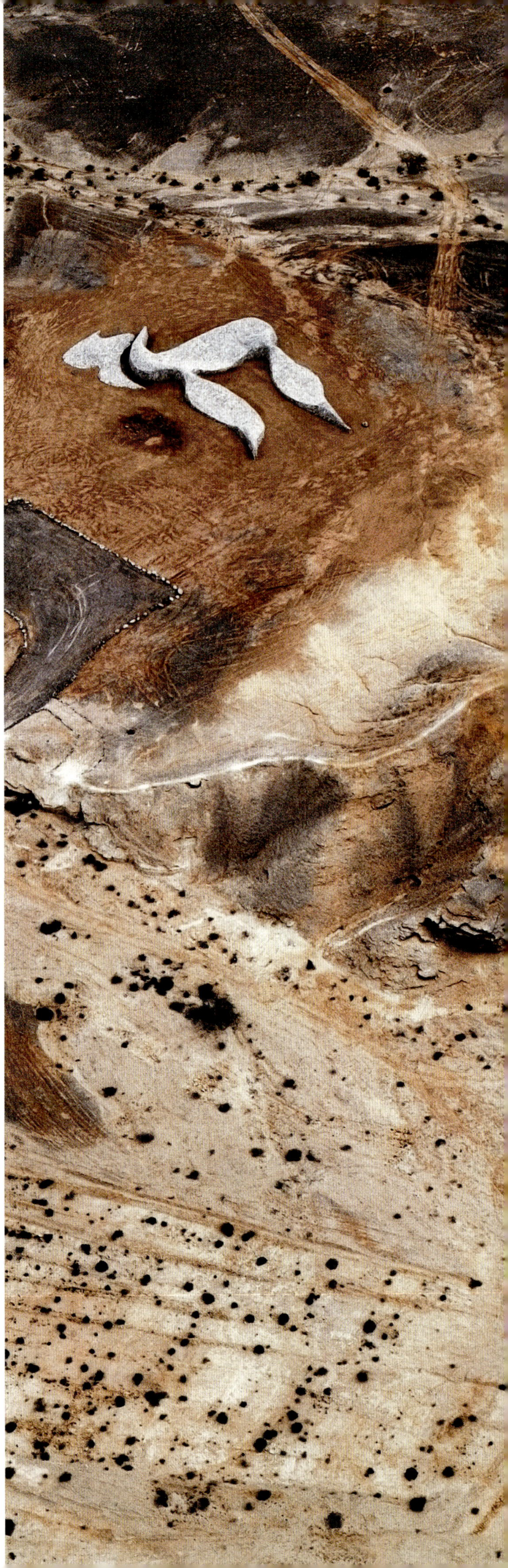

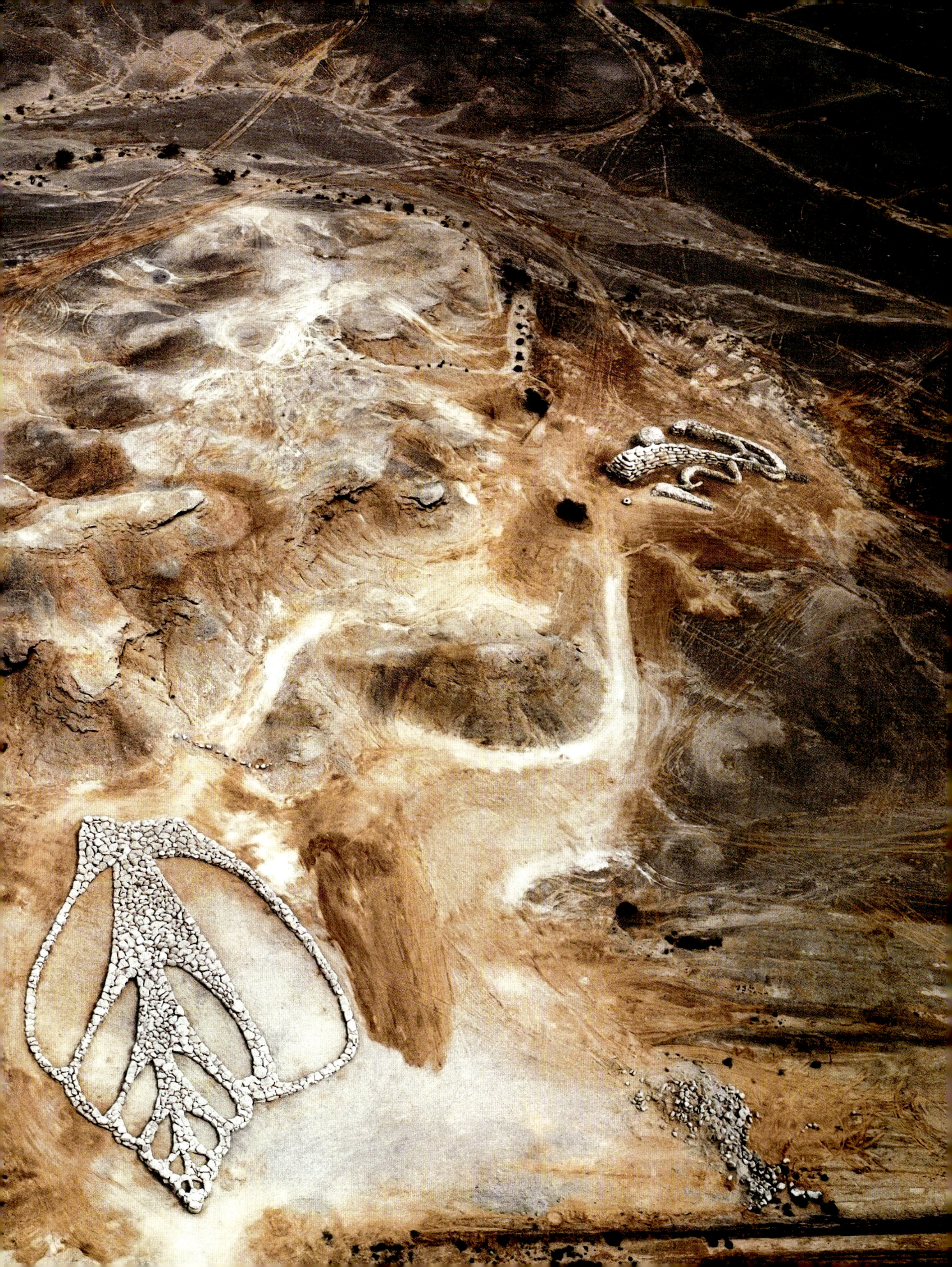

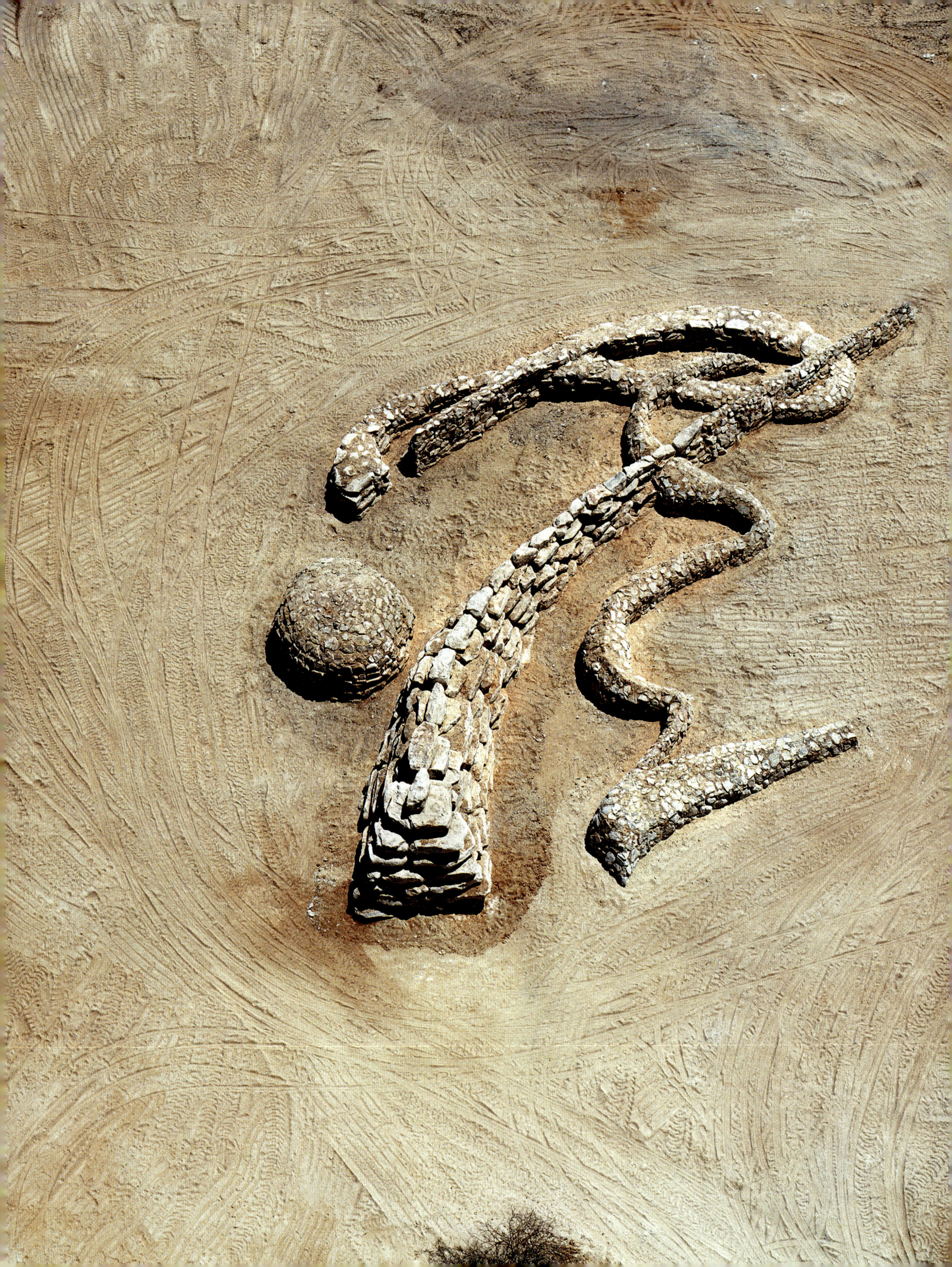

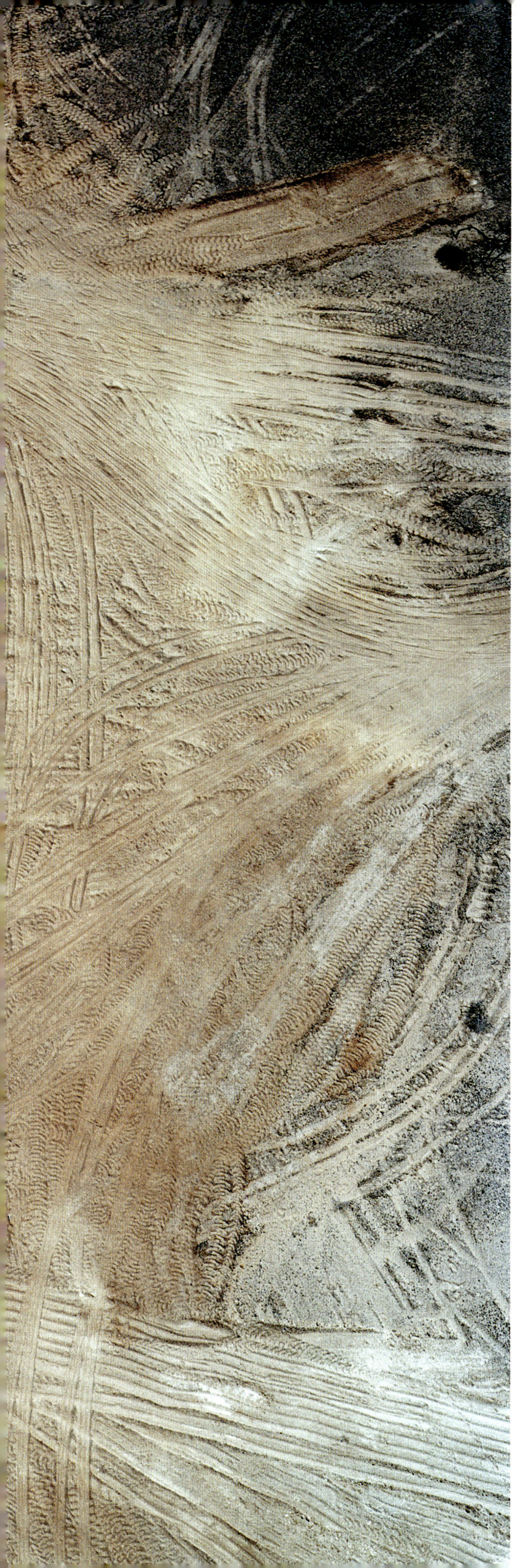

The vision for an ambitious global art project of this kind could truly not have been born in a better place than the Arava Desert, one of the most history-laden sites by far—a cradle of civilization. It was in this wide basin, which extends from the Dead Sea to the Gulf of Aqaba, that the Israelites wandered in search of the Promised Land. One of the most important trade routes in antiquity, the Incense Road, ran here from Petra to Gaza. And it was here, directly at the border to Jordan, that the geopolitically explosive peace agreement was concluded between Israel and Jordan in 1994.

The title of the first installation, *To Life*, derives from the Hebrew word *chai*, which it depicts. The figure consists of the two letters from the Hebrew alphabet that form the word *chai*, which Rogers erected on a rectangular area measuring 38 × 33 meters (125 × 108 feet) with stone walls up to 3.7 meters (12 feet) in height. He found the building material, boulders worn smooth over centuries by water, in the immediate vicinity.

He commenced work on the first geoglyph in 1999, a year after his visit to the Arava Desert. Under extreme working conditions with sandstorms and temperatures as high as 45° C (113° F), this monumental work of land art was a crash course in conception and implementation. Perseverance was required on everyone's part because the construction process was challenging due to the desert sand and extreme heat. "Because the steel bars got so hot from the sun that you couldn't touch them without suffering burns, you had to remember to wear gloves to handle them," said Rogers. Yet even before *To Life* was completed, it was already clear to him, the eternal optimist, that he would build more sculptures of this kind. "When halfway through the first, I knew that I would do a second, and a few minutes after starting the second, I knew there would be a third."

Hence *Slice* is located not far from *To Life*. Rogers also let himself be inspired by the geology of the site for this flat geoglyph made of giant rocks: the Arava Basin is a relic of a primordial ocean basin. Rogers renders this visible in the shape of a shell and thus at

RHYTHMS OF LIFE 2001 / Sandstone / 4.5 × 29 × 24 m (15 × 95 × 79 ft.)

the same time creates the connection to the overriding theme of rhythms of life, a tribute to life. The curves and spirals of a shell are not only one of the most beautiful marine creations, they are also considered the most perfect logarithmic spiral to occur in nature. They embody development, dynamics, the ancient, and the future.

The symbol *Rhythms of Life*, on the other hand, became the consistent formal component of Rogers's future projects, and thus is also the overall title of the global art project. With its intertwined spiral and ascending line, *Rhythms of Life* makes reference to an earlier bronze sculpture of the same name. It symbolizes dynamics and continuity, the foundations of all existence. In Israel, Andrew Rogers built the highly symbolic sculpture next to *To Life* with similar dimensions and with equally tall, swelling stone walls made of precisely layered slabs of limestone.

He completed the Arava project in 2004 with *Ratio*. Unlike the previous three geoglyphs, this one rises up as pyramid steps and crowns the top of a cliff face. Rogers had enormous blocks of stone hewn out of the local limestone and arranged them in such a way that they depict the Golden Ratio, the ideal principle of aesthetic proportion, in which the ratio of two parts is the same as that of their sum to the larger of the two parts. Rogers applied gold leaf to the edges on both sides of the seven-metric-ton stone steles. They reflect the progression of the sun and thus the life cycle as an equally relevant ideal principle.

In the end, Rogers underscored the eternal cycle of life with a ritual celebration of life and in doing so added another dimension to his land art project. Forty-two pregnant Israelis lined up in the bright light along the geoglyph in poses exposing their swollen bellies. Clad in white gauze, they symbolized the spark of life and celebrated the life-affirming message of Rogers's art. Thus the geoglyphs and the final celebratory ritual in the Arava Desert, one of the oldest centers of human civilization, constituted the prototype for Rogers's subsequent land art projects, with which he would like to connect people everywhere in the world.

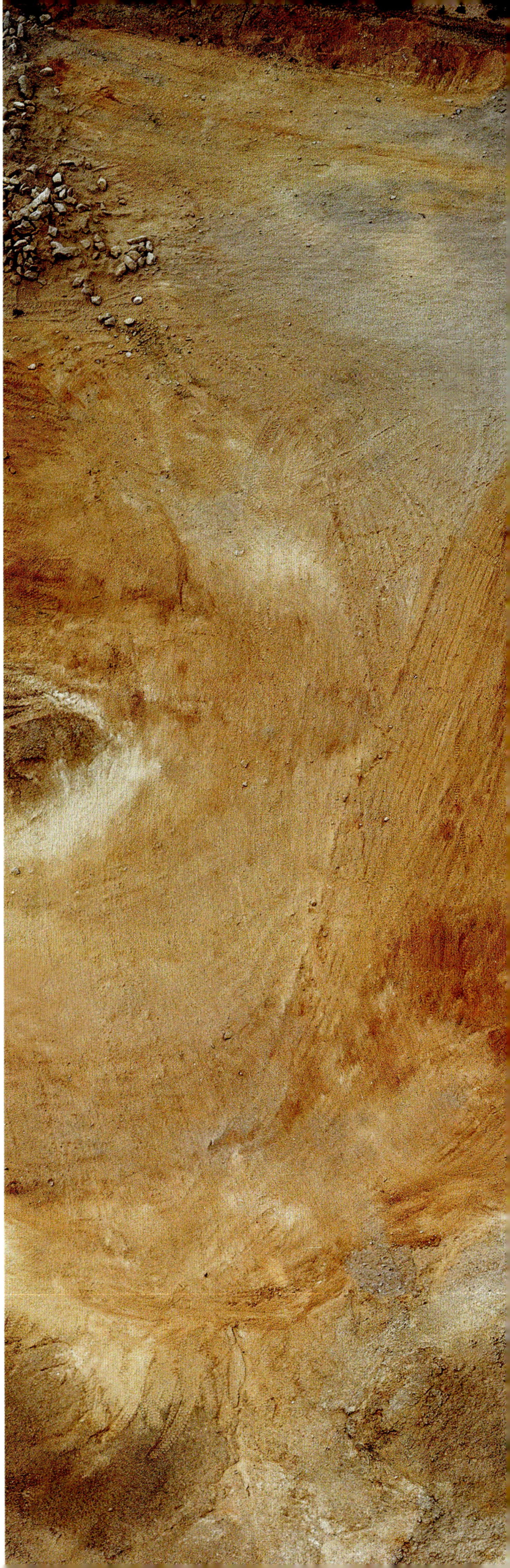

SLICE 2003 / Sandstone / 80 x 38 m (263 x 125 ft.)

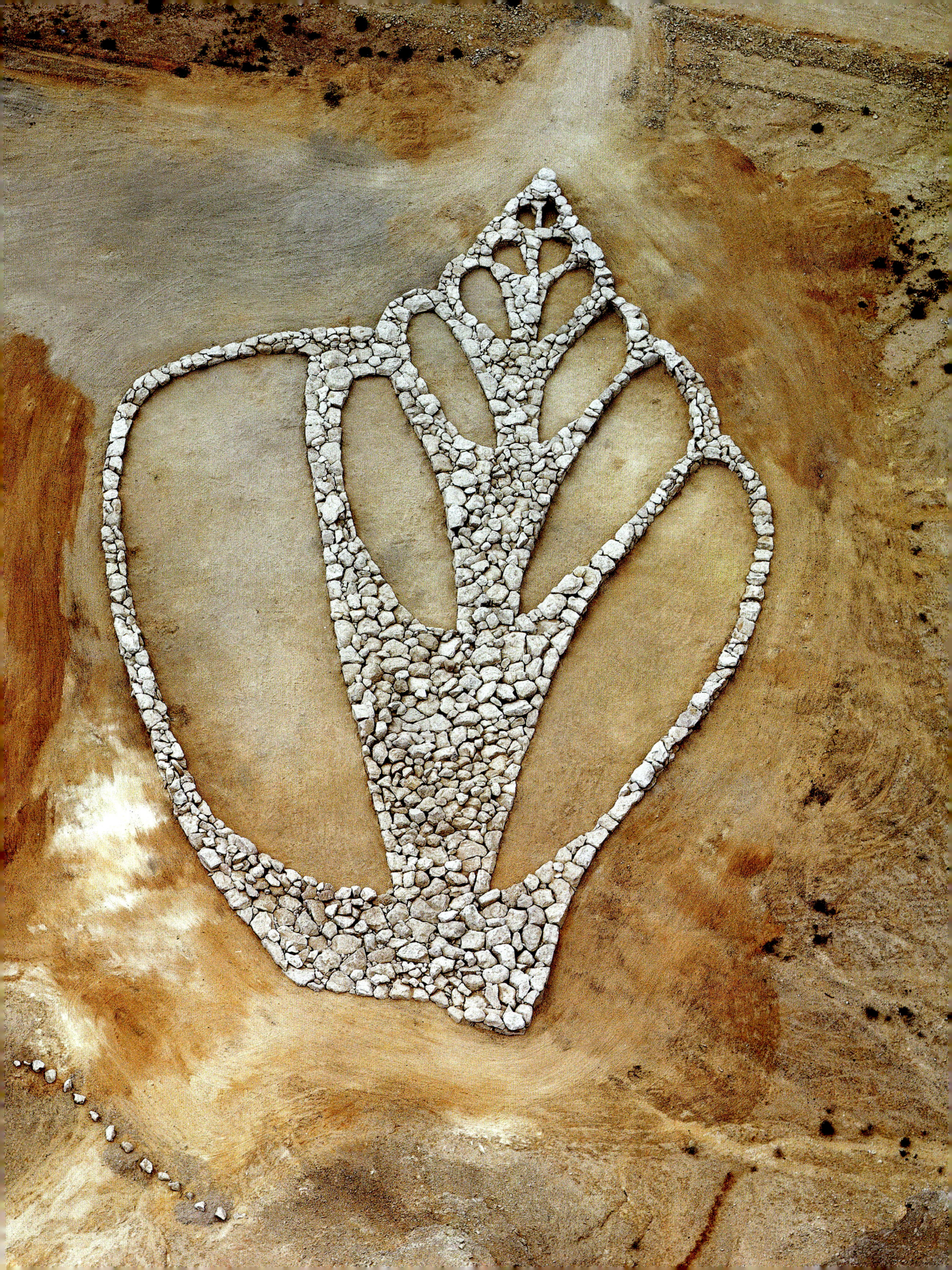

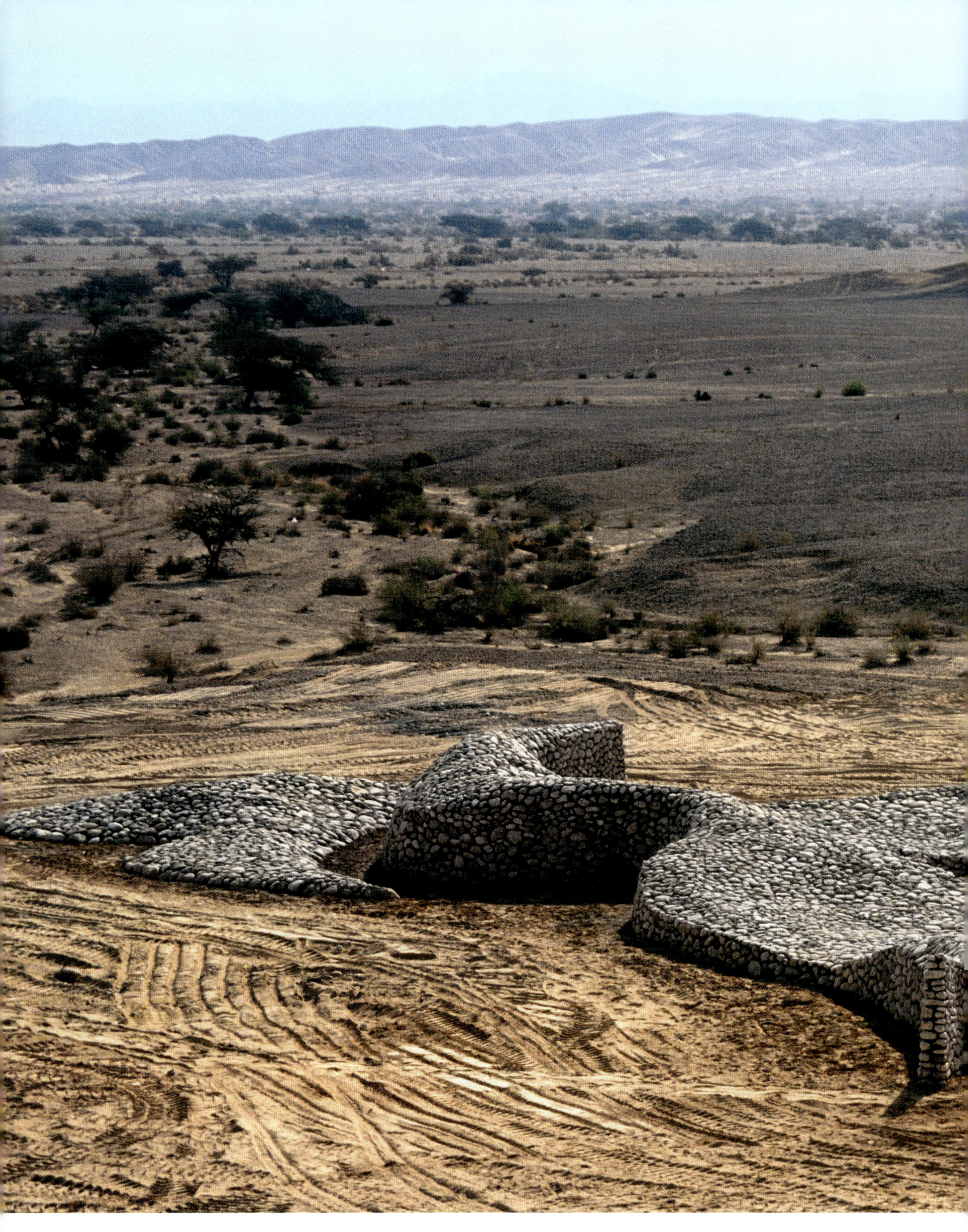

TO LIFE 1999 / Sandstone / 3.7 × 38 × 33 m (12 × 125 × 108 ft.)

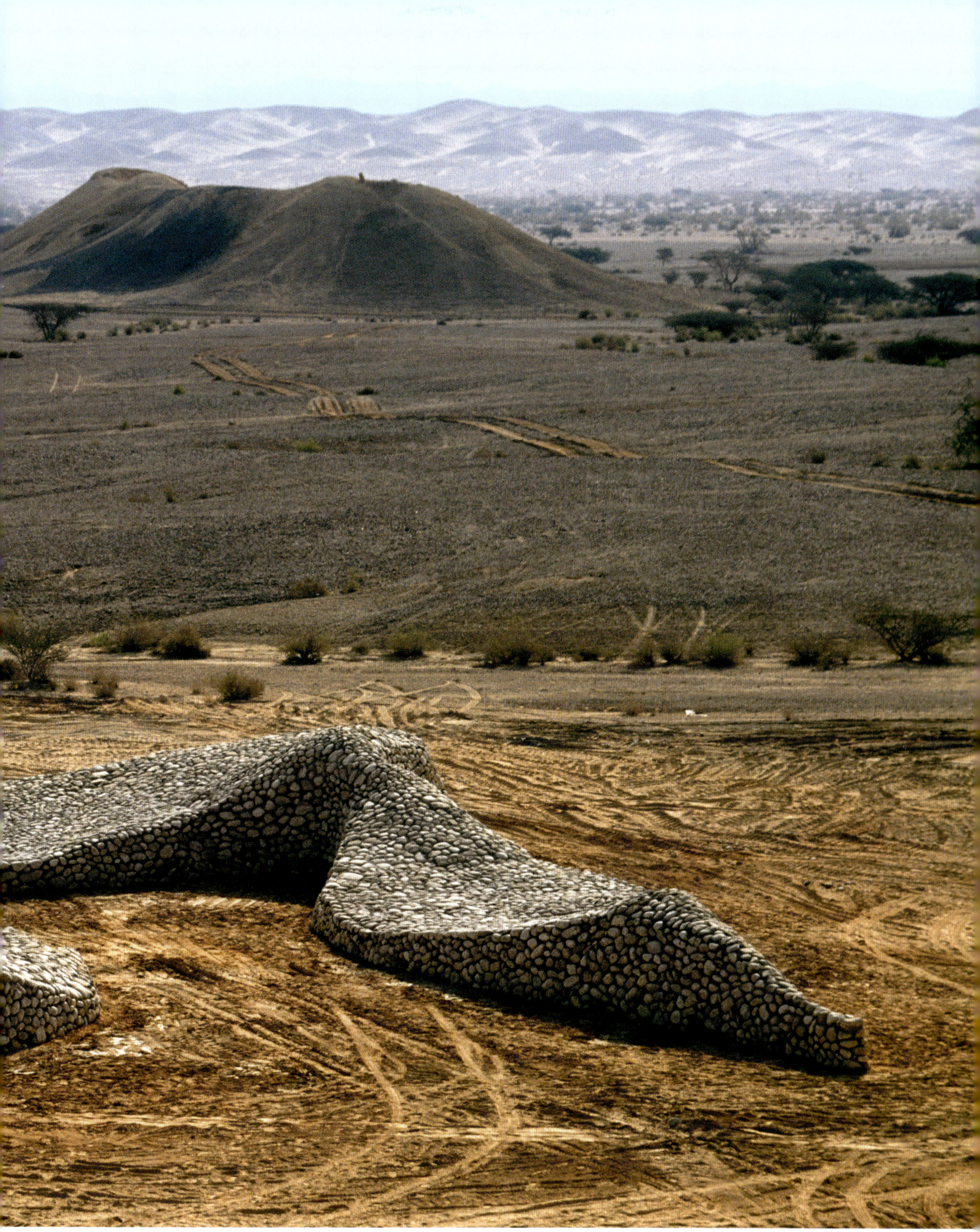

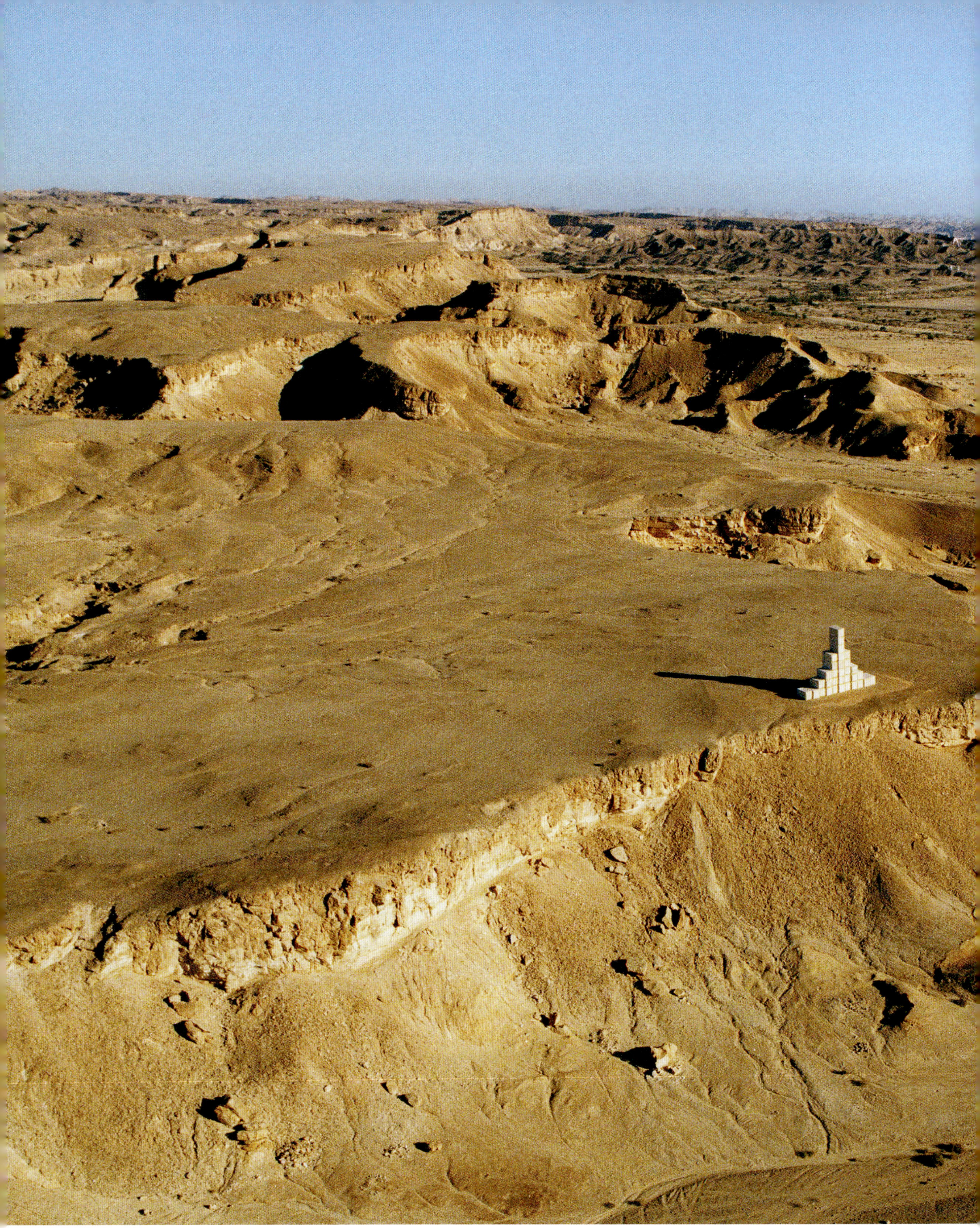

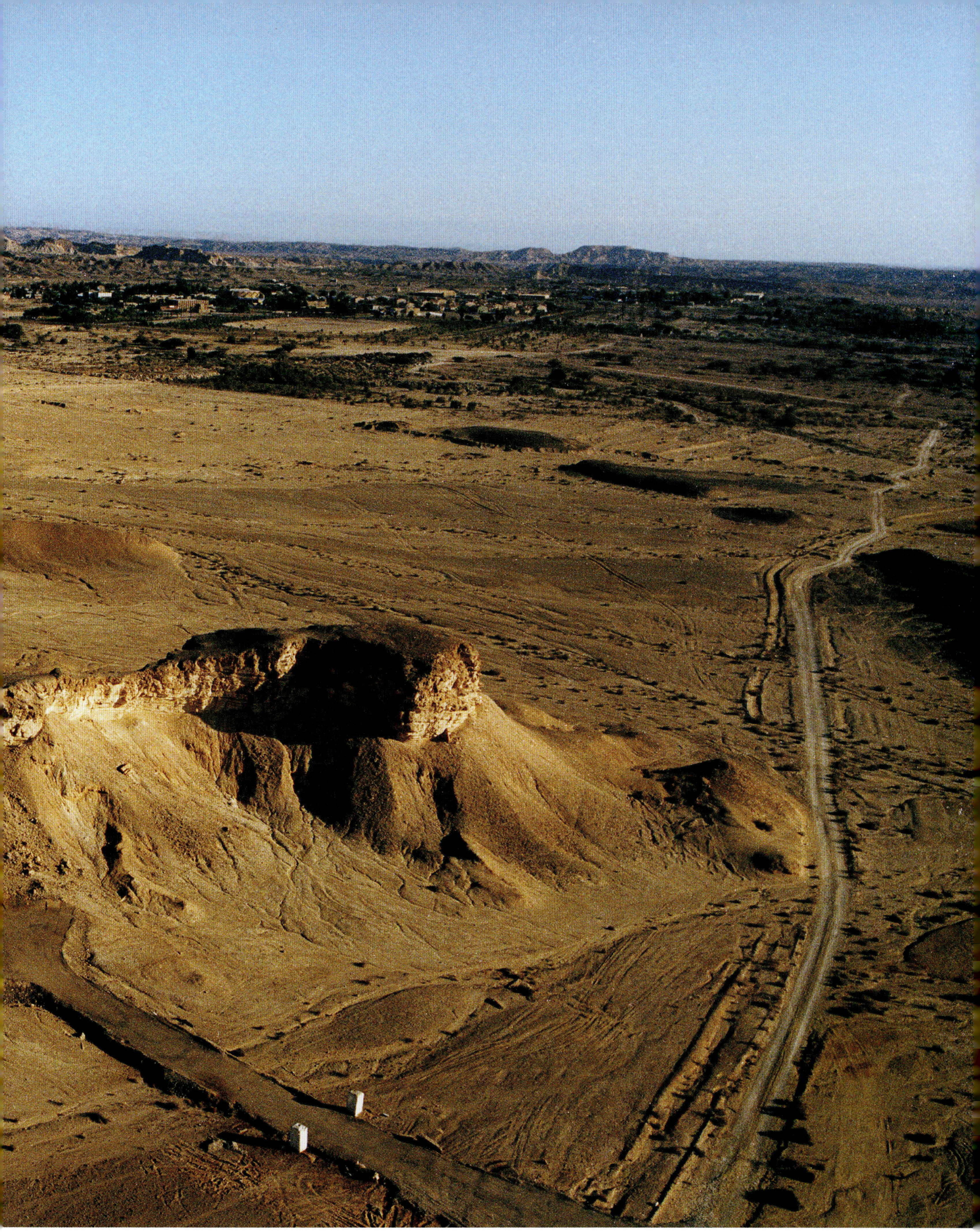

RATIO 2004 / Limestone / 8 × 32 × 2 m (26 × 105 × 6.6 ft.)

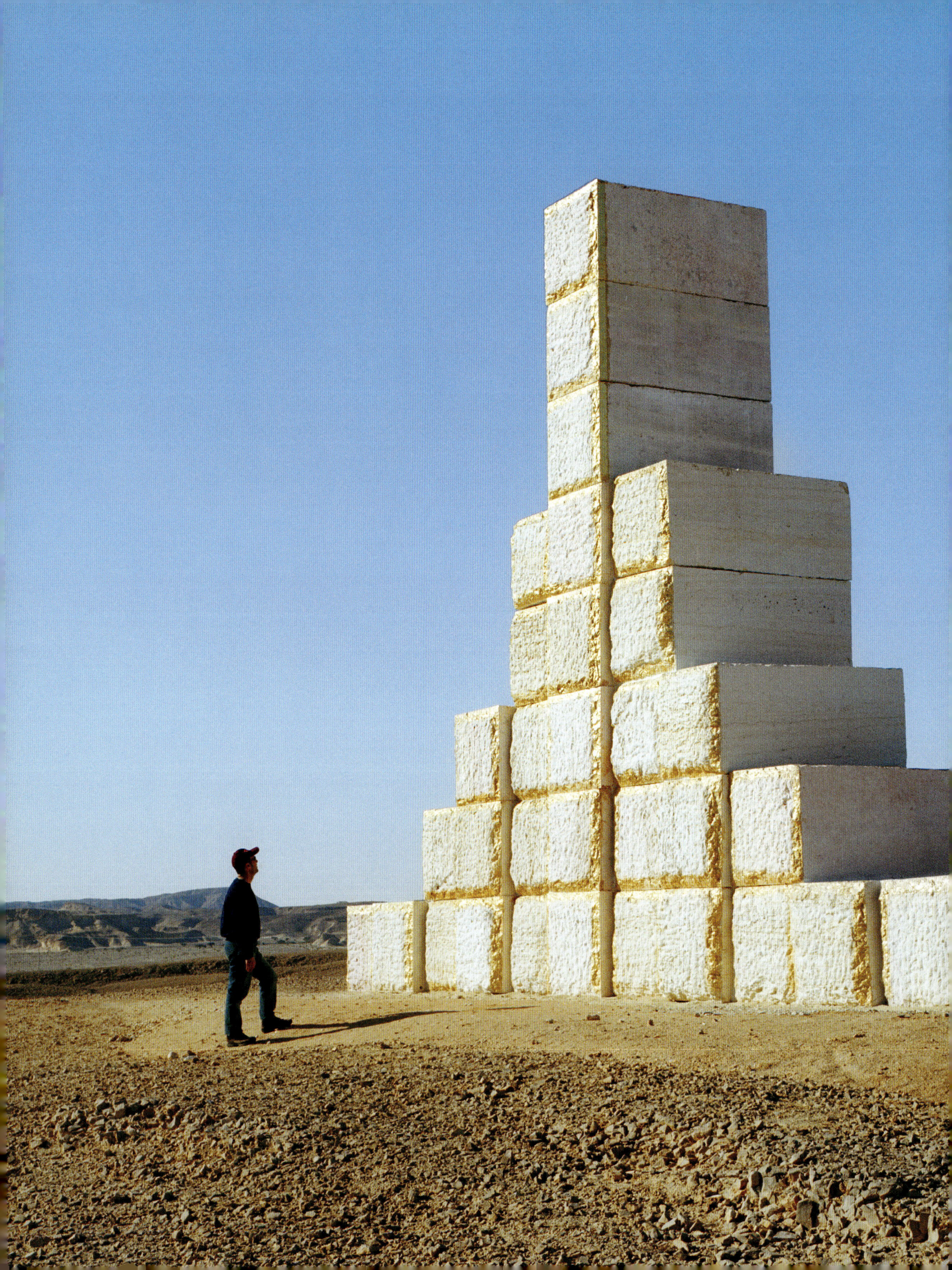

RATIO 2004 / Limestone / 8 × 32 × 2 m (26 × 105 × 6.6 ft.)

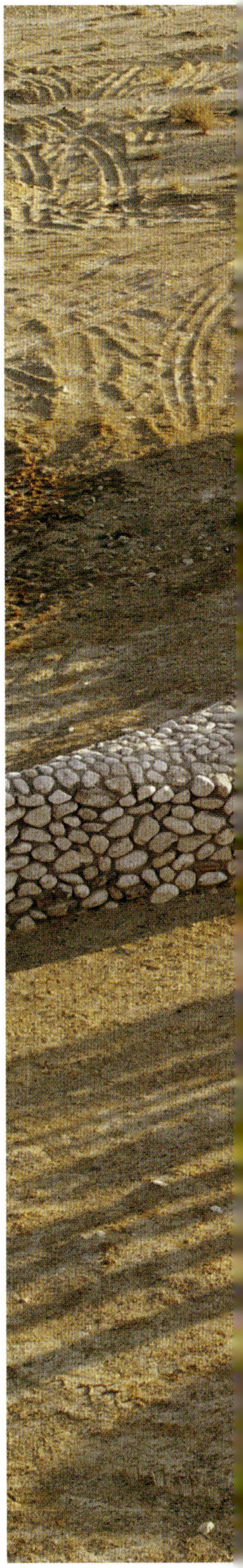

CELEBRATION OF LIFE, 2003: Forty-two pregnant women dressed in sheer white gauze reinforce the outline of *To Life*, thereby reaffirming the work's message of the celebration of life, continuity, regeneration and hope.

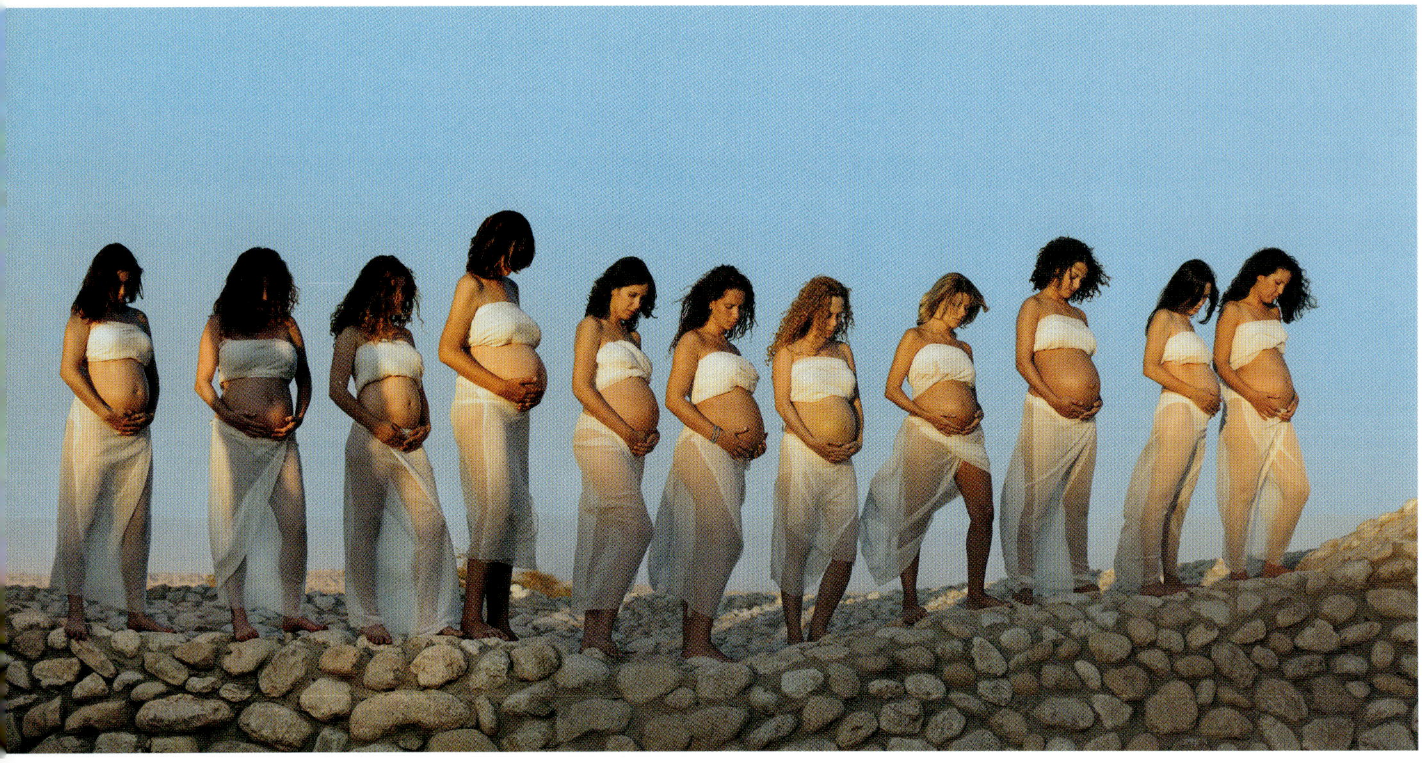

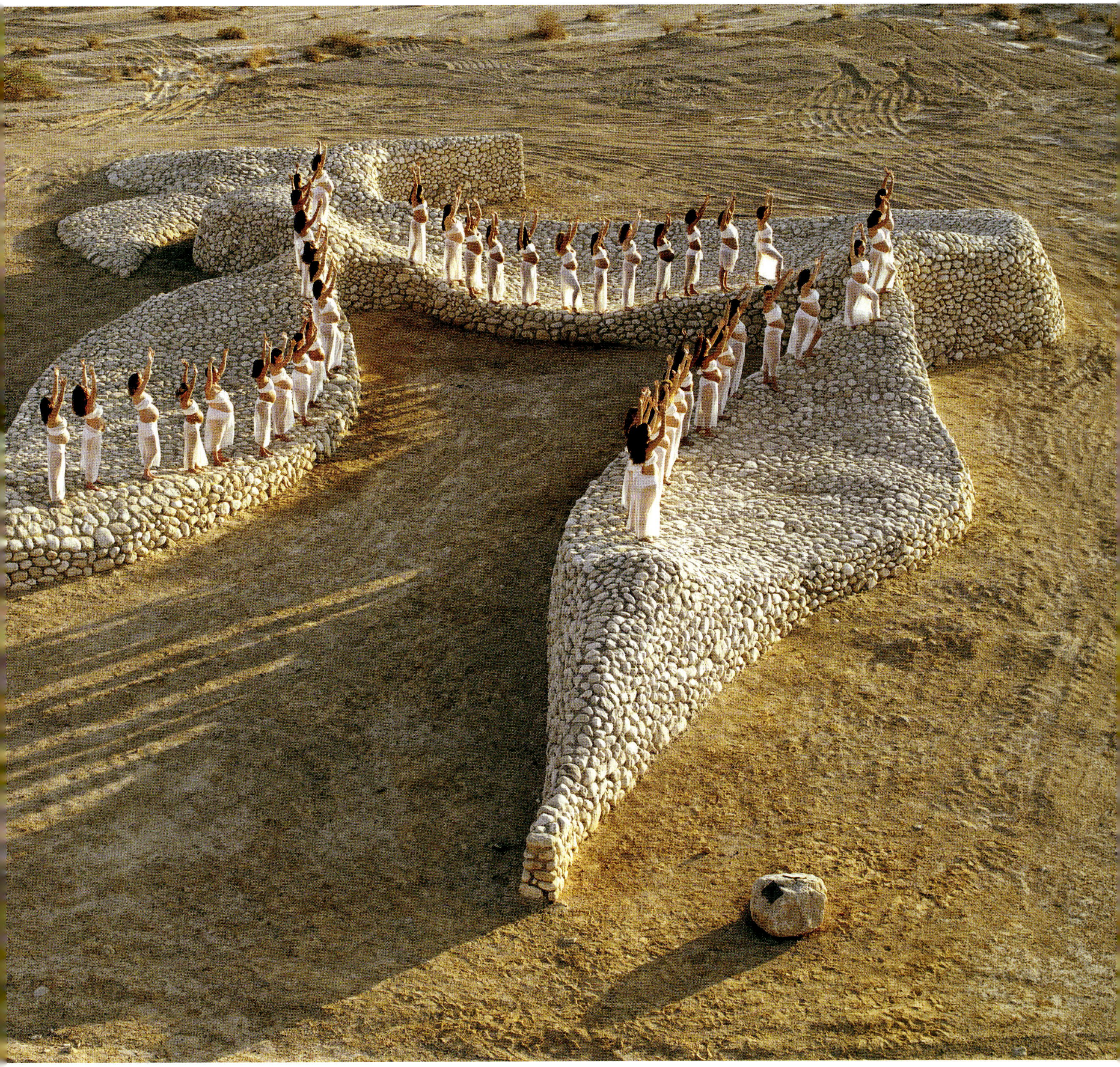

PRE-COLUMBIAN VISUAL LANGUAGE
ATACAMA DESERT, CHILE

Andrew Rogers sought out an inhospitable topography with traces of early civilization for his second *Rhythms of Life* project, and chose the Atacama Desert, in the Altiplano of South America. Not far from this area are the Nazca lines in Peru, one of the ancient land constructions that served as an inspiration for Andrew Rogers's *Rhythms of Life* land art project. The Atacama stretches along the Pacific coast from the south of Peru to the uppermost northern region of Chile. Estimated to have existed for fifteen million years, it is considered to be the earth's oldest and driest landscape. Due to its special location in the double precipitation shadow of the Andes and the Humboldt Current, there are places where it has not rained for more than two hundred years. Andrew Rogers produced three geoglyphs, *Ancient Language, The Ancients*, and *Rhythms of Life*, here in the Altiplano, the desolate Andean plateau that lies within Bolivia, Peru, Chile, and Argentina at an altitude of up to 4,000 meters (13,000 feet). The cold Humboldt Current and the Atacama's location on the western side of the Andes have created an extraordinary landscape with enormous salt lakes, geysers, vast sand dunes, perfectly formed volcanic valleys, and even a few fertile valleys. The American space agency NASA tests the prototypes of its Mars rovers here, as the conditions in the Atacama are very similar to those on the Red Planet. Moreover, the arid high valley has the clearest sky in all of the Southern Hemisphere: it is completely cloudless 340 days a year, an ideal site for some of the most important astronomical observatories in the world.

Despite the extreme conditions, people settled in the Atacama Desert relatively early. Cultic sites and irrigation terraces in the Altiplano indicate that it was a central settlement area as early as ten thousand years ago. Ethnic groups such as the Atacameño, the Aymara, the Diaguita, and the Chinchorro settled near the few oases, which has been confirmed by

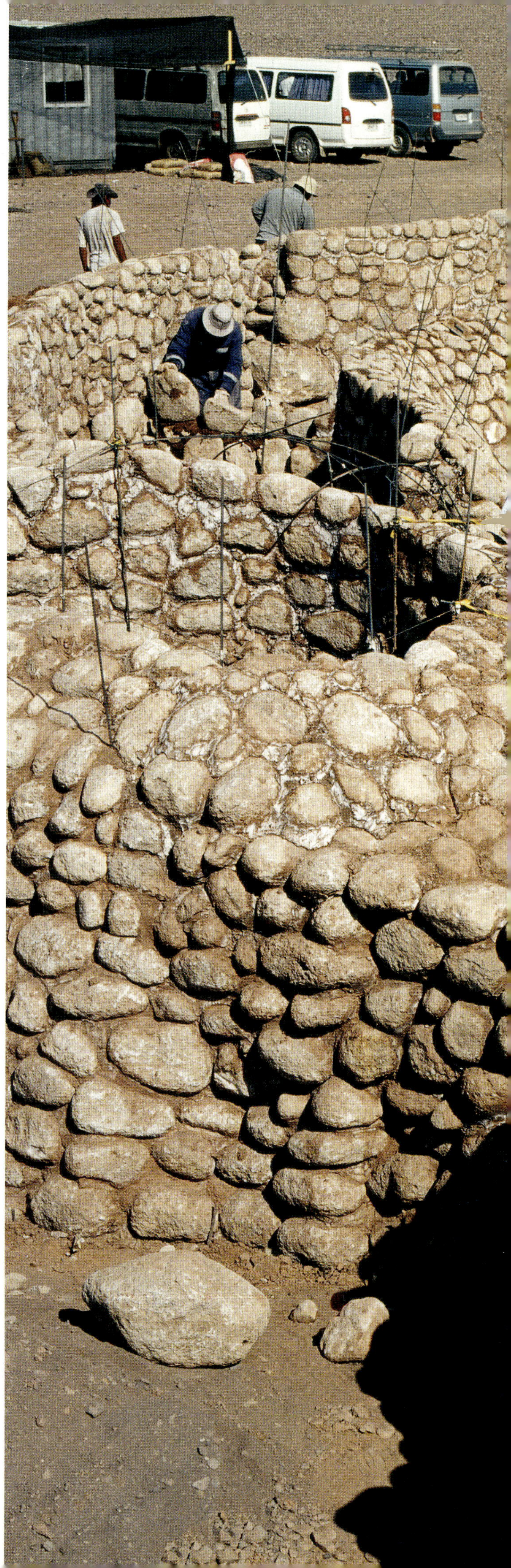

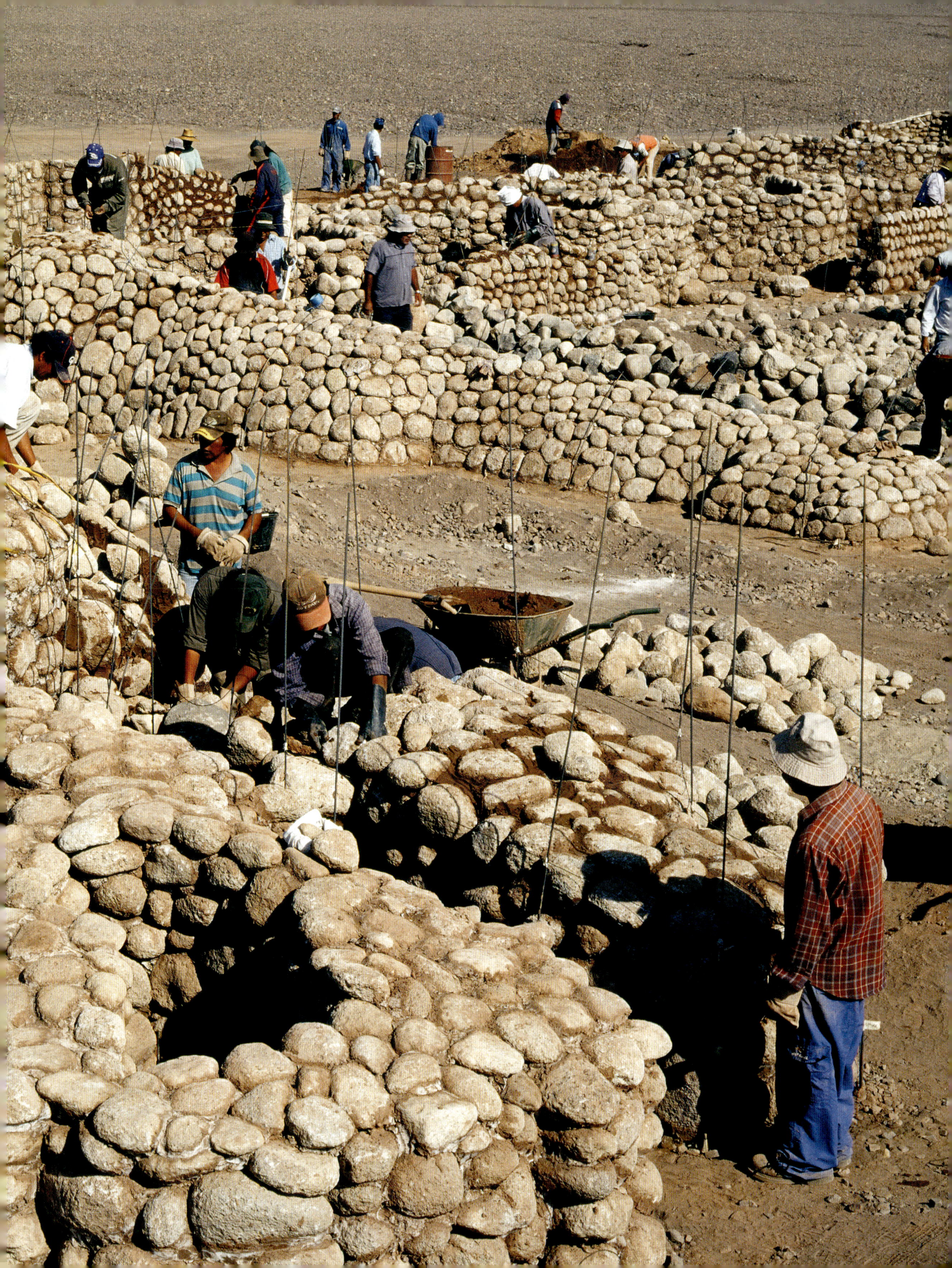

the discovery of mummies. In the fifteenth century, the region became part of the Inca Empire, one of the most magnificent advanced civilizations in the Americas. After its conquest in 1533 by the conquistador Francisco Pizarro, the former empire became a Spanish crown colony. Yet the excellent skills of the Inca Empire's stonemasons have survived to the present day, and Andrew Rogers relied on this when assembling his working party in the small town of San Pedro de Atacama. The five hundred Atacamians who built the three monumental geoglyphs over a two-year period used the ancient techniques of the Inca: elaborate, rounded stone walls are held together by a mortar of earth and the guano of the Guanay cormorant.

In the vicinity of San Pedro de Atacama there are numerous petroglyphs, which can be dated back as far as 1200 BC. Andrew Rogers found a bizarre depiction—a llama with two heads, one at each end of its body—at the Pampa Vizcachilla archaeological site near the small town of Yerbas Buenas and was immediately fascinated by it. Experts estimate that the drawing was created between 600 and 900 BC, providing an insight into the life of this prehistoric civilization. It is an example of the noticeably large number of naturalistic depictions of camelid species in the Atacama—llamas, alpacas, vicunas, or guanacos, animals that even today one runs into at every turn. At that time, they obviously had special meaning for the local inhabitants, both for their economic and cultural benefit and as religious symbols. For here, between San Pedro de Atacama in northern Chile and the towns in northwestern Argentina, is where one of the most important trade routes ran. The exchange of commodities and culture between the various tribes took place with these pack animals. On the one hand, in pre-Columbian art the two-headed llama is a religious symbol, indicating a special godlike power; on the other, it refers to the interaction between the tribal cultures of that period.

What is interesting is the interior zigzag drawn on the noticeably elongated body of the animal. Experts see it

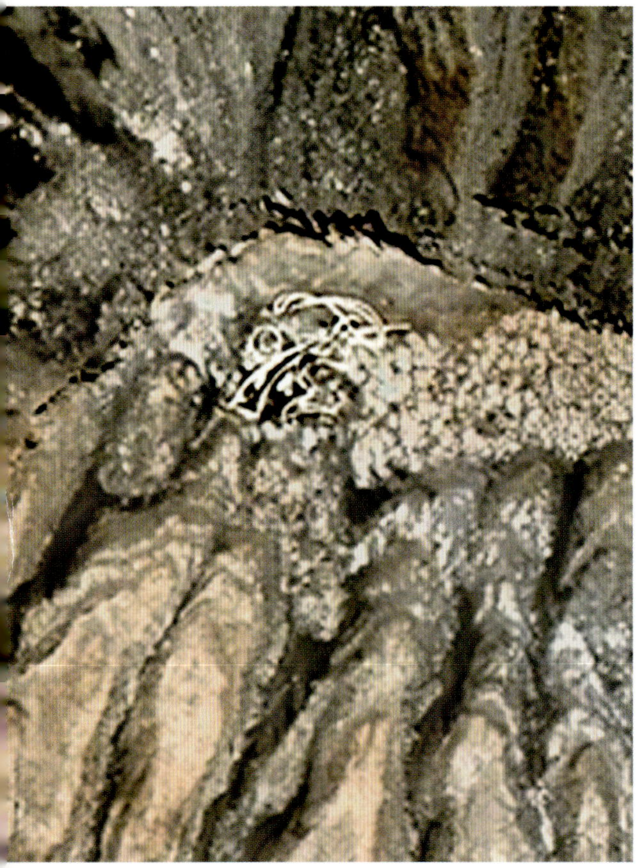

1

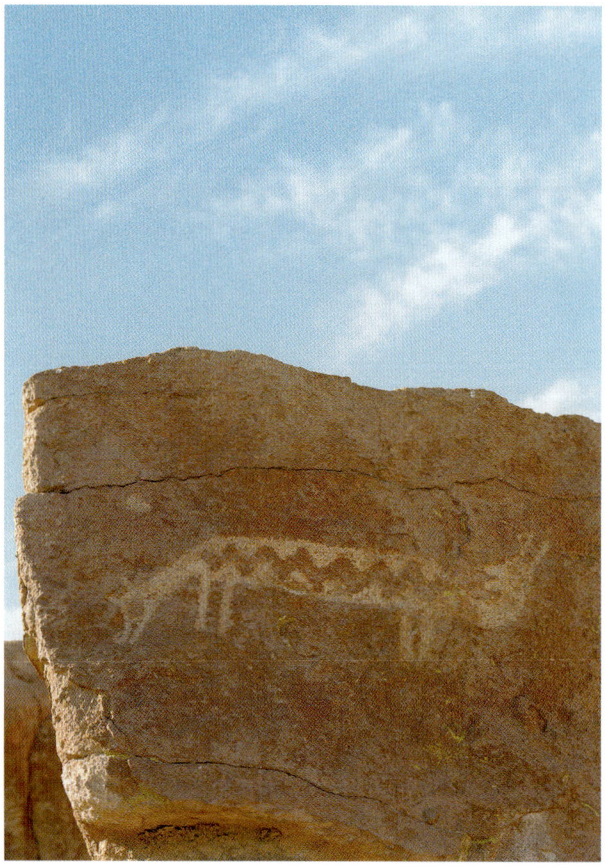

2

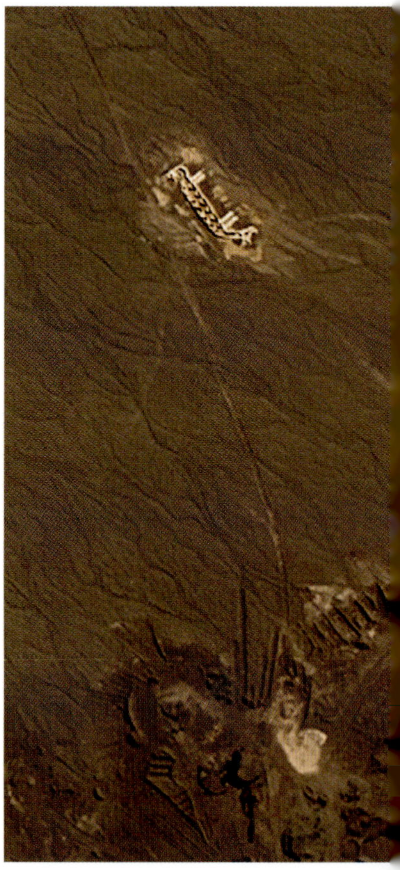

as a symbol for water, the most important element in this extremely arid desert site and thus a crucial power factor for any civilization. Rogers placed the geoglyph, which he symbolically called *Ancient Language*, on the Llano de la Paciencia (Plain of Patience) at the very end of the Valle de la Luna (Valley of the Moon), which is famous for its bizarre rock formations, on an area measuring 80 meters (263 feet) in length and with stone walls 3 meters (10 feet) high.

In contrast, the geoglyph *Rhythms of Life* is difficult to find. It is located approximately 10 kilometers (6 miles) west of San Pedro de Atacama, hidden at an altitude of 2,603 meters (8,540 feet) on the broad ridge of a rock overhang.

For *The Ancients*, Andrew Rogers again let himself be inspired by the petroglyphs that he found in the vicinity of the small town of Calama. This time it was a drawing carved into the rock with red pigments known as *El Señor de los Báculos* (Lord of the Scepters), a divinity who wears a sun crown on his head and holds lightning bolts in his hands—symbols

1 RHYTHMS OF LIFE, satellite image taken 440 km (275 miles) above the earth

2 Ancient pictoglyph of the double-headed llama

3 ANCIENT LANGUAGE, Satellite image taken 440 km (275 miles) above the earth

4 Ancient petroglyph of El Señor de los Báculos

5 THE ANCIENTS, satellite image taken 440 km (275 miles) above the earth

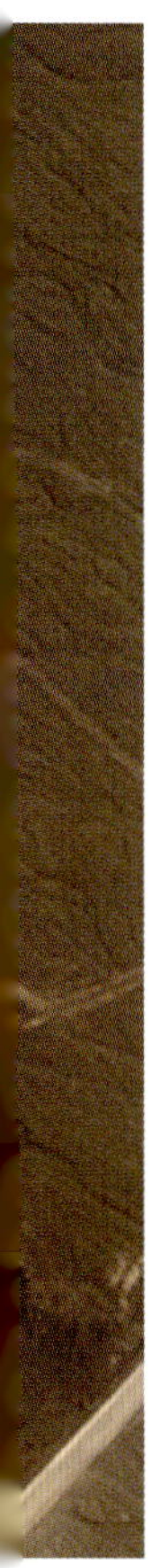

3

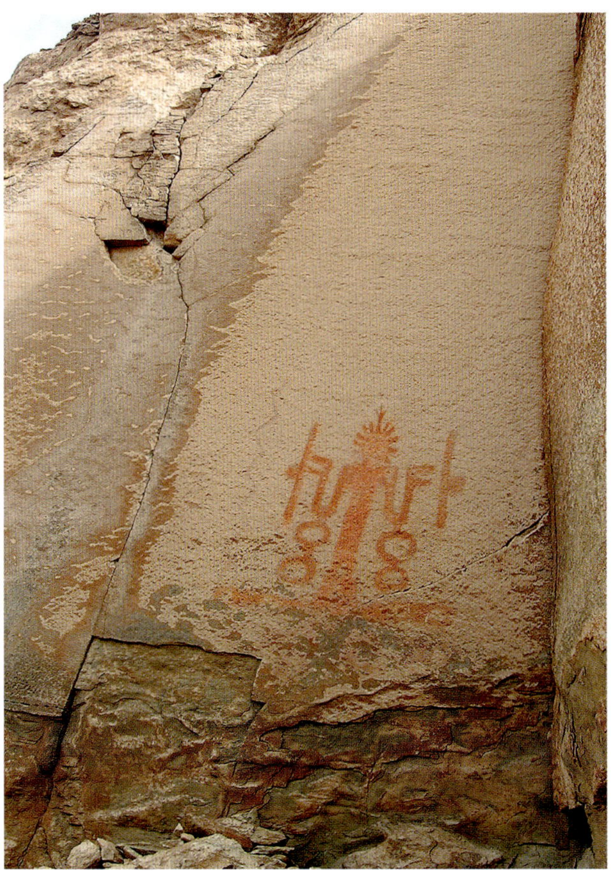

4

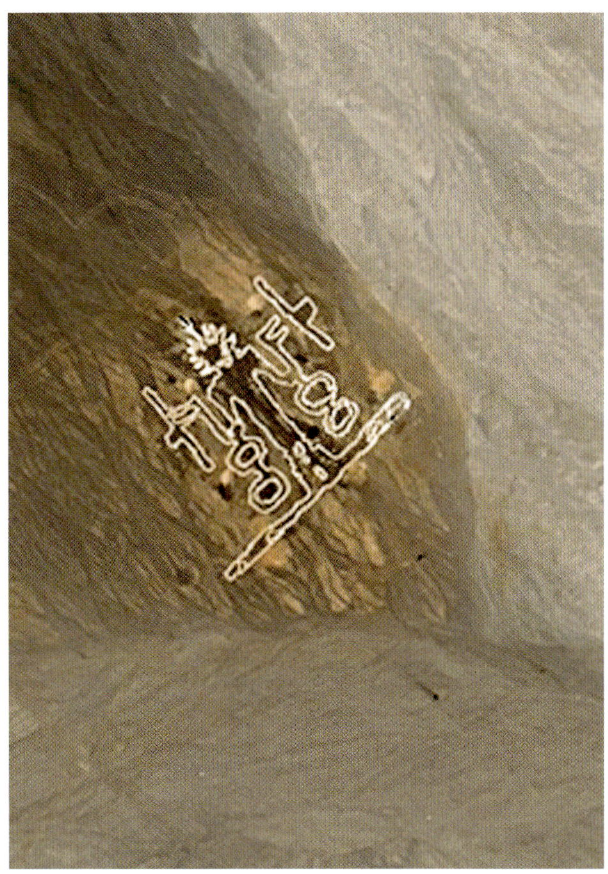

5

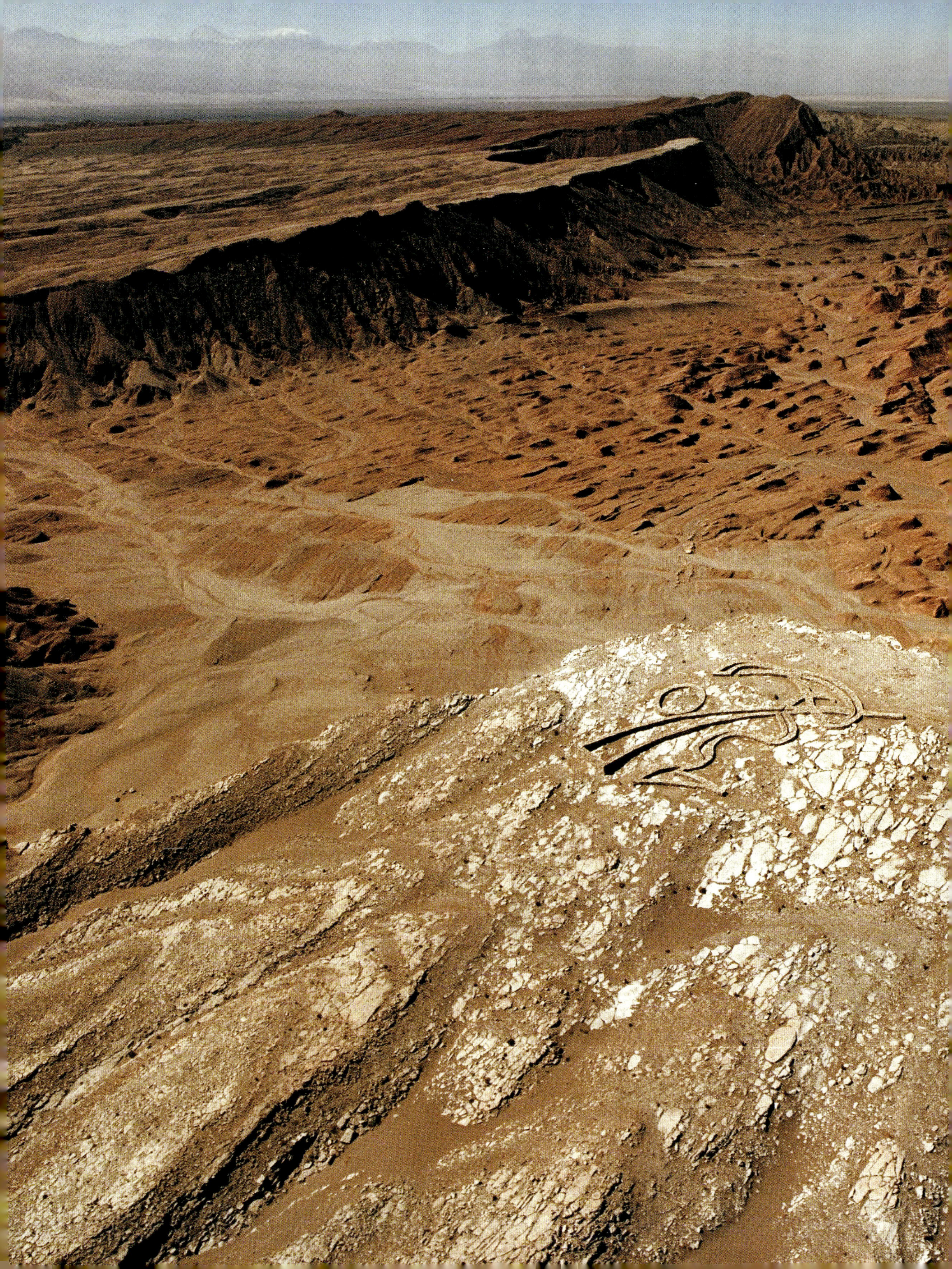

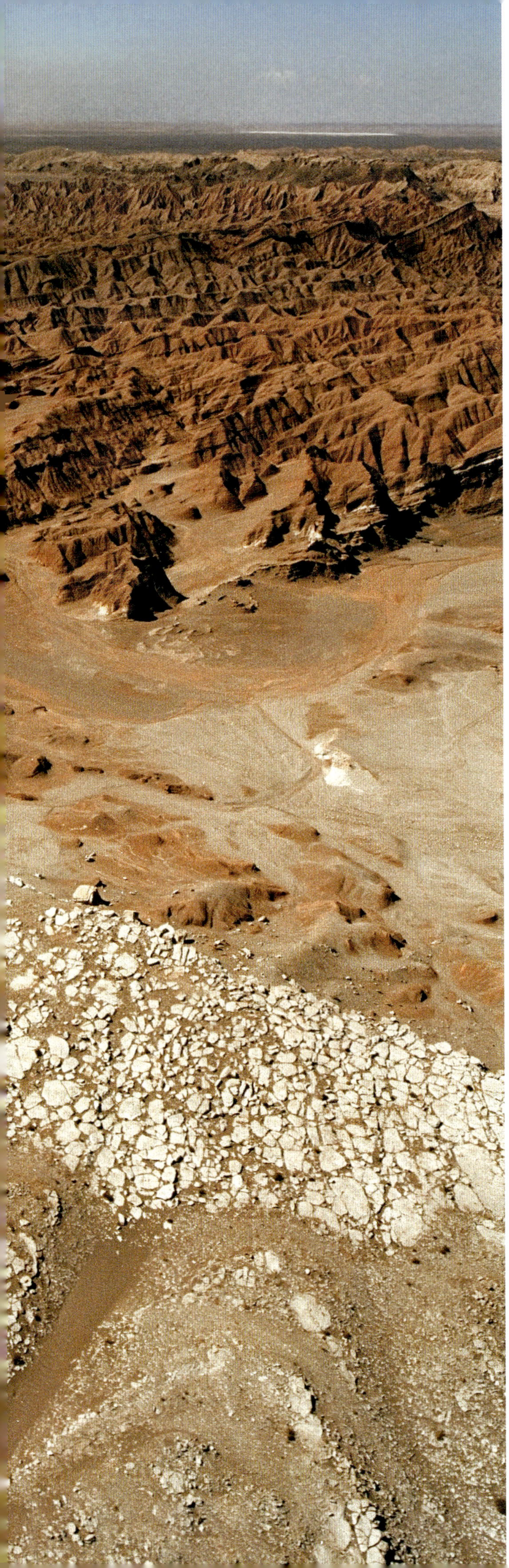

for the creator of the universe. The Inca called him Viracocha and also worshipped him as god of the sun and storms. It is interesting to note that they had already adopted the divinity from their predecessors, the Tiwanaku. According to legend, it was Viracocha who created giants to move rocks for the large buildings of his subjects. But the undertaking failed, and Viracocha imposed a flood that would engulf the giants forever—a myth that, thank God, had no relevance in connection with Andrew Rogers's visionary large-scale project. During the building of *The Ancients*, Rogers closely adhered to the drawing as a visual source material. He therefore also deliberately dispensed with an accurately drawn contour for the continuous stone wall made of volcanic rock, because only in this way does the geoglyph at the base of the massive Cordillera de la Sal (Salt Mountains) convey the fragility of the early petroglyphs despite the enormous extent of its 90 × 90-meter (295 × 295 feet) base. In order to introduce an extra dimension, suggesting people climb closer to the sky and enabling viewers to have an optimum overhead view of the enlarged installation, the artist integrated stairs into the geoglyph, "the only stairs in the entire Atacama Desert," as he remarks with a smile.

The Incan worship of depictions of Viracocha, which were traditionally celebrated with ritual acts and mythic dances, fits in perfectly with Andrew Rogers's artistic concept for his global *Rhythms of Life* project, which provided for a ceremony upon the completion of each individual project. In Chile, the descendants of the Inca that had worked for him consecrated the building of all three geoglyphs with a ritual for Pachamama, the Mother Earth goddess. The Challa ritual is a ceremony of reciprocity with Pachamama and the local inhabitants. It begins with casting in four directions a mixture of alcohol and symbolic ingredients such as crushed coca leaves onto the earth before drinking the rest. For Rogers, "drinking a concoction of strong alcohol and a questionable substance from the same earthenware vessel that two hundred workers have drunk from before me" was more of a dubious, albeit impressive pleasure.

RHYTHMS OF LIFE 2004 / Volcanic rock, clay, guano / 40 × 30 m (131 × 98 ft.)

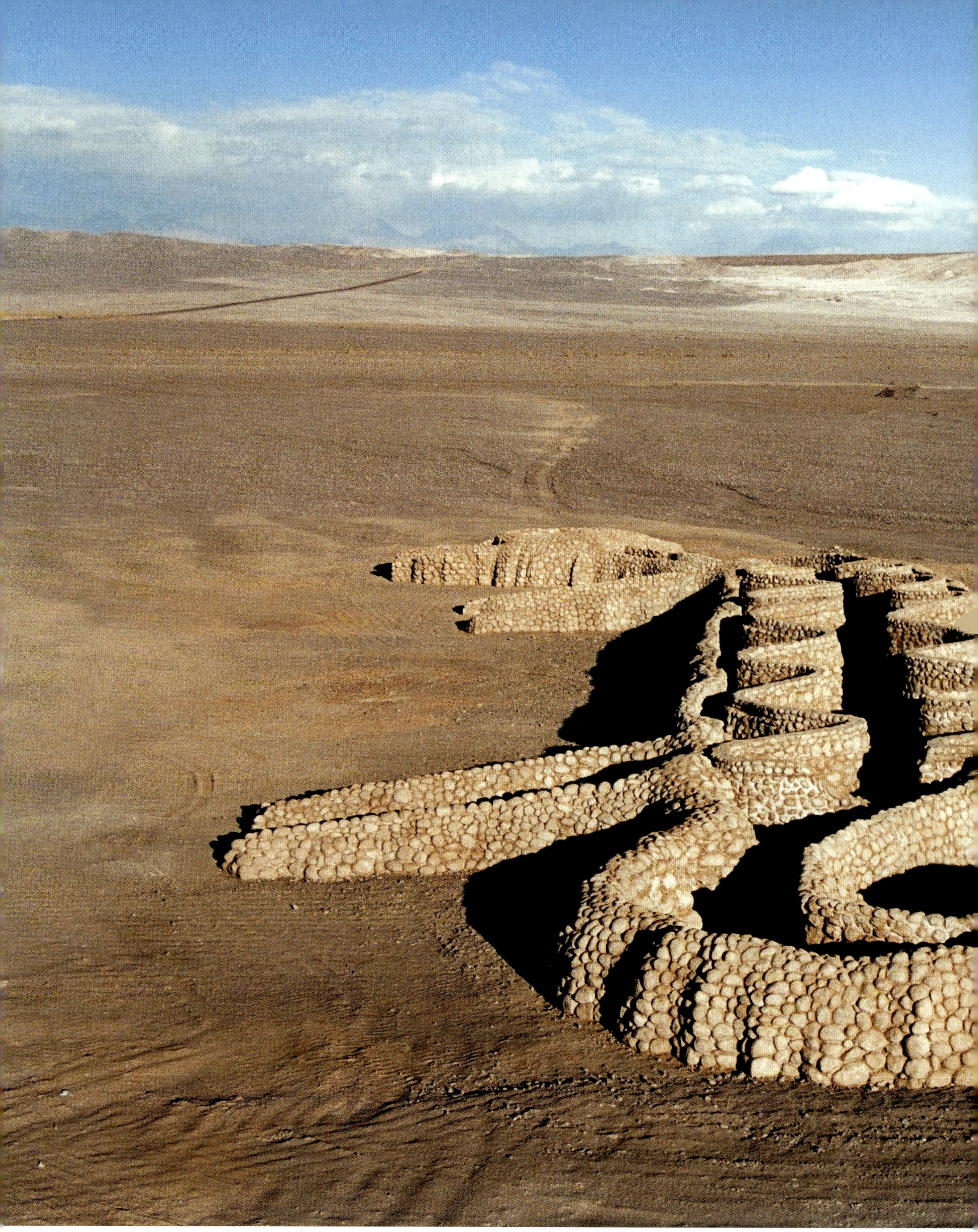

ANCIENT LANGUAGE 2004 / Volcanic rock, clay, guano / 3 × 80 m (10 × 263 ft.)

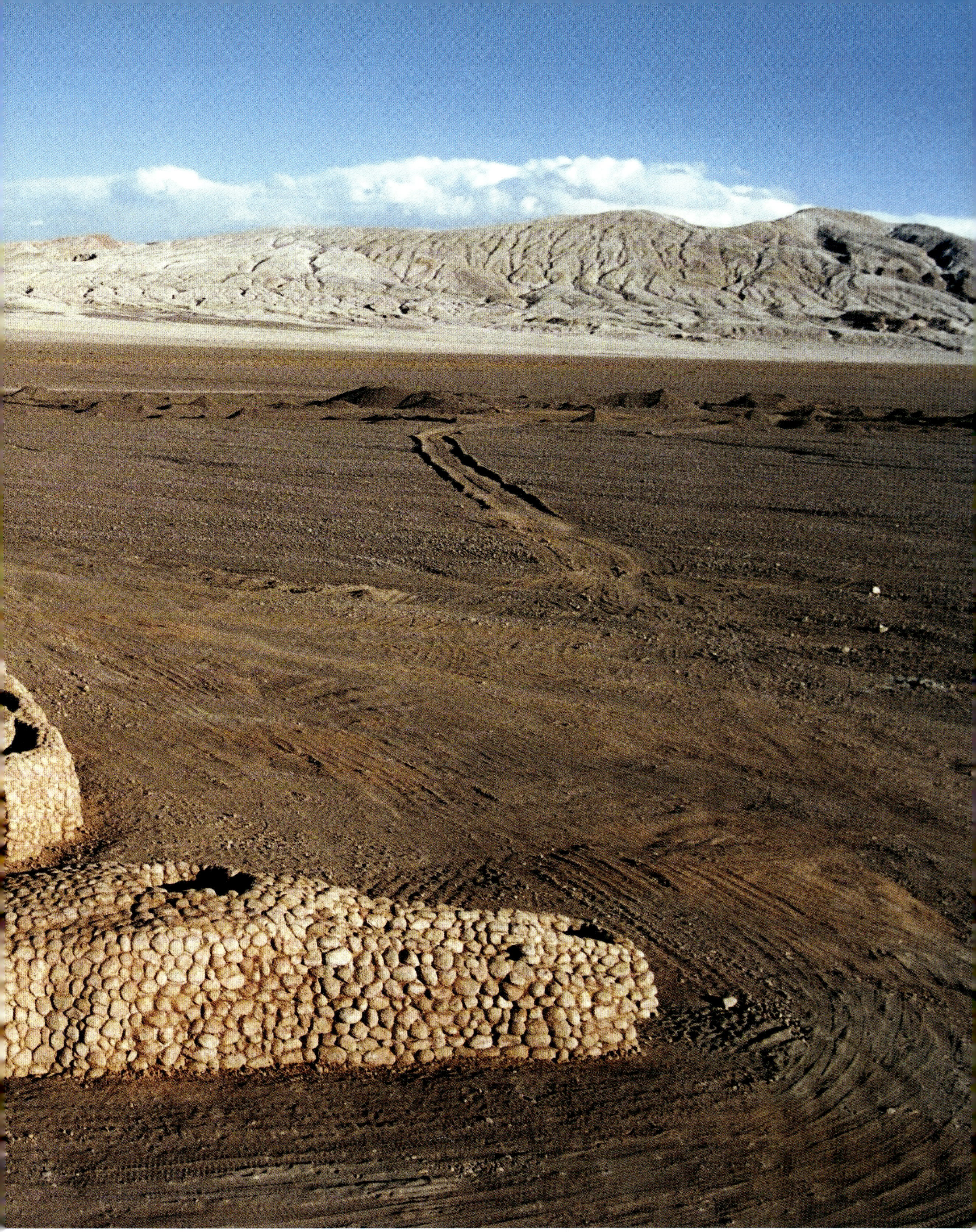

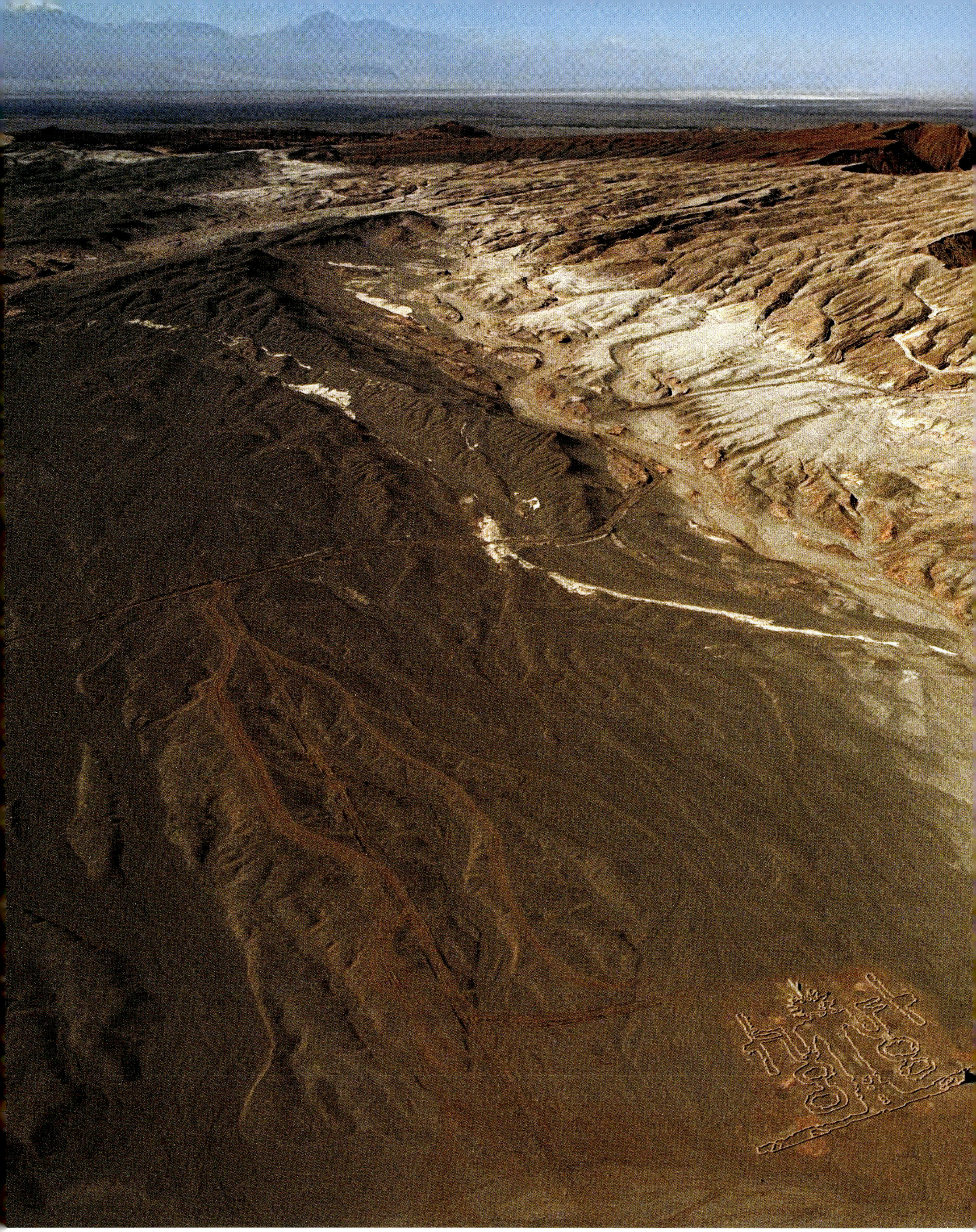

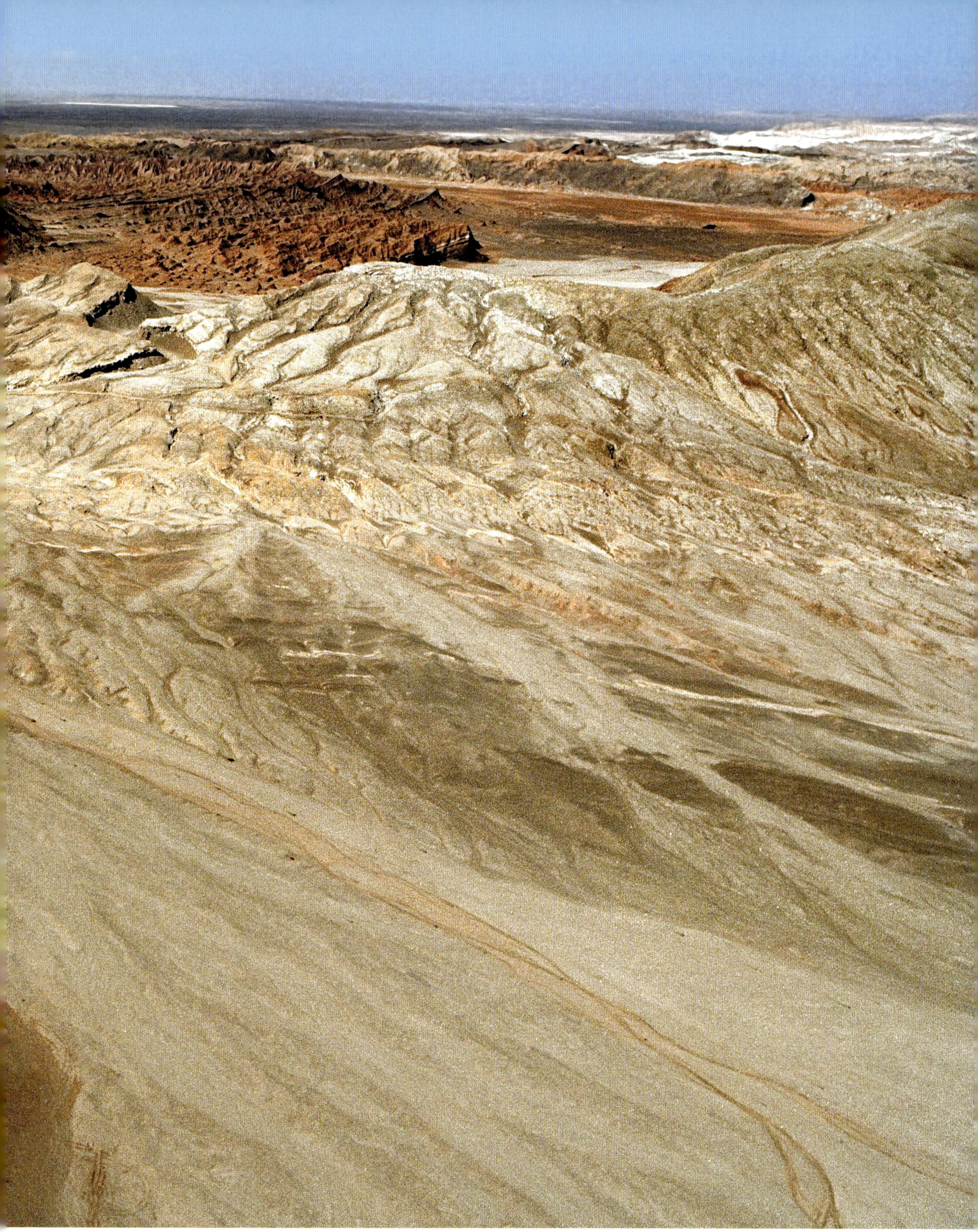

THE ANCIENTS 2004 / Volcanic rock, clay, guano / 90 × 90 m (295 × 295 ft.)

ABOVE THE SILVER MINES OF POTOSI
ALTIPLANO, BOLIVIA

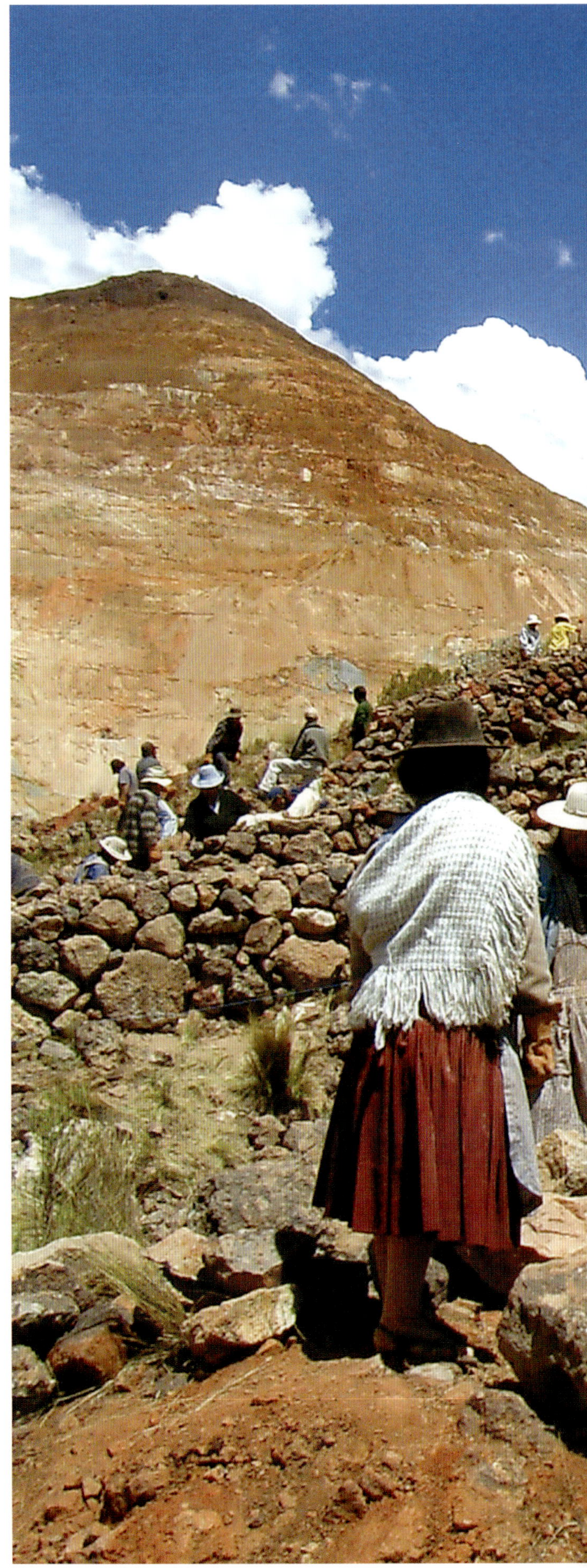

For his next geoglyphs, *Circles, Presence*, and *Rhythms of Life*, Andrew Rogers shifted his attention to Bolivia, Chile's neighbor in the Andes region, a country on whose extremely high plateaus the Incas erected the center of their 300-year empire, leaving behind numerous famous ruins, such as those at Tiwanaku. The Inca Empire is without equal in South America to this day. By the fifteenth century, it ruled over more than 250 ethnic groups and 9 million people. Its north-to-south extension was longer than the distance between Norway's North Cape and Sicily. Humankind has been fascinated not only by the legendary wealth of the Inca, but also by their regimented body politic, brilliantly developed road network, and settlements whose dimensions and splendor surpassed many European cities of that time. Rogers chose a spectacular site for his geoglyphs in this historico-culturally dense environment: various precipices at an altitude of 4,360 meters (14,304 feet) on the highest level of Cerro Rico. At the base of the mountain lies Potosi, a mining town that was initially one of the most important economic centers of the Spanish Empire due to the silver mines at Cerro Rico ("rich mountain"). It also became a synonym for the exploitation and eradication of the Inca's advanced civilization. The people of Potosi have yet to recover from the repercussions of what was then the New World Spanish Empire; today it is one of the most impoverished cities in South America. Even young women, many carrying infants on their backs, asked Rogers for employment when he was assembling working parties for Cerro Rico. Rogers was glad to be able to help them. In the end, 500 women and 300 men joined forces to build a contemporary land art installation of major scale at the highest altitude in the world. They formed human chains and passed the heavy stones upward over the extremely steep and rough slope, where stonemasons then assembled them to create enormous, works of art.
For Andrew Rogers, petroglyphs of the region again served as his source material. In the nearby region of

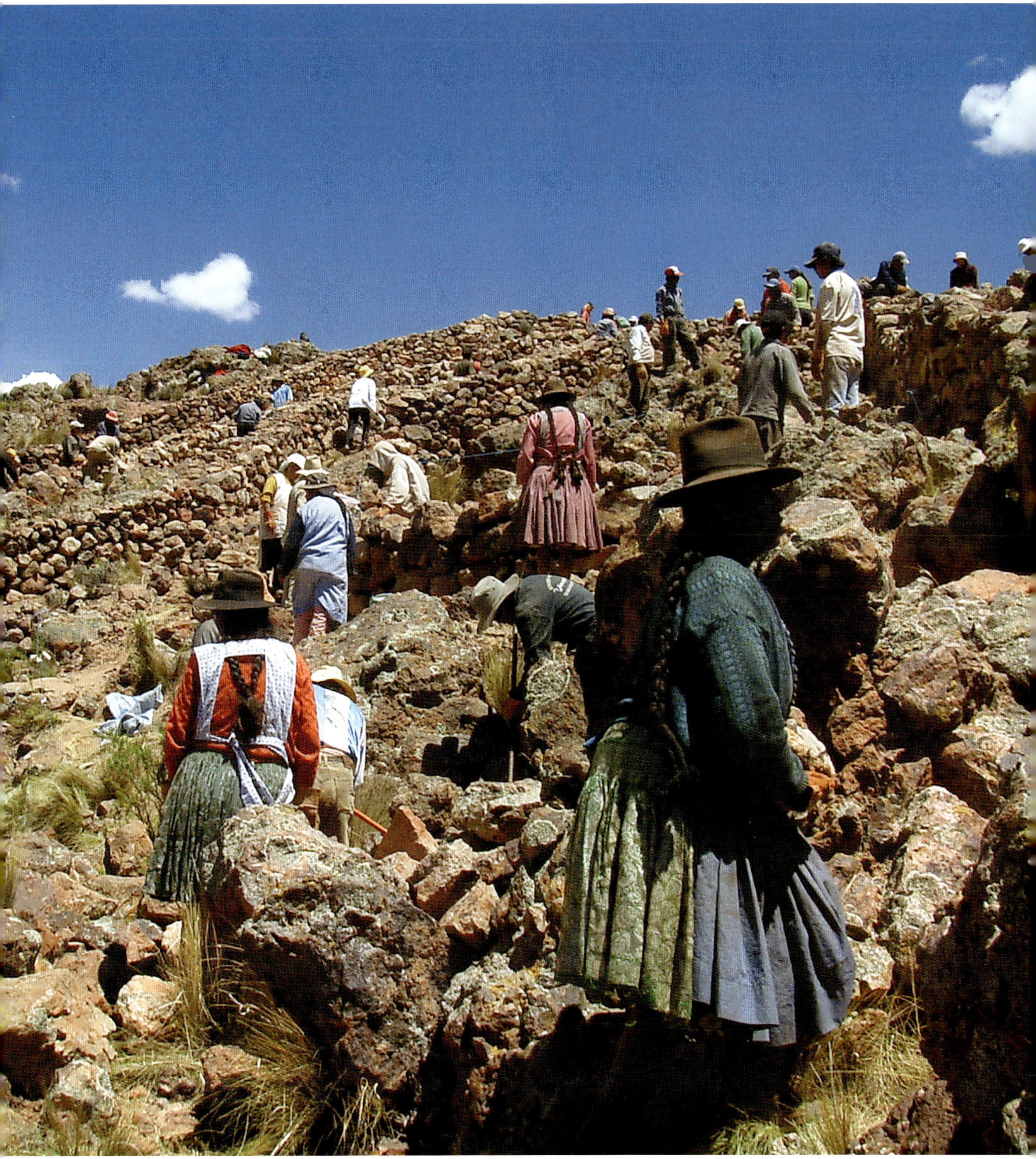

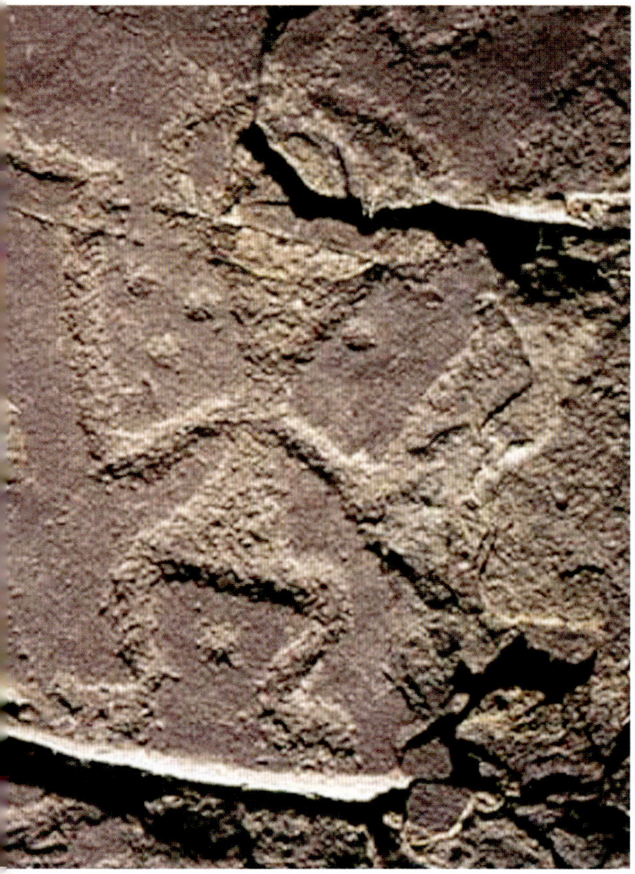

1

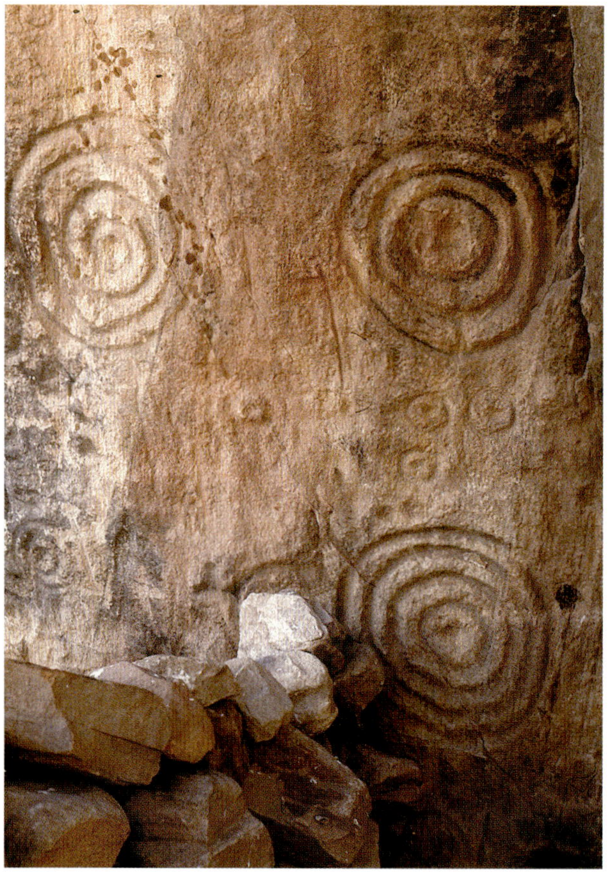

2

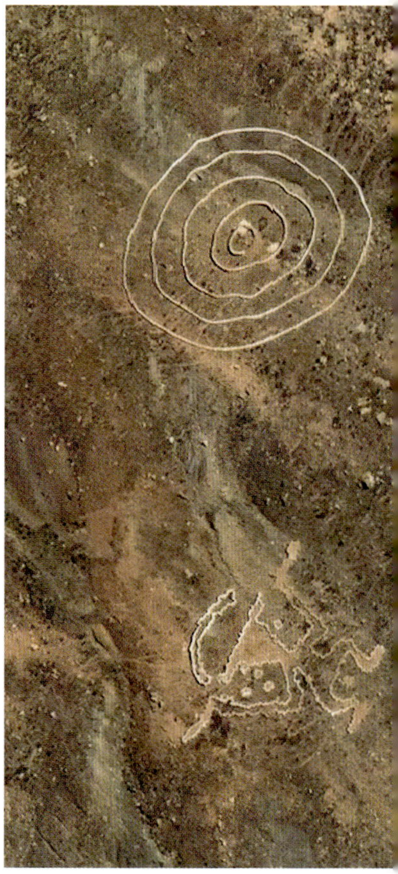

1 Petroglyph, dancing shaman

2 Petroglyph, circles

3 PRESENCE and CIRCLES, satellite image taken 440 km (275 miles) above the earth

4 RHYTHMS OF LIFE, satellite image taken 440 km (275 miles) above the earth

Betanzos, one of the village elders took him on a long hike and proudly called his attention to several concentric rings that were precisely carved into the rock face eight thousand years ago. In a folkloric context they symbolize many things: groups or families, the documentation of a first-born child, fertility, female genitals, and the solar or lunar cycles. Others see them as referring to a gravestone. Interestingly, the minimalist symbol can be found at a wide variety of places in the world, from North and South America all the way to Central Asia. This would be the original model for *Circles*.

With his enormous structure, Rogers presents posterity with a further example of interpretation. The symbol with circles placed one inside the other is layered out of compact stone walls, a powerful image that sets itself apart from the steep mountain ridges.

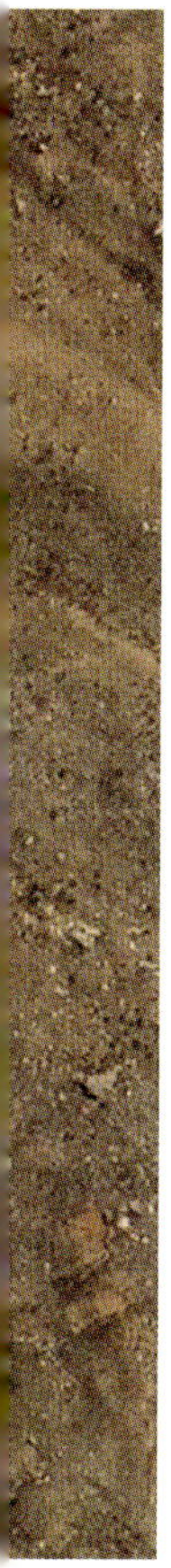

3

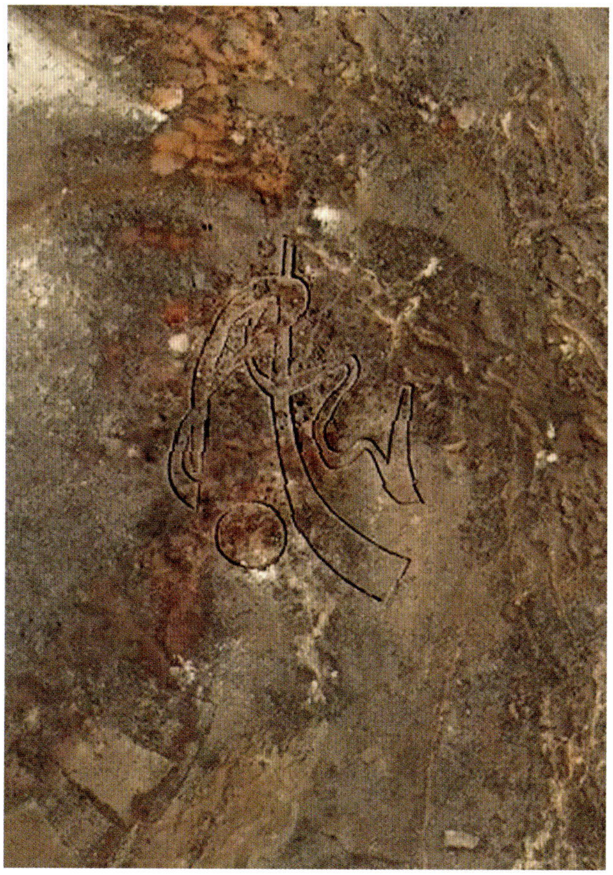

4

In the case of the *Presence* geoglyph, Andrew Rogers also enlarged his model, a petroglyph with the dancing figure of a shaman, to measure 100 × 100 meters (330 × 330 feet). What is striking is the figure's oversized, triangular headdress and raised hands, which hold instruments of power or assume a posture of worship. As in Chile, Rogers drew on the idea of a delicate image. However, in addition to the corresponding state of the original source, he wanted to render visible the aspect of impermanence. He therefore consciously and constantly varied the diameter of the continuous wall. This gives the impression of a fragile drawing that takes off from the ground. Or as Rogers puts it: "I wanted it very loose, like a calligraphy."

The *Rhythms of Life* geoglyph is on a steep slope located 6 kilometers (3.7 miles) away from *Presence* and *Circles*. Yet thanks to the clarity of the air at the high altitude, they are all within sight of one another and once again demonstrate the content-related reference to the long history of the Bolivian site.

As in Chile, the local inhabitants held a Pachamama ritual at the beginning and at the end of the creation of the structures. This rite, performed before commencement of work, can be traced back to the Inca period and requires the sacrifice of a llama. A shaman pours its blood onto the site of the geoglyph, and then its entrails are cooked and afterward burned and buried along with its bones. This was an expression of gratitude to the creative primal sources of the earth and the sun for their blessings. One sees how deeply the indigenous people's belief in and adherence to rituals continues to be: they remain strongly connected with their old culture. Hence they ideally bring the central idea of the entire *Rhythms of Life* project to life and in their own way render it visible—and palpable.

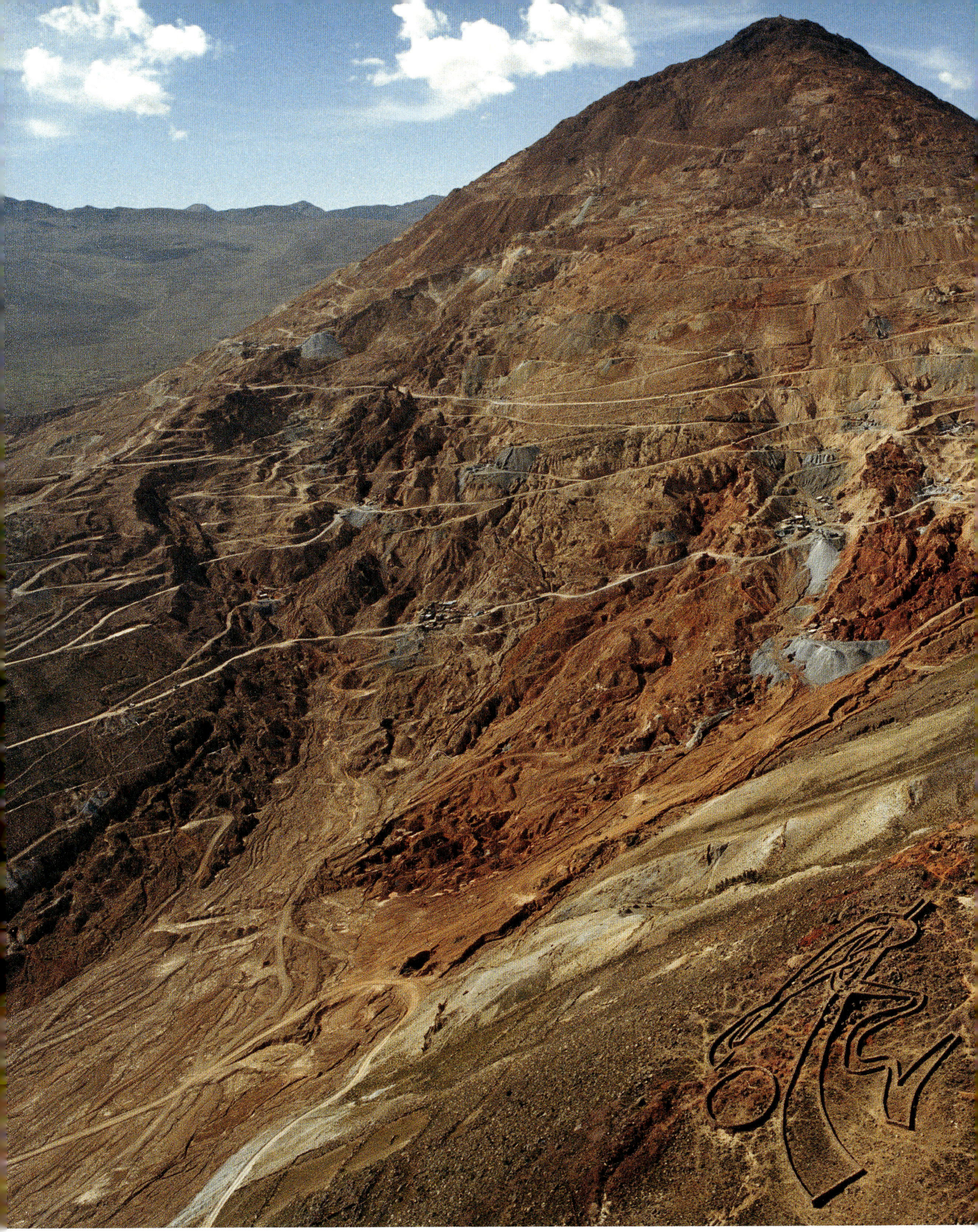

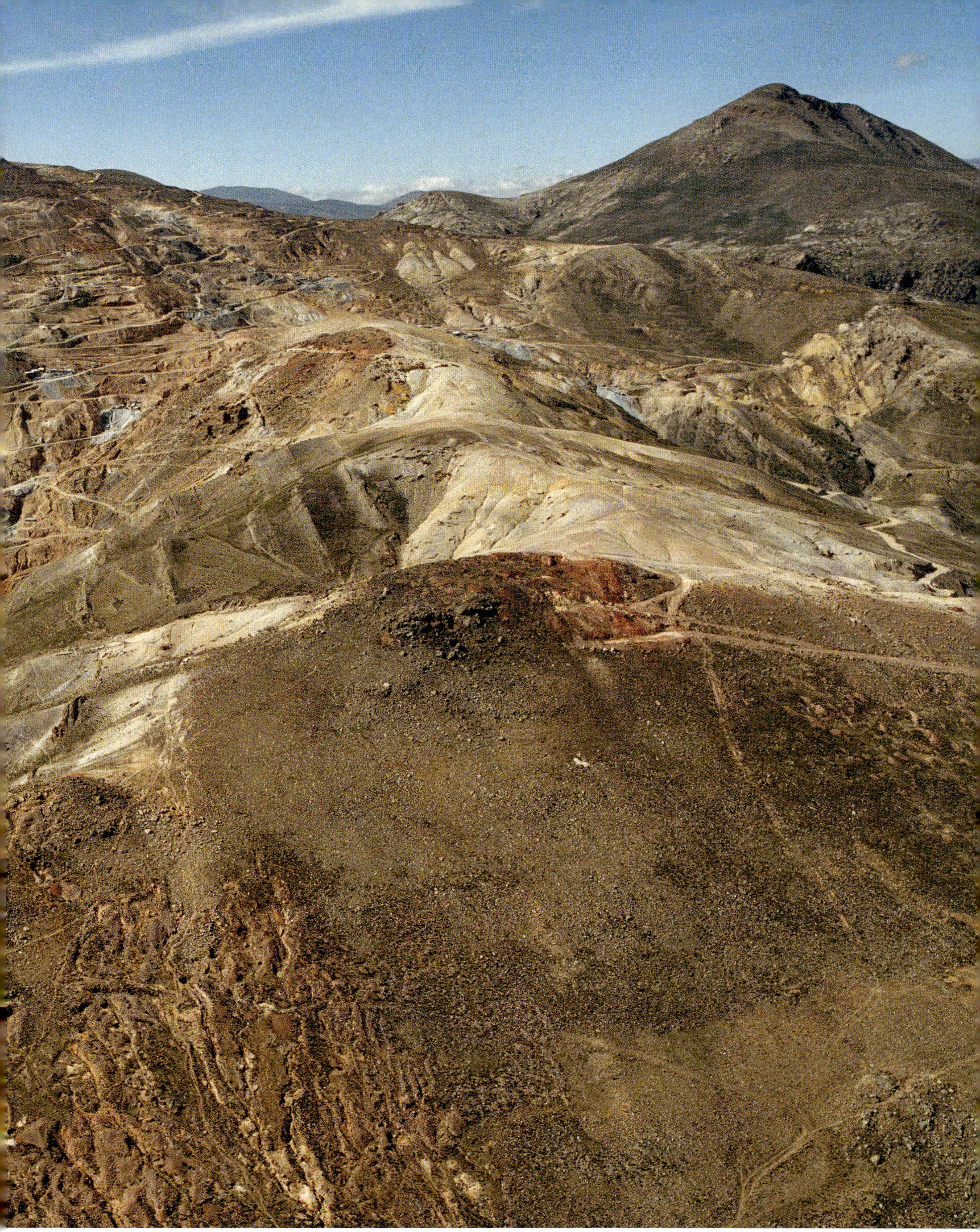

RHYTHMS OF LIFE 2005 / Volcanic rock / 100 × 100 m (330 × 330 ft.)

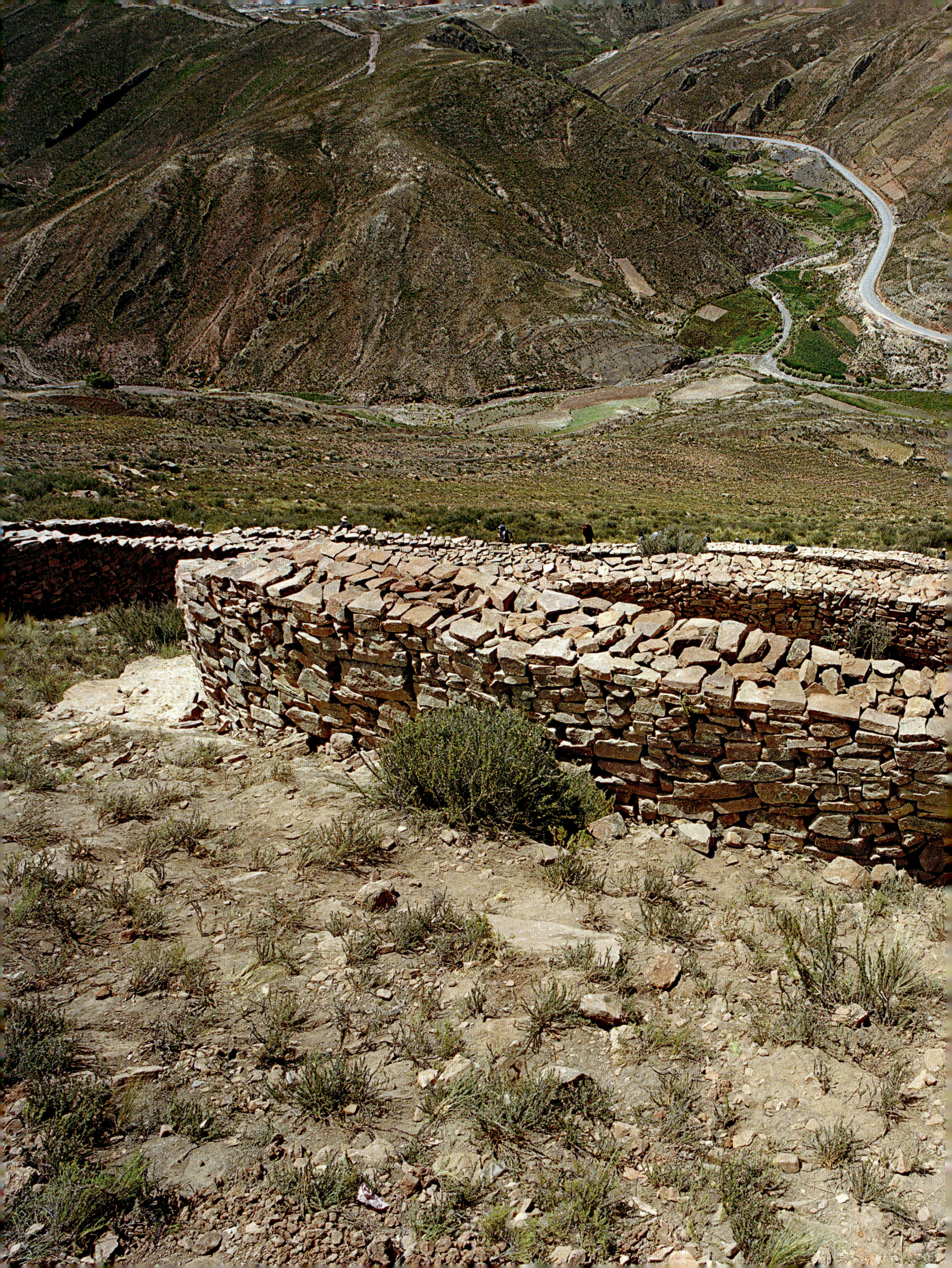

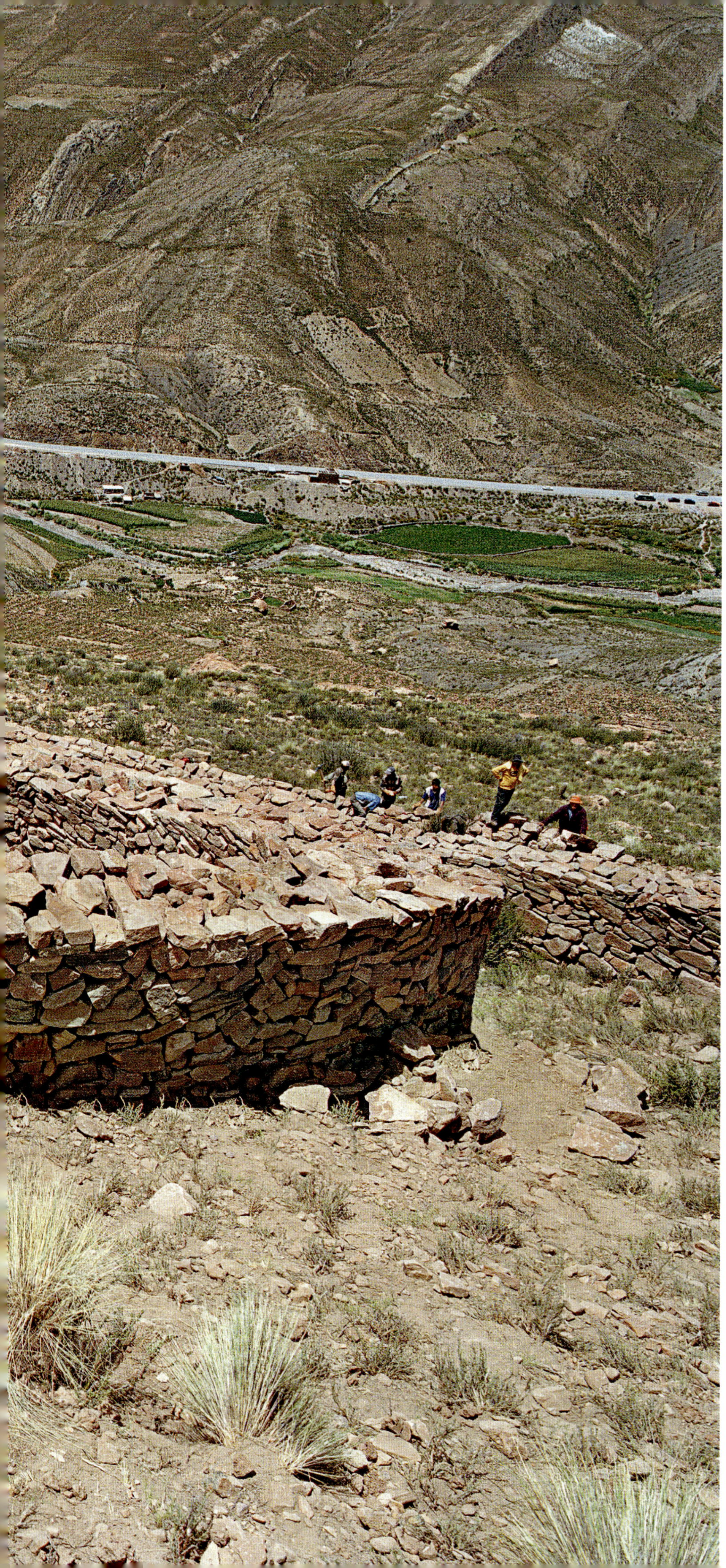

PRESENCE 2005 / Volcanic rock / 100 × 100 m (330 × 330 ft.)

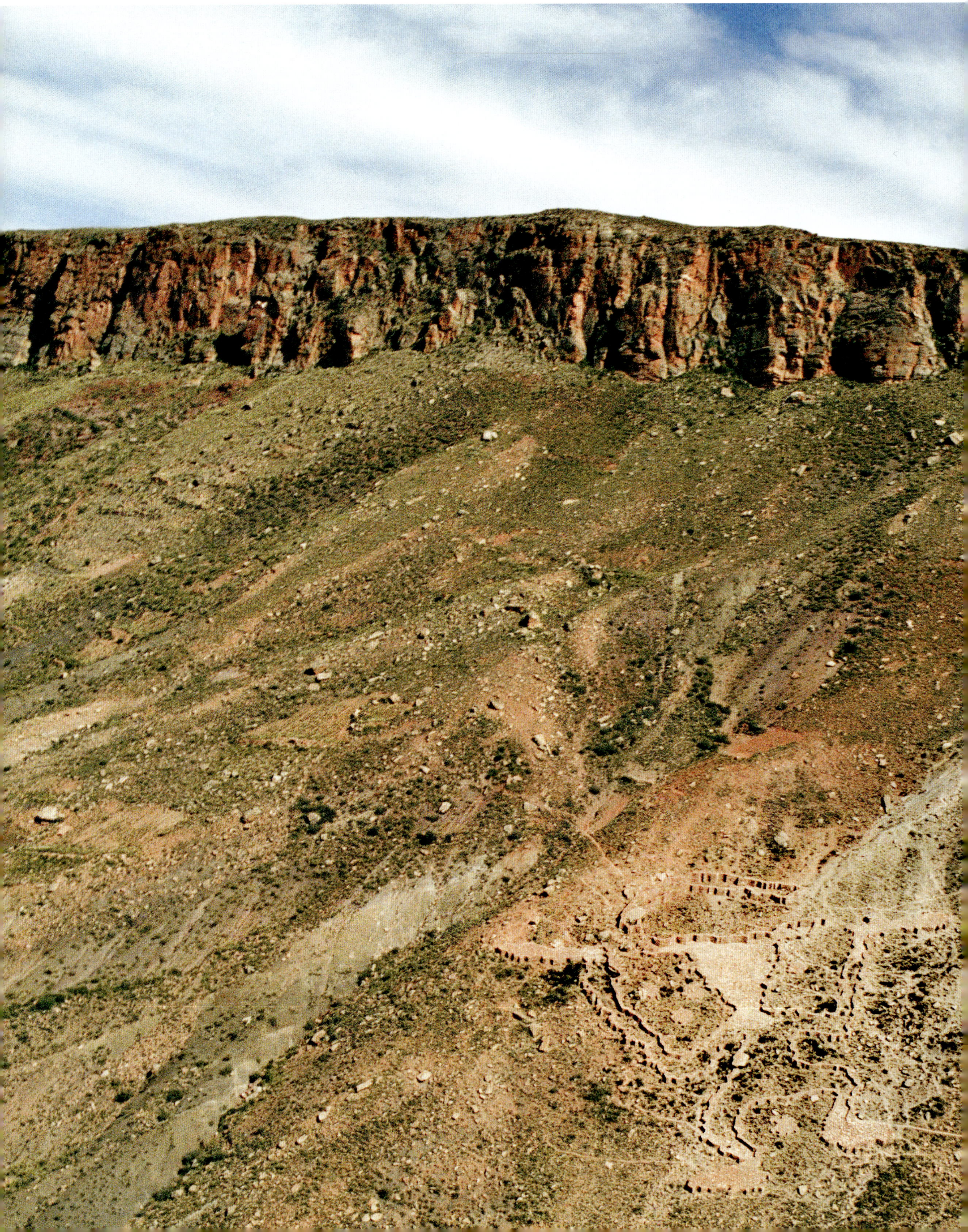

CIRCLES 2005 / Volcanic rock / 100 m (300 ft.) diameter

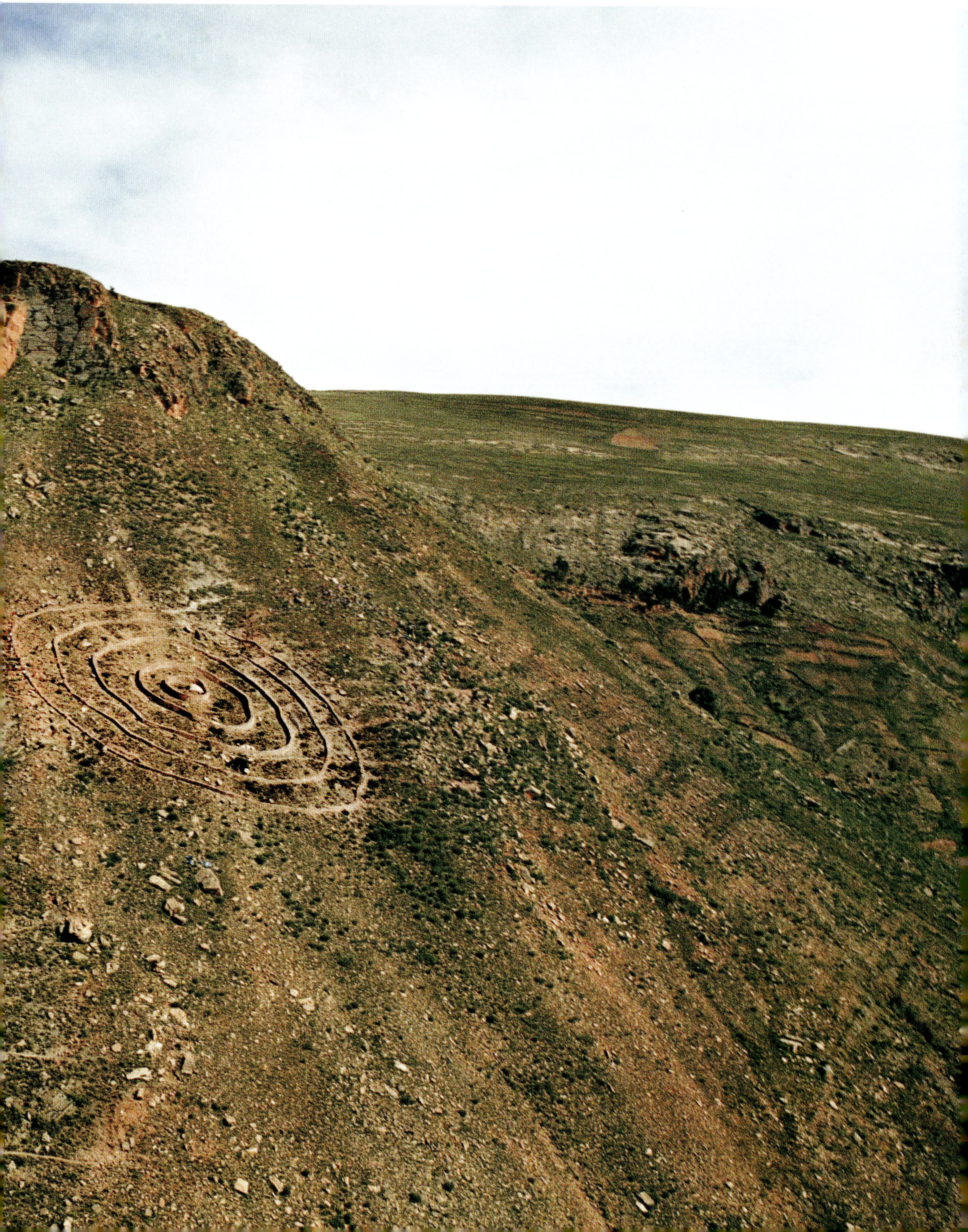

ON BARE ROCK
KURUNEGALA, SRI LANKA

The site for Rogers's next project could not have been more different: instead of the arid steppe climate and barren expanses of Bolivia's Altiplano, there was the humid tropical monsoon climate of Sri Lanka and its almost unbridled flora. Instead of the Inca mythology, there was the vibrant symbolic world of four of the world's largest religions: Buddhism, Hinduism, Islam, and Christianity. Andrew Rogers was fascinated by the numerous new facets presented to him by this island in the Indian Ocean: Merchants brought Islam from the Middle East to what had originally been a Buddhist country; the Tamils from neighboring India introduced Hinduism, and with the British and the Dutch came Christianity. However, the majority of the population, the Sinhalese, continues to practice Buddhism to this day.
Rogers chose the site for his geoglyphs near the small town of Kurunegala, not far from the coast in the northwestern part of the island. He was captivated by the site's being next to a large placid lake, around which eight enormous, bare ridges rise to a height of up to 350 meters (1,148 feet) and radiate as imposing highlights out of the deep green of the tropical palm forests. This is where the two geoglyphs *Rhythms of Life* and *Pride* were to be built, as well as the vertical stone structure *Ascend* within sight of the lake. Six of the eight rocky hills bear characteristic names; the largest was christened Ethagala (Elephant Rock). Giving names to the hills can be traced back to an old folk legend according to which the city once suffered from a terrible drought. The animals exacerbated the situation—they needed so much water that the city's water reserves were seriously threatened. Yet with the help of a witch, the largest animals—such as, for example, an elephant or a tortoise—were turned into stone, liberating the people from their hardship.
Water was also a source of hardship for Andrew Rogers, however in quite a different way: torrential rainfall, heat and the resultant high humidity made the extremely steep slopes almost impossible to negotiate. Rogers had no other choice than to build a

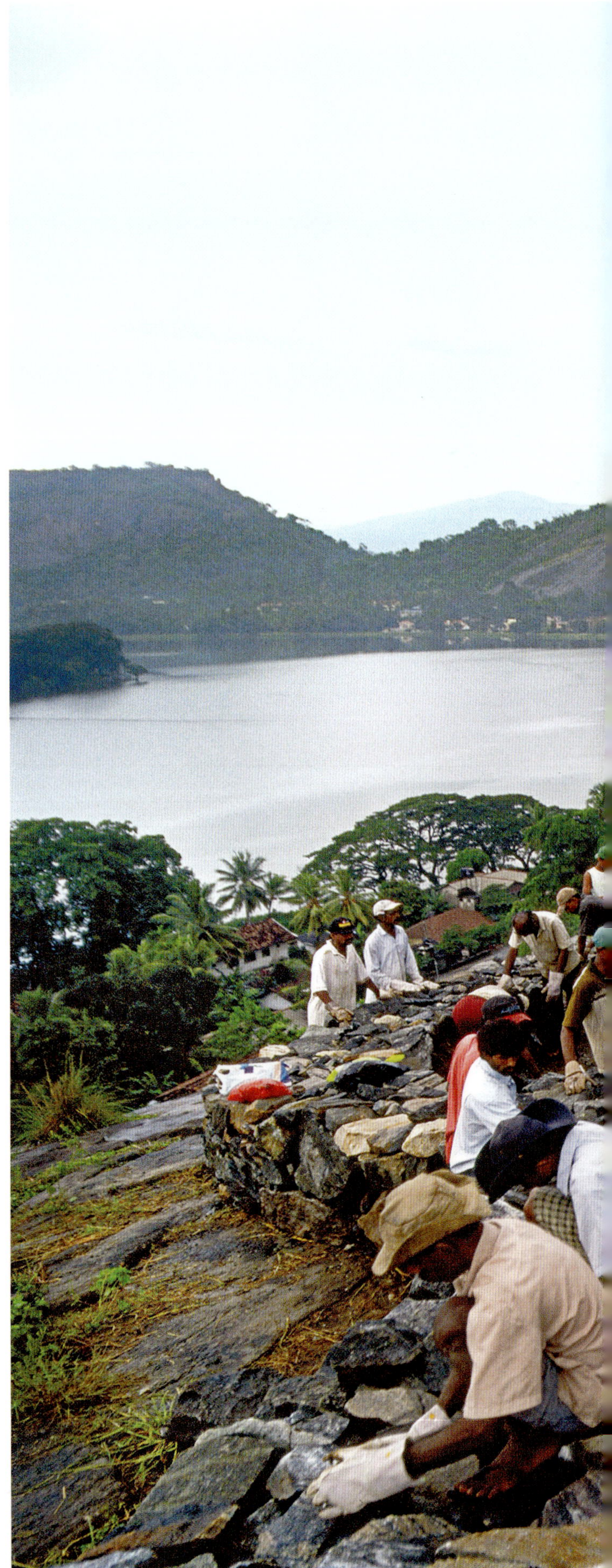

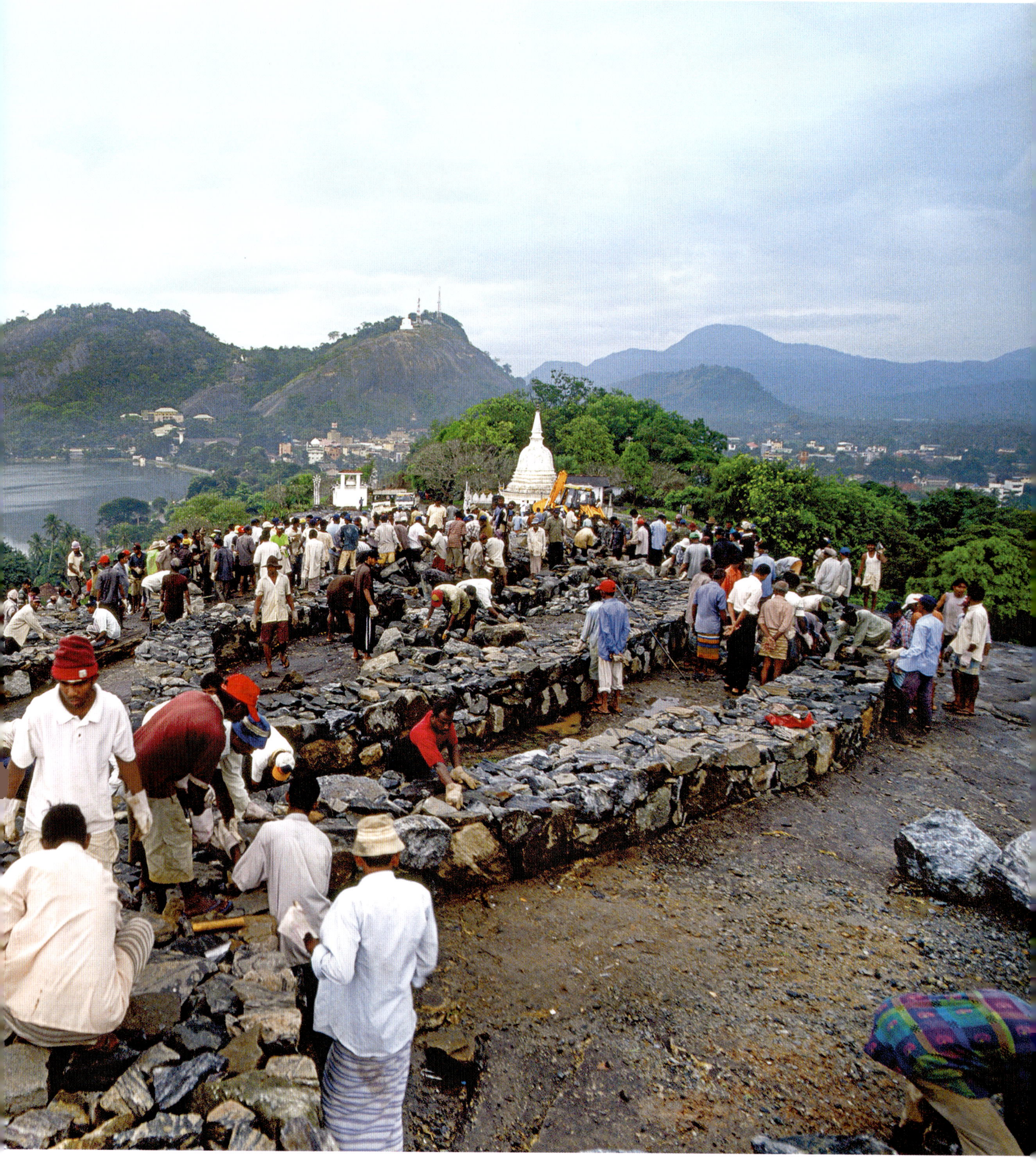

road for the transport of the rocks and to draw up an elaborate logistical plan for organizing the 850 local laborers before actual construction work could begin under such inhospitable conditions.

"We had to feed them three meals a day, breakfast, lunch, and dinner, and needed to create cooking sheds. Just getting the necessary amount of drinking water for the people working in the 30- to 34-degree [86–93°F] heat and 80 percent humidity was a logistical nightmare," the artist recalled. Hardly any of the laborers had proper footwear. A physician was employed to look after those who sustained cuts from the sharp pieces of rock. He also became a general health consultant to the workers and their families.

The surface of the giant rock faces were slippery from the rains, which made them difficult to work on. The smooth surface of the rock faces did not present any grippable foundation whatsoever for the erection of walls. Stainless steel rods had to be inserted deep in the rock for the purpose of supporting the construction.

The first geoglyph is situated on the steepest incline next to a temple complex with a stupa on a uniformly rounded ridge. The symbol, made of layered granite stone walls, extends over nearly the entire ridge on a surface area of 60 × 60 meters (197 × 197 feet). For safety reasons, the largest flat-surfaced rocks possible were used for the walls; the laborers had to pass them carefully, one at a time, in a long human chain over the slippery rock surface.

The second geoglyph, *Pride*, a gigantic stylized lion comprised of stone walls the same size as those used for *Rhythms of Life*, was situated on the same rocky ridge. Rogers based the form on an ancient painting that local inhabitants had shown him in one of the numerous old Buddhist temples in the area. The lion is the most important symbol for the Sinhalese, Sri Lanka's largest ethnic group. In their language, *sinha* means lion, and it adorns the country's national flag, which is why it is also referred to as the "Lion Flag." According to legend, Vijaya, the first king of Sri Lanka, is alleged to have brought it along after returning from India in 486 BC—as the Buddhist symbol of strength and power. Rogers chose the title *Pride* for his depiction of the lion and also underscored this by means of the particularly thick outline and by dispensing with any interior contours.

The shape of the third geoglyph, *Ascend*, resembled the pyramidal stone structure *Ratio*, which Rogers built in the Arava Desert in Israel in 2004. Like *Ratio*, *Ascend* was built according to the Fibonacci sequence; however, the steps reach a height of 6.5 meters (21 feet) on one side only. Rogers's stairs reference the remarkably tall flights of stairs at the numerous local Buddhist temple complexes, the Buddhist symbol for striving toward the infinite—the universe.

Ascend rises in a spectacular way and almost like a monument on the narrow stone ridge of the famous Ethagala, one of the longest stones in the world. It required three attempts before he and his laborers succeeded in finding their way up and along the steep cliff. They had to chop their way up the mountain through the completely overgrown, jungle-covered terrain with machetes, and it was only possible to climb up the rock faces with the use of tightly braided ropes made of coconut fiber. This transport route for the building material again required a great deal of caution on the part of the laborers. "There were snakes, and swarms of big red ants which constantly fell on us and stung," the artist recalled with discomfort. The rocks for *Ascend* were left over from a gigantic, 20-meter-tall (65.6 feet) Buddha statue that had recently been hewn in the rock at the Monaragala Viharaya Temple in Rambodagalla, about 20 kilometers (12.5 miles) away from Kurunegala. (It is meant to resemble one of the famous Buddha statues in Bamiyan, Afghanistan, destroyed by the Taliban in 2001.) With his work made of such symbolically charged building material, Rogers joined the ranks of those who want to make the continuity between new and old cultures visible for everyone.

The elaborate festivities that took place before and after the construction of the artworks on the rocky ridges also underscored this aspect. Acrobats, dancers, and officials performed at the opening ceremony wearing traditional costumes, and priests from all four main religions consecrated the project with hot milk. More dancers, drummers, and local inhabitants assembled for the closing ceremony. Many of them even arrived on the backs of elaborately decorated elephants so as to expressly and extensively celebrate the continuity of life with the community of celebrants.

1 Rogers studying the painting of a lion in a local Buddhist temple

2 PRIDE and RHYTHMS OF LIFE, satellite image taken 440 km (275 miles) above the earth

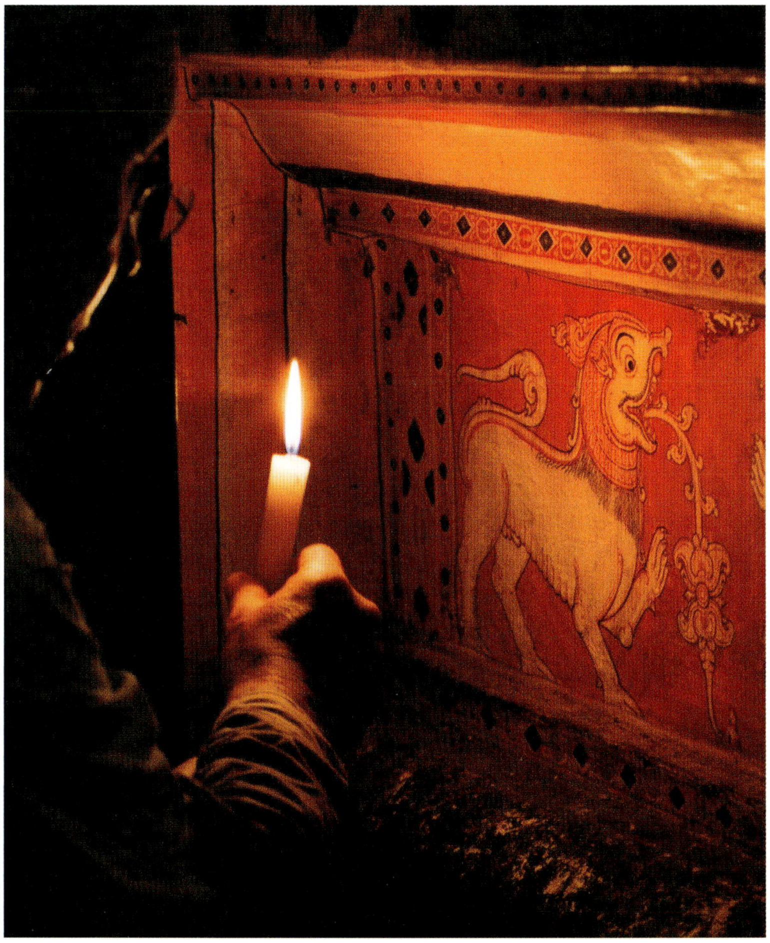

1

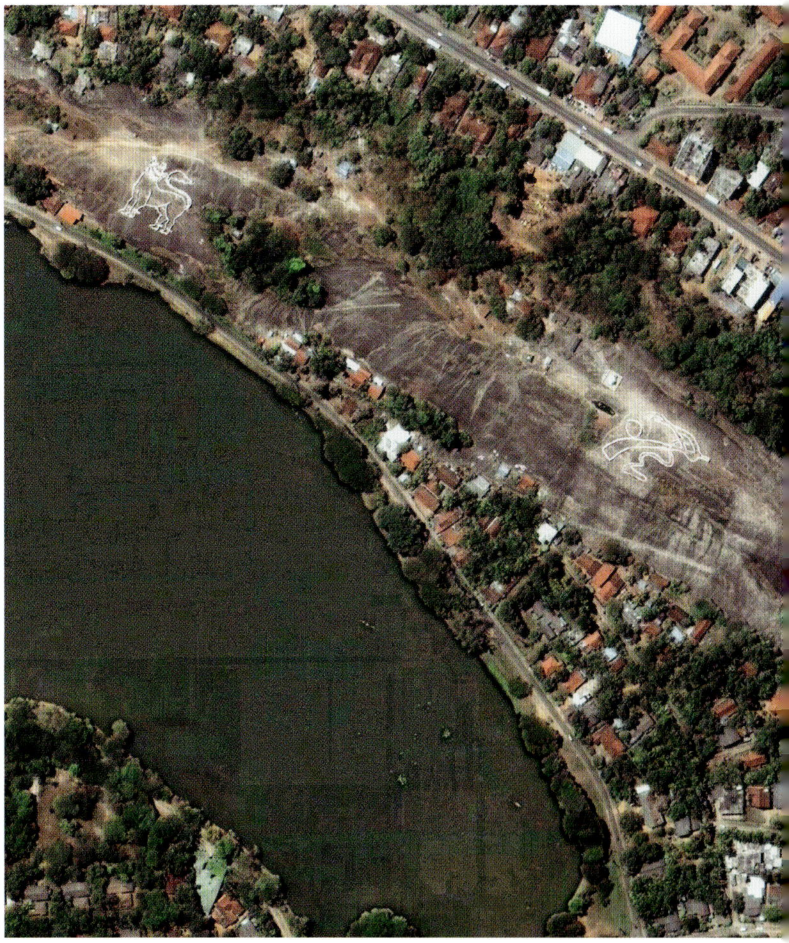

2

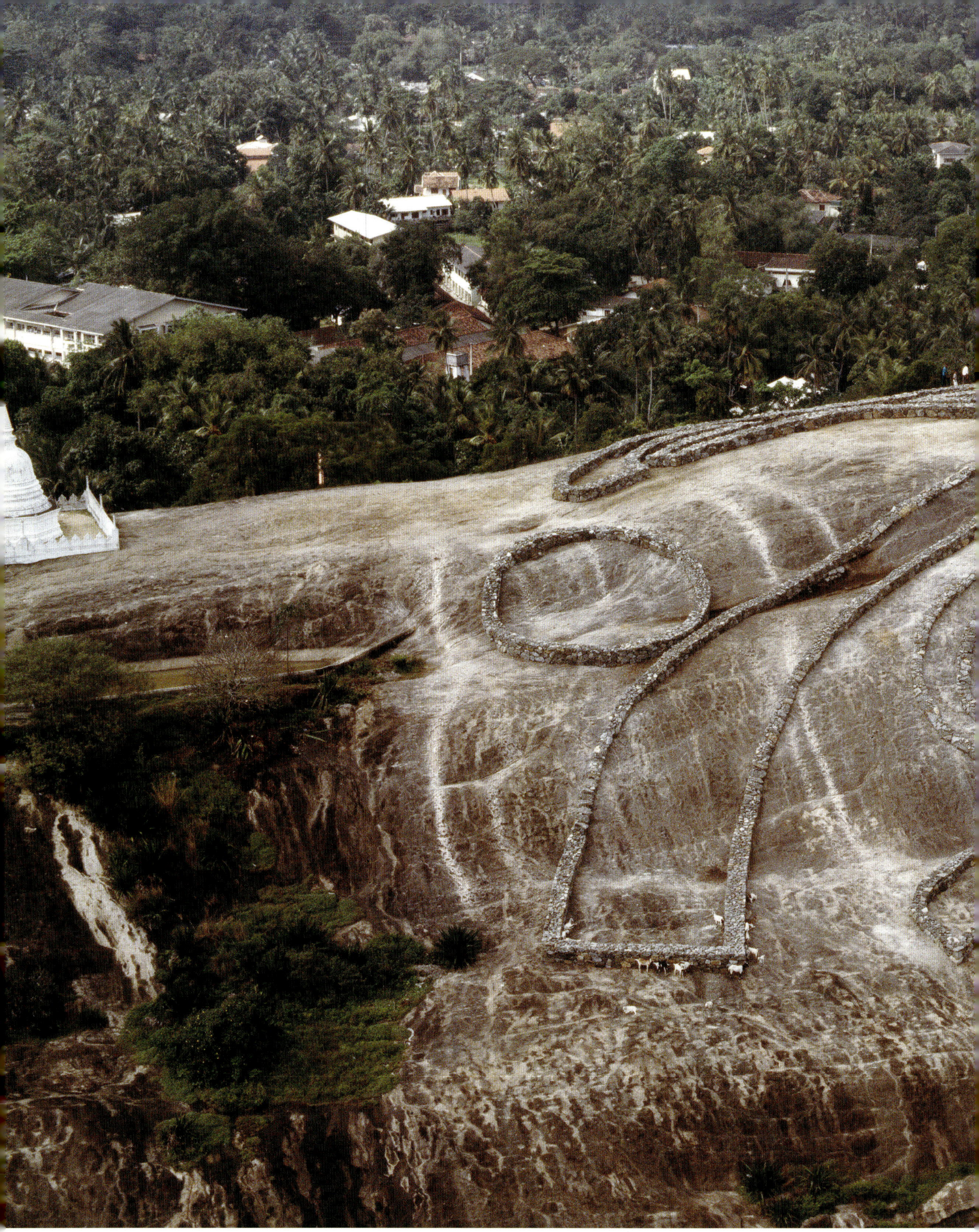

RHYTHMS OF LIFE 2005 / Granite / 60 × 60 m (197 × 197 ft.)

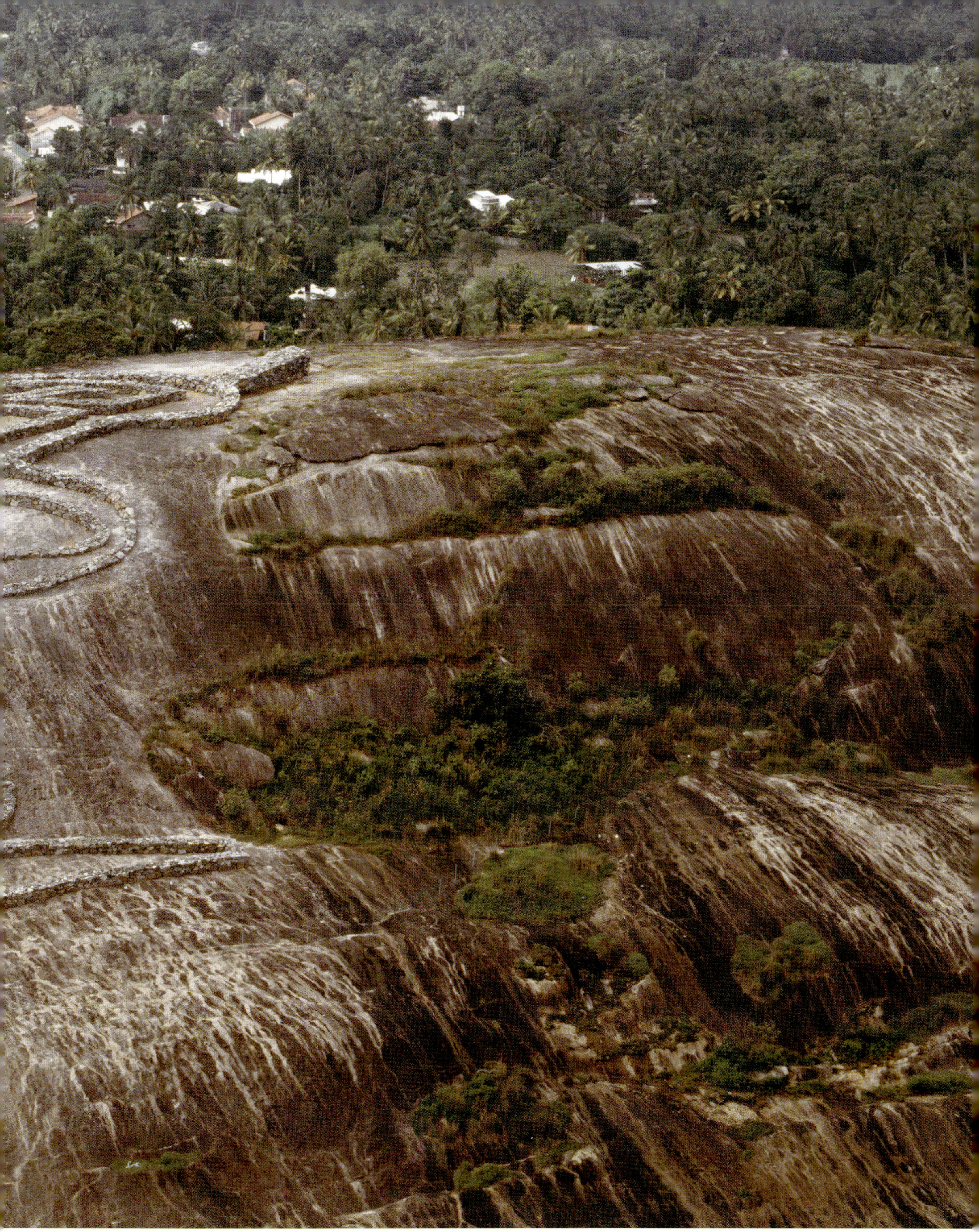

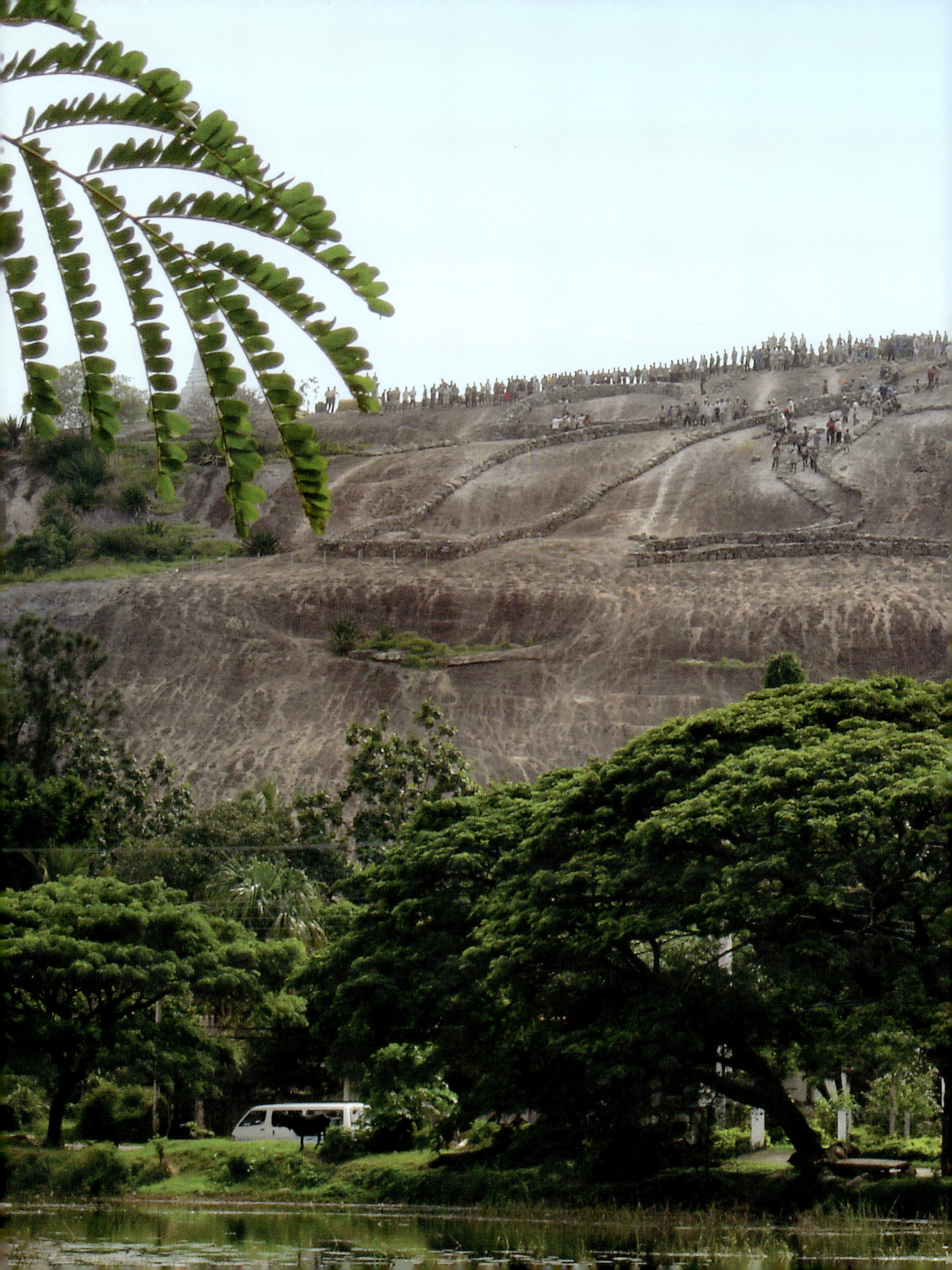

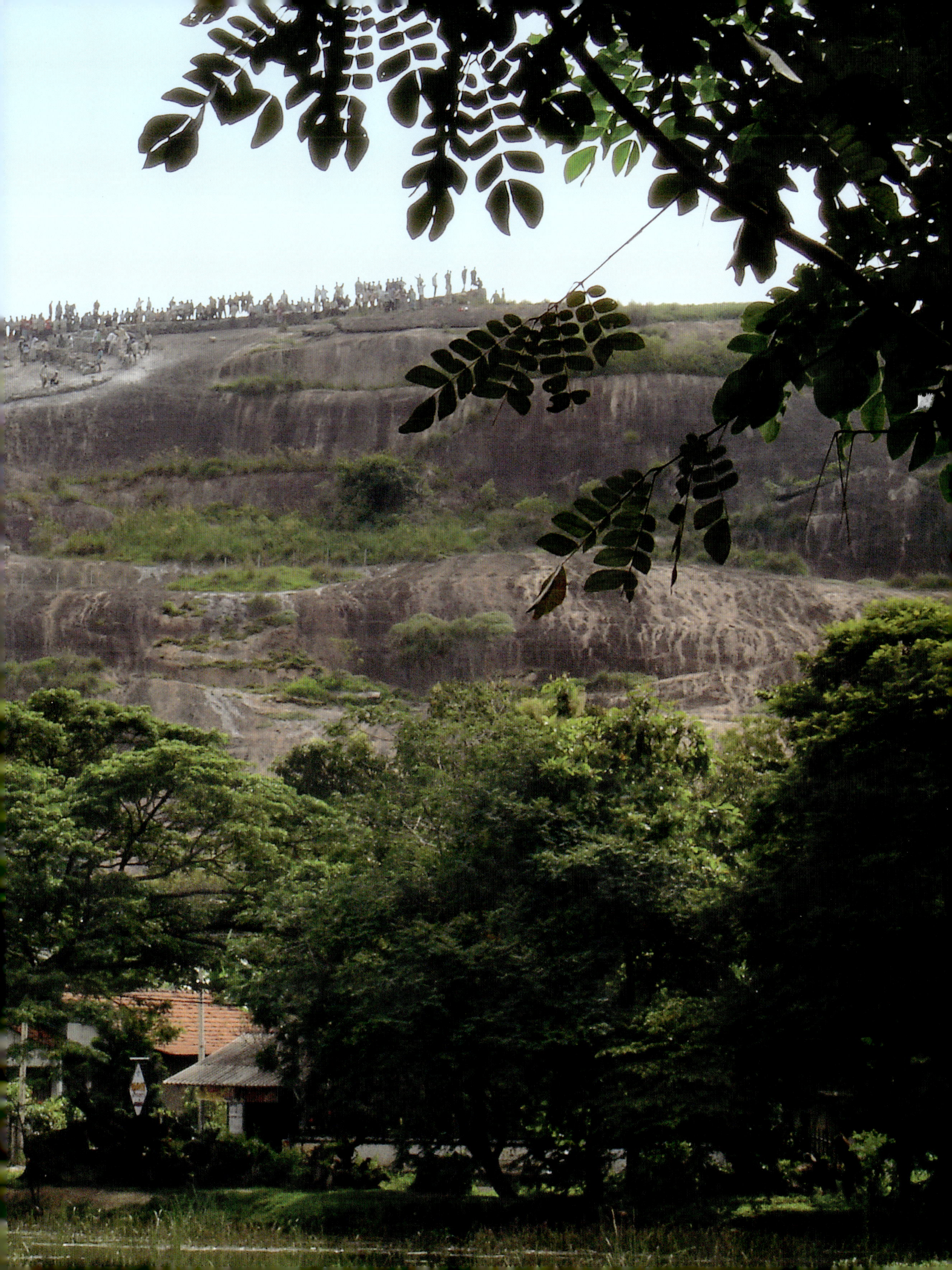

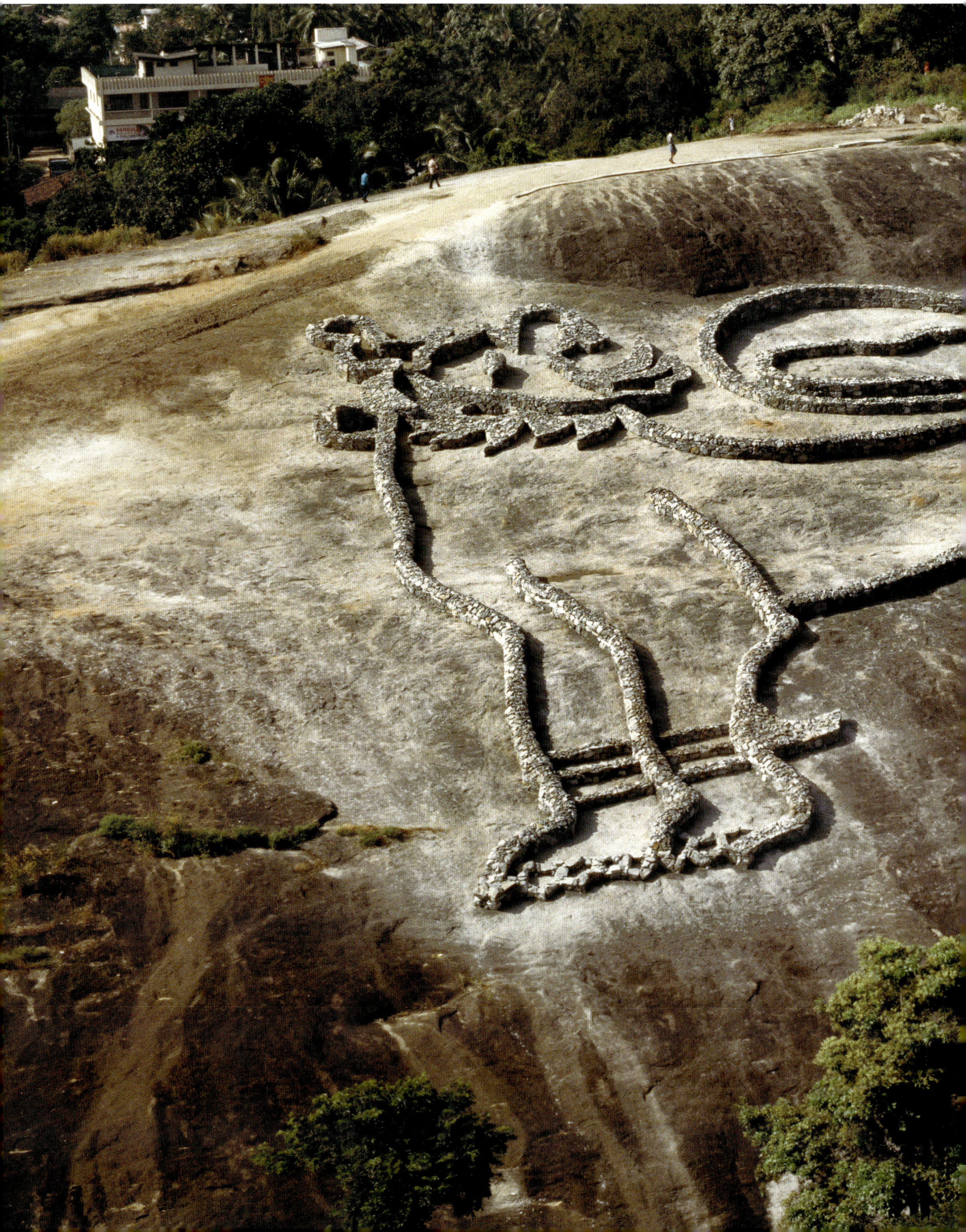

PRIDE 2005 / Granite / 60 × 60 m (197 × 197 ft.)

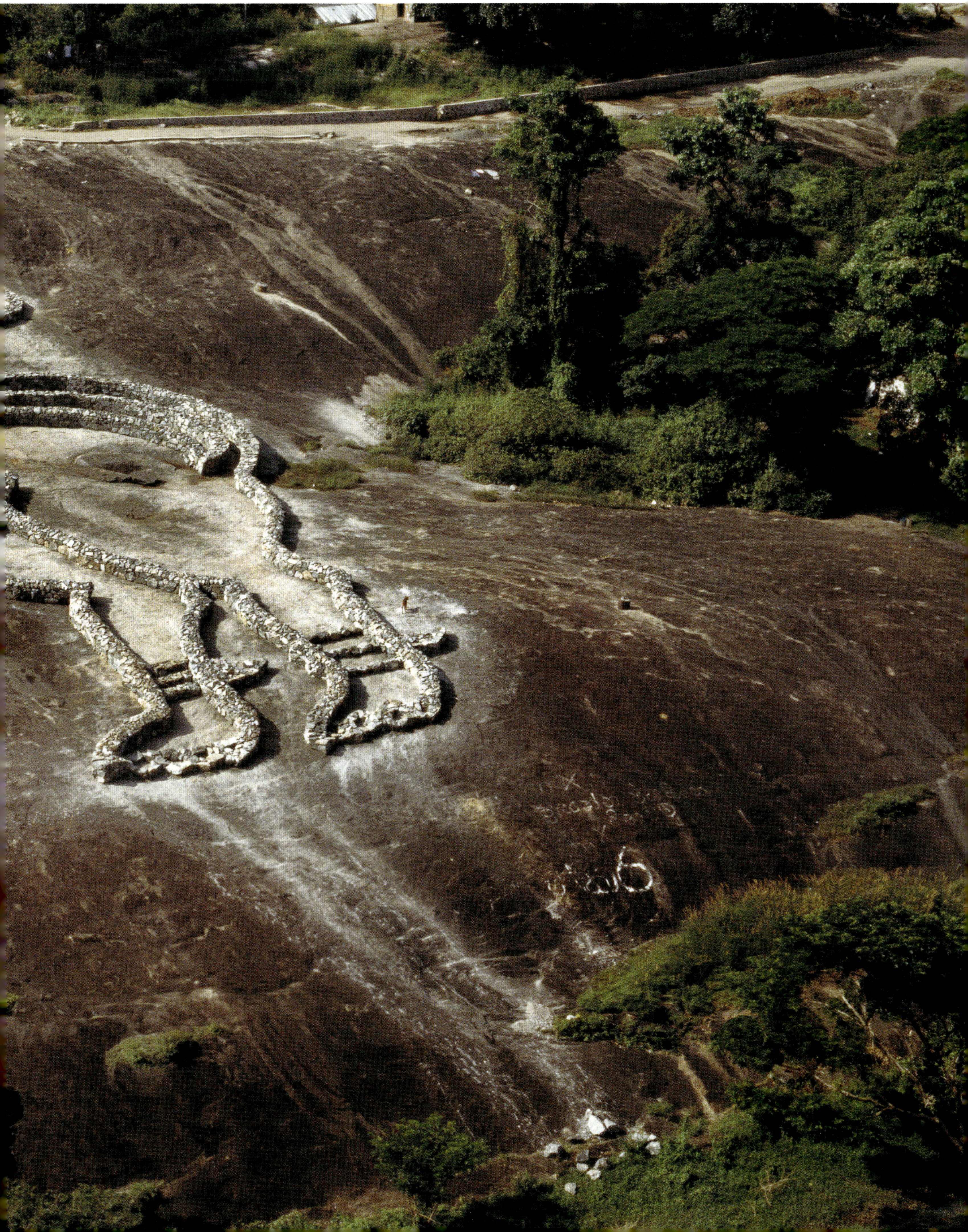

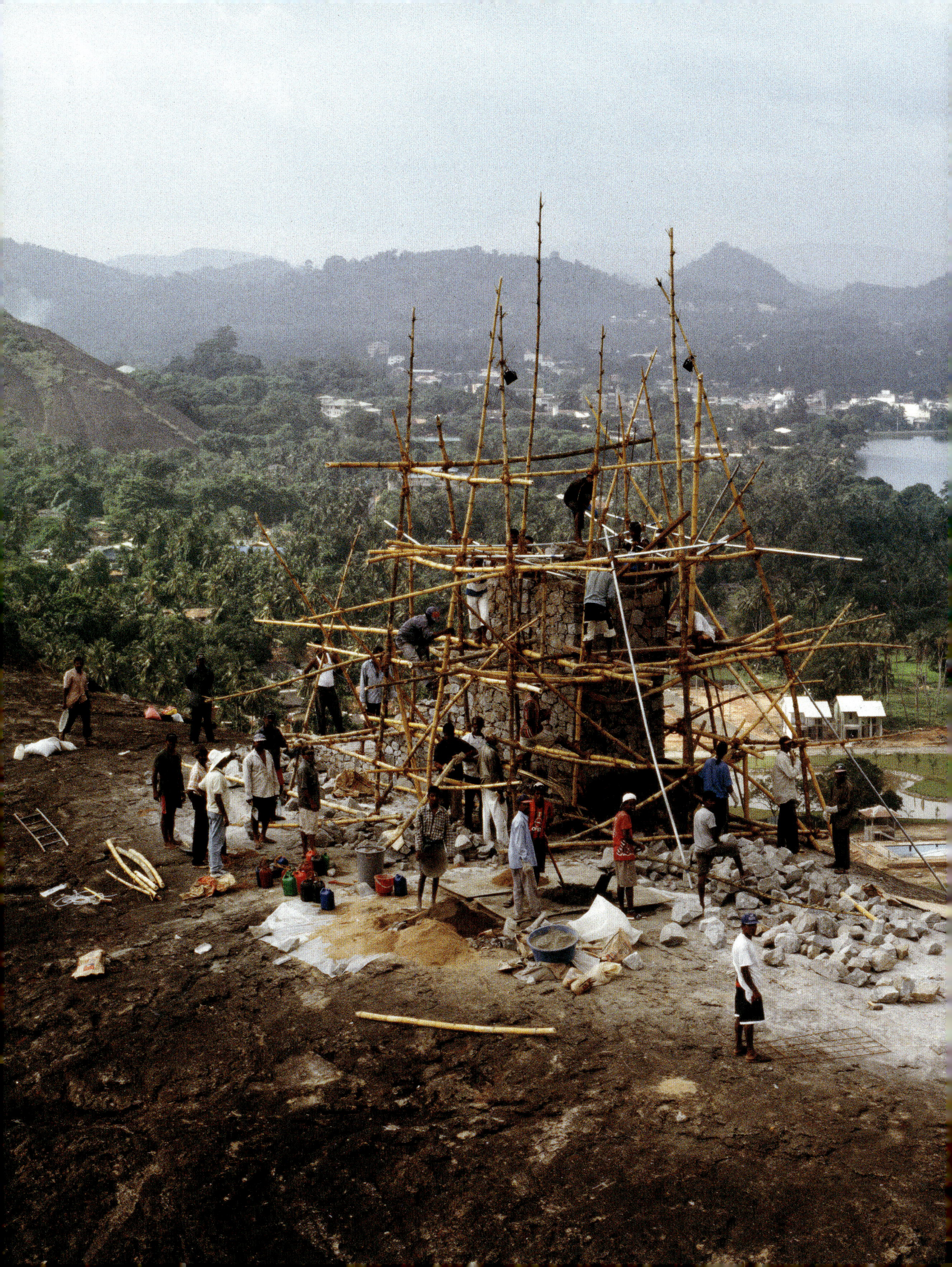

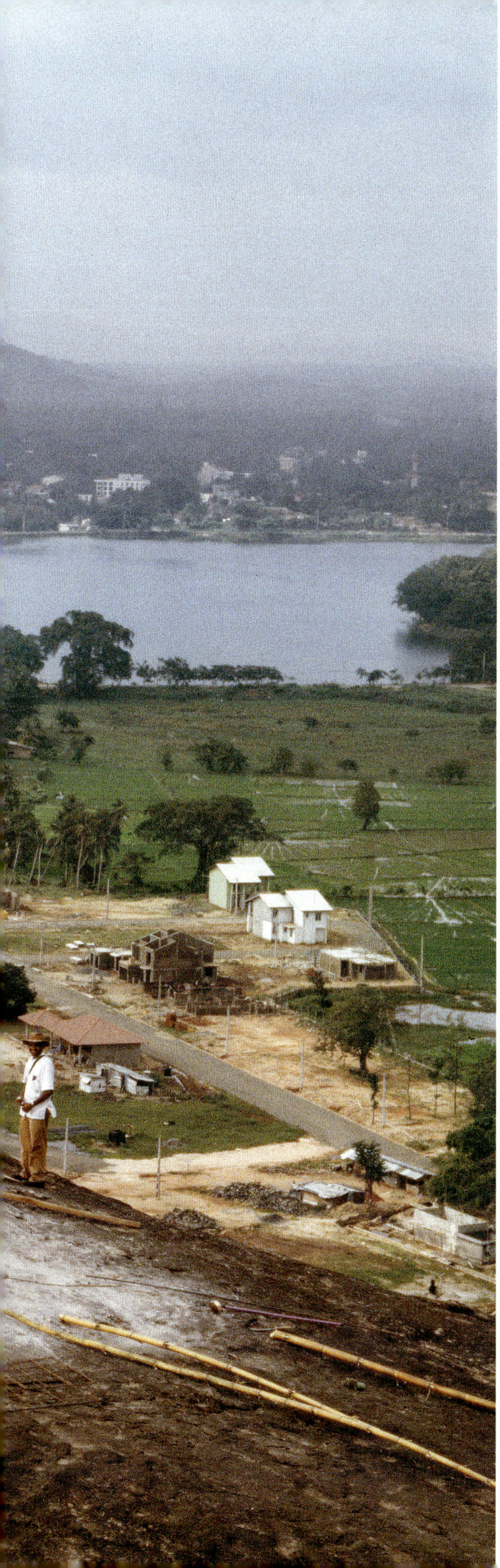

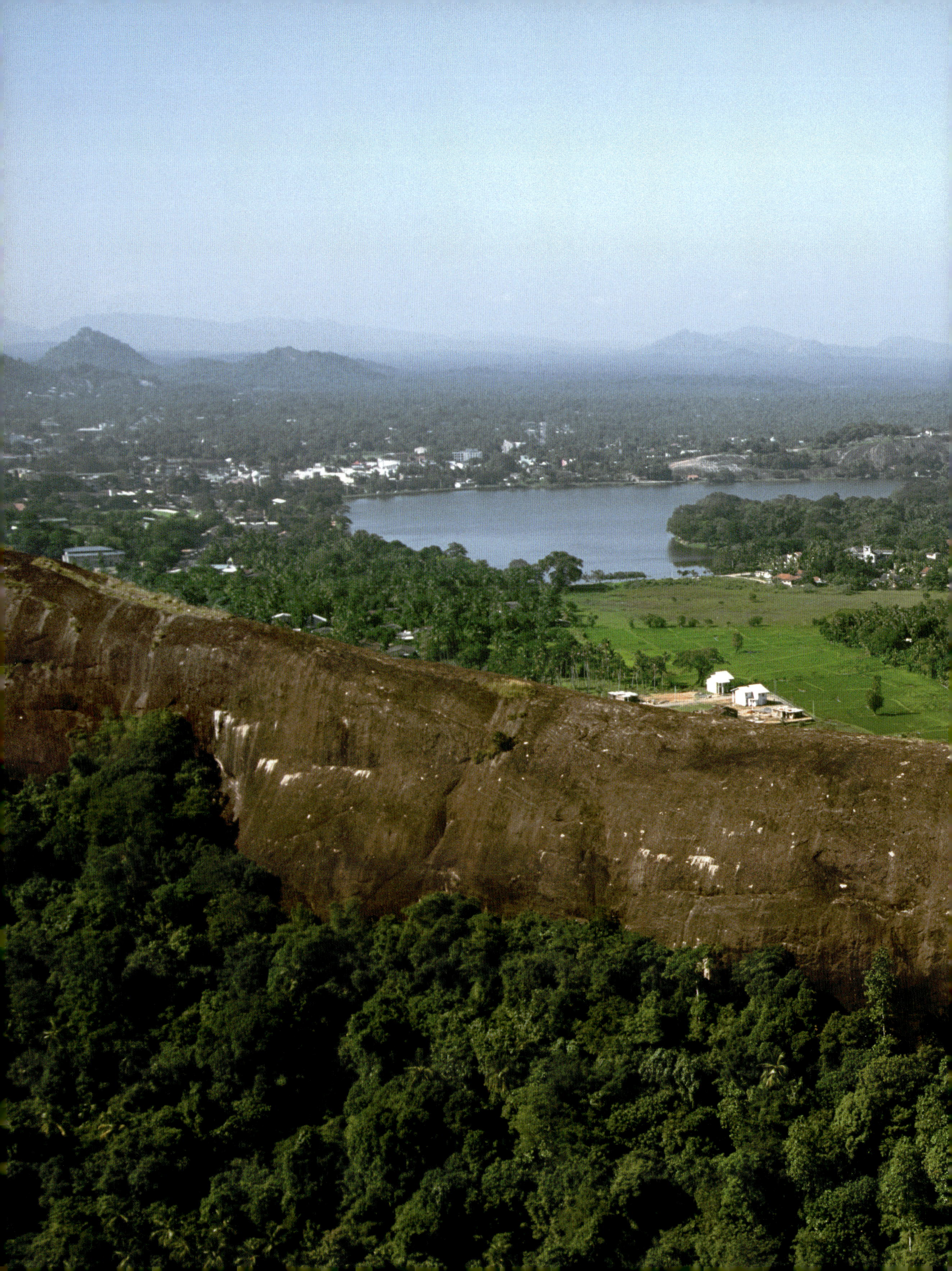

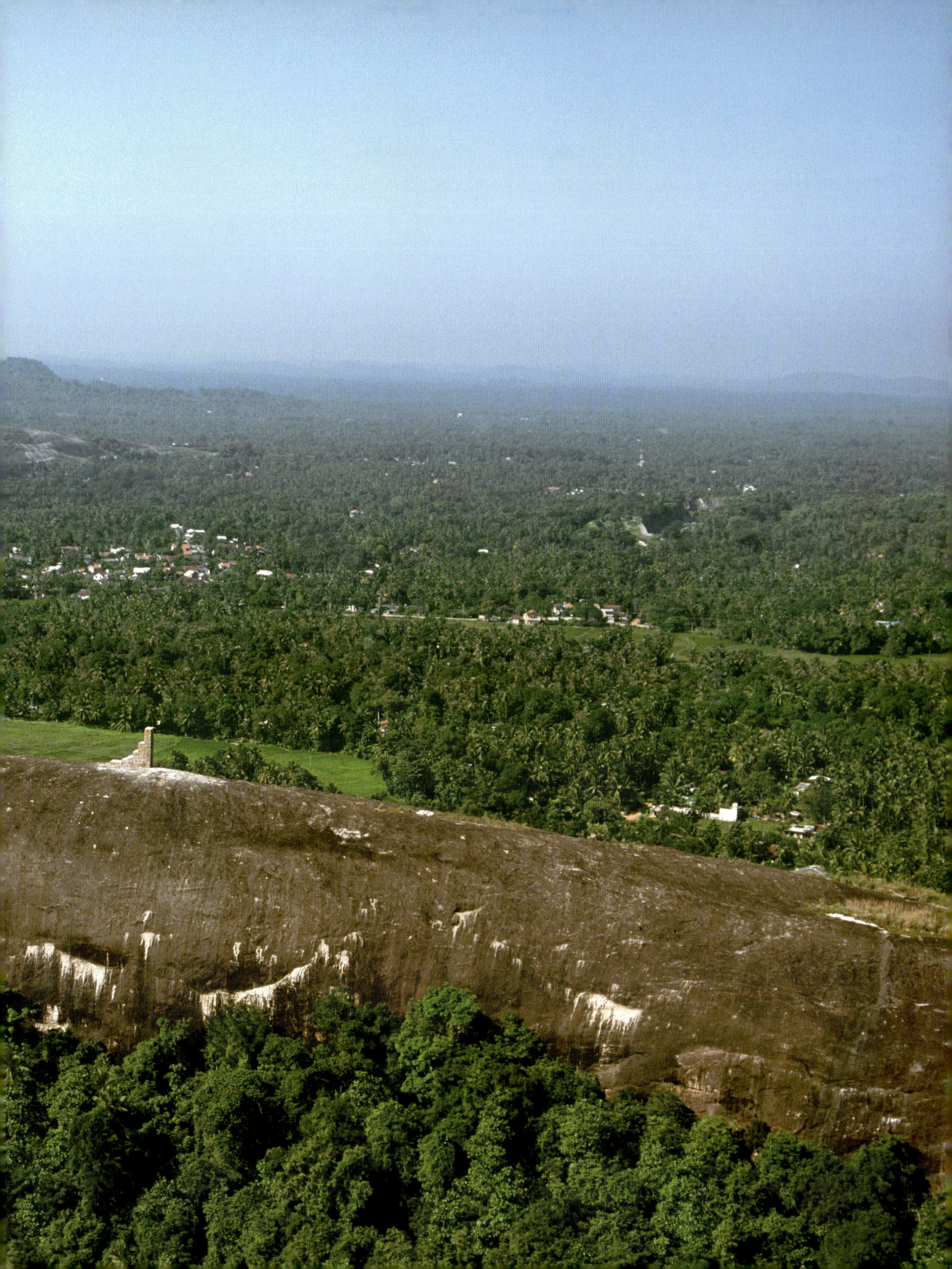

ASCEND 2005 / Granite / 6.5 × 6.5 m (21 × 21 ft.)

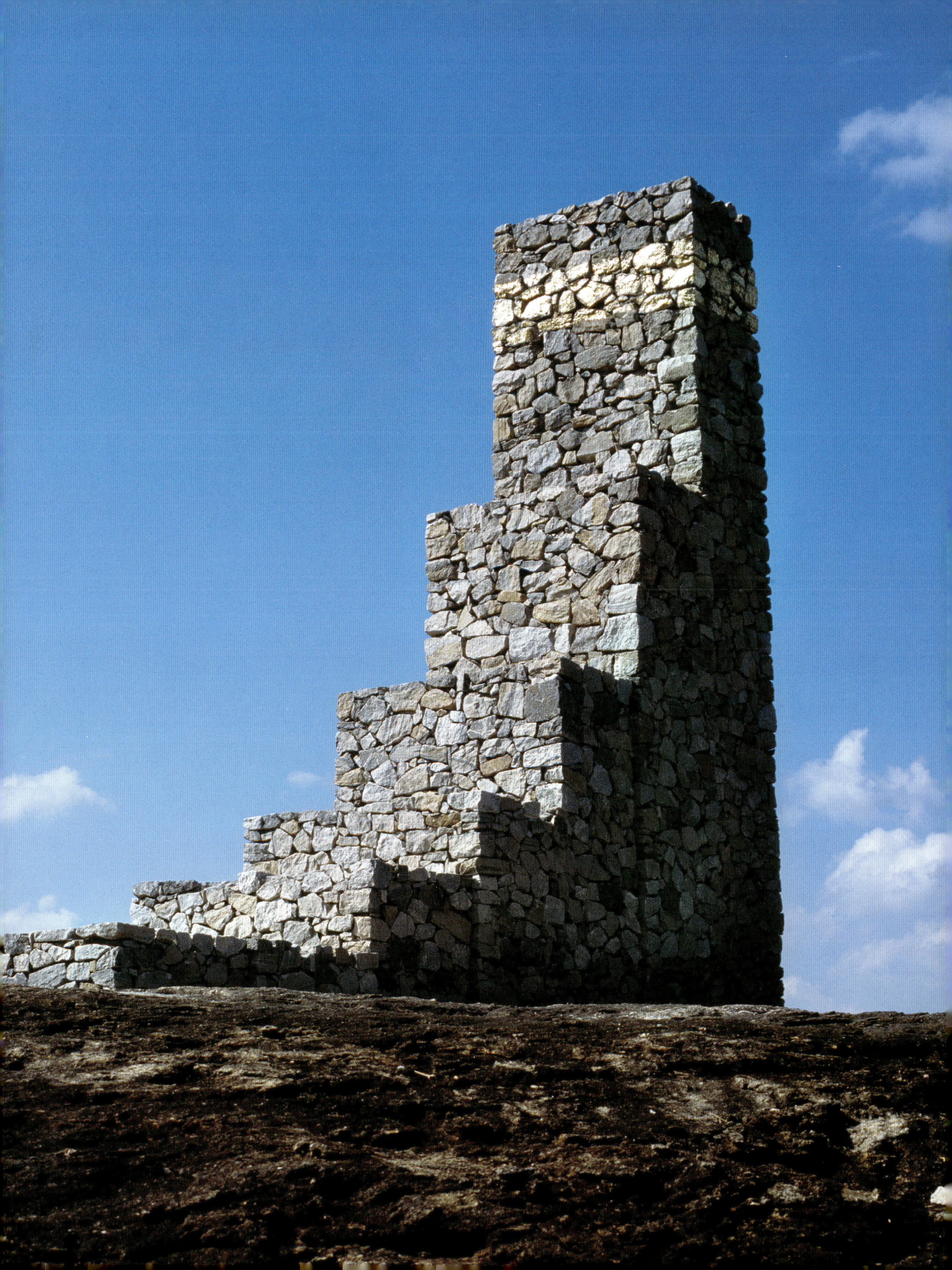

A LINK TO INDIGENOUS AUSTRALIA
GEELONG, AUSTRALIA

It needs no comment that the continent of Australia, Andrew Rogers's homeland, would be a site for his global land art project—a country whose infinite expanse and wealth of pristine landscapes continue to exert an unabated pull on pioneers from the Western world. The artist's ancestors emigrated from Poland, where Jews were being persecuted, in the early twentieth century. Rogers has recalled the trauma of the Holocaust in large-scale sculptural memorials, creating five such outdoor works alone for public spaces in Melbourne, capital of the State of Victoria, where Rogers has lived for years.

However, independent of the artist's personal, close relationship to Australia, the country is synonymous with his core artistic message: the importance of memory. "Without memory we are nothing," is repeated in the context of his artistic oeuvre *Rhythms of Life*.

As the descendant of European immigrants to Australia, this statement has very special relevance for him, for it was European settlers who lastingly destroyed relations with the indigenous population, the Aboriginal people. Initially, the English penal colonies were established in the late eighteenth century. A short time later, the Australian gold rush flushed people from every corner of the globe into the country, who brought along diseases against which the Aboriginal people had no immunity. In the mid-nineteenth century they were forced to migrate to specially created protectorates or to adapt to modern ways of life in cities. Even today, the Aboriginal people, one of the oldest surviving indigenous cultures in the world, have to fight for their land, for the preservation of their customs, their languages, and their traditions. For Rogers, raising awareness about this issue is a concern.

On the occasion of the Commonwealth Games in Melbourne in 2006, the Australian government commissioned him to produce *Rhythms of Life*

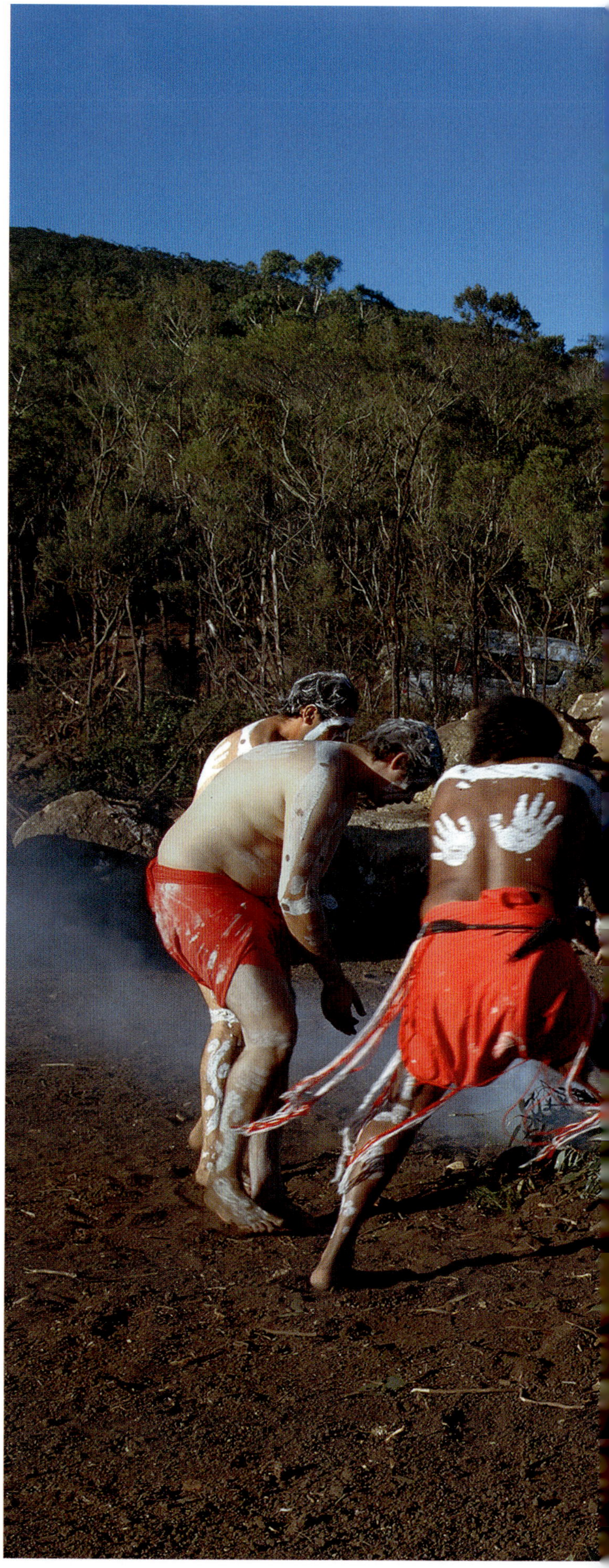

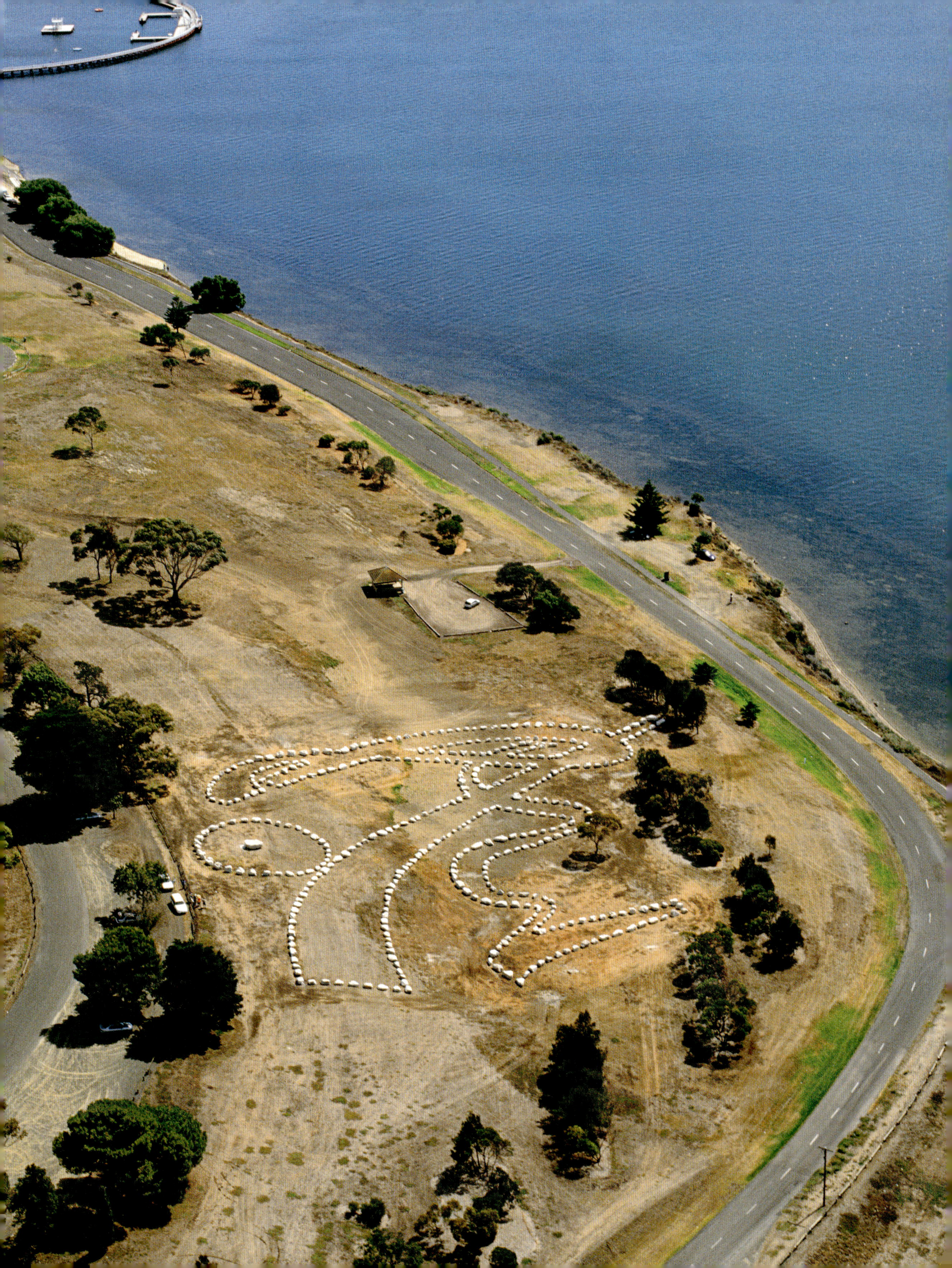

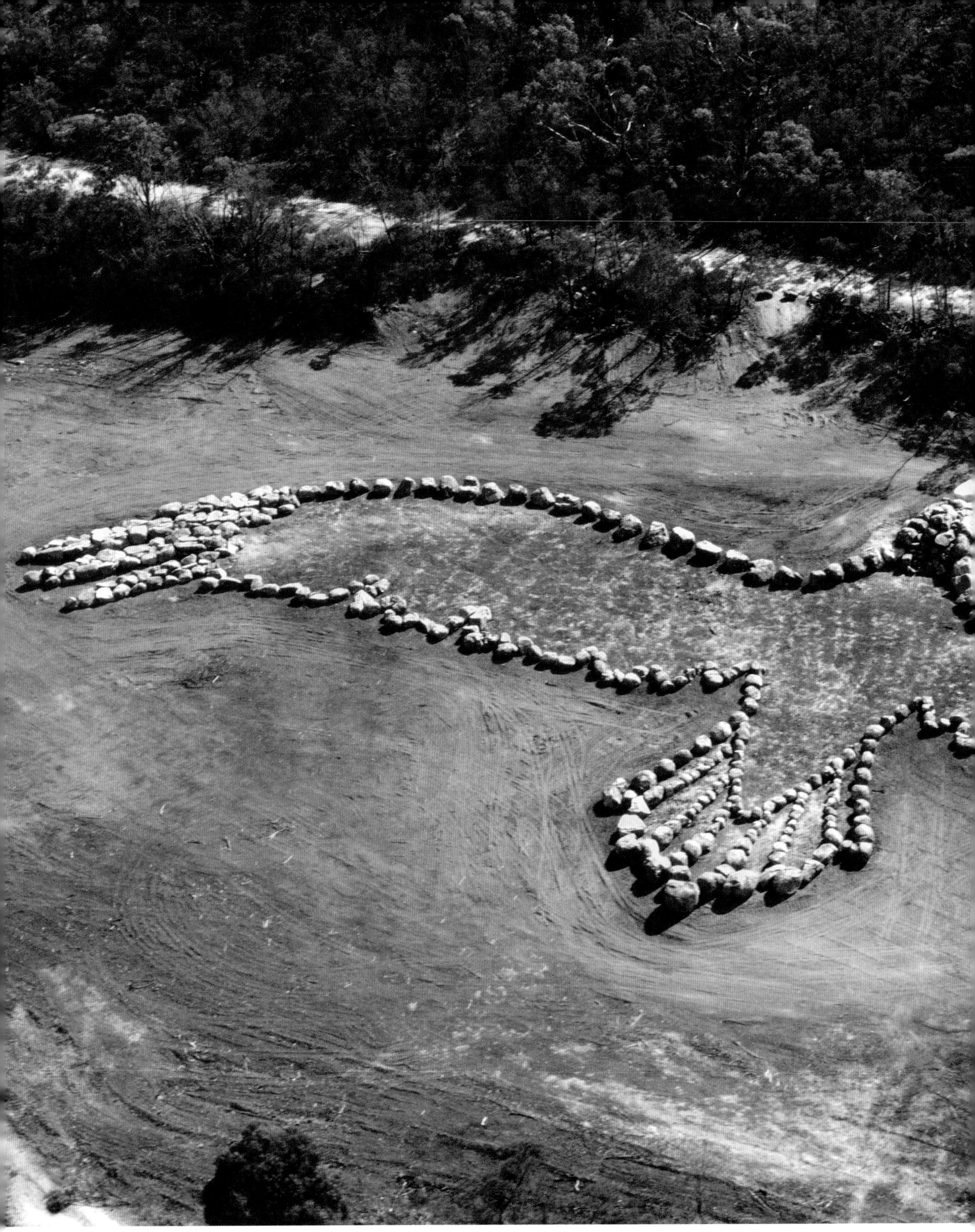

BUNJIL 2006 / Granite / 100 × 80 m (330 × 263 ft.)

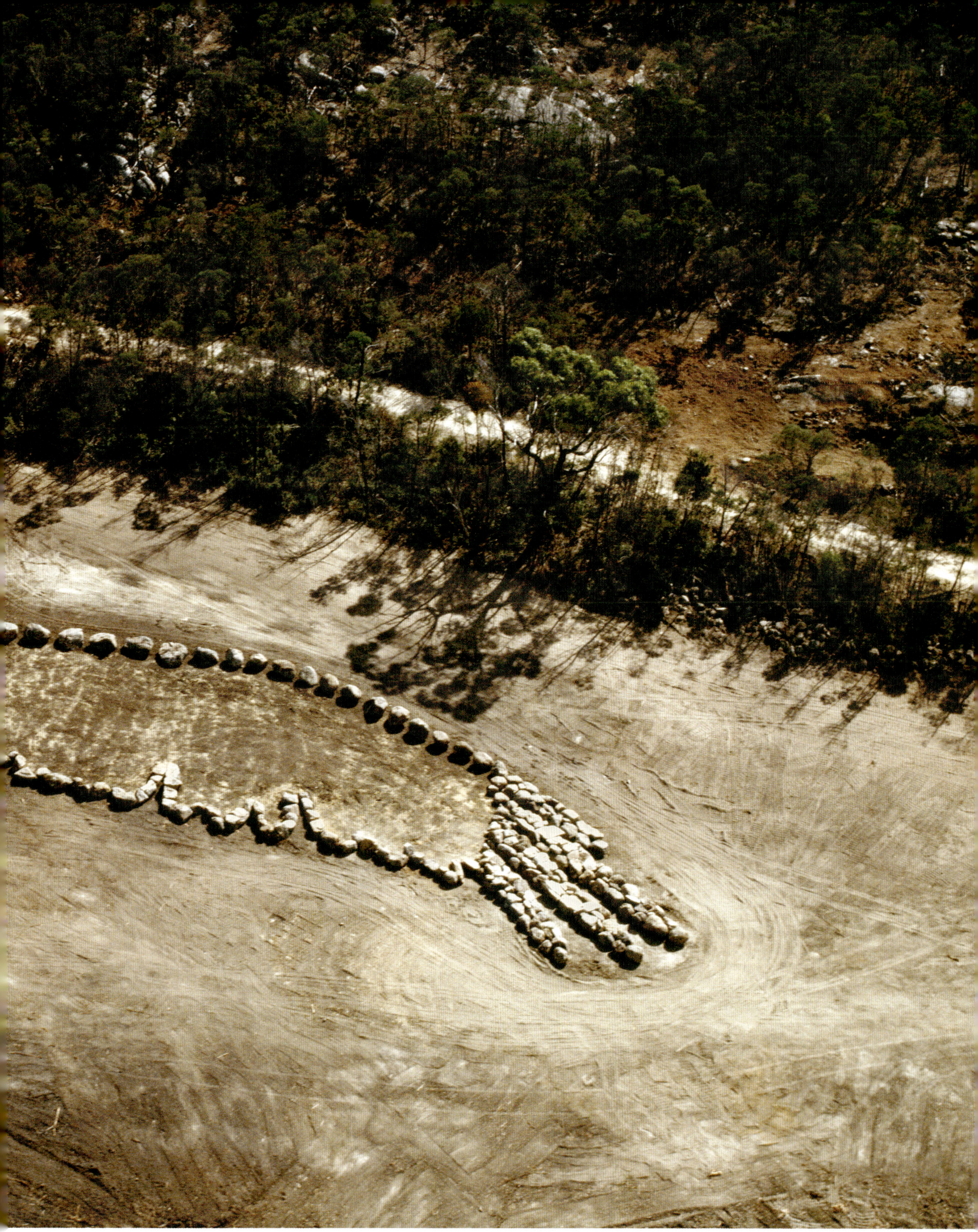

AT THE MERCY OF NATURE'S ELEMENTS
AKUREYRI, ICELAND

From one extreme to another: Andrew Rogers's next project was as far away from Australia as possible. He traveled from the extreme south of the globe to a country at the Arctic Circle: Iceland. Located between the Eurasian and the North American tectonic plates, Iceland is exposed to constant geological activity—earthquakes, volcanic eruptions, and steaming geysers. There is nowhere else in the world with a wider range of active natural elements. It is a land of ice and fire in a perpetual struggle. There are arctic snowscapes here, with hot volcanic springs in which one can bathe outdoors in the middle of an ice-cold winter. Said Rogers, "Why I chose Iceland is because it has a lot of mythology and history. It's wonderful to see the Atlantic out there and see snow-capped islands and the snow-capped mountains all around. It's got lots of history and heritage. It is a very, very beautiful area." For his land art project he chose the city of Akureyri at the end of the 60-kilometer-long Eyjafjörður, Iceland's longest fjord, not far from the Arctic Circle, a place in which for millennia people have defied the extreme climate, worked hard for their livelihood, and lived with the elements of nature. And despite a history that is characterized by poverty, hunger, isolation, and constant volcanic eruptions, the descendants of the Vikings in Akureyri have developed a special connection to art. After Reykjavik, Akureyri is Iceland's most important cultural metropolis. A ten-week arts festival takes place every summer with an impressive platform consisting of concerts,

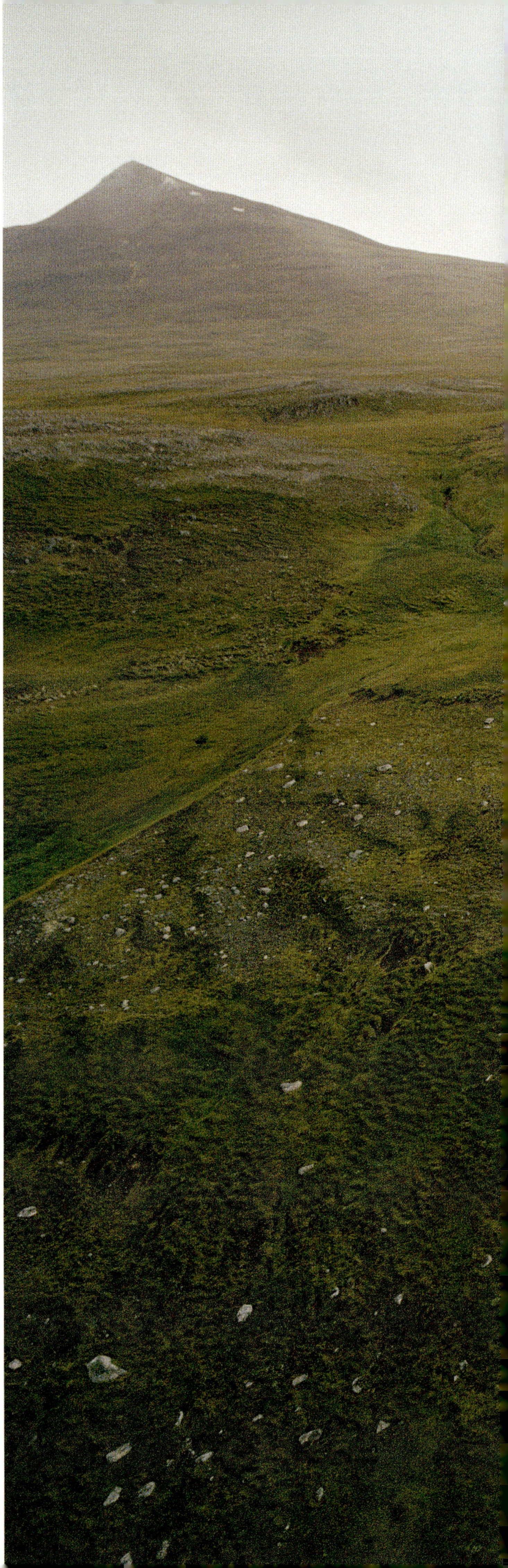

RHYTHMS OF LIFE 2006 / Volcanic rock / 100 x 100 m (330 x 330 ft.)

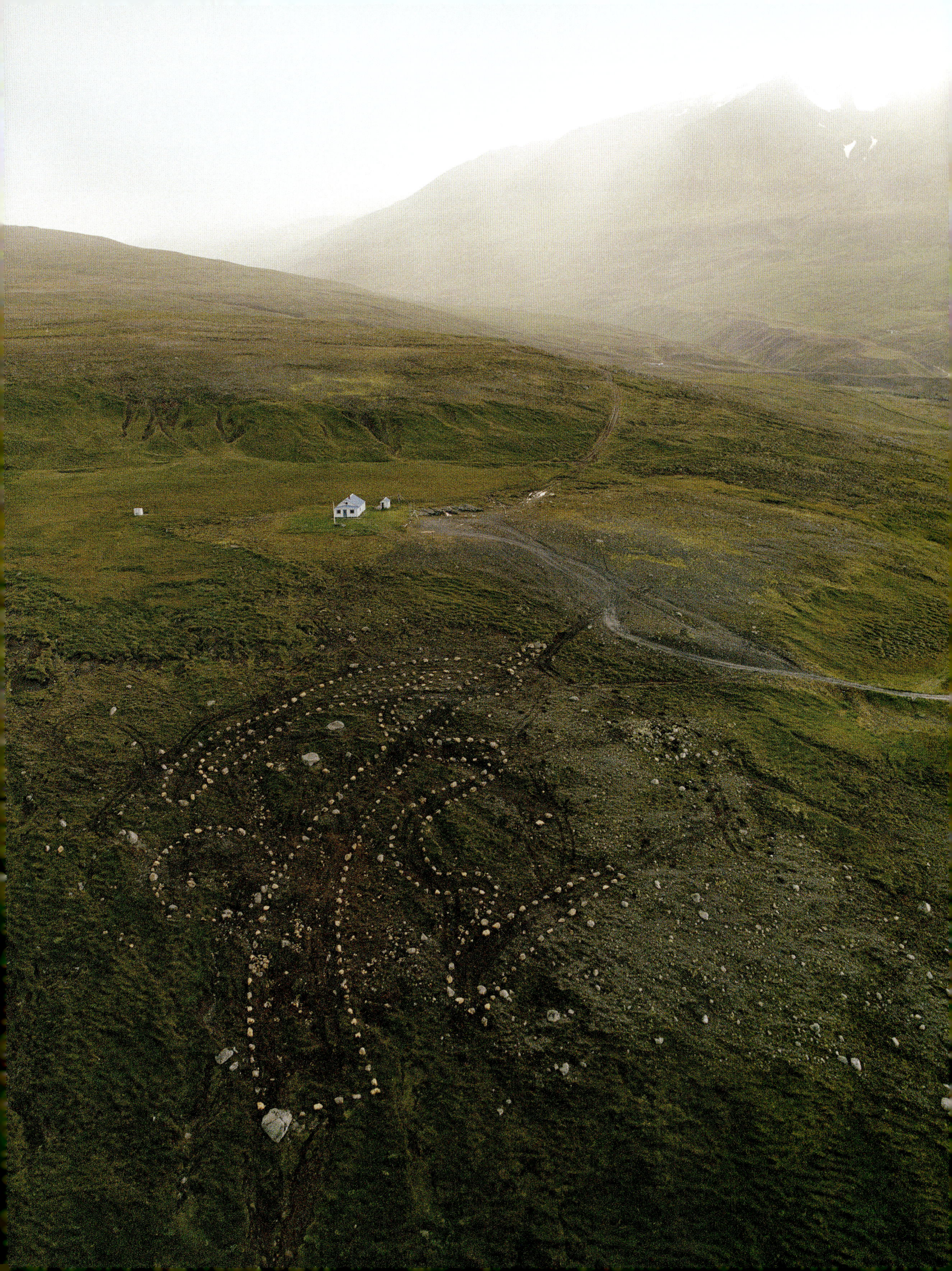

performances, exhibitions, and art competitions. "The people here have an extraordinary interest in art. They also have an open mind about my land art projects," said Rogers enthusiastically.
As might be expected, the residents were instrumental in the realization of the installations. All of them wanted to play a part, to be involved when the international art celebrity built the site-specific works. Besides the sculpture *Rhythms of Life*, two geoglyphs were planned for Iceland. They were to specifically incorporate Icelandic mythology, which continues to be deeply rooted in the everyday lives of the local inhabitants. In their minds, elves, giants, trolls, and gods—whose dwellings lie below large, prominent rocks, which are protected by law—still preside over nature.
For the first geoglyph, the majestic eagle, which enjoys special relevance in Iceland, was relatively quickly agreed on. The eagle not only adorns Akureyri's ubiquitous coat of arms, but also is a protector of the entire nation, alongside the bull, the dragon, and the giant. It plays a key role in the *Heimskringla*, a collection of medieval sagas about Norwegian kings and still an important source on Norse pre-Christian beliefs. And last but not least, by depicting the eagle Rogers referred to the important, endangered species of bird as the result of the increasing destruction of the ecological balance in Iceland. "There is only 100 pairs left," remarked Rogers.
In contrast, finding a second symbol proved to be considerably more difficult. Rogers wanted something that was devoid of specifically religious or political connotations but by all means symbolically represented Iceland's history and identity. He repeatedly rejected ideas until Hannes Sigurdsson, the director of the local museum and one of his major supporters, finally made an unusual suggestion that fascinated him: the rendering of an old Icelandic rune that means "now." The early Germanic tribes believed that magical powers inherently emanated from writing that influenced their actions. Rogers transferred this idea to his artistic project: the rune as a built, symbolically charged symbol for the purpose of raising awareness of the past and connecting it to one's future actions—namely now. Thus with respect to Rogers's project *Rhythms of Life*, the rune fits in perfectly with his approach to memory, which implies the theme of time and fuels the cycle of the three components of past, present, and future. Rendering the fleeting moment, which stands between the past and the future, occurs with large boulders that are themselves part of a ten-million-year-old past and are placed in the "now."
In keeping with the pictographic model, the form consists of a widely flared hook with a short diagonal line on the handle. What Rogers saw in this is the ambiguity of time as well as a linear and a circular dimension. He in turn tied it in with his first geoglyph, *To Life*, which he built in the Arava Desert of Israel: it is based on a Hebrew word *chai* meaning "to life," in which all three tenses combine.
After the choice was made for the symbols for the two structures, sites had to be selected. The three geoglyphs were to be situated and visible to all along the city's lifeline, the Eyjafjörður. However, due to tight environmental constraints, the final determination of the sites had to be changed repeatedly. Ideal sites were

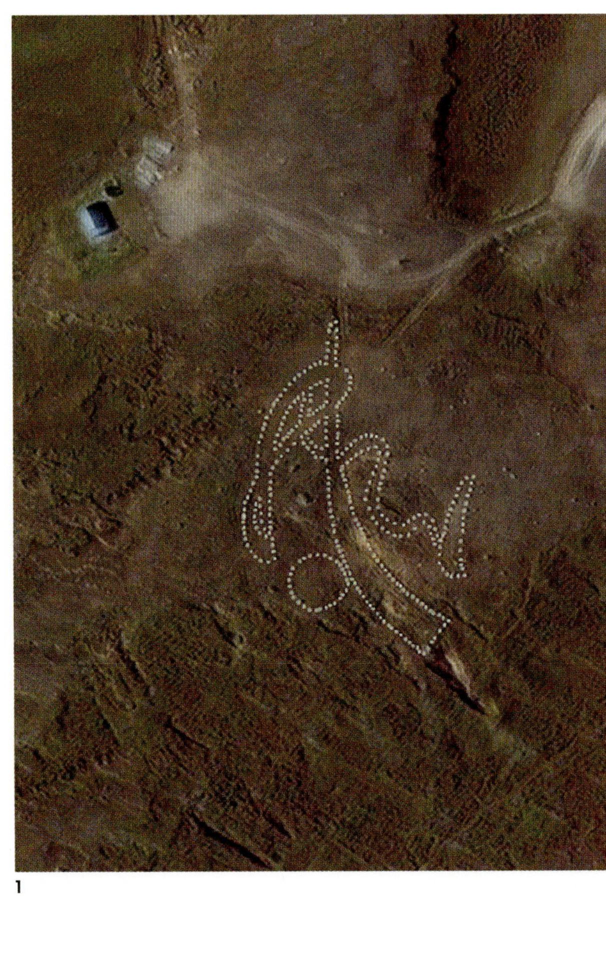
1

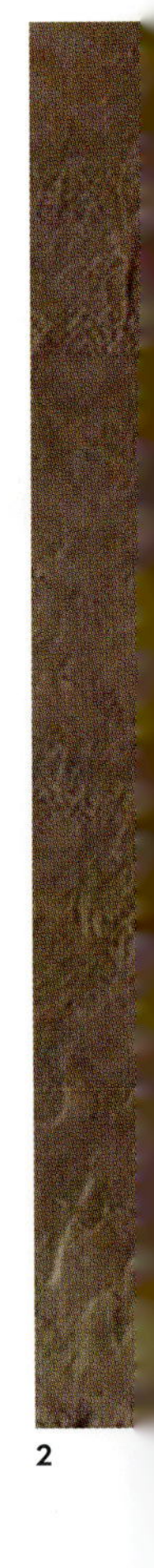
2

ultimately found for all three geoglyphs on different hillsides along the fjord. Yet as spectacular as the view of the water and the snow-covered islands and mountains on the horizon is from each of the sites, the building work on the permanently wet, muddy meadows proved difficult. This was complicated by unusually poor weather with fog and snow—at the height of summer.

"It was a typical summer in Iceland, as if the elements of nature almost wanted to conspire. We often couldn't see our markings for the boulders in the ground, let alone recognize the geoglyphs later as complete forms." In fact, the artist created a schematic depiction of the three geoglyphs that is discernible only if one looks closely. This was deliberate to be in harmony with the delicate nature of the terrain. It is uncertain whether one is wandering through rocks that have been deliberately placed or are laying about randomly. It is an impression, however, that is thoroughly in the spirit of the land art artist, because when he assembles his installations out of boulders found locally, he never grows tired of explaining "that land art means we only take parts of nature, rearranging it."

As was the case in Israel, on completion of the project Rogers organized a performance of the celebration of life. Whereas in Israel, pregnant women exposed their bellies in the heat of the desert and raised their arms in honor of the sun and to pay homage to the cycle of life, in Iceland the women now did the same in Arctic temperatures. With this second act of celebrating life on the other side of the globe, Rogers once more underscored the importance of the spark of life as well as the shared themes of all of his installations.

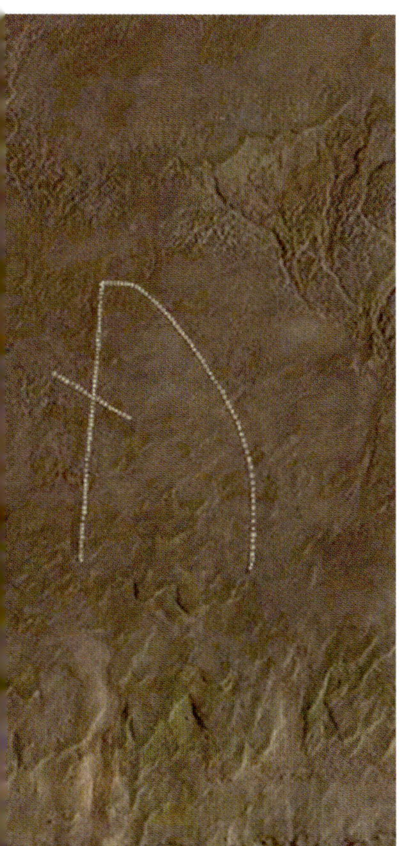

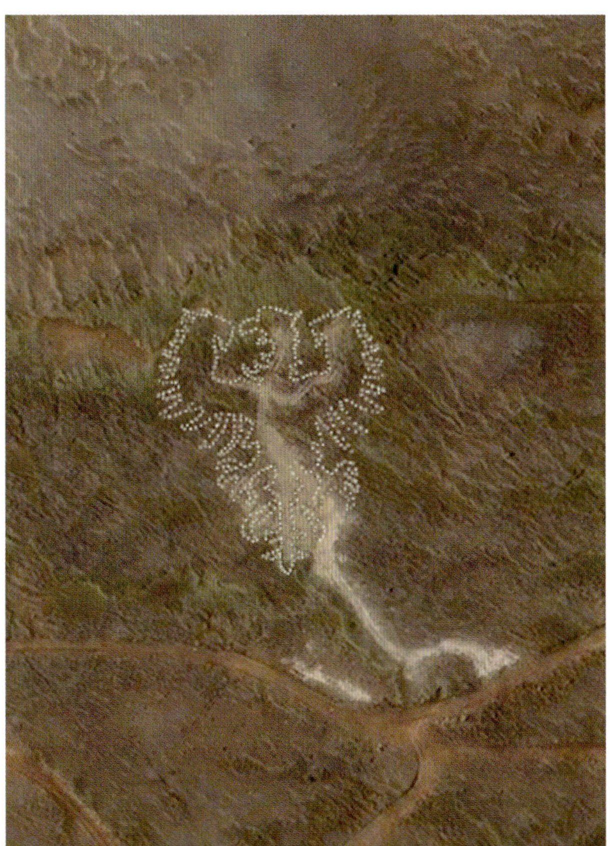

3

1 RHYTHMS OF LIFE, satellite image taken 440 km (275 miles) above the earth

2 RUNE, satellite image taken 440 km (275 miles) above the earth

3 EAGLE, satellite image taken 440 km (275 miles) above the earth

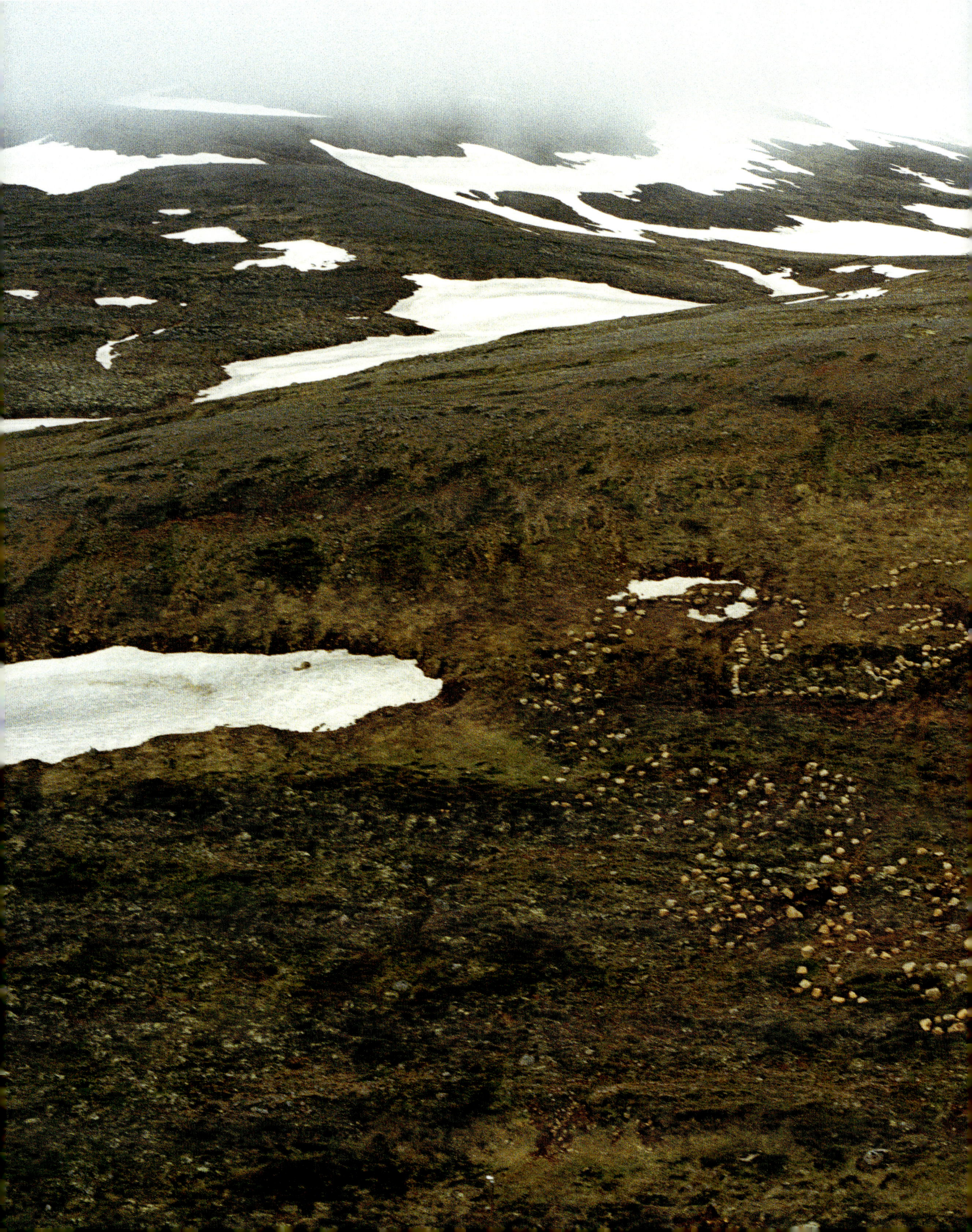

EAGLE 2006 / Volcanic rock / 100 x 100 m (330 x 330 ft.)

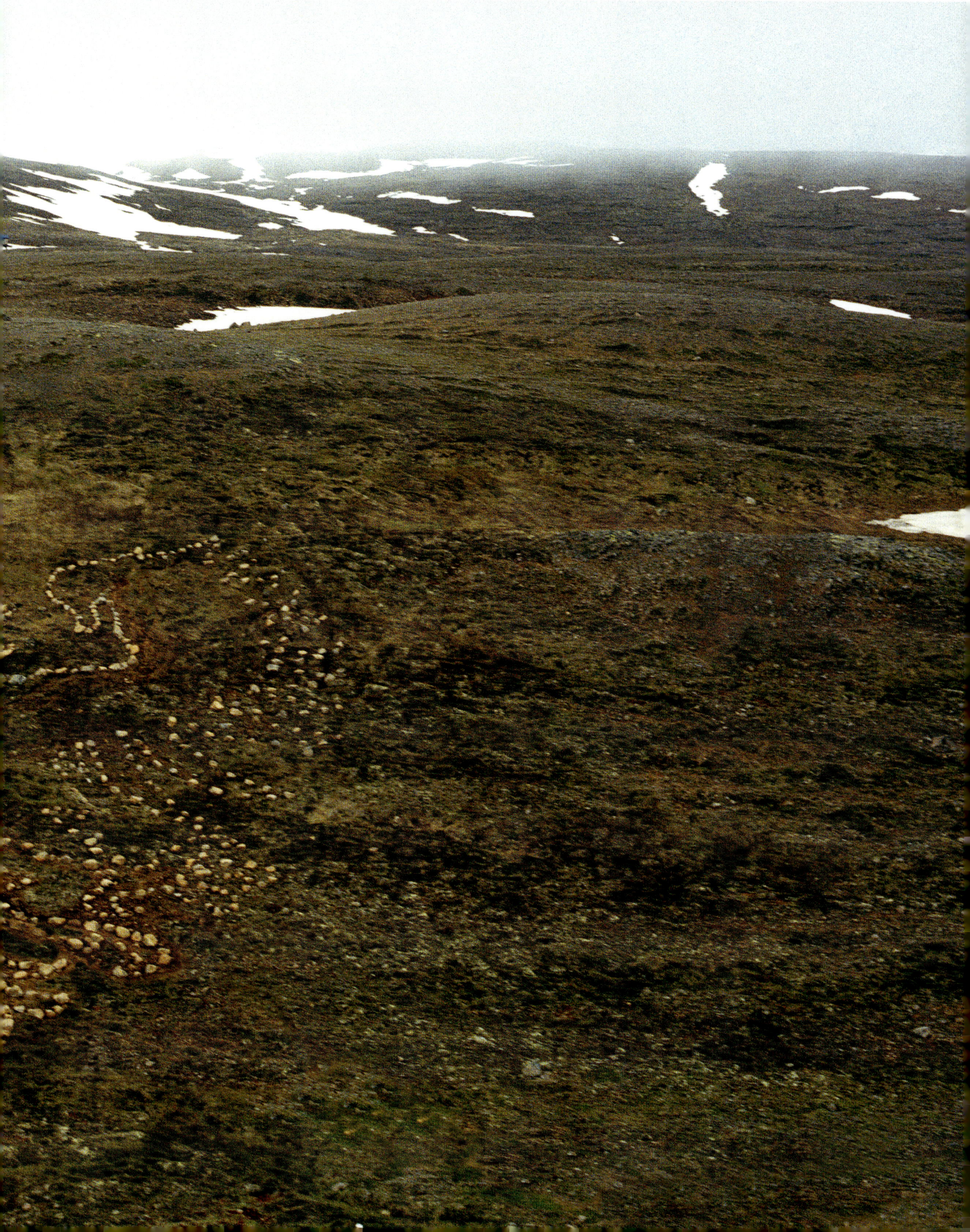

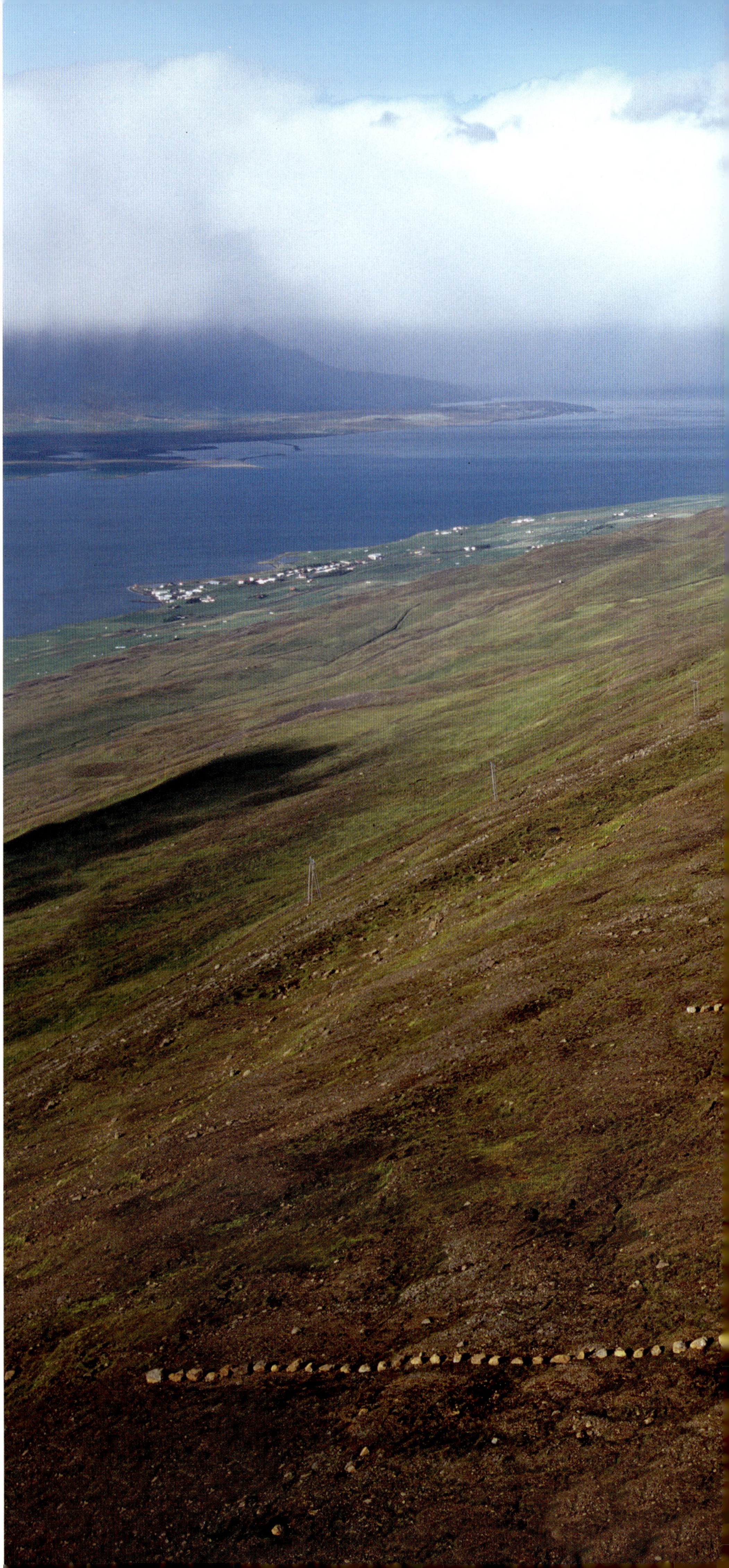

RUNE 2006 / Volcanic rock /
100 × 100 m (330 × 330 ft.)

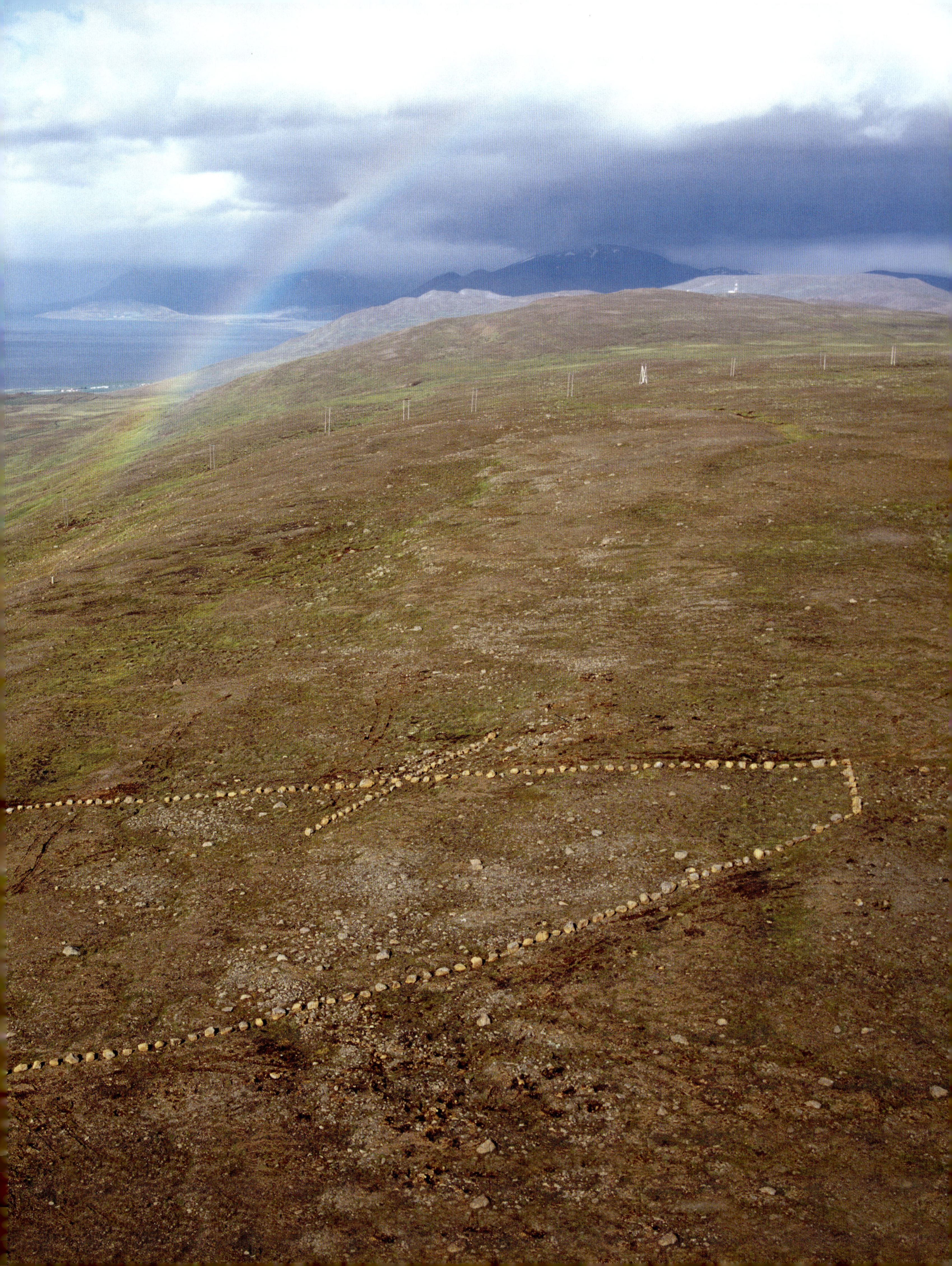

CELEBRATION OF LIFE 2006

Three degrees Celsius (37°F), threatening to snow, cloudy skies; densely grassed slopes dotted with a pattern of volcanic boulders and beautifully distended bodies celebrating life and nature.

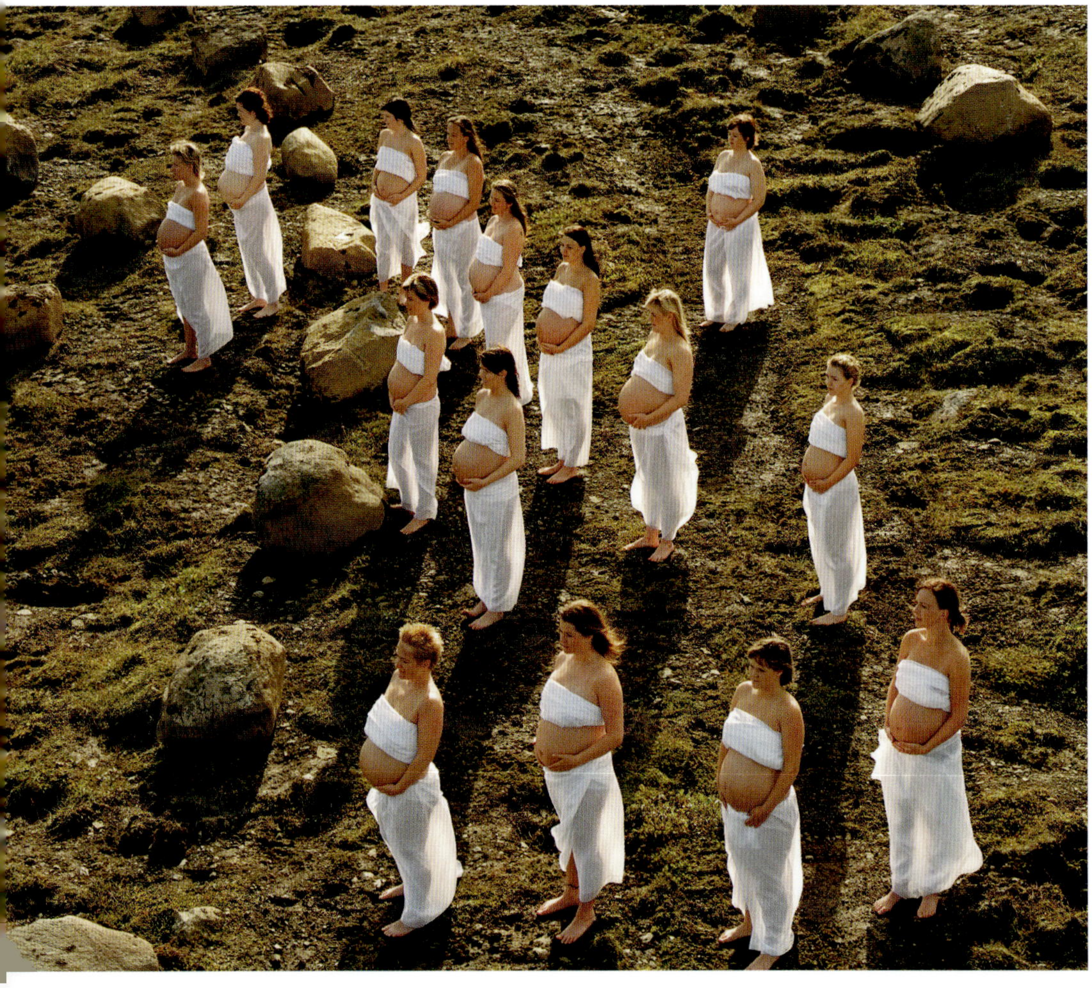

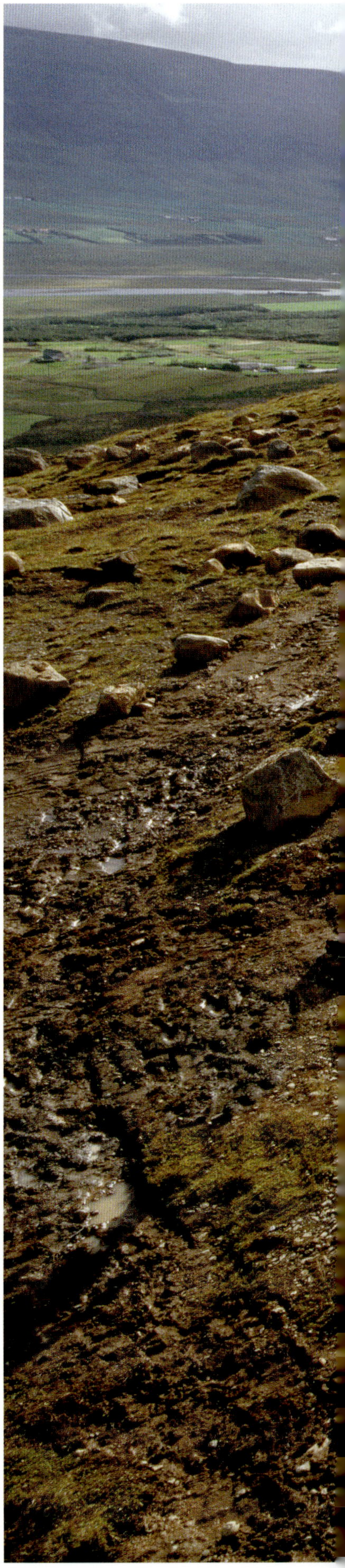

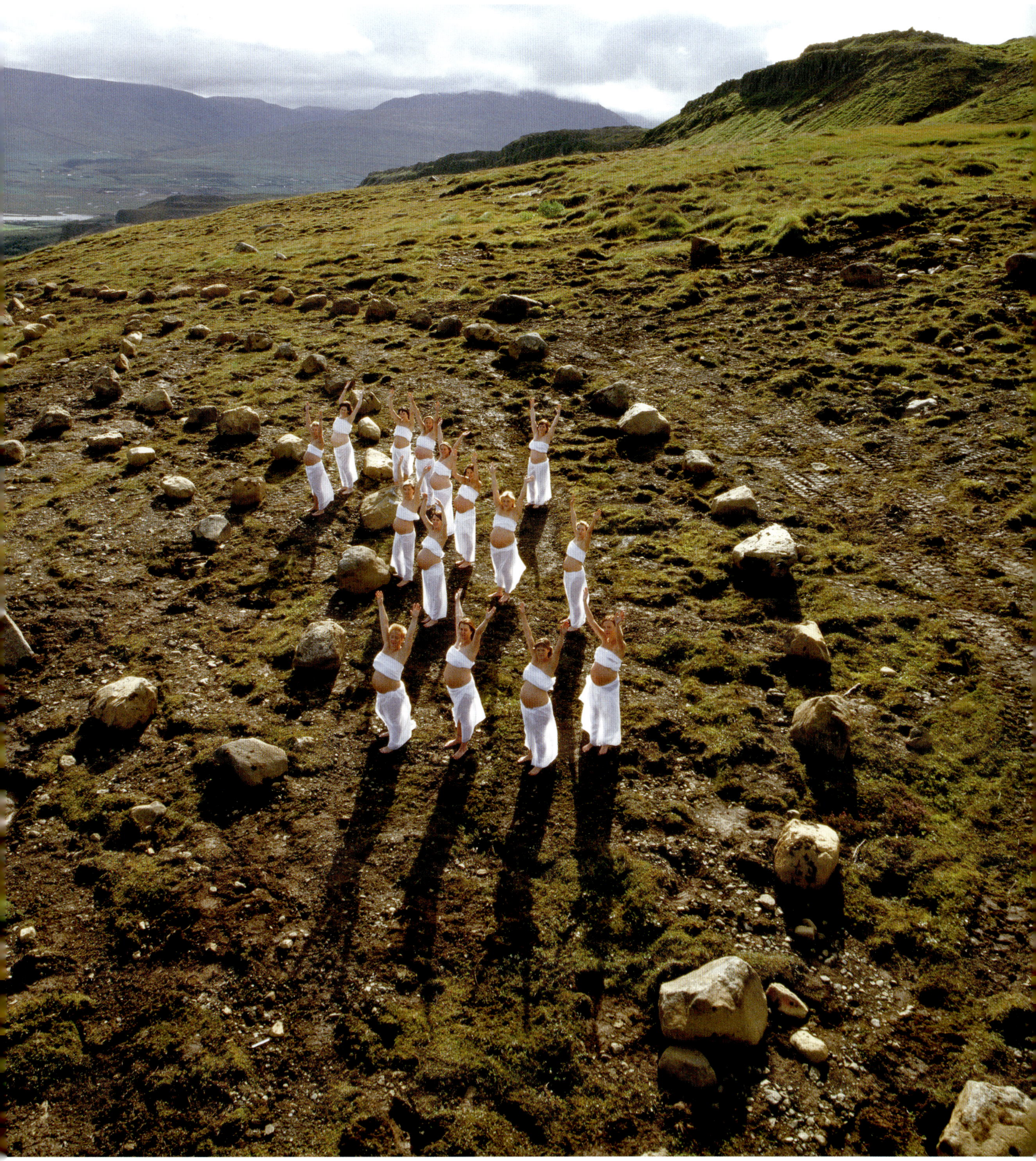

ALONG THE SILK ROAD AT THE END OF THE WORLD
GOBI DESERT, CHINA

Andrew Rogers's decision to install three geoglyphs in China's Gobi Desert is based on the profound history of this stretch of land. The sculptures are situated not far from the city of Jiayuguan, in a pass that played a key role as a way station along the Silk Road. Here there is an impressive, large fortress which was one of the numerous caravansaries on the land route from the Mediterranean to East Asia. In addition to merchants like Marco Polo, who traveled the trade route with valuable goods, including fabrics, precious stones, and spices, scholars, monks, and armies disseminated new ideas, religions, and entire cultures over the European and Asian continents.

Thus the Silk Road implemented the idea of today's globalization as early as pre-Christian times, and it lent itself to Andrew Rogers to build his geoglyphs for the *Rhythms of Life* project in the spirit of this consonant body of thought with respect to worldwide cultural exchange.

Jiayuguan is also located at the western end of the Great Wall of China, a fact that led people in ancient times to believe that the world ended here. As the artist of a global project of gigantic stone installations, Andrew Rogers felt both inspired and challenged by this work, the largest ever to have been created by human hands. His geoglyphs, with dimensions up to 200 × 200 meters (656 × 656 feet), therefore became the largest and most elaborate of any of his structures. A masterly logistical performance was required for the project in the Gobi Desert, which could only work with the aid of the strict hierarchy and discipline of an army. Andrew Rogers worked with 1,000 soldiers from China's People's Liberation Army. These "descendants of the original builders of the Great Wall of China," as he called them, effortlessly built a total of 4 kilometers (2.5 miles) of accurately layered stone walls in the endless expanses of the hilly desert landscape. "The various teams were so motivated that they spurred each other on!"

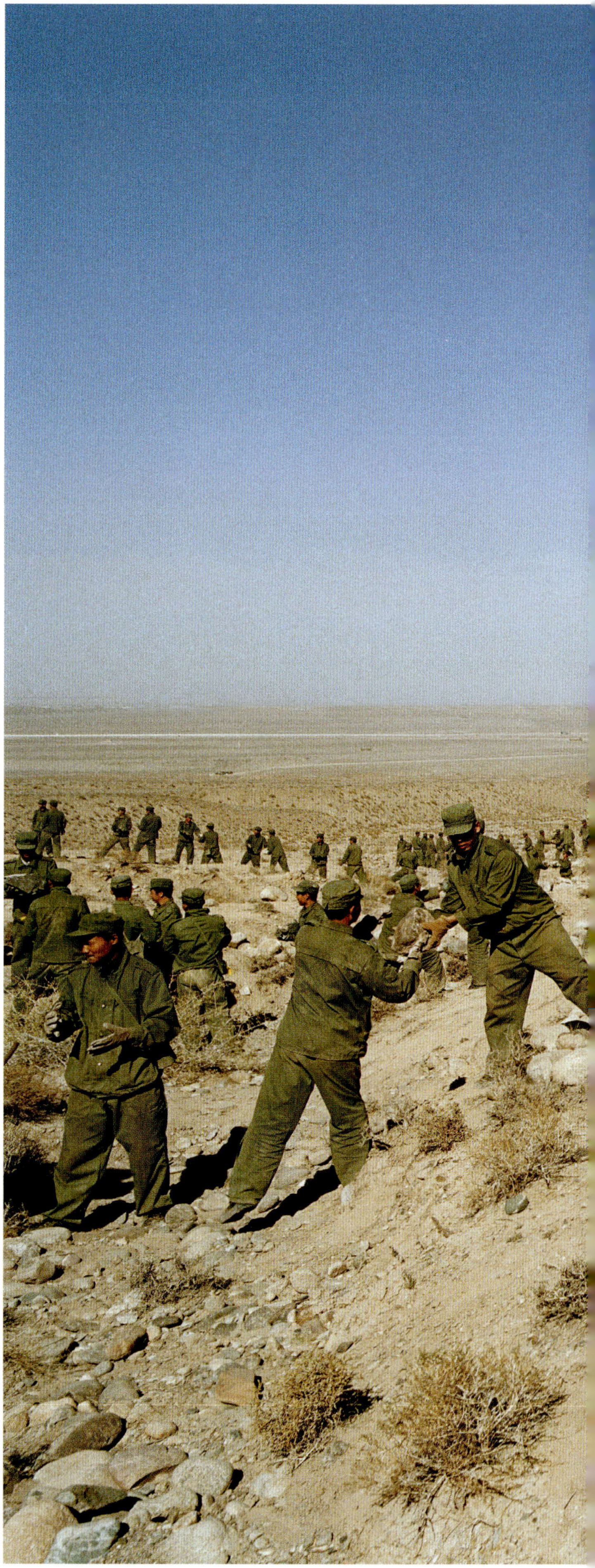

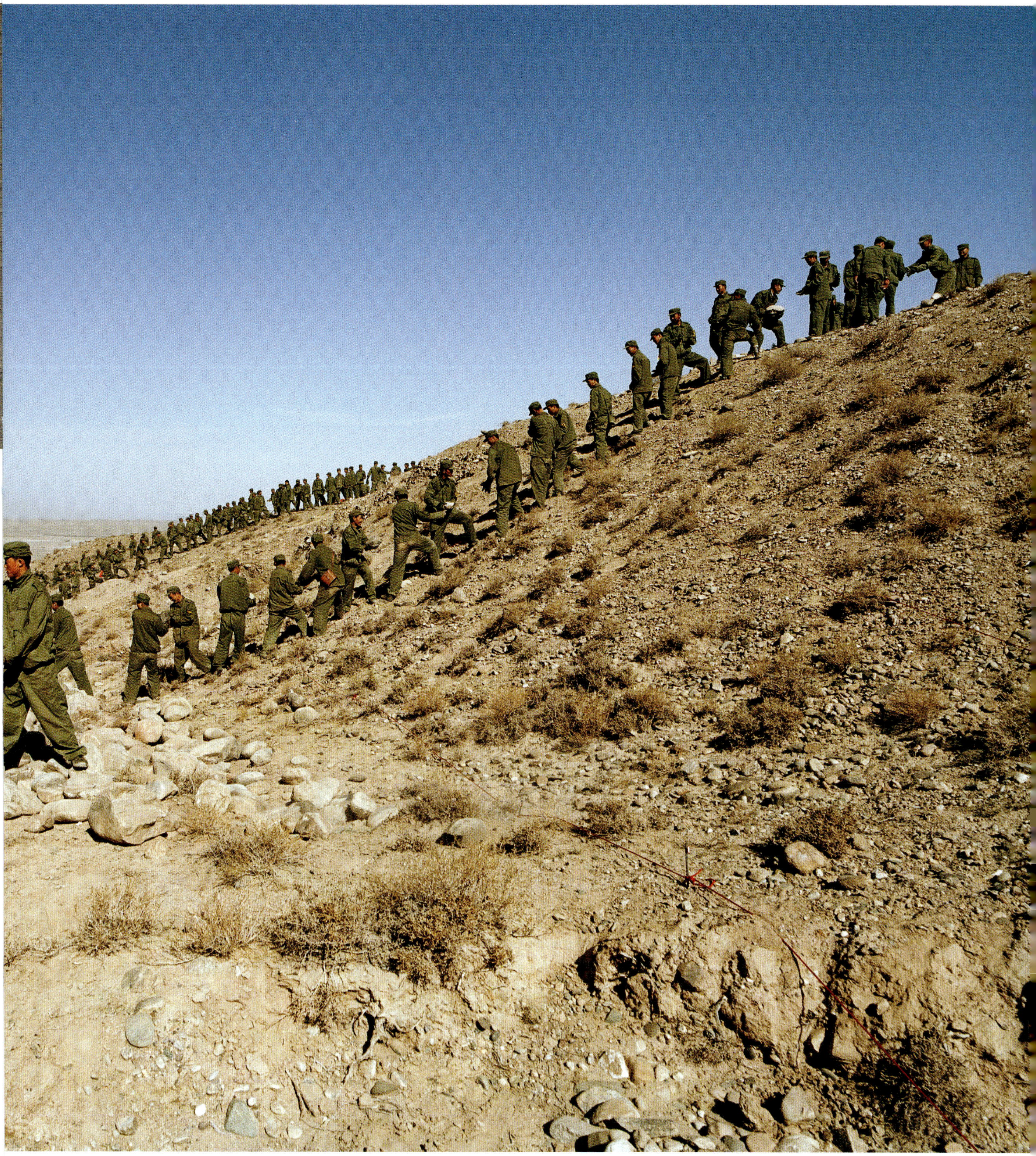

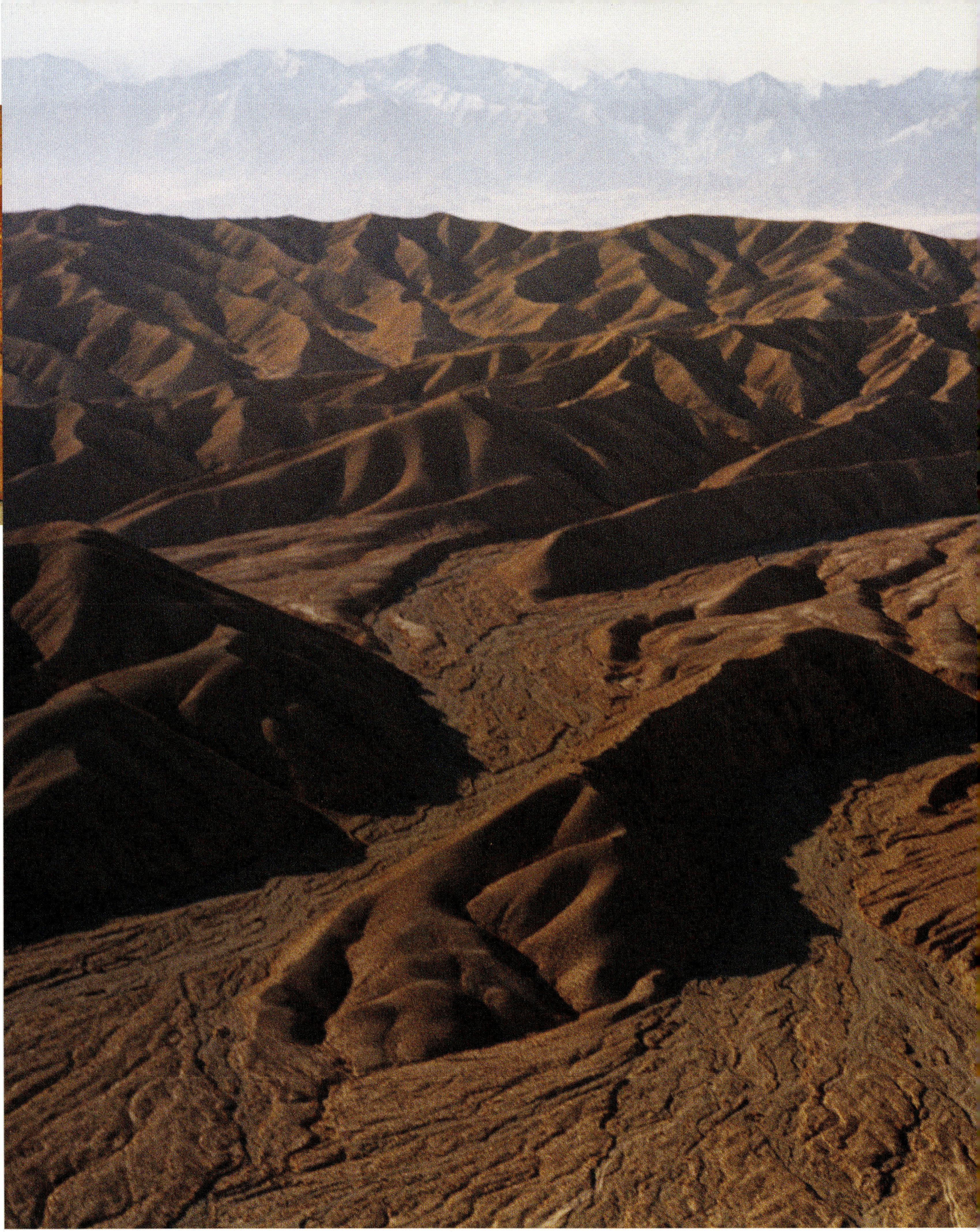

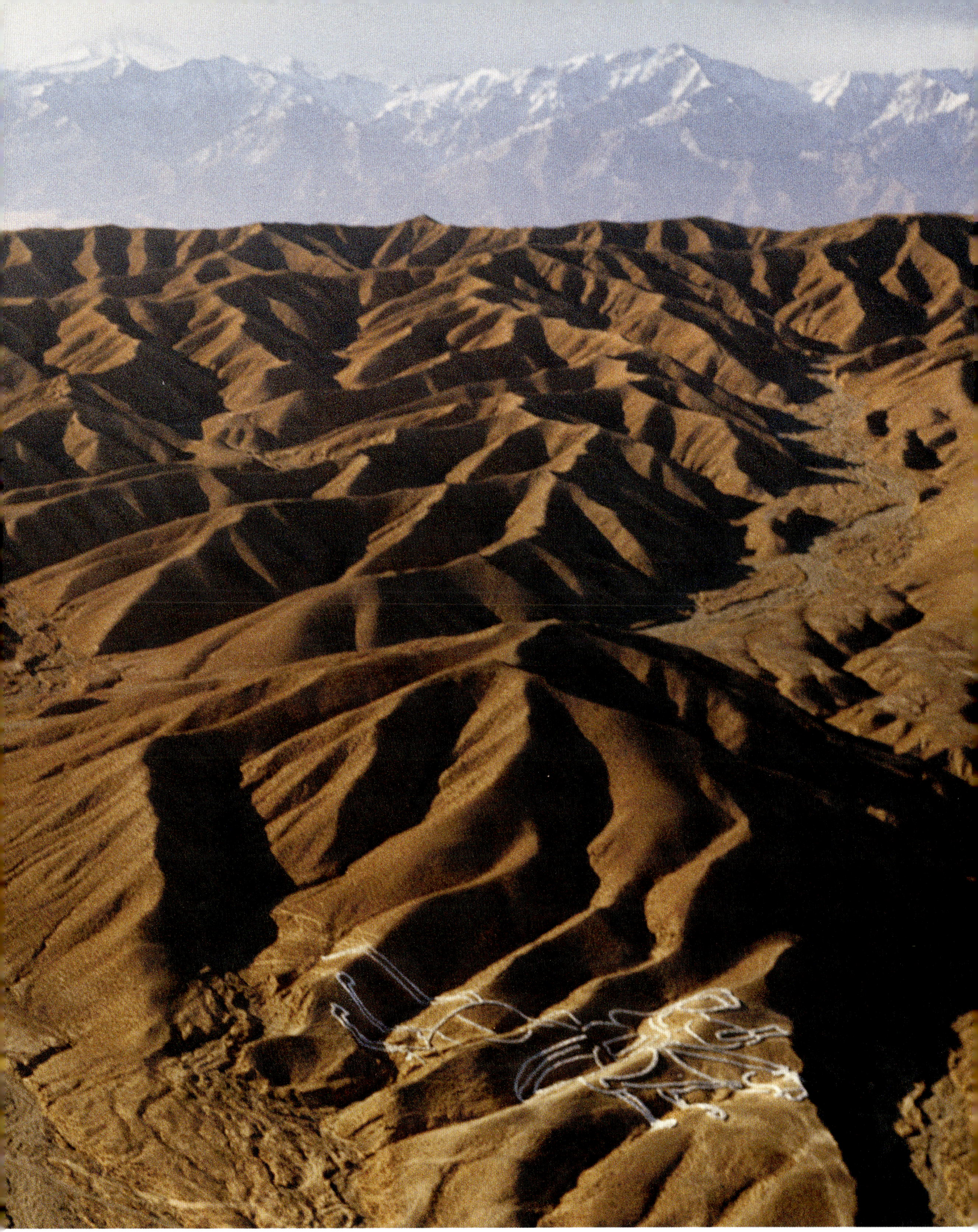

THE MESSENGER 2006 / Sandstone / 150 × 150 m (492 × 492 ft.)

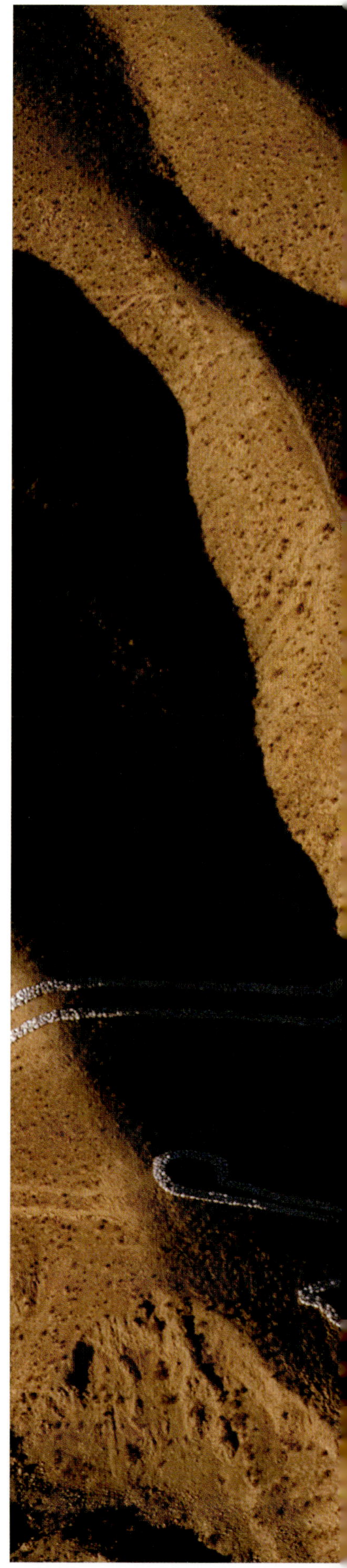

THE MESSENGER 2006 / Sandstone / 150 × 150 m (492 × 492 ft.)

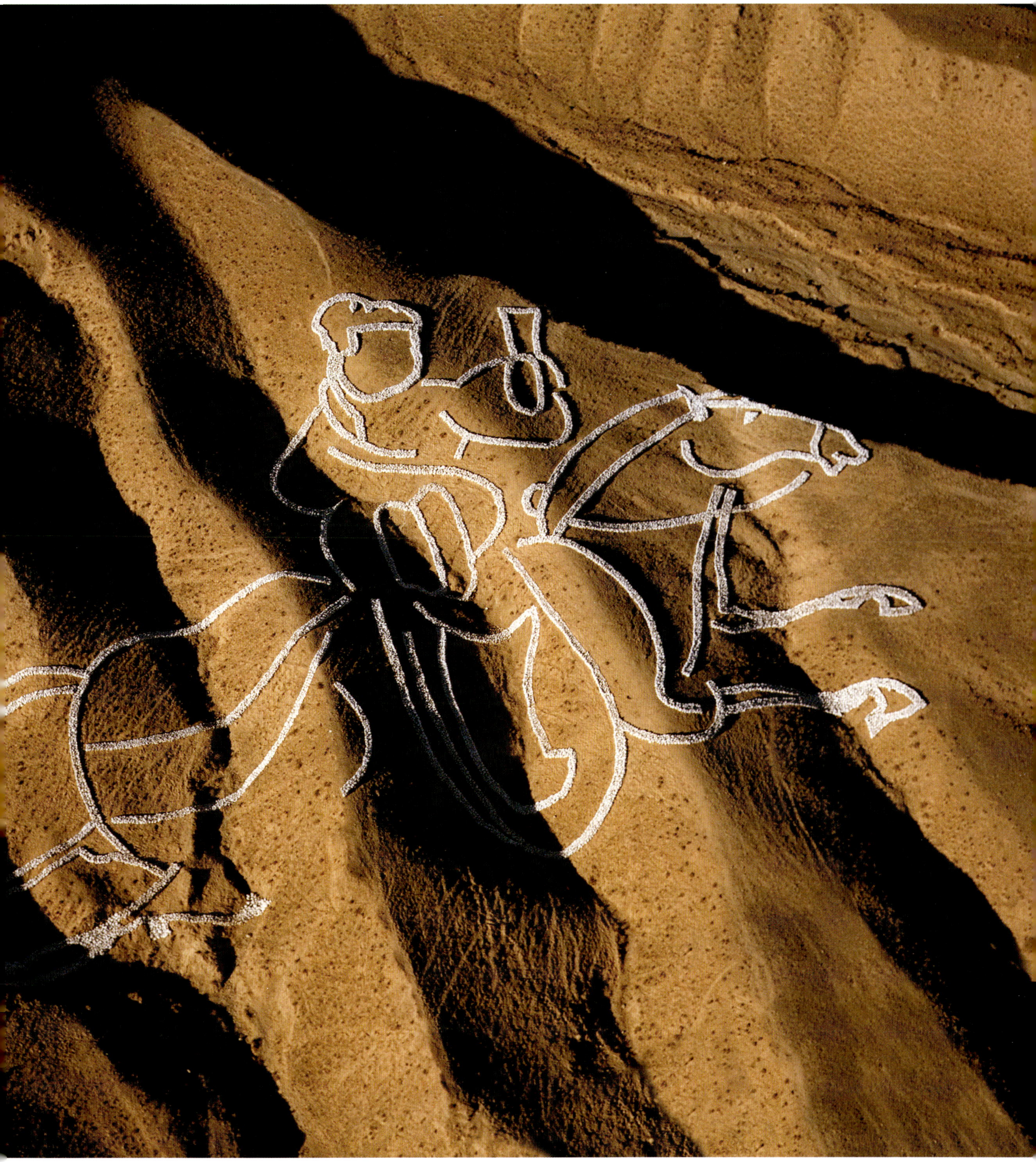

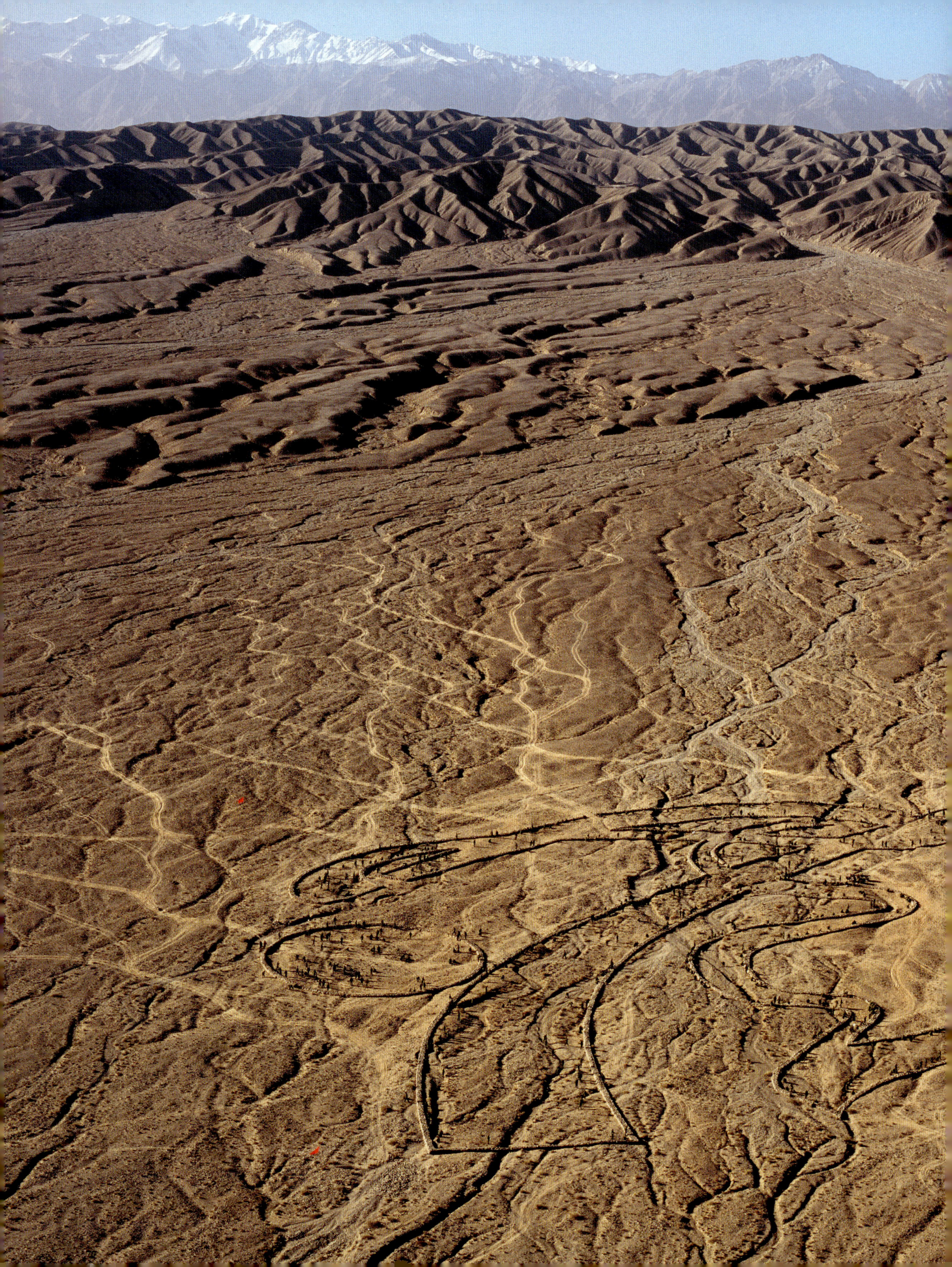

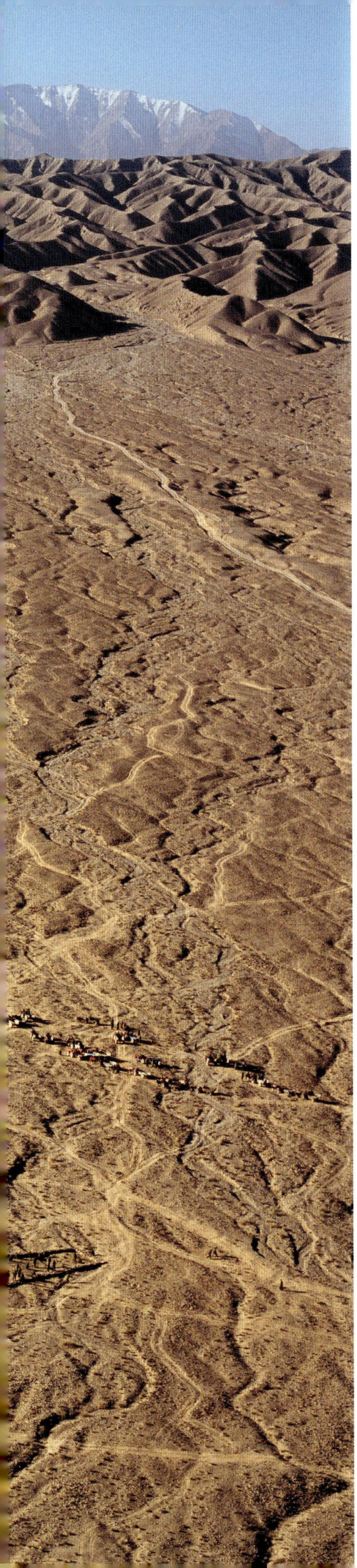

RHYTHMS OF LIFE 2006 / Sandstone / 200 x 200 m (656 x 656 ft.)

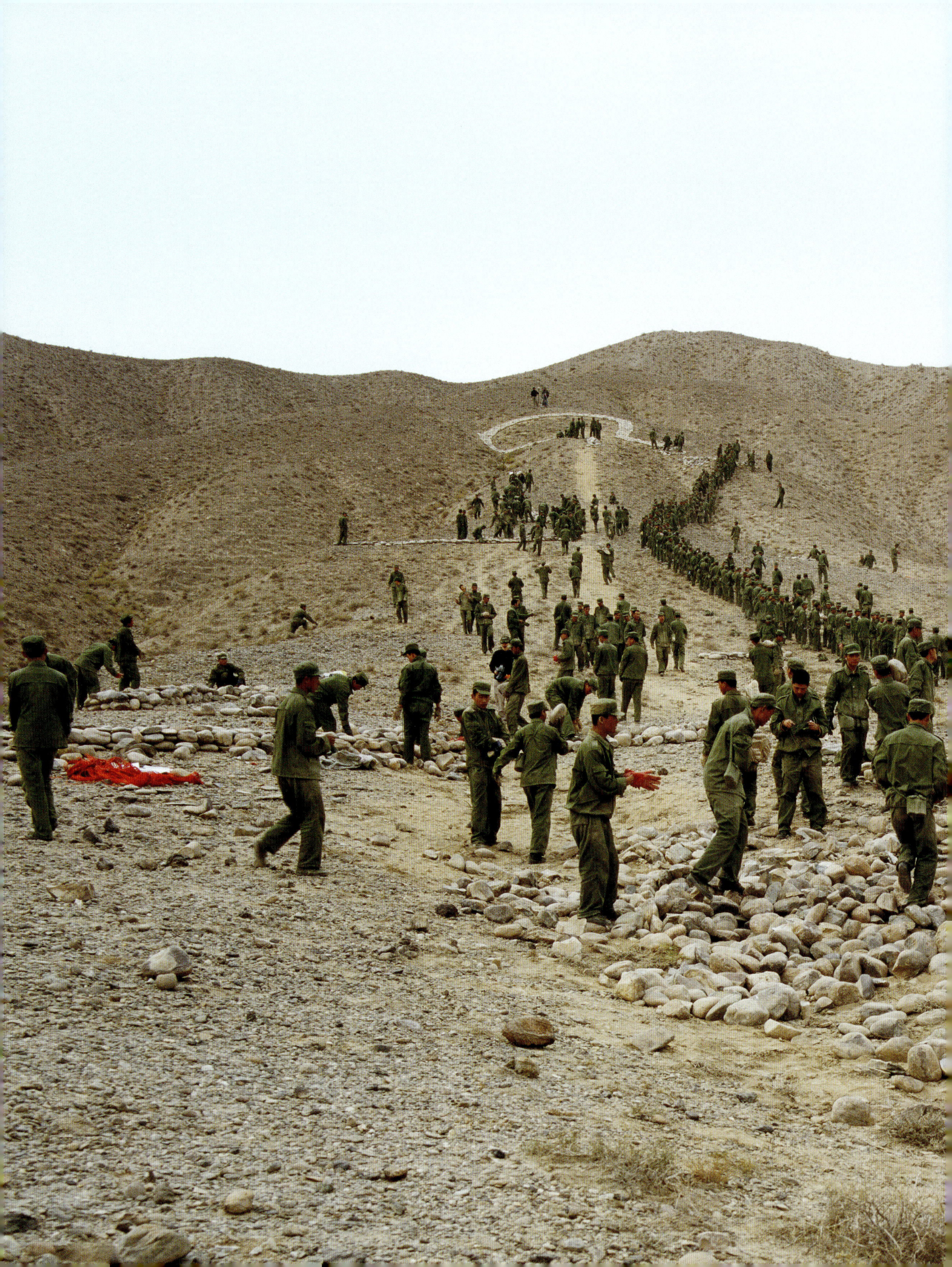

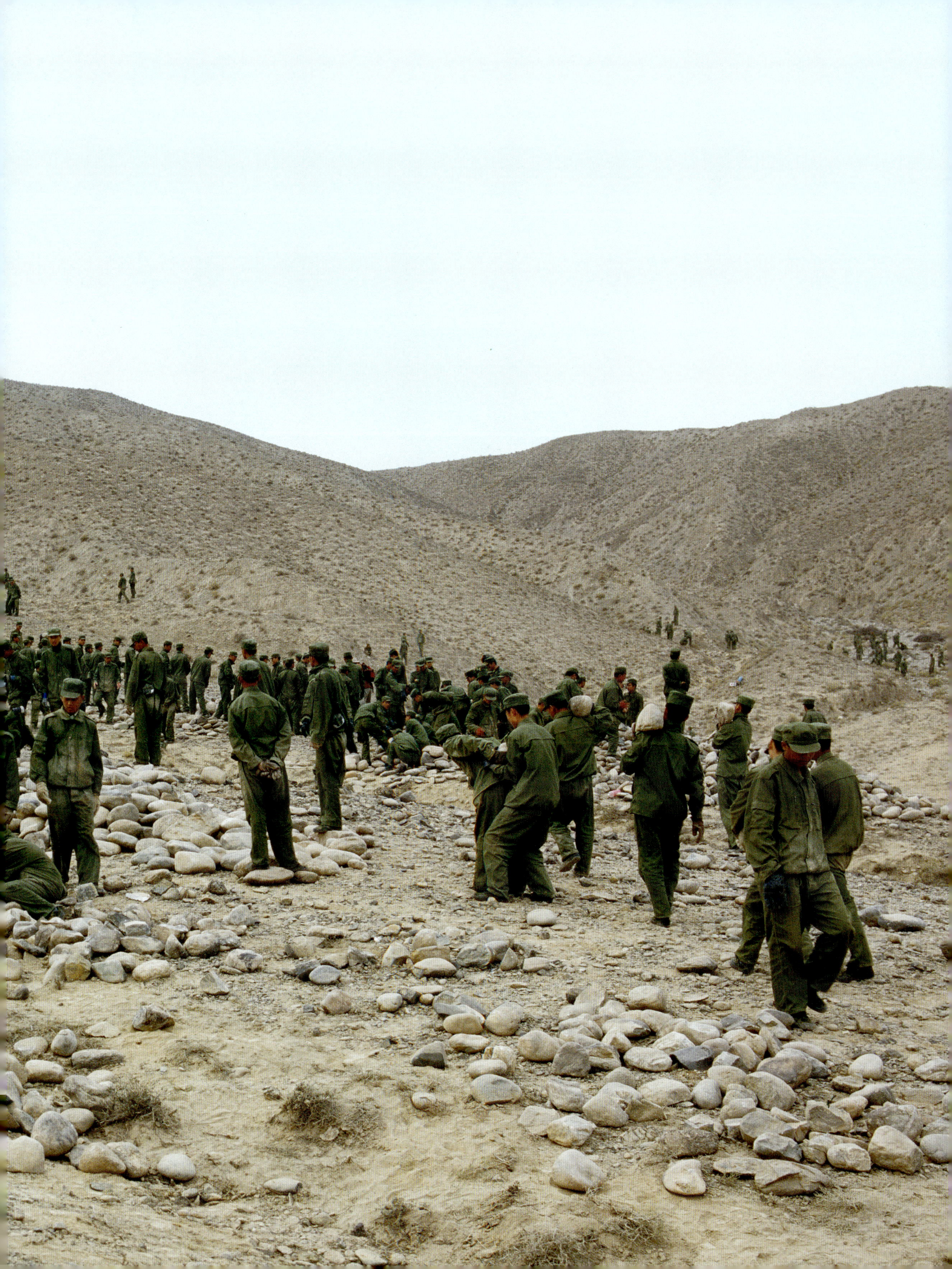

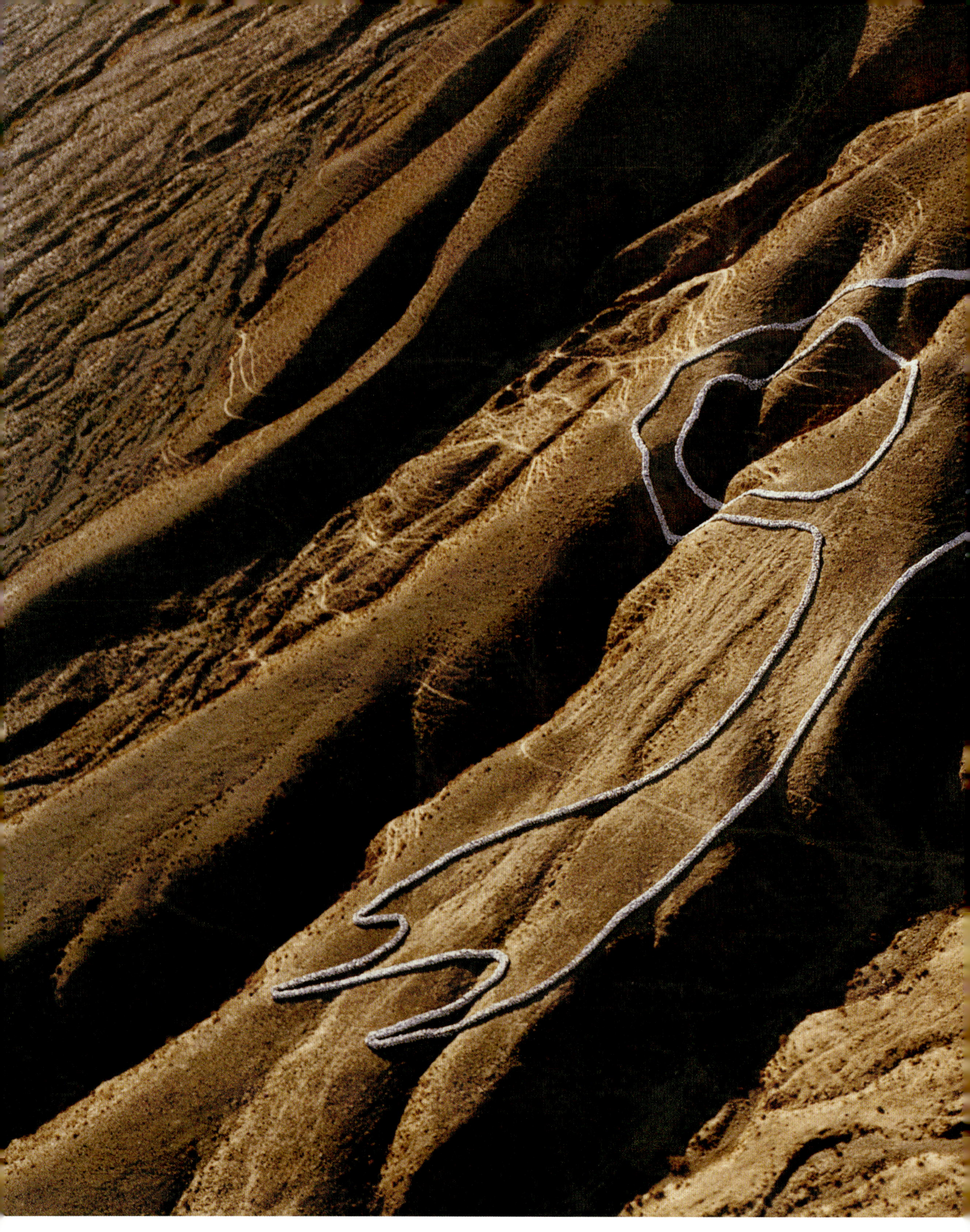

CAVEMAN 2006 / Sandstone / 150 × 150 m (492 × 492 ft.)

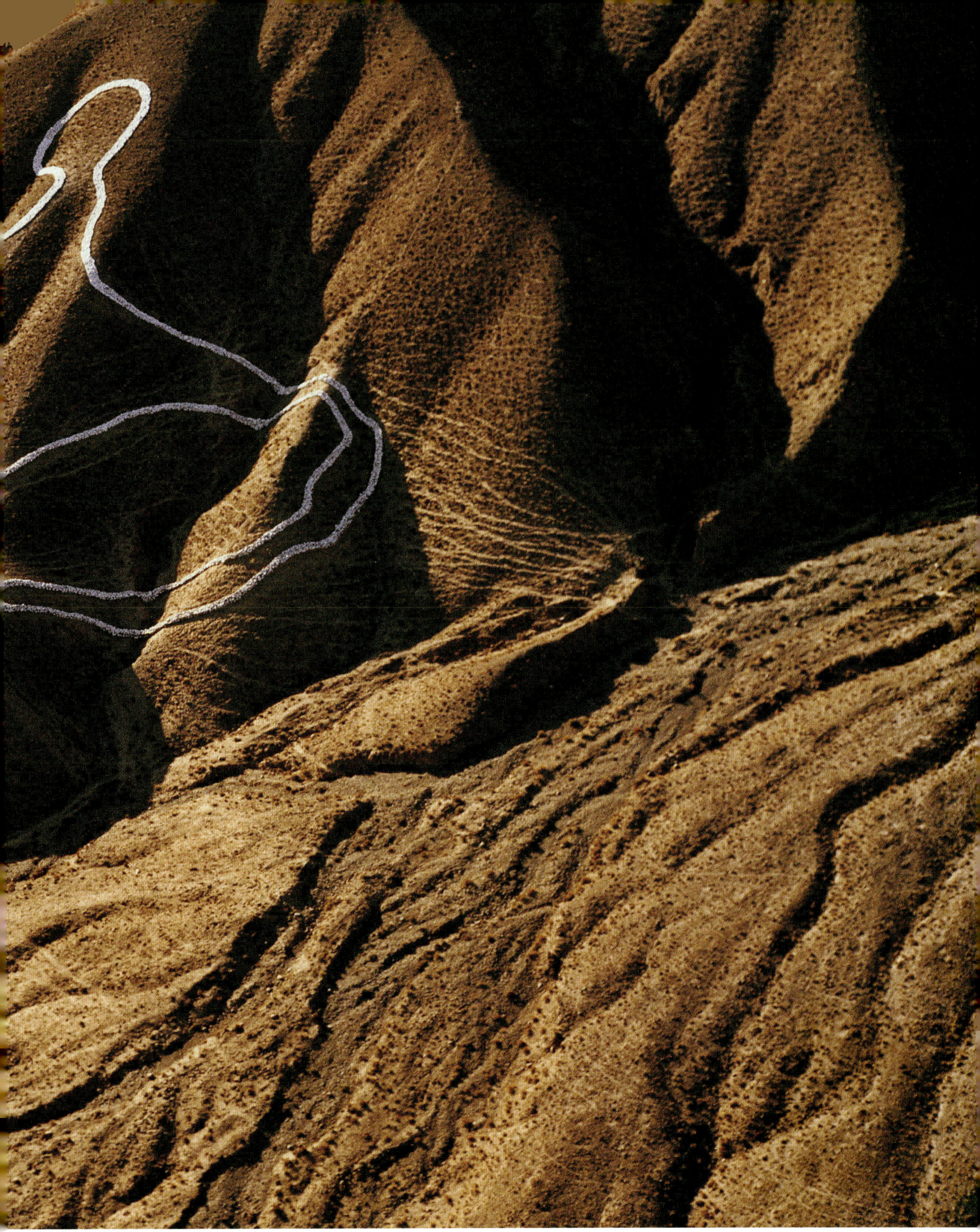

ON THE TRAIL OF THE MAHARAJAS

RAJASTHAN, INDIA

Rajasthan, in northwest India, the second-largest state on the subcontinent, seems to unite all of the images of a fairy-tale land: palaces embellished with gold and jewels; camel caravans against the silhouette of the setting sun in the middle of endless desert landscapes; women in colorful saris and men wearing turbans; and magnificent festive parades with decorated elephants, jugglers, and musicians. The land of the maharajas continues to excite fantasies of *One Thousand and One Nights* in anyone who visits India. At the same time, Jaipur, its capital, offers a marked contrast. This industrial metropolis in the middle of the desert is one of the fastest-growing cities in the world—with all of the disadvantages that accompany rapid growth, such as pollution and chaotic living conditions among an exploding population. Yet the cliché of picturesque India is still a reality in the historical city center, with its playful mogul architecture and building façades of delicate pink, the traditional color of hospitality; its wide streets are full of the richness of Oriental life. The Maharaja Sawai Jai Singh, who founded Jaipur in 1727, had all of the structures in what is today's historical city center built from shimmering pink sandstone.

Rogers deliberately sought a site that united everything: the desert landscape, the remains of a culturally charged history, and a place in which most people master their lives day after day on the edge of chaos. He found all of these conditions in the lively city of Jobner, 35 kilometers (22 miles) west of Jaipur and accessible only via a rutted dirt road.

In Jobner, the Hindu temples and imposing castles from which the maharajas once ruled their princedoms look toward the Aravalli Range and the Thar Desert beyond. Like the buildings in Jaipur, they are also built from shimmering sandstone. Here, in the immediate vicinity of the four-hundred-year-old Jobner Fort and the important Hindu temple Jwala Mata Ka Mandir, Rogers built two striking works: *Rhythms of Life* and *Ratio*. With both works, Rogers incorporated the multilayered historical and

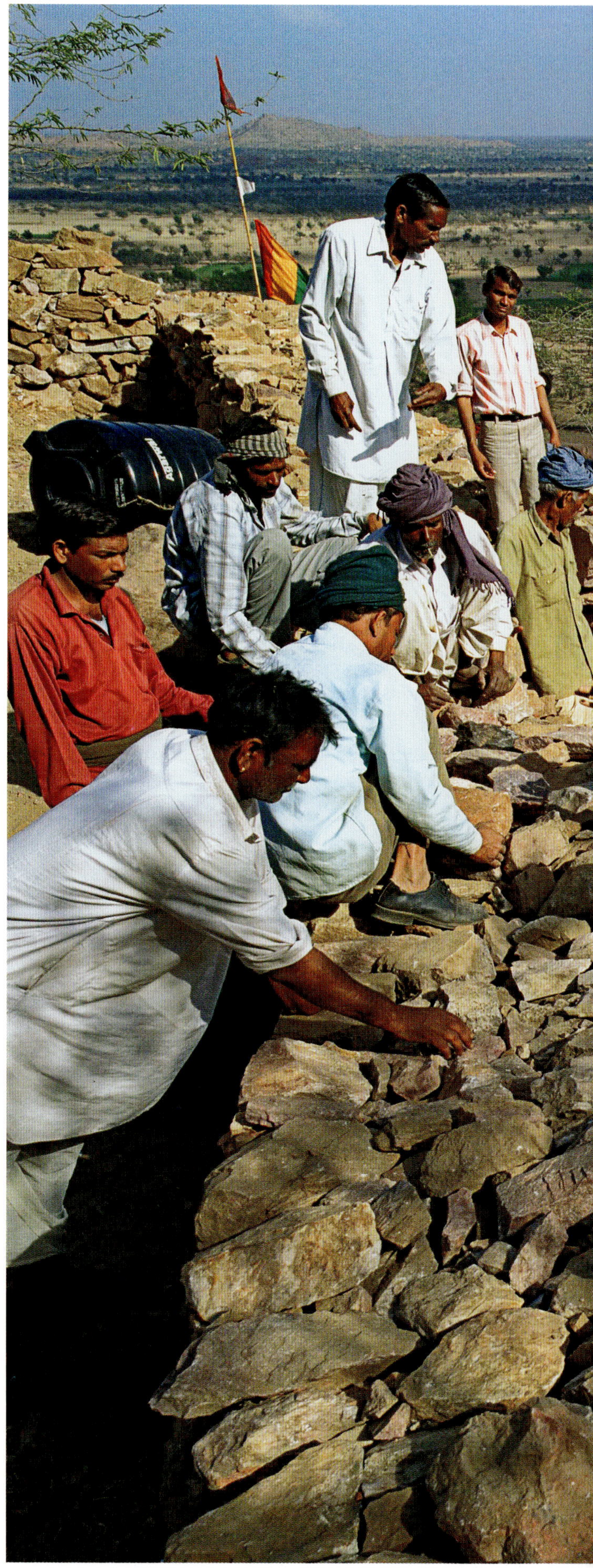

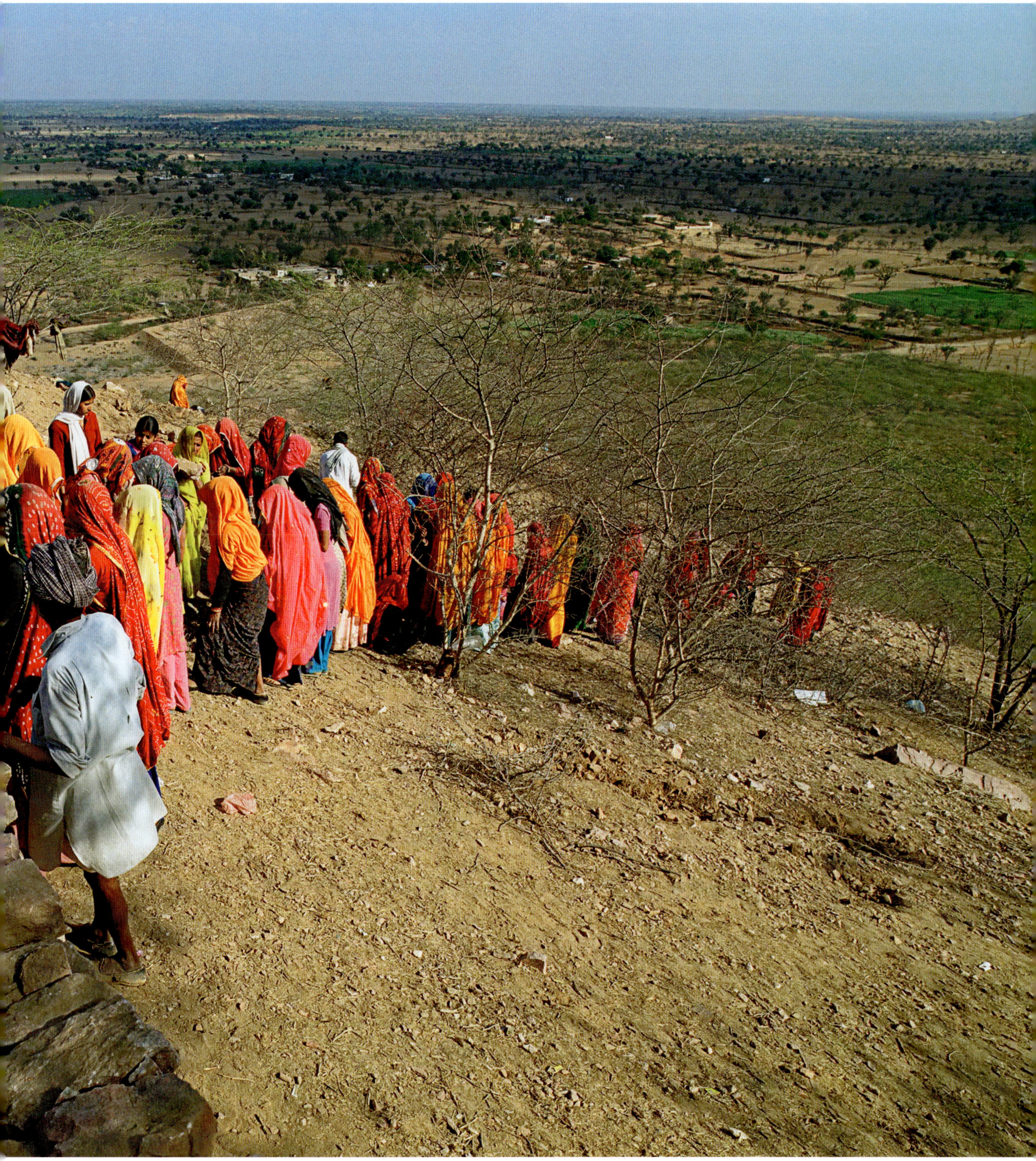

cultural parameters that characterize the country and its people, from the ancient Hindu religion and the culture of the maharajas to the British Raj and India's independence and growth in the modern era. Working in India was far from well organized and disciplined. The caste system frequently makes cooperation between laborers of different social origin impossible; there was wrangling and corruption. "We even had to call the police several times," recalled Rogers. "And people always suddenly disappeared who had just been hired. Or others came who wanted to get paid and had not even worked. It was simply chaotic." Those who worked hardest in the unrelenting sun were usually women. Draped in colorful saris and wearing loose slippers on their feet, they tirelessly collected and shifted the rocks up to the building site. For *Ratio*, the artist consciously used the same building method that he had executed in a similar manner in Sri Lanka: a stepped stone structure which has proportions based on the Fibonacci sequence. The mathematical formula explains the hidden order in nature, from growth patterns all the way to finiteness, but also the Golden Ratio, the ideal principle of aesthetic proportion in art and architecture. The structure is located above the Hindu temple Jwala Mata Ka Mandir, dedicated to Jwala Mata, the goddess of fire, one of the most important divinities in the Vedic religion. Thousands of believers assemble there every year during the festival of Navratri to pay homage. But the temple is also popular for weddings, and young couples who wish to have children make a pilgrimage there with offerings. Rogers's workforce used the pilgrims' path in order to transport rocks, sacks of cement, and sand up to the building site. The stone structure's 8.5-meter-high (28 feet) flight of stone stairs is also made of the same pink sandstone as the palaces from the maharaja period. Rogers placed importance on concealing the mortar used on the steps by placing small stones in the joints. It was imperative to create the impression of a wall joined without the use of cement so that the artwork did not differ outwardly from the historical buildings in the vicinity.

As in Sri Lanka, with the stone steps *Ratio* Rogers references the stair motif of the Hindu temple and elevates it in the truest sense of the word by placing it on the highest range of hills: as a simplified symbol of striving upward into infinity, as an expression of divine expectation. Moreover, in iconographic terms the works of art, designed like a powerful monument, relate to the former maharajah's fort only meters below it as a simple symbol of power or, put more positively, as a sentinel of the people who live in the valley. The geoglyph *Rhythms of Life* is embedded in a rough escarpment. With its extreme slope, rocky surface, and thorny bushes, this site was barely accessible to the laborers, let alone suitable for creating a large-scale stone drawing. Yet Rogers insisted on it. With tremendous physical effort, the laborers succeeded in laying the foundation walls between the stunted bushes in such a way that the geoglyph is clearly visible from above as an image, but which has been adapted to the landscape so it appears as a natural occurrence.

As always, Andrew Rogers respected the customs and traditions of the laborers, which were particularly elaborate in this case. Before work could even commence, the project had to be consecrated with a puja, a Hindu purification ceremony. Women drew a colorful mandala on the ground, and the stones were purified with curd, vermilion, and water from the Ganges. When, as was so frequently the case during the construction phase, chaos got the upper hand and the project threatened to come undone, Ganesh, the benevolent Hindu god with an elephant's head who helps remove all obstacles, was invoked by the locals. Peace and discipline eventually set in among the laborers—first and foremost thanks to the village elder, who as the foreman enjoyed the necessary authority among his compatriots—and the project was completed. Reason enough for everyone to celebrate. For this ceremony, a further 2,500 people from the surrounding area assembled on the hill in order to be present at the magnificent parade of decorated elephants and horses, with music, jugglers, and dancers in traditional attire, adorned with elaborate brocade embroidery.

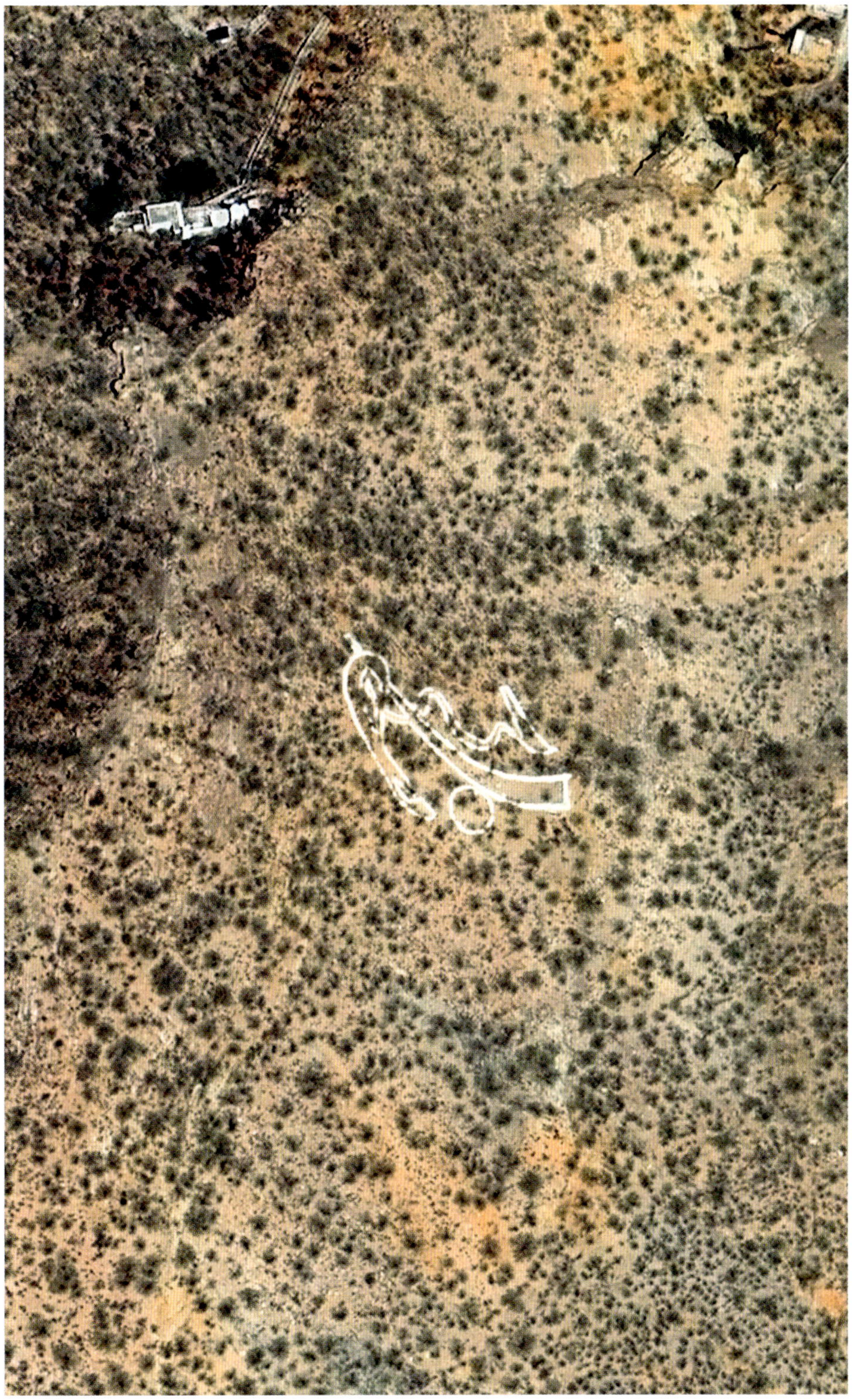

RHYTHMS OF LIFE, satellite image taken 440 km (275 miles) above the earth

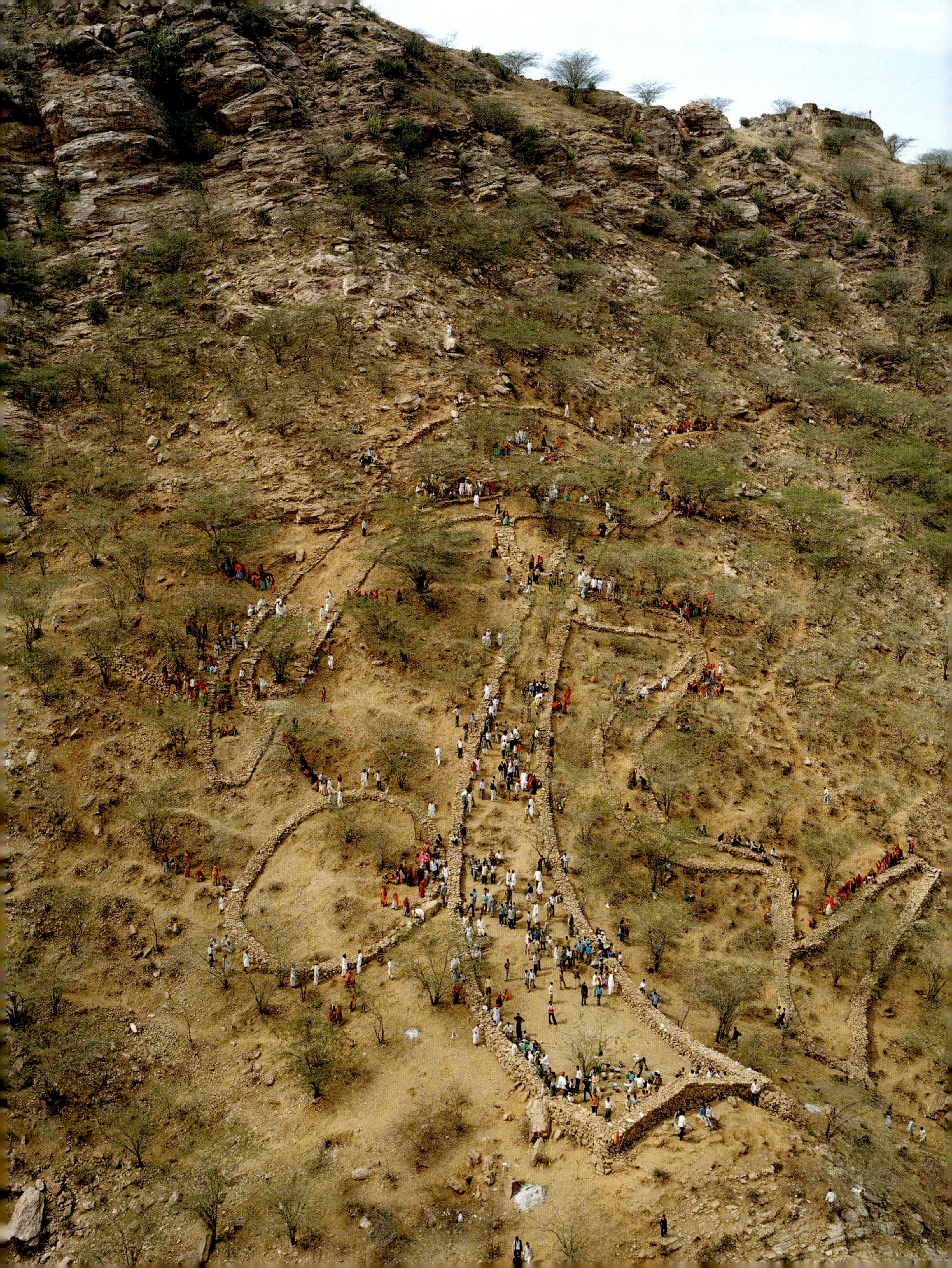

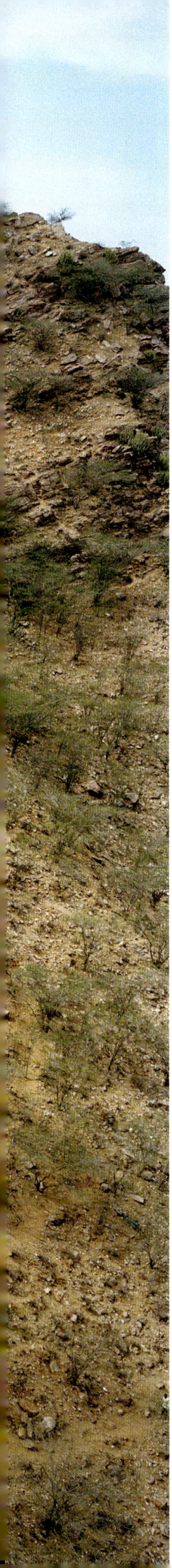

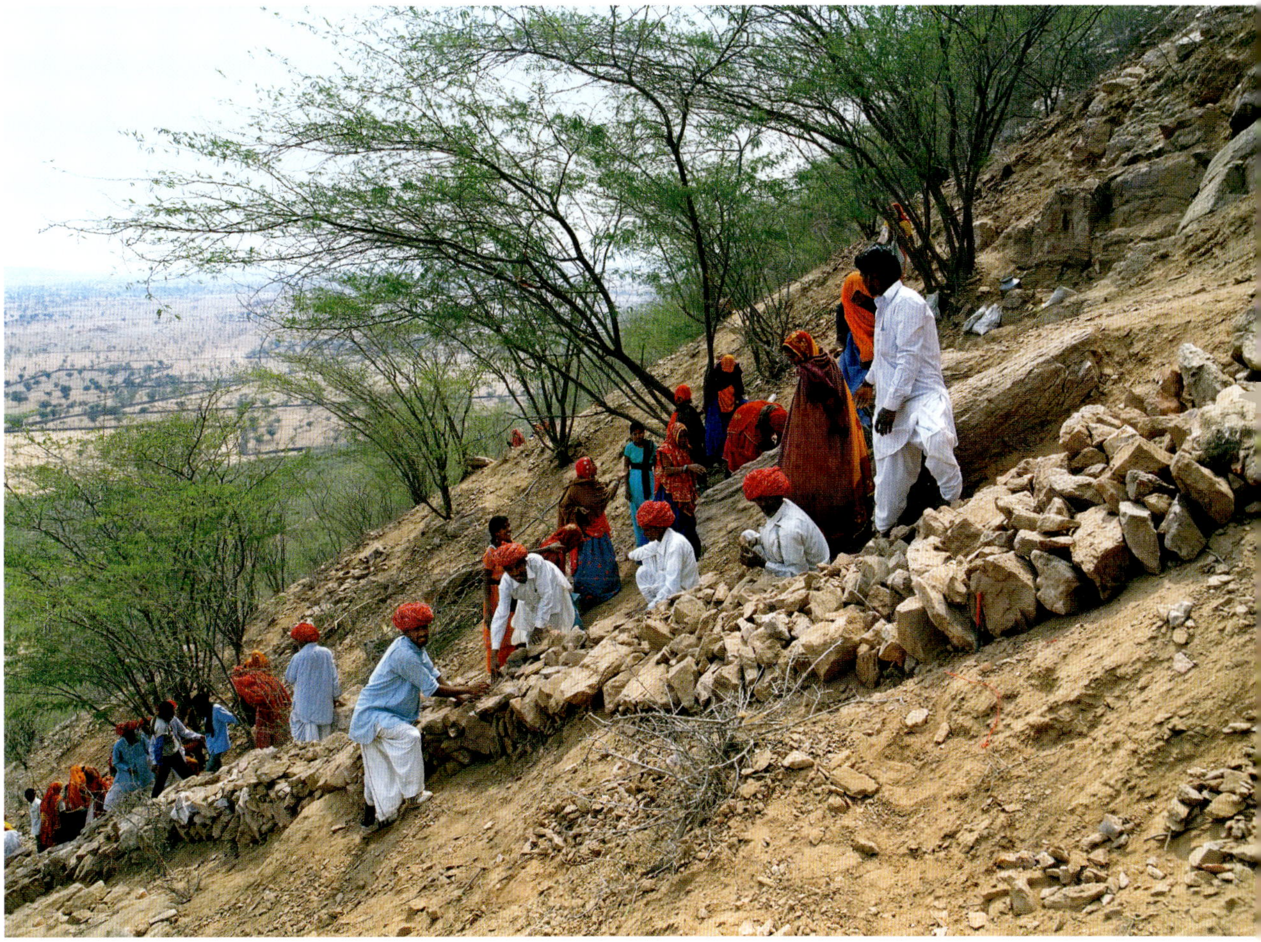

RHYTHMS OF LIFE 2007 / Sandstone / 90 × 75 m (295 × 246 ft.)

RATIO 2007 / Sandstone / 6.5 × 8.5 m (21 × 28 ft.)

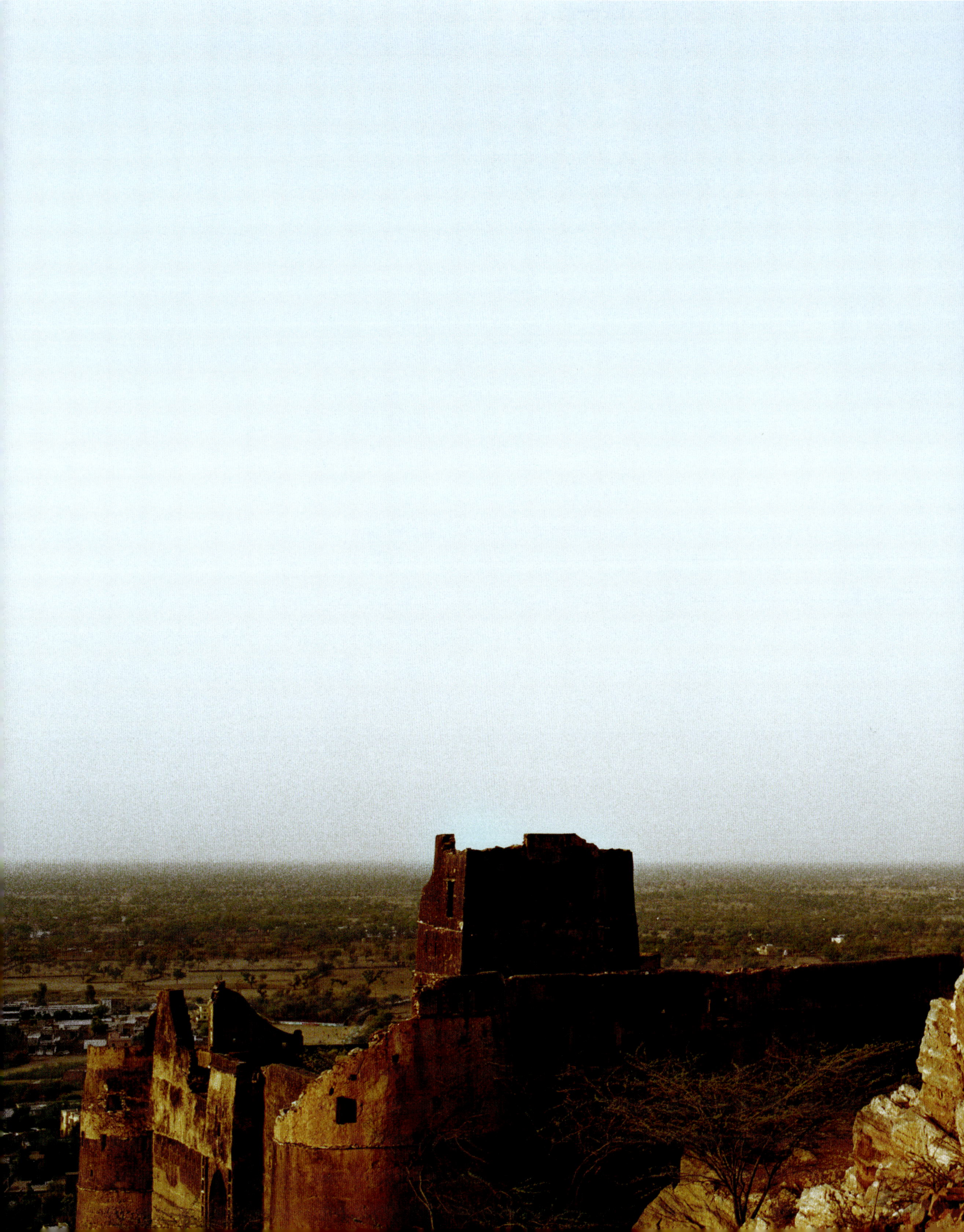

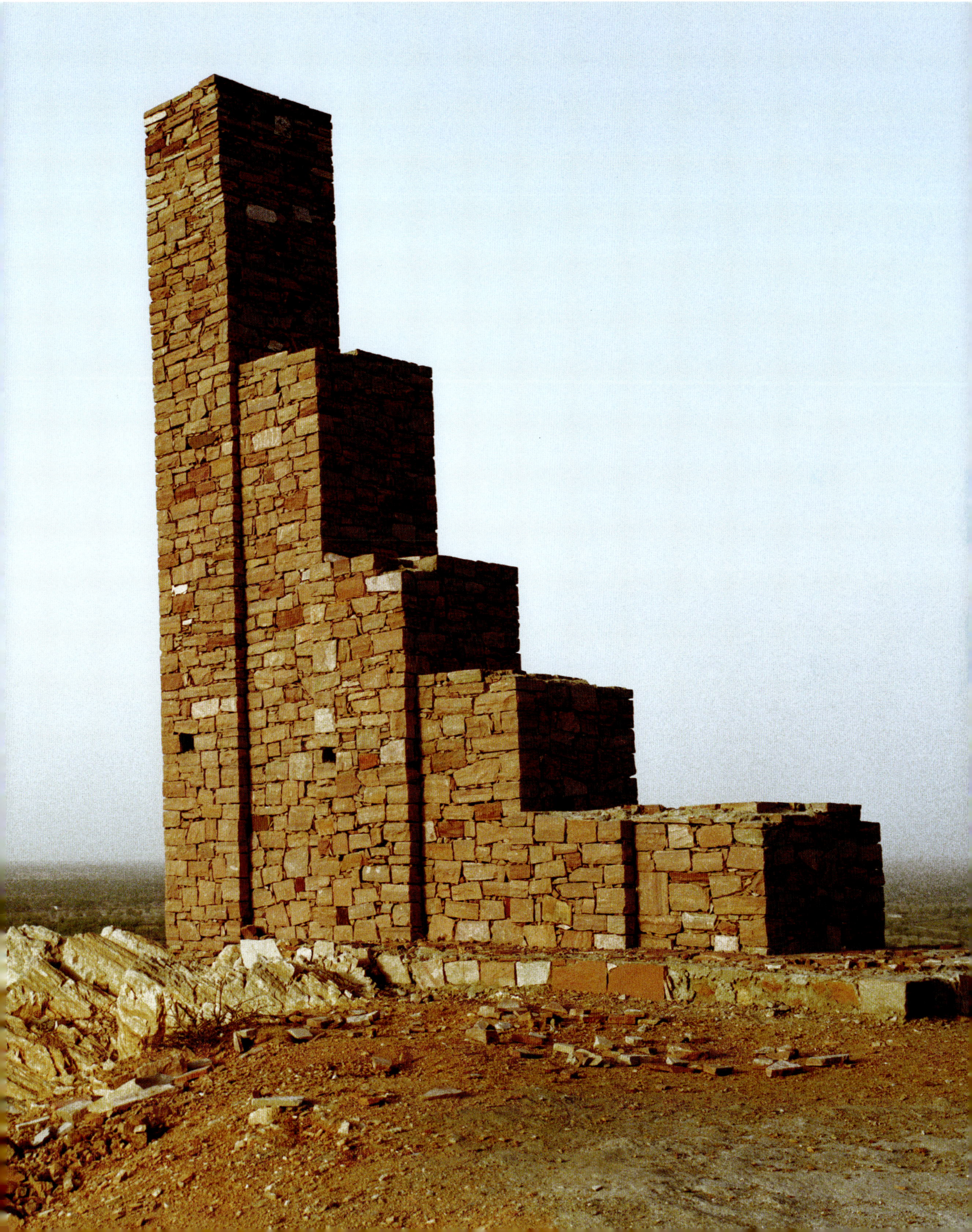

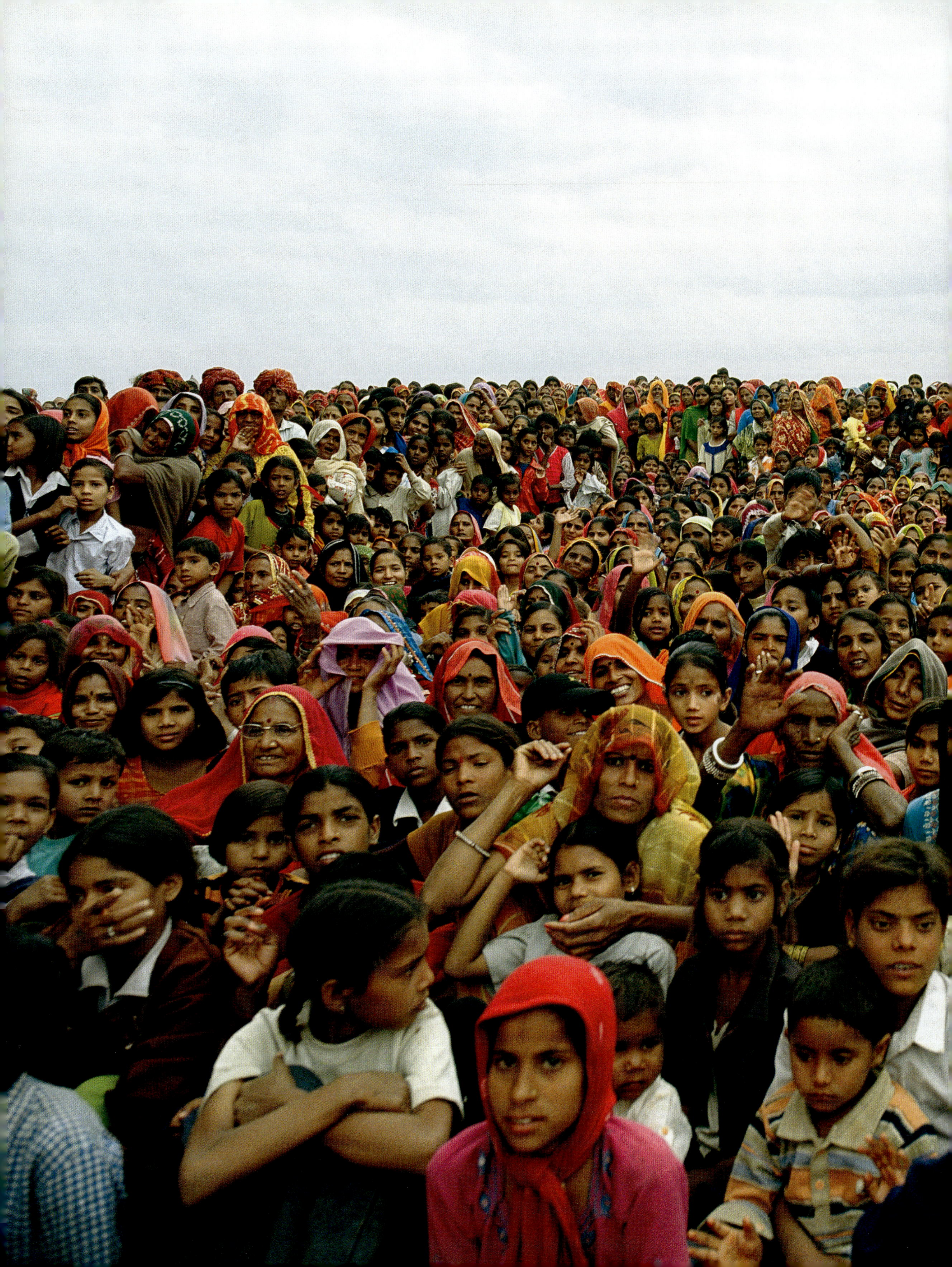

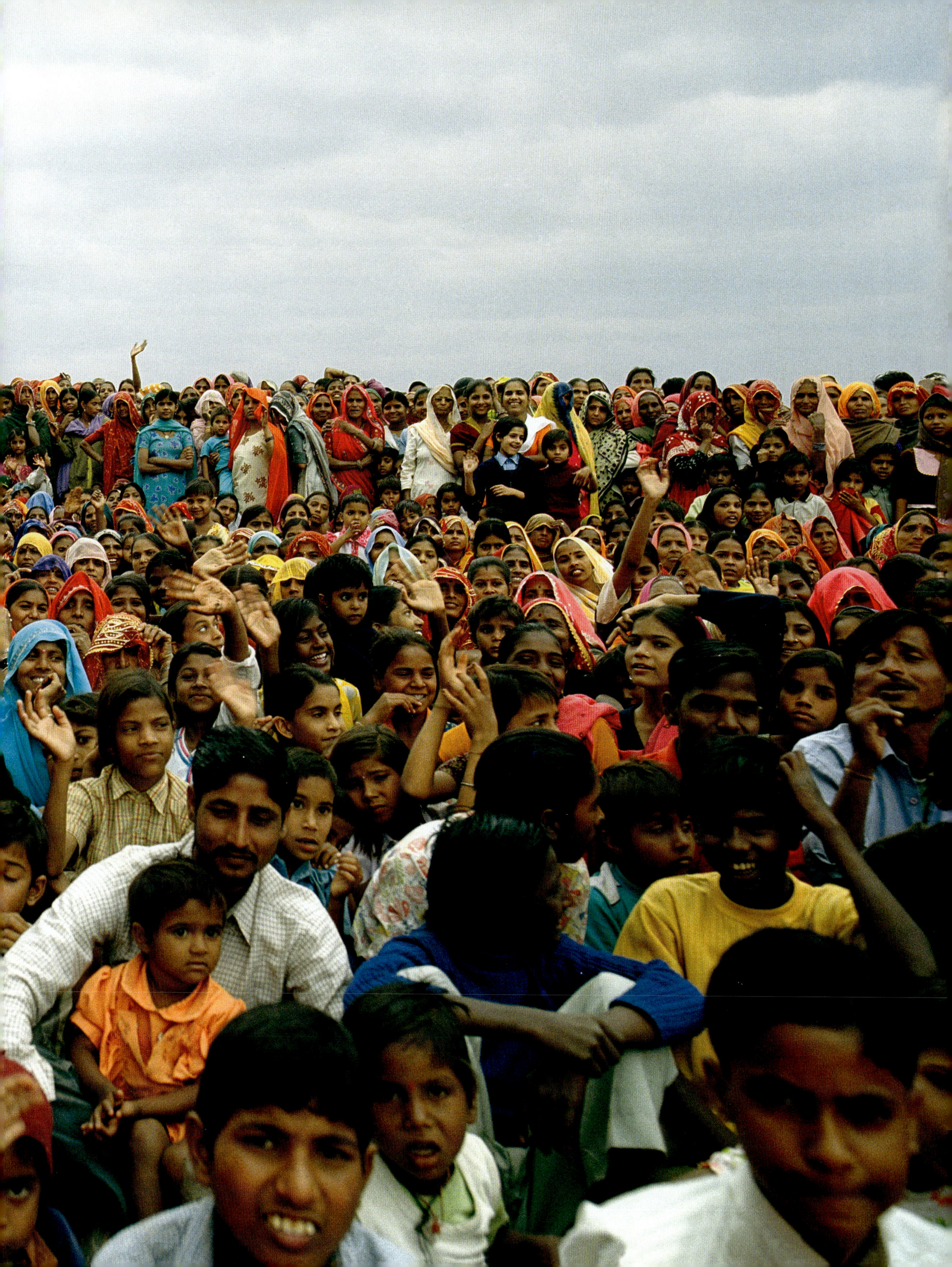

AT THE FOOT OF THE EIGHT-THOUSANDERS

POKHARA AND JOMSOM, NEPAL

Religion and everyday life are inseparably connected in the region between India and China. The puja, a prayer in honor of the gods, is part of everyday life in Nepal, where Hinduism and Buddhism peacefully coexist with the still vibrant religions of the mountain dwellers from ancient times. Hindu and Buddhist cultic sites are often even situated side by side and are visited together. Lumbini, the birthplace of the Buddha, who lived there as Prince Siddhartha before his enlightenment and foundation of the Buddhist doctrine, is also one of the most important pilgrimage sites for Hindus.

For an artist like Andrew Rogers, who is moved by the spirituality of all cultures and deliberately seeks out sites where it can still be actively experienced, it was natural to produce a sculpture in Nepal.

Added to this is Nepal's spectacular landscape: there is no other place in the world where the contrast between the tallest mountains and the deepest gorges is greater than in Nepal. Only here is there such a close juxtaposition of a majestic backdrop with the colossal mountains of the Himalaya, the highest mountain massif and the deepest gorges in the world: "I wanted to come to the Himalayas because they are one of the most significant topographical features in the world. And the spirituality that is drawn from them by the people that live here is so very special," recalled Rogers.

Near Pokhara, a city 200 kilometers (124 miles) west of Nepal's capital, Kathmandu, and almost exactly in the geographic middle of the country, he found the site in Pokhara Valley's Seti River Gorge. In the background are the white giants of the main crest of the Himalaya, with three of the fourteen eight-thousanders (mountains more than 8,000 meters (26,247 feet) above sea level), Dhaulagiri, Annapurna, and Manaslu.

RHYTHMS OF LIFE 2008 / Granite / 100 x 100 m (330 x 330 ft.)

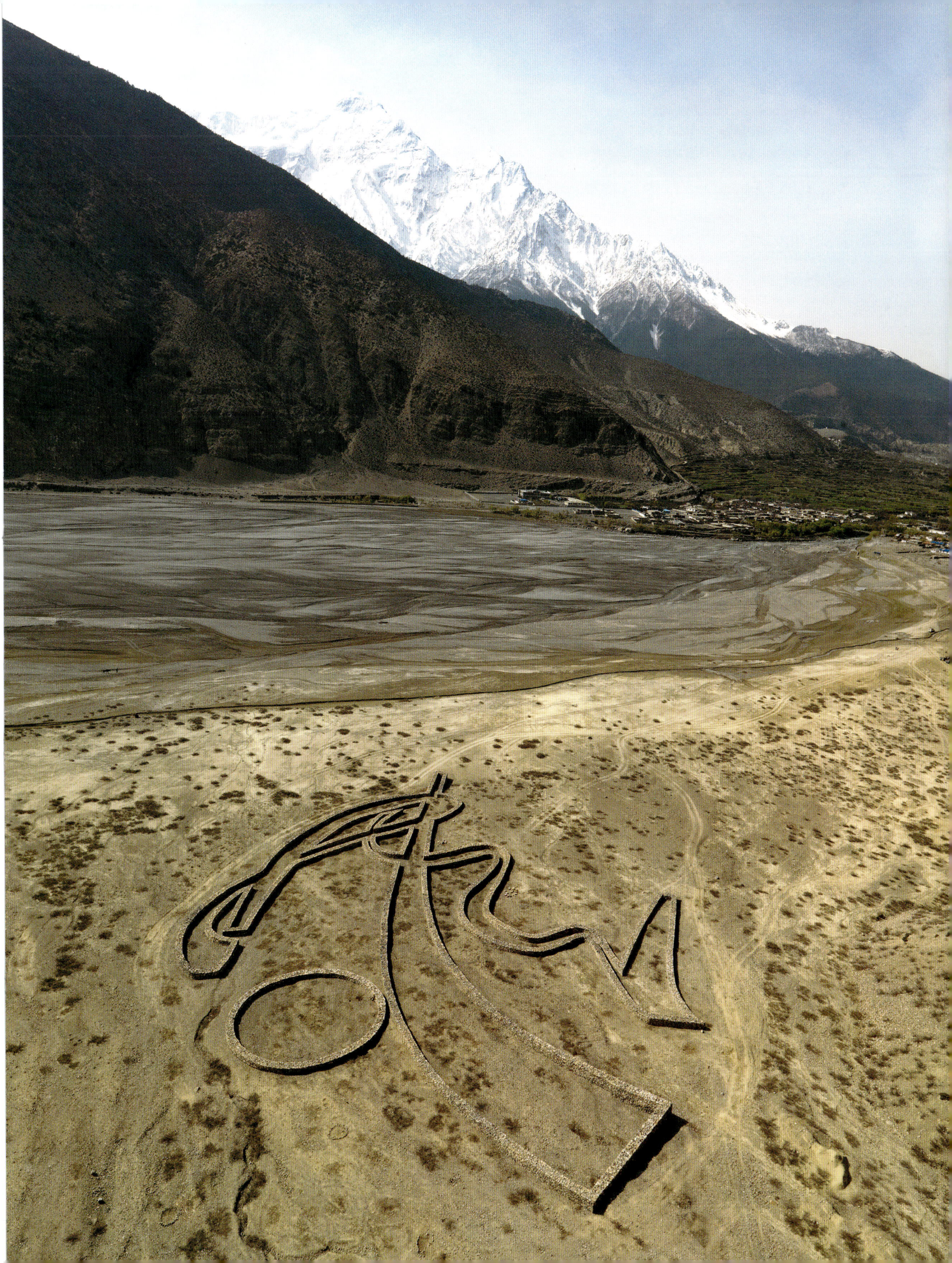

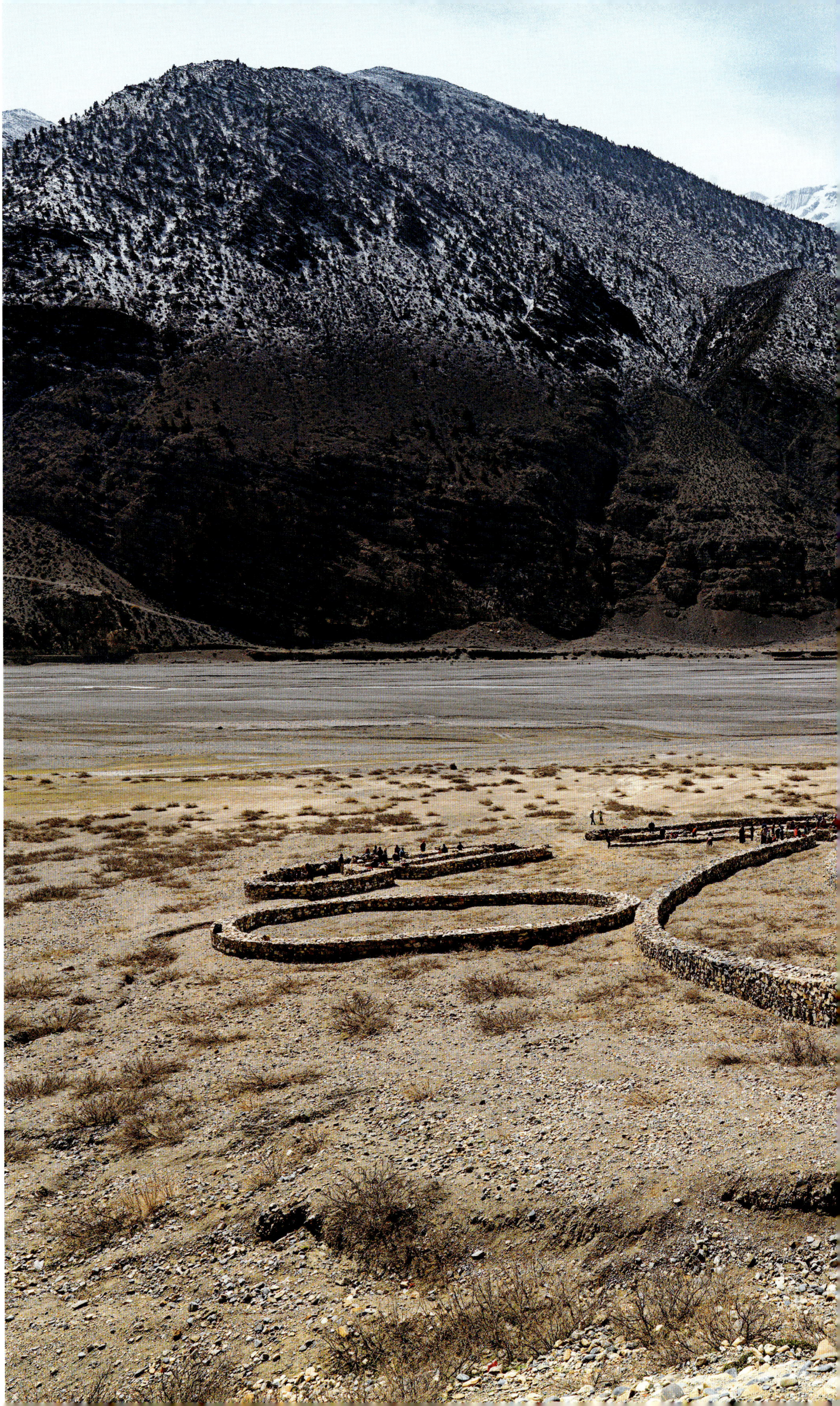

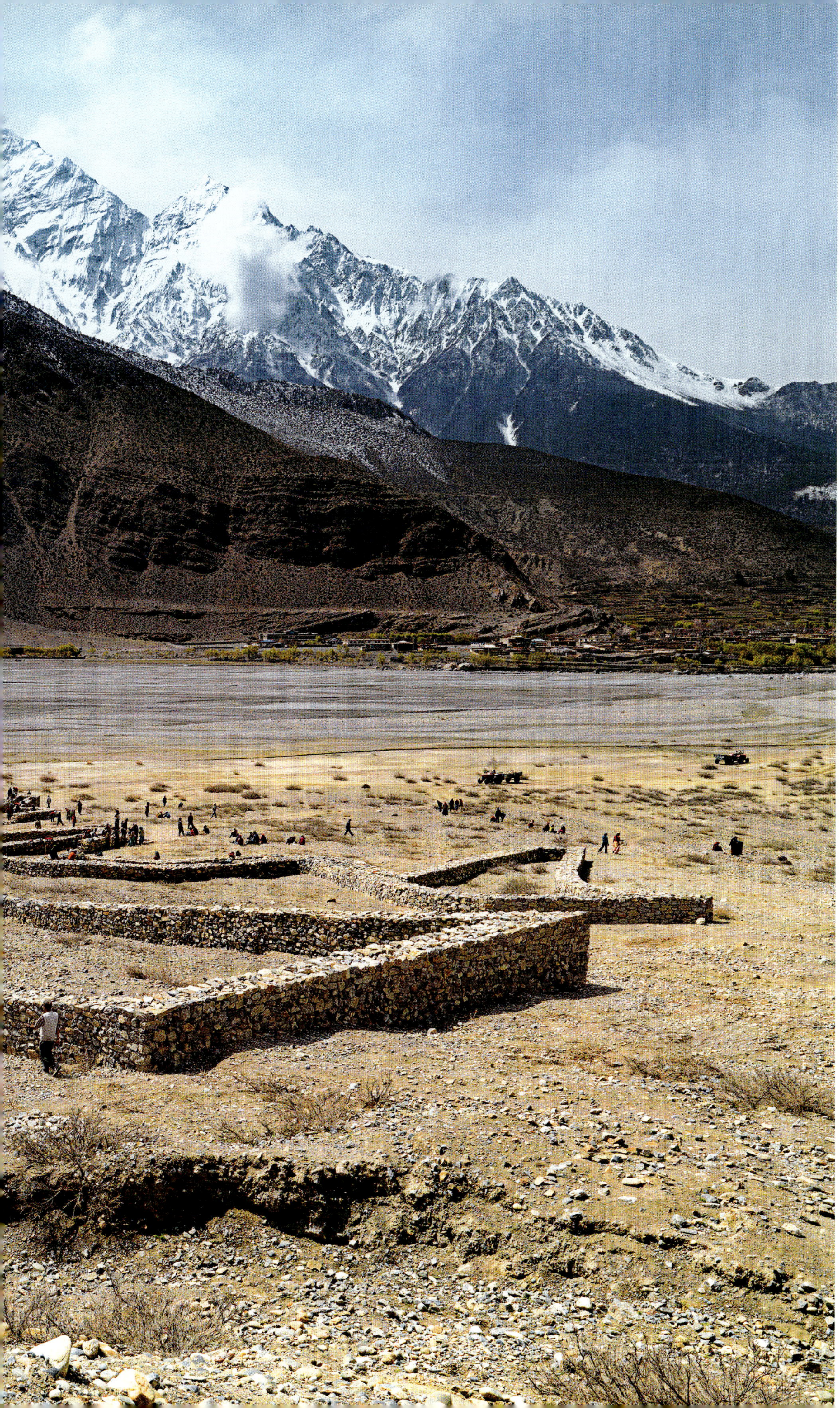

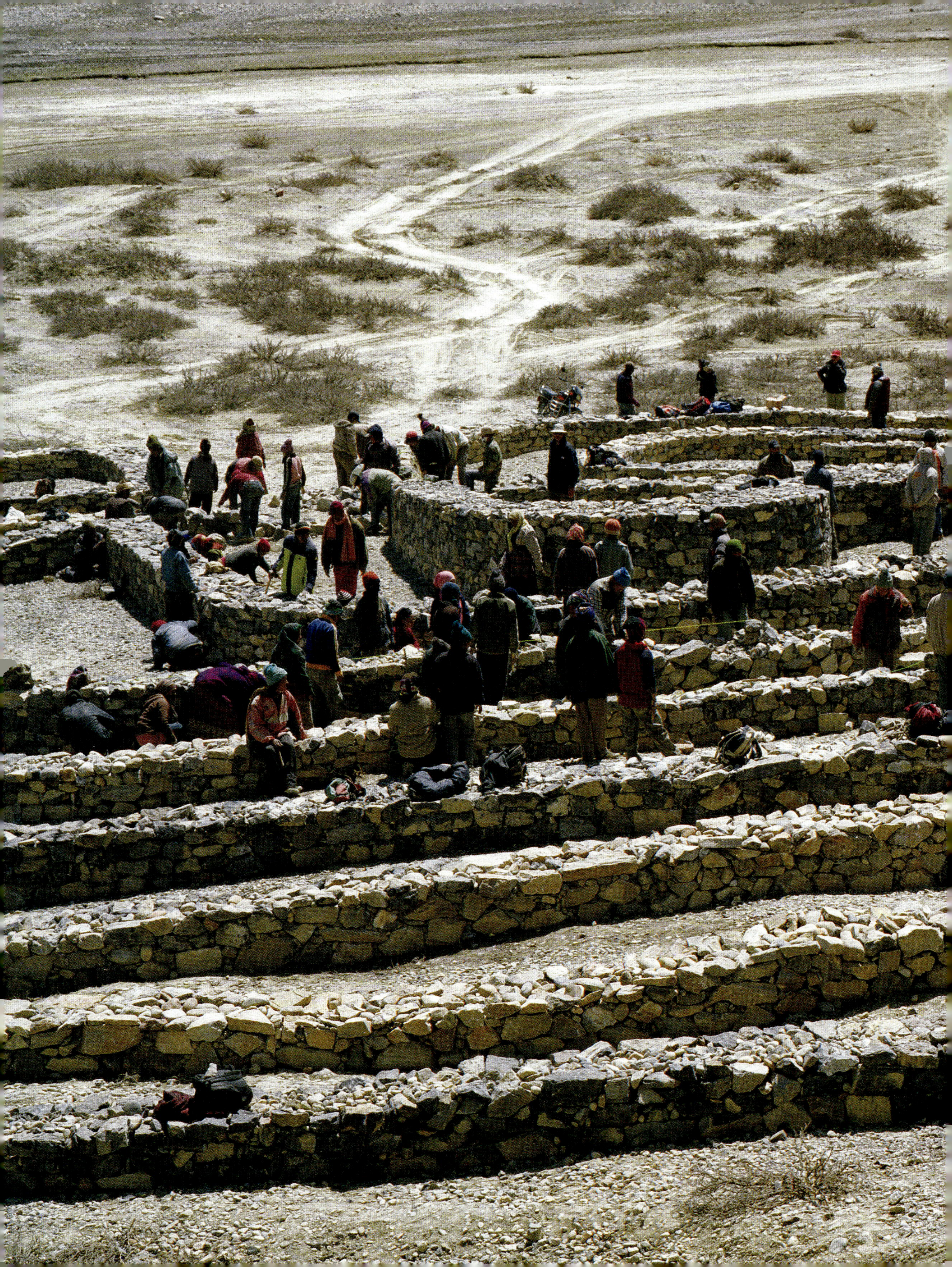

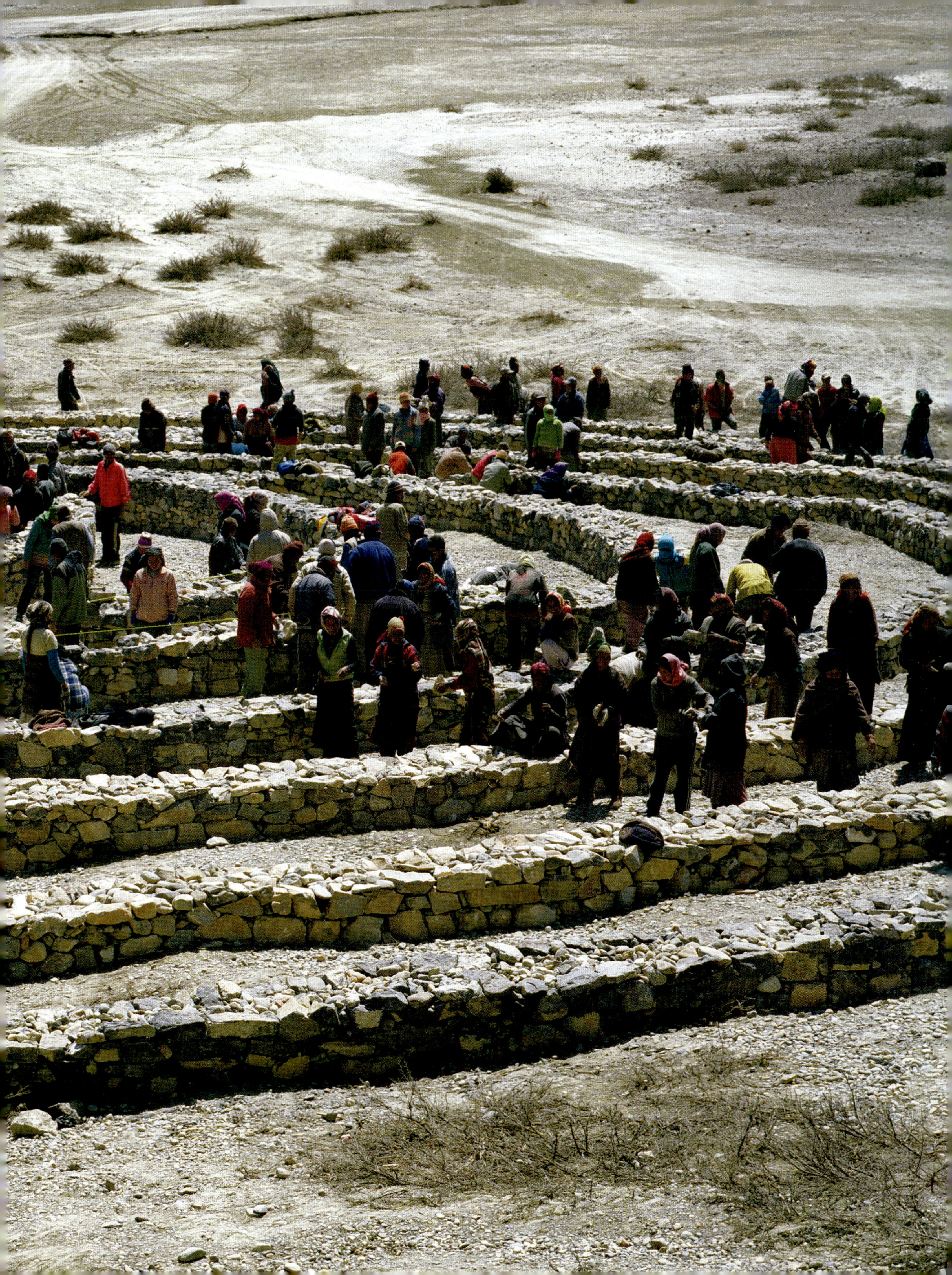

LABYRINTH 2008 / Granite / 60 × 60 m (197 × 197 ft.)

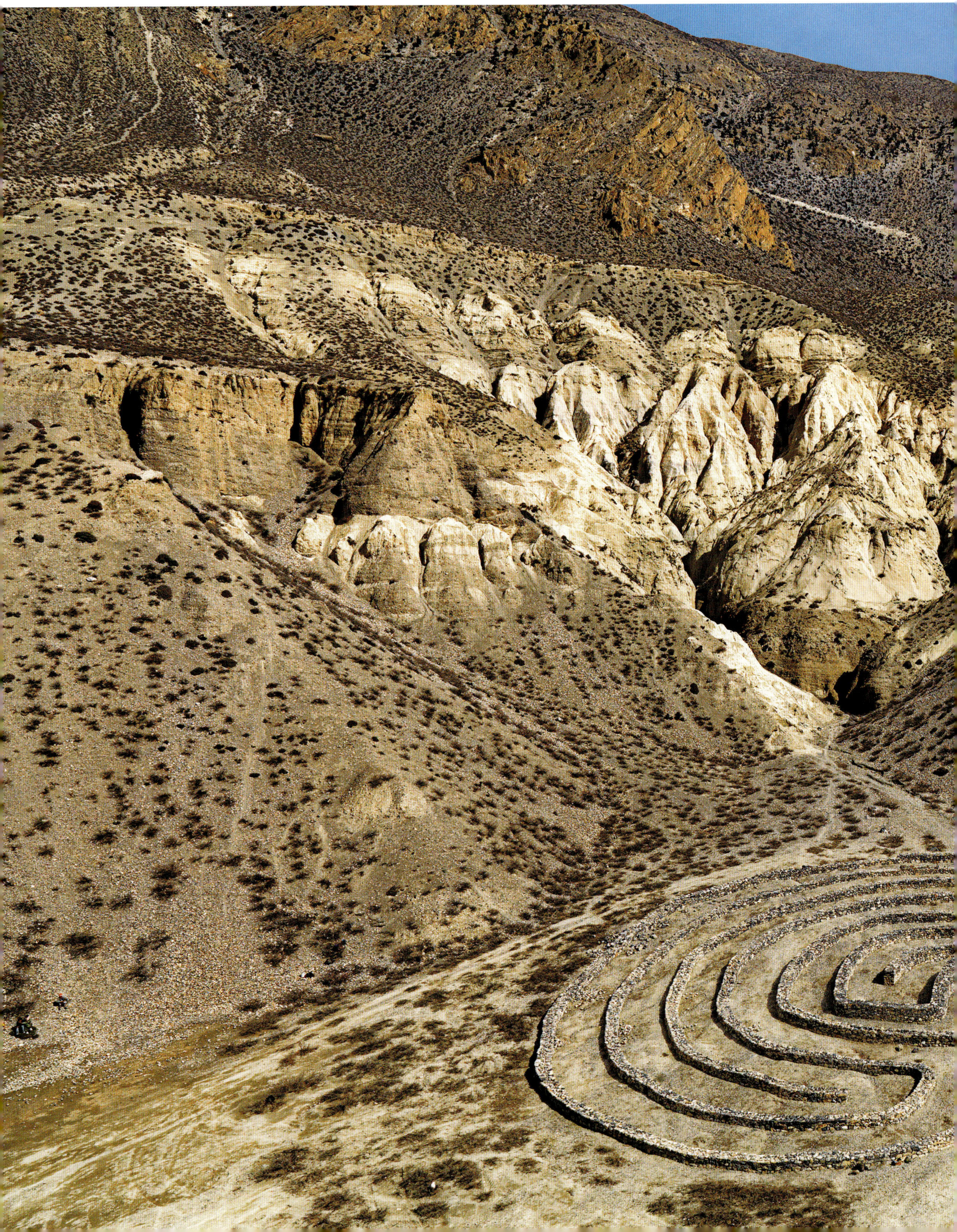

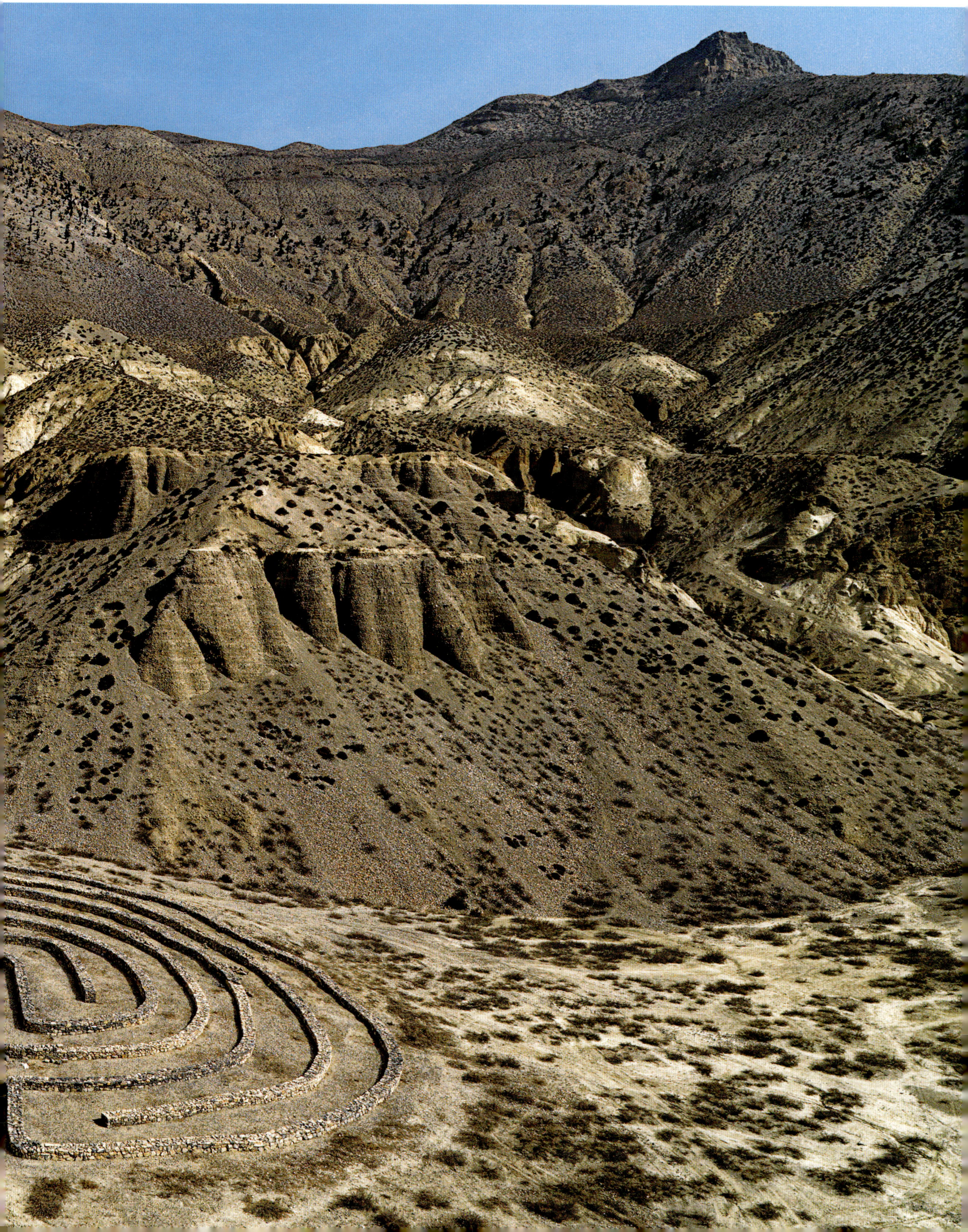

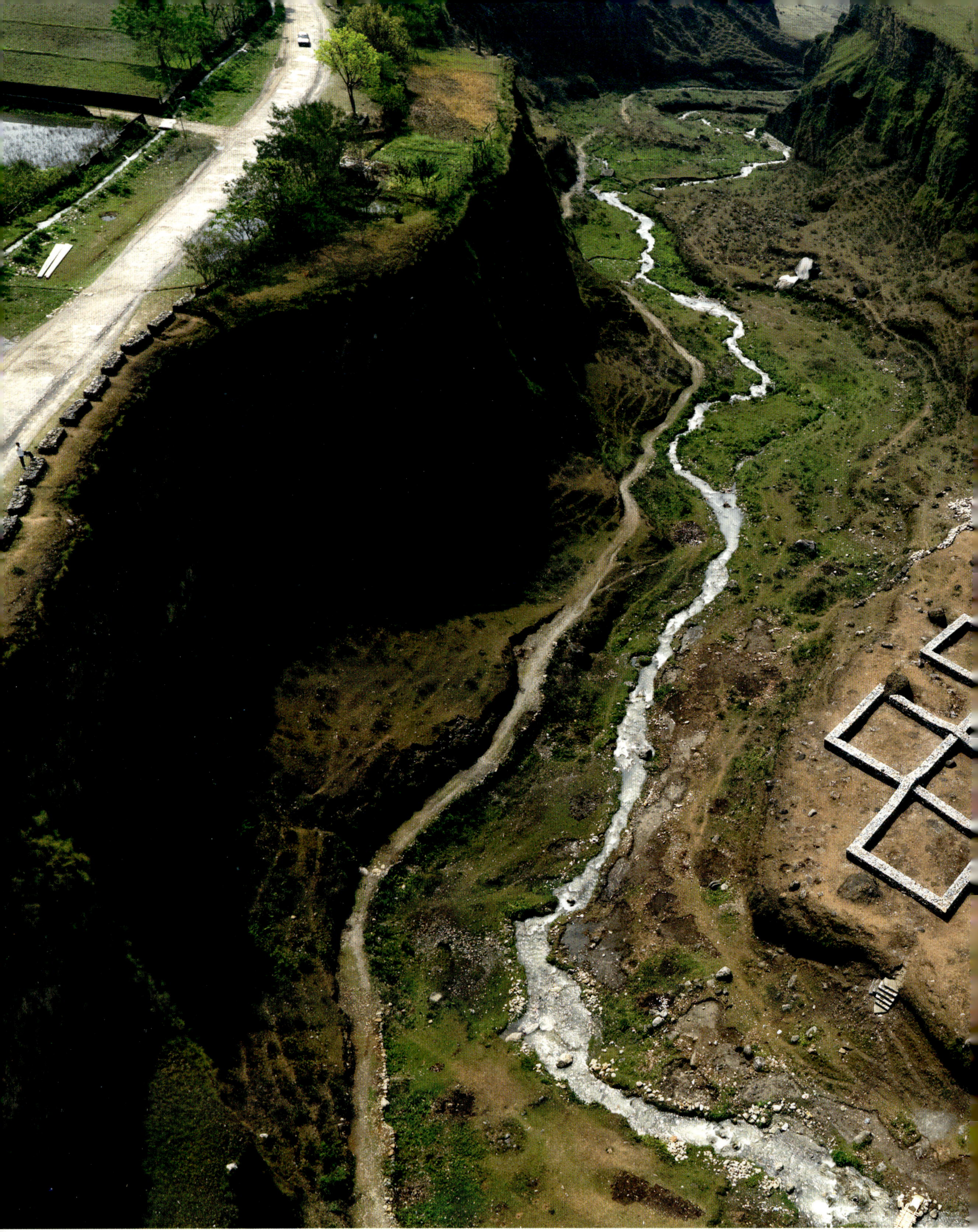

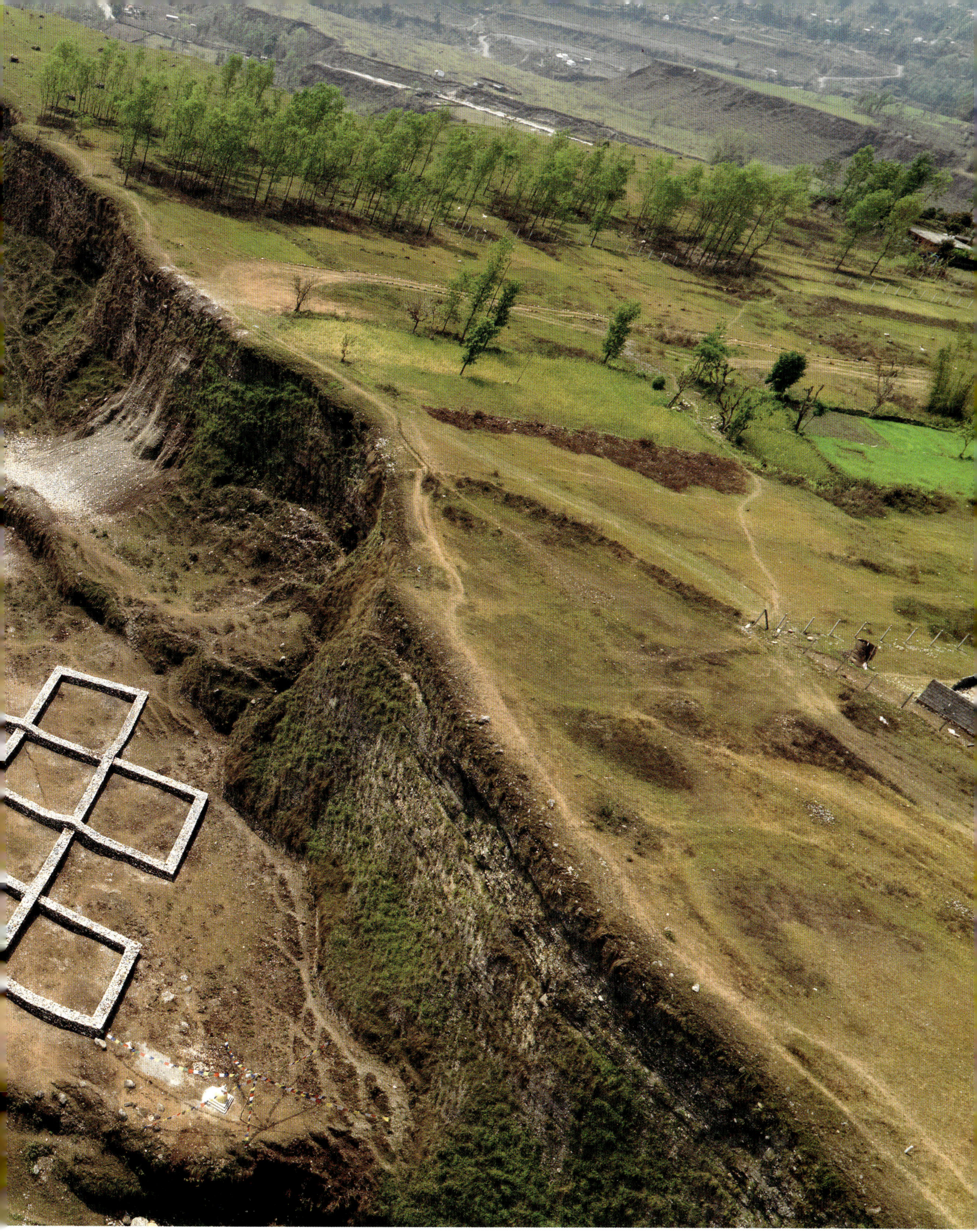

KNOT 2008 / Granite / 60 × 60 m (197 × 197 ft.)

THE CELTS

SPIŠSKÝ HRAD AND THE HIGH TATRAS, SLOVAKIA

With its lush, green hill country and snow-covered mountains, white meadows, endless forests, and clear rivers above which mighty castle complexes rise, the Spiš region in the northeastern part of Slovakia is reminiscent of Switzerland. Yet what seems so idyllic is misleading, because this region has always been an important hub due to its location between Europe and Asia and was therefore continually overrun and ruled by new peoples, including the Romans, the Mongolians, the Turks, and the Habsburgs. When the Habsburg Empire was dissolved at the end of World War I, the Czech and Slovak republics joined to form a single country, Czechoslovakia, which was fragmented during World War II and partly reunited after the war under Communist rule. In 1993 the union of the Czech and Slovak republics was dissolved and both republics celebrated their independence. This rich history, in connection with the country's almost archaic nature in the middle of what is otherwise a densely populated and highly civilized Europe, prompted Andrew Rogers to render visible the message of his *Rhythms of Life* project with two land art installations.

He chose two geographically dispersed places in the east and the west of the country, each of which is spectacular in its own right: *Sacred* is located on the escarpment below the medieval castle ruins of Spišský Hrad, one of Europe's largest castle complexes, which was named a UNESCO cultural heritage site in 1993. *Rhythms of Life*, on the other hand, is situated an hour's drive to the west, at the foot of the High Tatras, the tallest massif in the Carpathian Mountains, which, alongside the Alps, is a defining mountain range in Central Europe.

Spišský Hrad, built completely of white travertine, almost seems to grow out of the rock as the crown of a 365-meter-high (1,197 feet) hill. An extensive complex with towers, bridges, palace-like buildings, a chapel, and its own water reservoir in the large castle

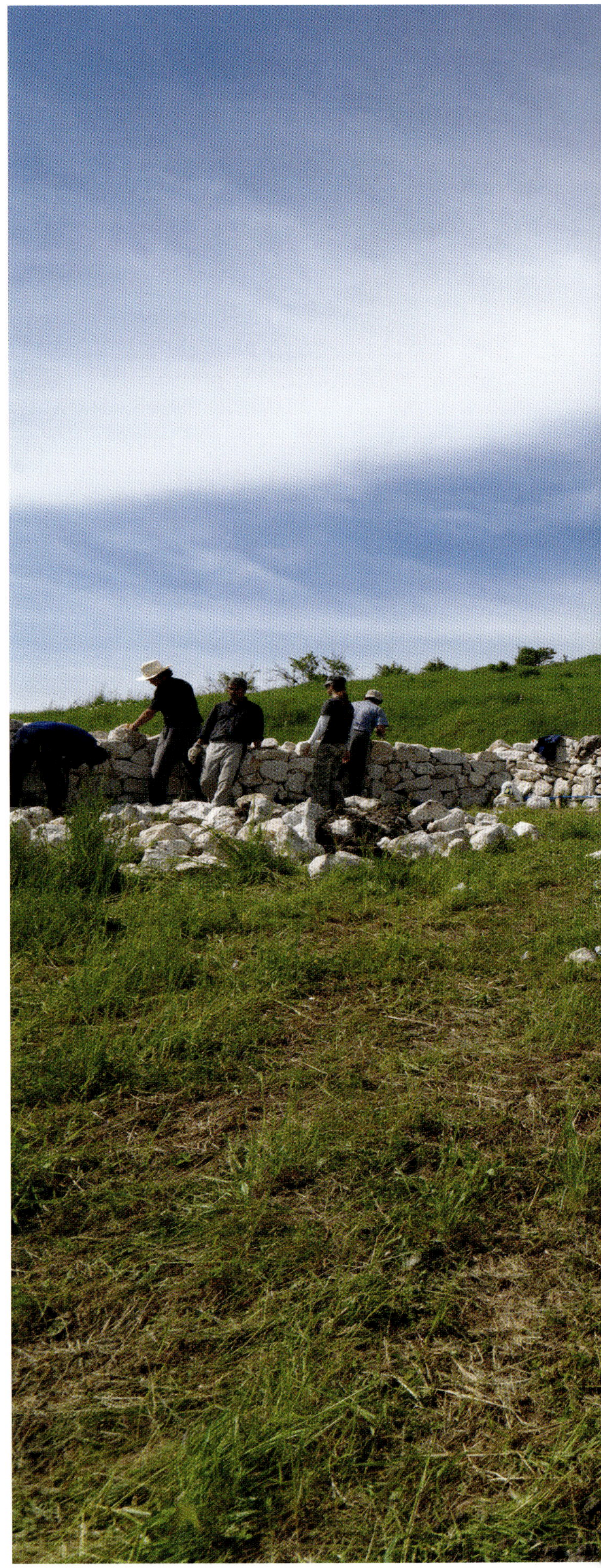

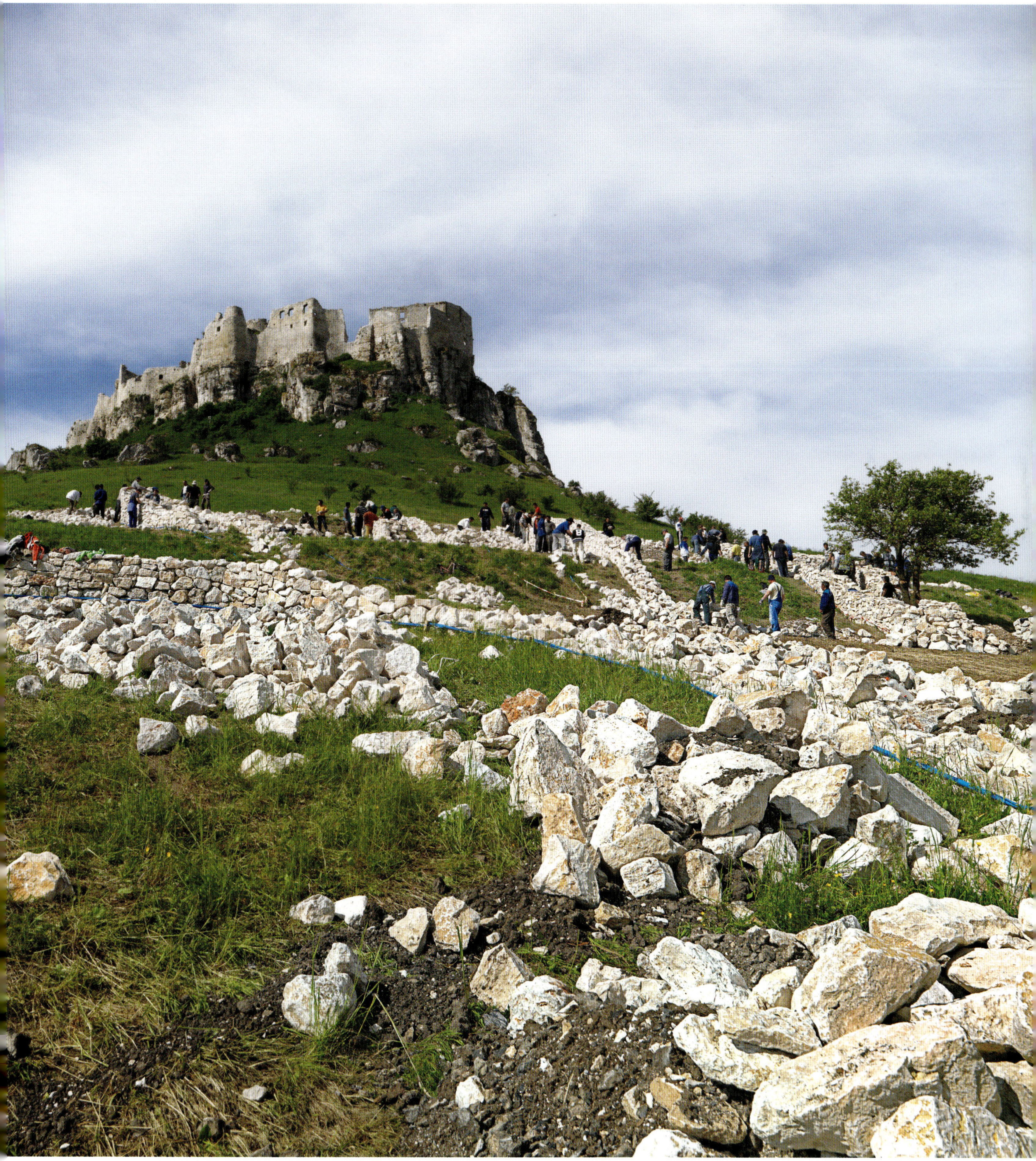

1 SACRED and the Spišský Hrad castle complex, satellite image taken 440 km (275 miles) above the earth

2 RHYTHMS OF LIFE in the High Tatras, satellite image taken 440 km (275 miles) above the earth

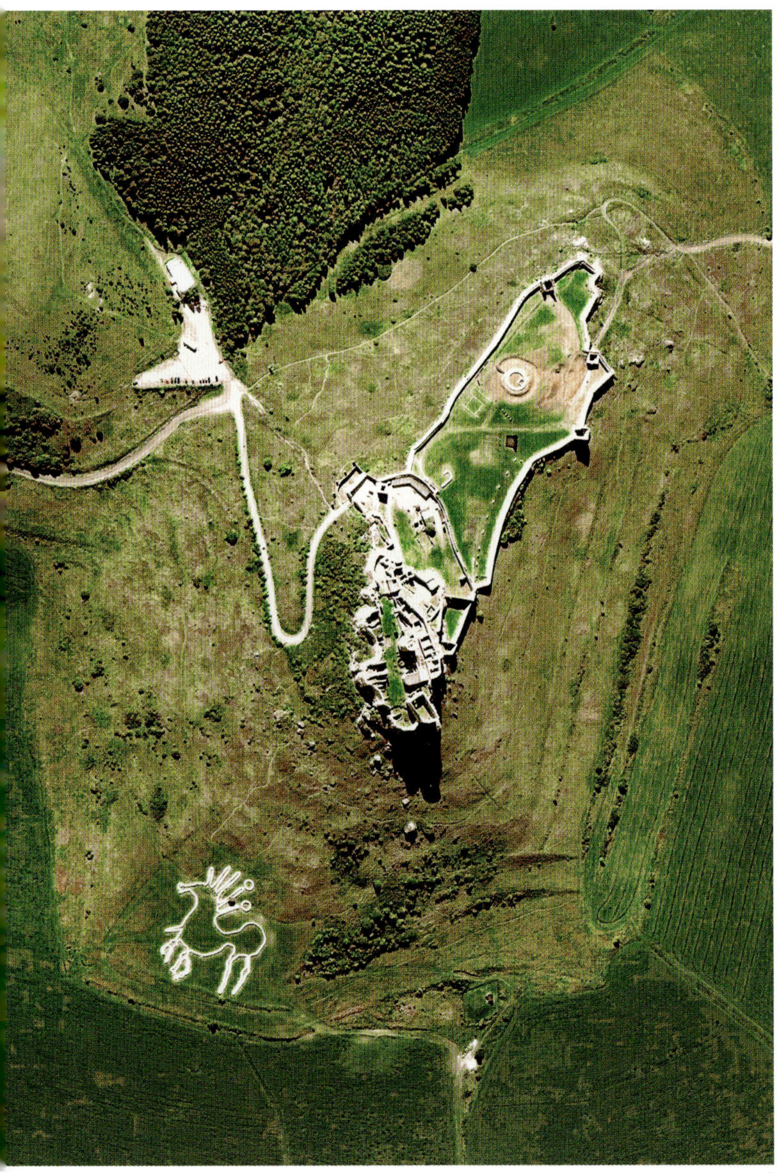

1

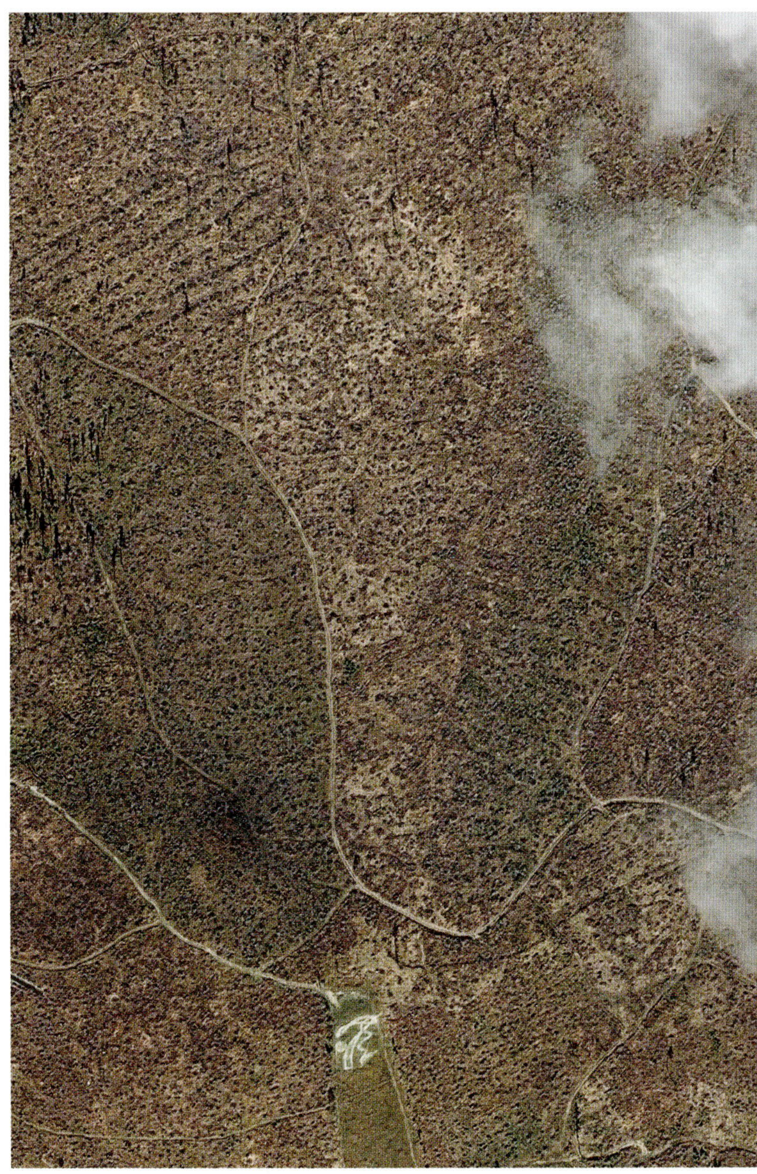

2

courtyard, it is the perfect backdrop for medieval knights' games and grand fairy-tale and fantasy films. The Celts, combative tribes that left traces across all of Europe from Anatolia to Ireland, had originally settled there. They were the first Central European people to use horses in many respects—above all against their archenemies, the Romans. Rogers used a two-thousand-year-old coin in a local museum, a find from the castle grounds, as the model for this Slovakian geoglyph. It features a stylized, galloping horse. In Celtic mythology the horse was so important that it represented a separate deity, which explains the title, *Sacred*, that Rogers selected. It is a reference to the history of the Celts as well as to the castle ruins, which are considered a national, sacred cultural artifact—the pride and joy of the Slovakians, and one of the greatest tourist attractions in the country. The drawing of the horse, enlarged to measure 100 × 100 meters (330 × 330 feet), is built of the same light-colored travertine as the castle ruins up on the crest of the hill; its shoulder-high, white walls radiate out of the lush green of the castle meadow from a distance.

Besides the Slovakian workers, Andrew Rogers deliberately hired masons from the neighboring village of Žehra, men from the Romani minority. From time immemorial they have been derogatorily called "gypsies" due to their nomadic lifestyle, and have suffered discrimination and persecution for centuries. During World War II, 80,000 Romani were exterminated in Slovakia alone. Their relationship to the Slovakians, the largest ethnic group in the country, is tense even today. "Romani people normally in this area are not given a lot of opportunities," explained Rogers, "so one thing I wanted to address there was that situation. I wanted to give them the opportunity to be part of the history and heritage of this area. I hope that the work helps to generate a fulcrum of contemplation where these sorts of atrocities are not forgotten."

Rogers was able to experience just how much the Romani appreciated his commitment when he was invited to be the honorary guest at a big first communion celebration in the village.

Rogers received permission to build the second geoglyph, *Rhythms of Life*, within the Tatra National Park, the country's oldest. Named after the mountain range, it is famous for its unique, largely virgin landscape with numerous craggy summits higher than 2,000 meters (6,500 feet), deep blue glacial lakes, waterfalls and caves, and above all its rare flora and fauna. Rogers decided in favor of a wide, green valley surrounded by tall, snow-covered mountains, "a wonderful natural theater for the dramatic sculpture, a giant metaphor for life and the human journey."

Here Rogers also used chunks of granite from the surroundings that had been polished by the weather into large, round boulders, most of which had to be dug up—an enormous effort, but one that was worth it. Using these well-proportioned stones, Rogers succeeded in enshrining his dynamically drawn form as a perfectly homogenous, totally compact surface in the rocky substratum of the wide valley.

In the end, everyone joined together in a joyful celebration of the success of this large-scale, joint art project. Even though it took a while until the workers, with their different ethnic backgrounds, accepted one another and could work together harmoniously, Rogers acknowledged with satisfaction: "It is wonderful to be able to share the lives and cultures of our workers, it makes the work interesting. There is more appreciation and understanding of differences."

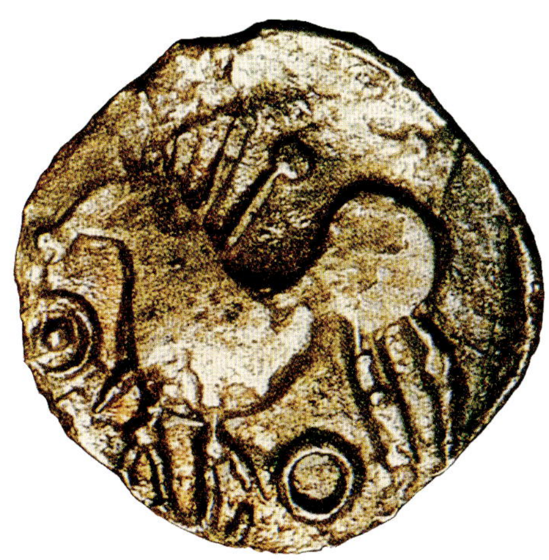

Two-thousand-year-old coin featuring the image of a horse. This coin was found in the grounds of Spišský Hrad castle, and is now in the collection of the local museum.

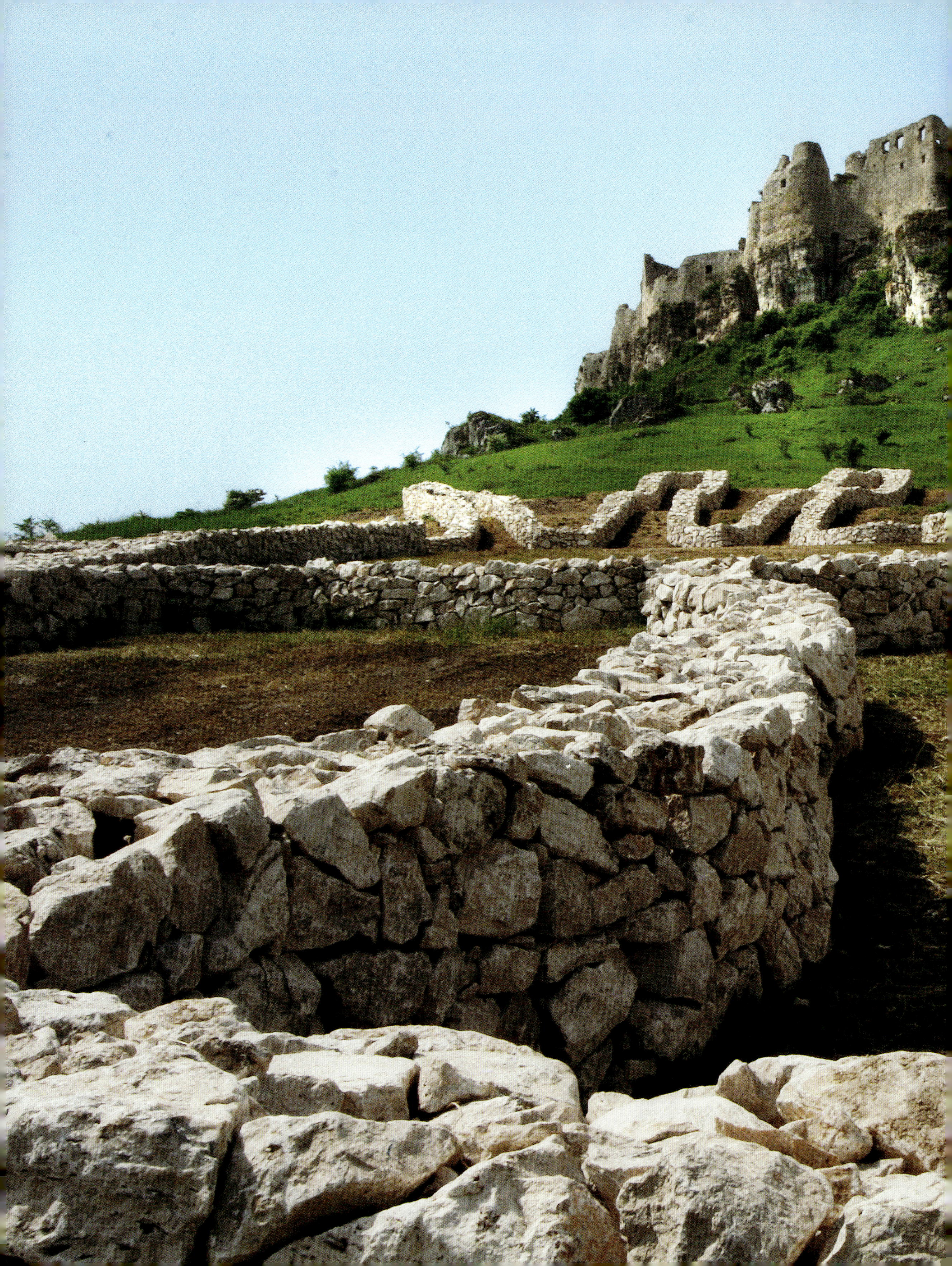

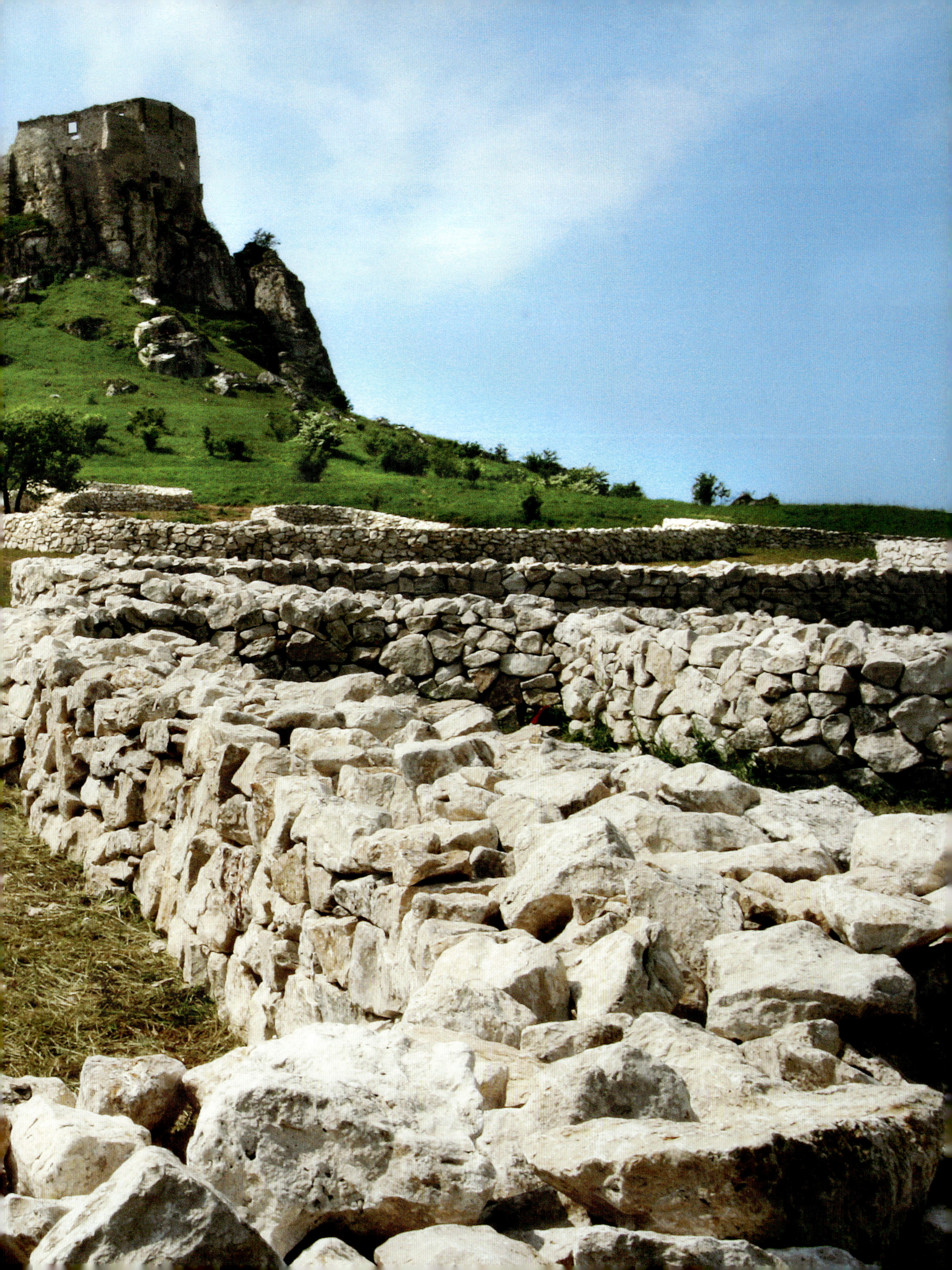

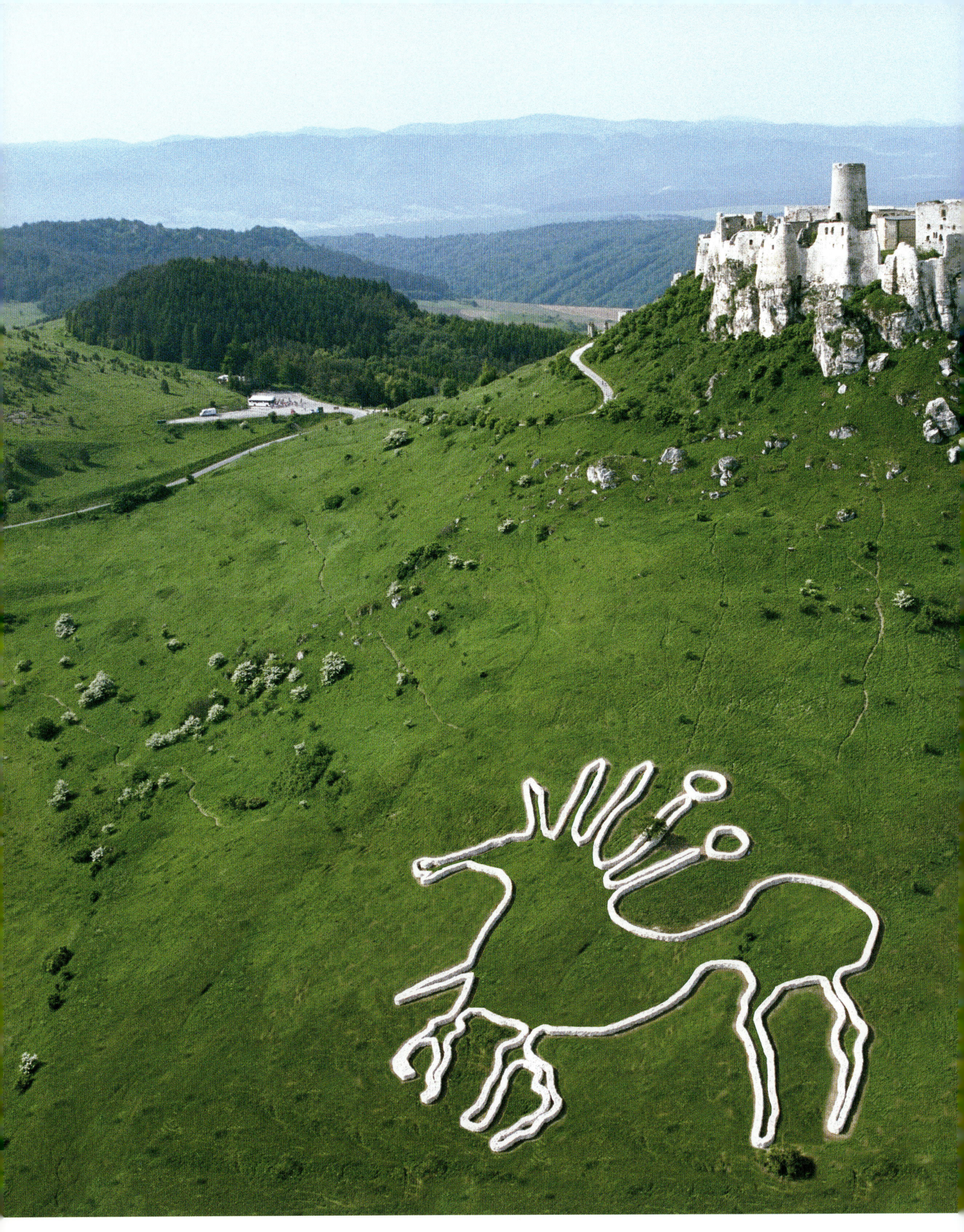

SACRED 2008 / Travertine / 100 × 100 m (330 × 330 ft.)

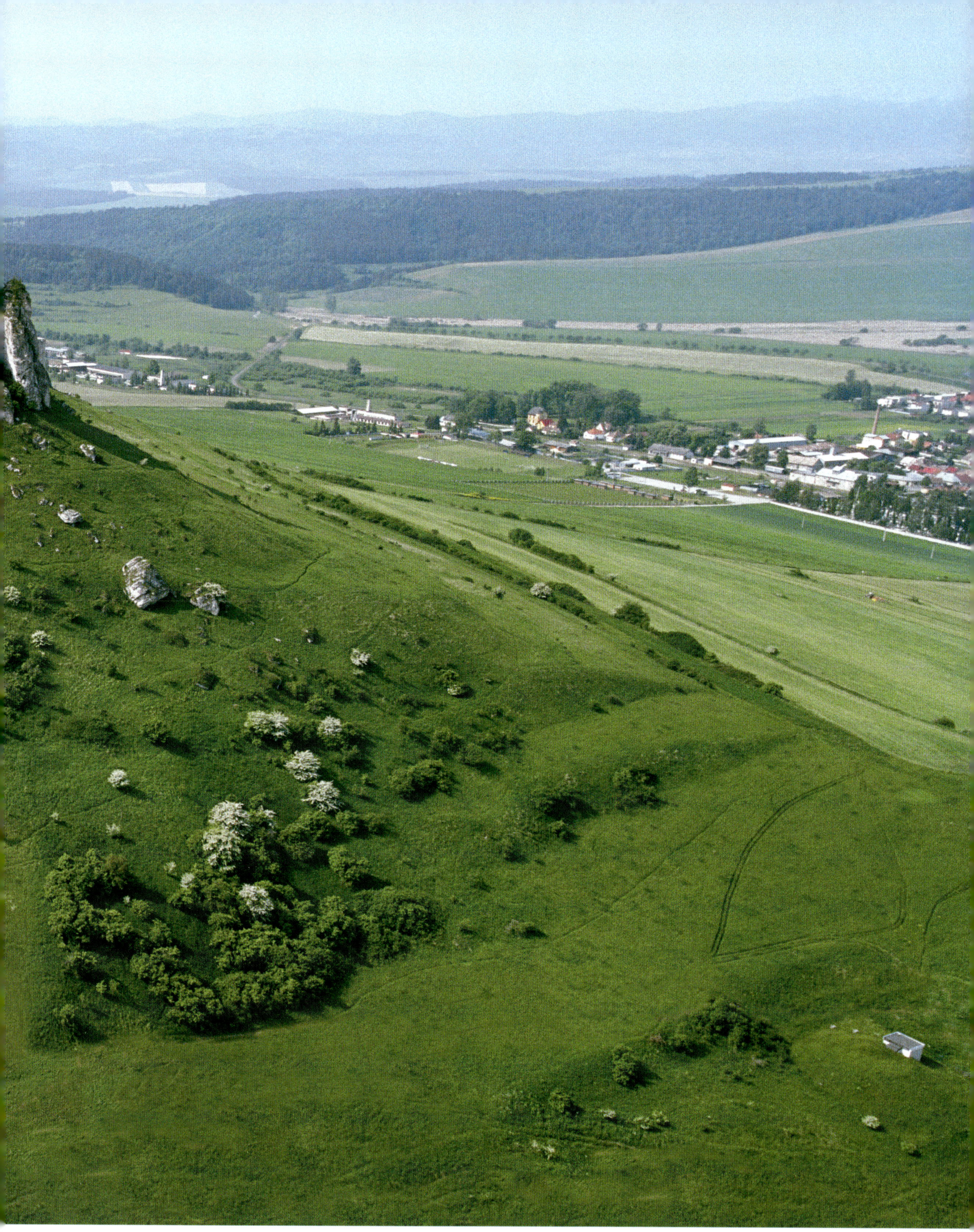

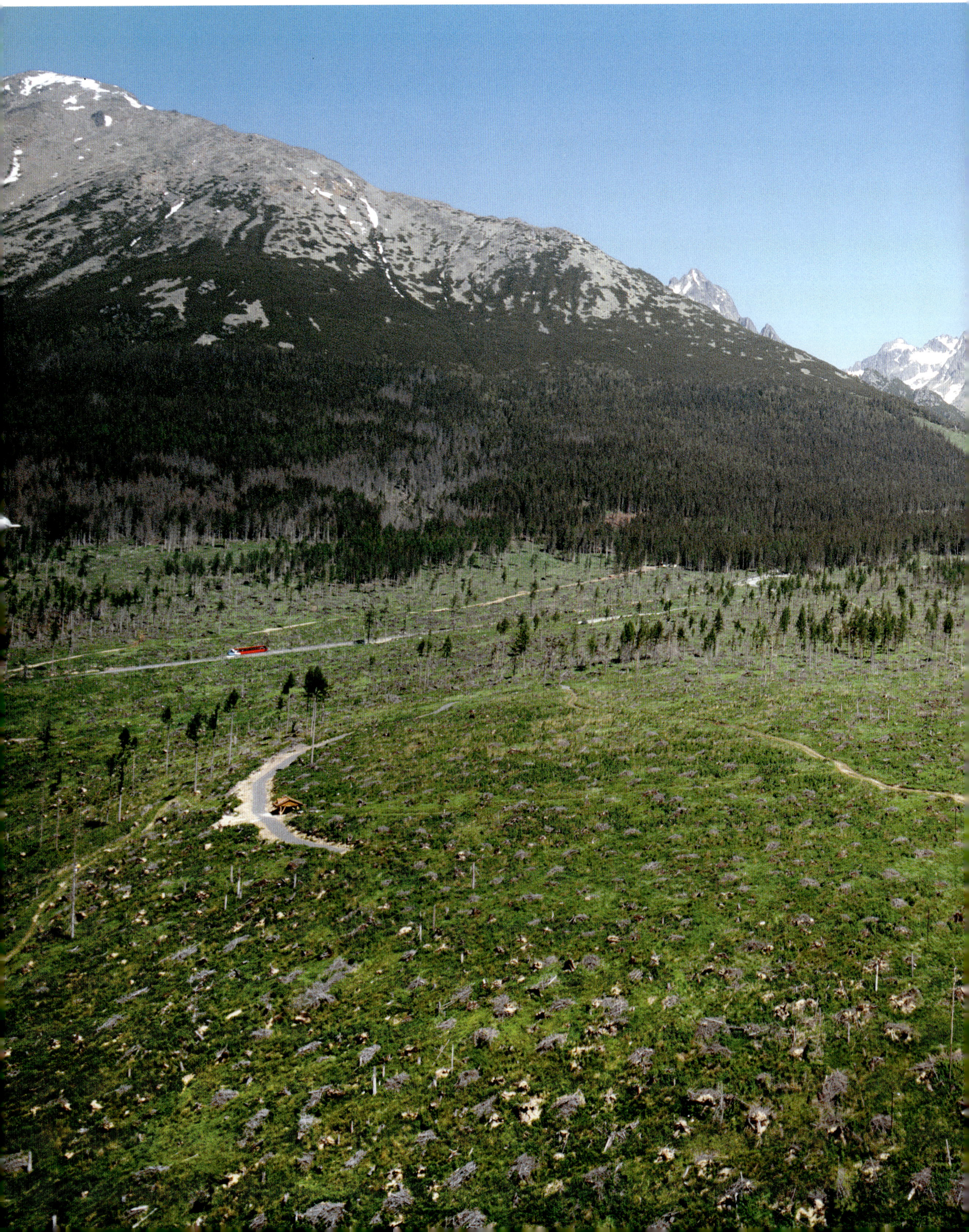

RHYTHMS OF LIFE 2008 / Granite / 35 × 45 m (115 × 148 ft.)

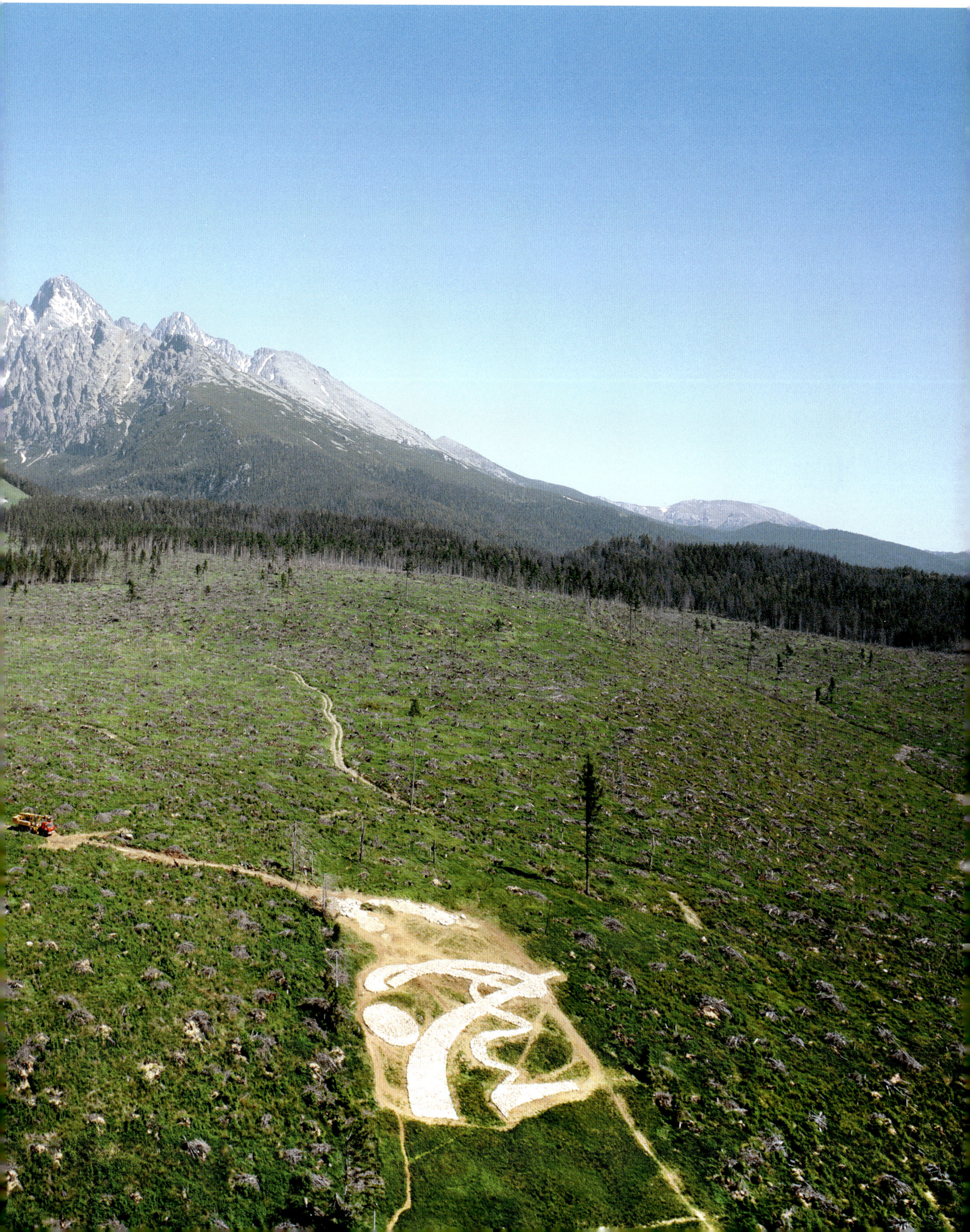

IN THE SPIRIT OF THE ANCESTORS

MOJAVE DESERT, UNITED STATES

For the next part of *Rhythms of Life*, Rogers traveled to the Mojave Desert; the driest desert in the US, the Mojave is 35,000 square kilometers (13,514 square miles) in size and extends over four states: California, Utah, Nevada, and Arizona. Enormous mountain chains border the huge desert basin. In California it is the San Bernardino Mountains, which consist of different kinds of rock, including a great deal of lava. The desolate, inhospitable landscape is otherwise characterized by countless bizarre, tree-like agave plants: Joshua trees, after which a national park in the Mojave is named. This area was for millennia the heartland of the Serrano and Cahuilla Indians, whose descendants still live there today. One continues to find petroglyphs and pictoglyphs that are thousands of years old. The carved and painted drawings symbolize elements that have to do with the everyday lives of the native Indian populations. They are above all depictions connected with their livelihood: collecting and hunting. On one of his scouting expeditions with descendants of the Serrano and Cahuilla Indians, Rogers was shown a three-thousand-year-old model for the abstract motif of *Atlatl*, a spear thrower and the earliest hunting and combat weapon, realized as a circle with a long vertical line drawn through it. By no means are all of the petroglyphs so clearly decipherable, since the passing down of the traditions and culture of the Indians was historically done orally. Much of their knowledge has therefore been lost due to attrition and forced assimilation into a Western lifestyle.

Interest in their cultural legacy is surging among younger Cahuilla and Serrano Indians. They are again reviving their native languages and songs and learning to respect the higher power of the spirits they perceive behind all natural phenomena—be it the wind, the rain, or lightning and thunder. And belief in supernatural forces is pronounced—they believe that everything has a soul, be it a living creature or an inanimate object.

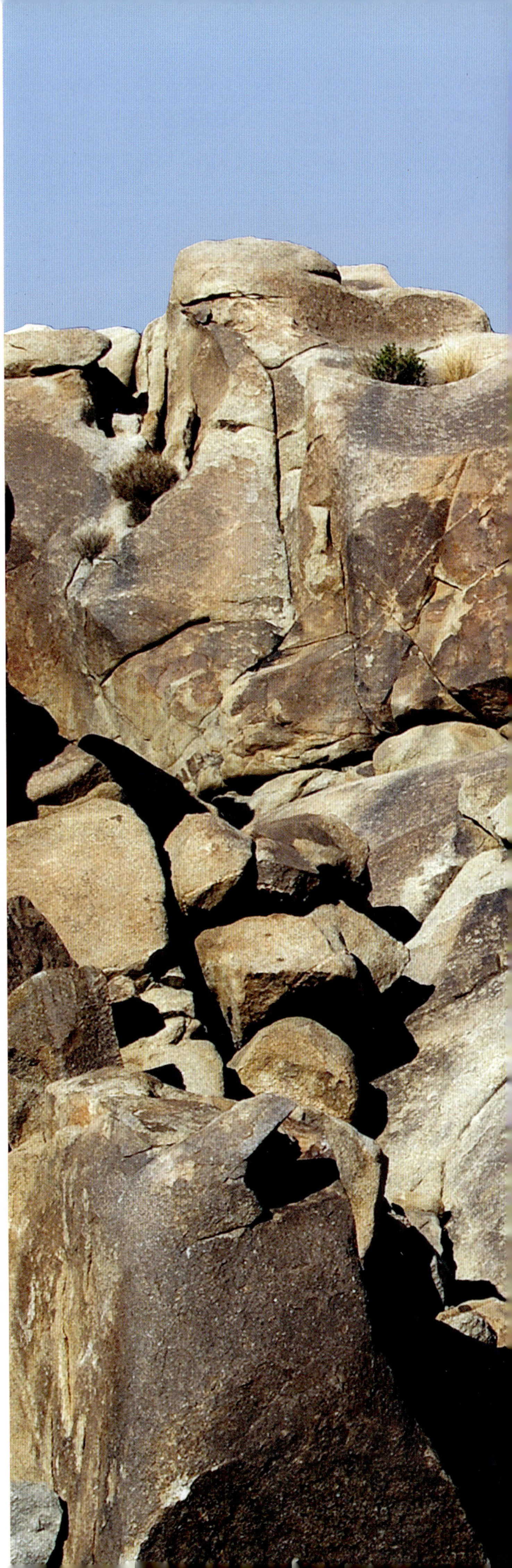

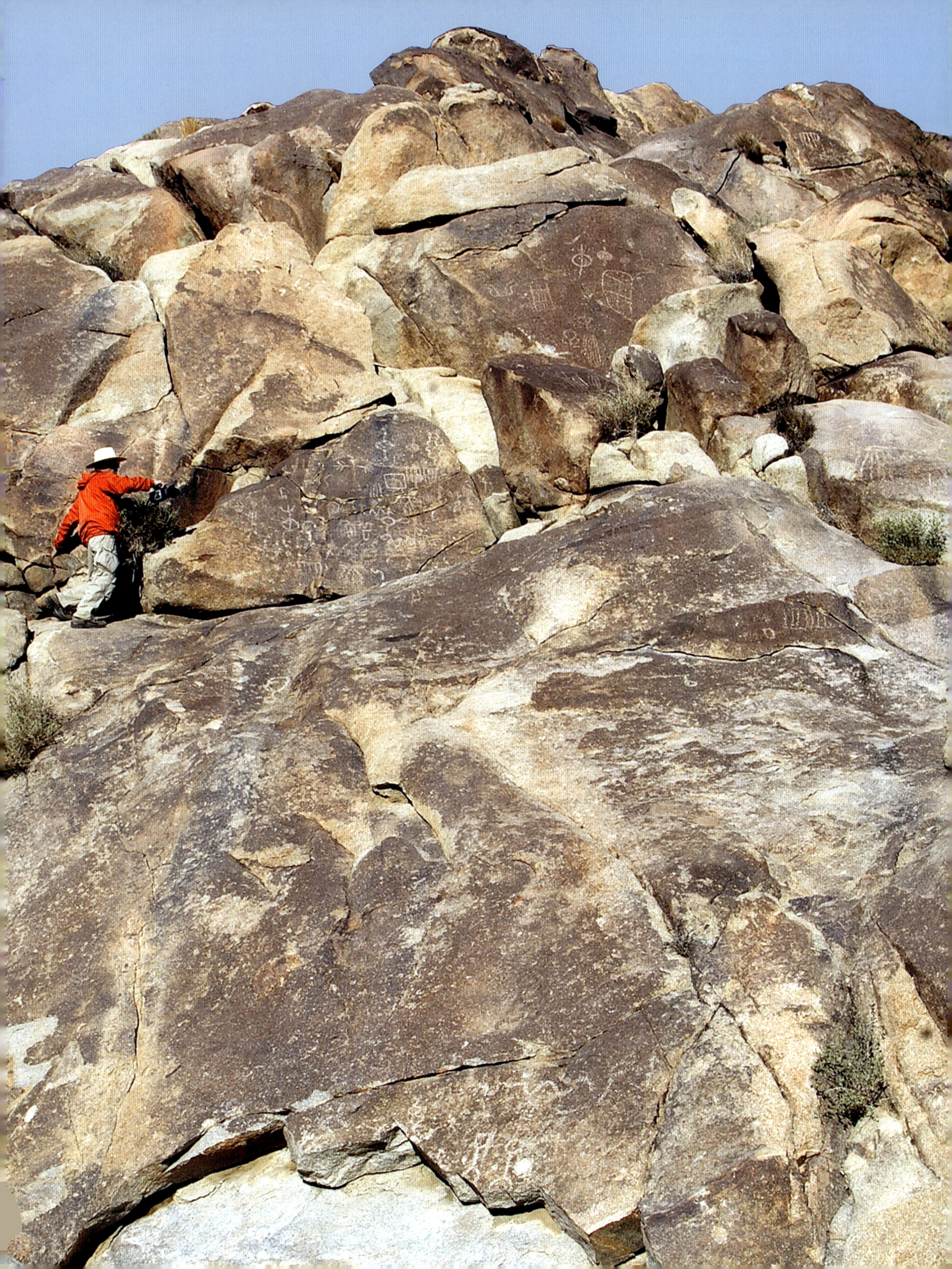

Rogers's *Rhythms of Life* message as a symbol for the diverse impulses of human life, the inner bond with the past as well as the future, naturally fits in with this notion. He is familiar with the Indians' special relationship to rocks, which Steve Reevis, one of their representatives, defined as follows: "There is a strong spiritual presence in the rocks. The rock is our oldest living relative on this Mother Earth. It is almost to me like a grandfather or grandmother."

The willingness to build geoglyphs, drawings on the earth, immediately met with enthusiasm among the local inhabitants—Americans, descendants of the Indians, but also several Mexicans wanted to help. Before construction of the two works of art commenced, Rogers met with a tribal elder to explain the project to him and receive his blessing. He experienced how the chief, holding a rattle in his hand and with sustained chanting, spiritually connected with the earth and his ancestors.

The artist selected a wide slope outside the town of Yucca Valley on the Black Mesa, a large hill consisting of volcanic rock that can be seen from the whole valley, as the site for the geoglyphs. In order to clearly visually set the two works *Rhythms of Life* (50 × 50 meters/164 × 164 feet) and *Atlatl* (61 meters/200 feet) apart from the dark substrate, he used only light-colored slate slabs from the surrounding areas, which means that by way of exception, Rogers deliberately did not use material from the site itself. Moreover, for *Atlatl* he altered his building method in order to achieve an effect similar to the Nazca Lines in Peru, the inspiration for all of his geoglyphs. The Nazca Lines are some of the very earliest geoglyphs on the earth's surface. At the time, the lines were carved into the ground with sharpened sticks. Rogers modified his approach somewhat and had the surface soil and stones along the circle and the extended line removed, and laid the light-colored slate slabs as the foundation in the indented groove, above which the masons erected the low stone wall. Scorpions and poisonous snakes, such as the sidewinder rattlesnakes that populated the building site, made it a dangerous undertaking.

When the two monumental works of art were completed, the Indians invited Rogers and his helpers

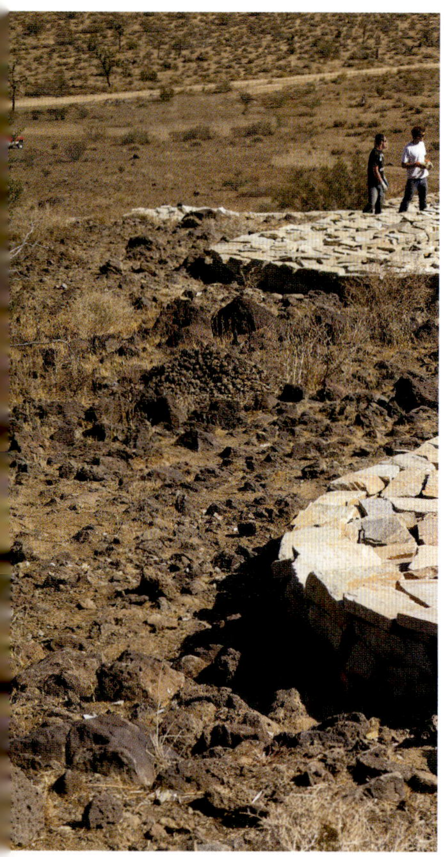

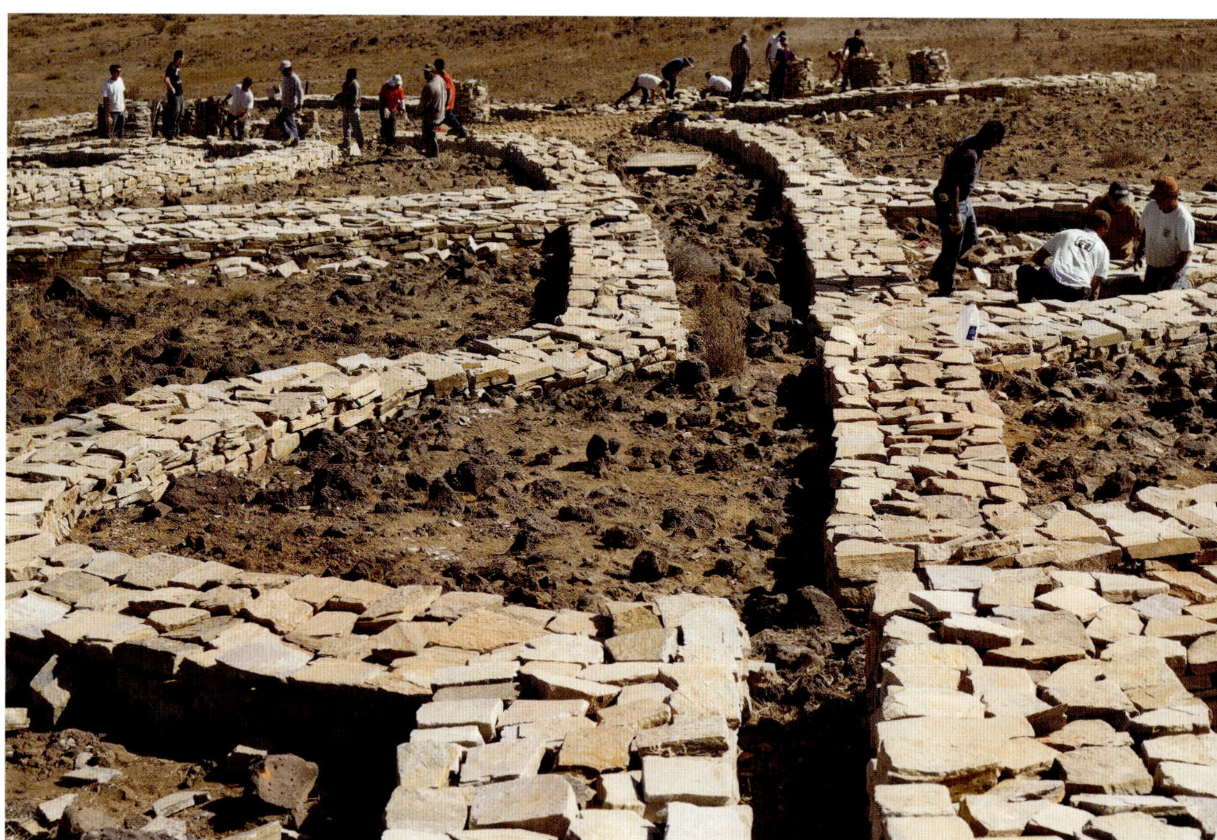

to a closing ceremony. They not only wanted to celebrate the new artworks, but above all to honor all of their ancestors who had once lived on the patch of earth where the two geoglyphs stood. They donned headdresses made of eagle feathers and put on their traditional, colorful garments with impressive patterns, and embroidered moccasins. Traditional songs were struck up and together with Rogers and his helpers, ritual dances were performed. This culminated in a smoking ceremony for Rogers, blessing him and his monumental art project, which had now also become theirs—an art project that honors the creative spirit of the land and their people in the past, the present, and the future.

1 RHYTHMS OF LIFE and ATLATL, satellite image taken 440 km (275 miles) above the earth

2 RHYTHMS OF LIFE, work in progress

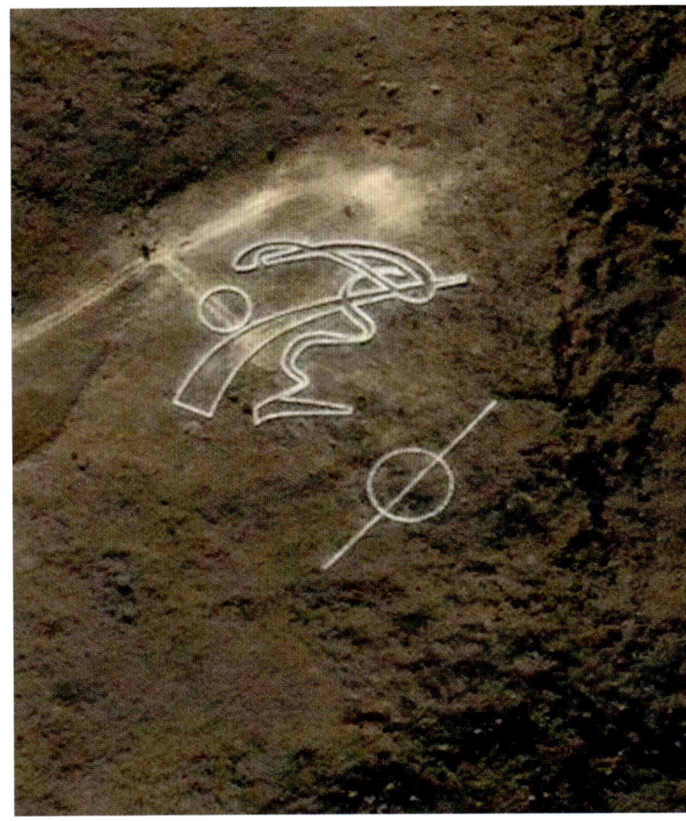

1

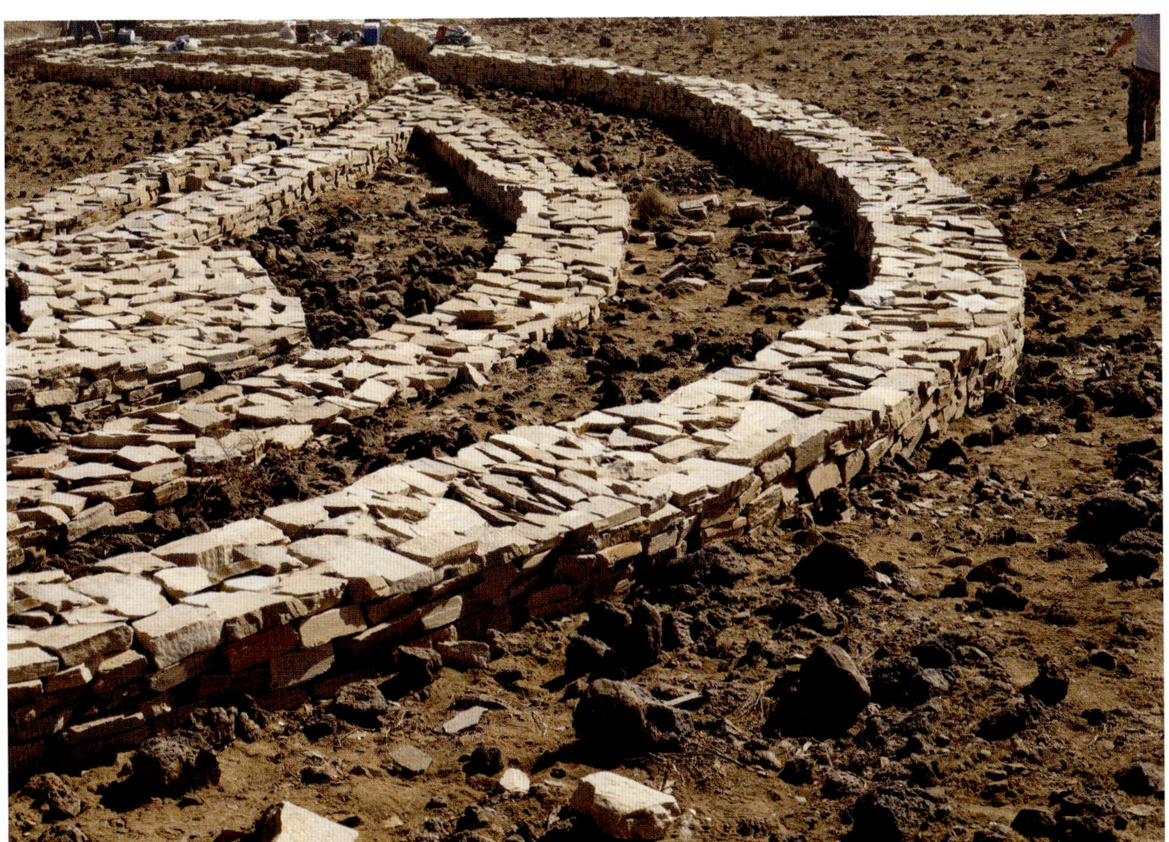

2

RHYTHMS OF LIFE 2008 / Slate, quartzite / 50 × 50 m (164 × 164 ft.)

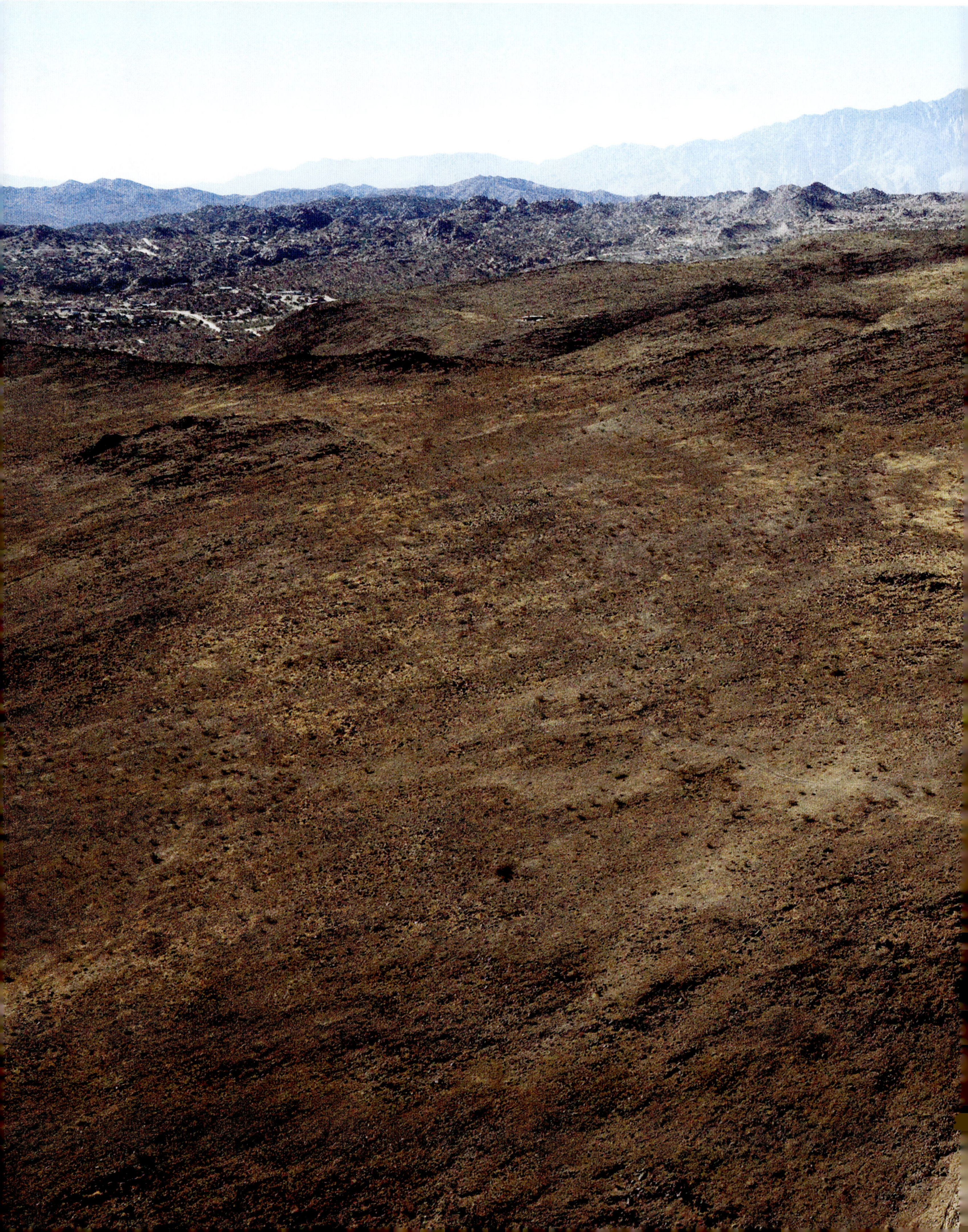

ATLATL 2008 / Slate, quartzite / 0.75 × 61 m (2.5 × 200 ft.)

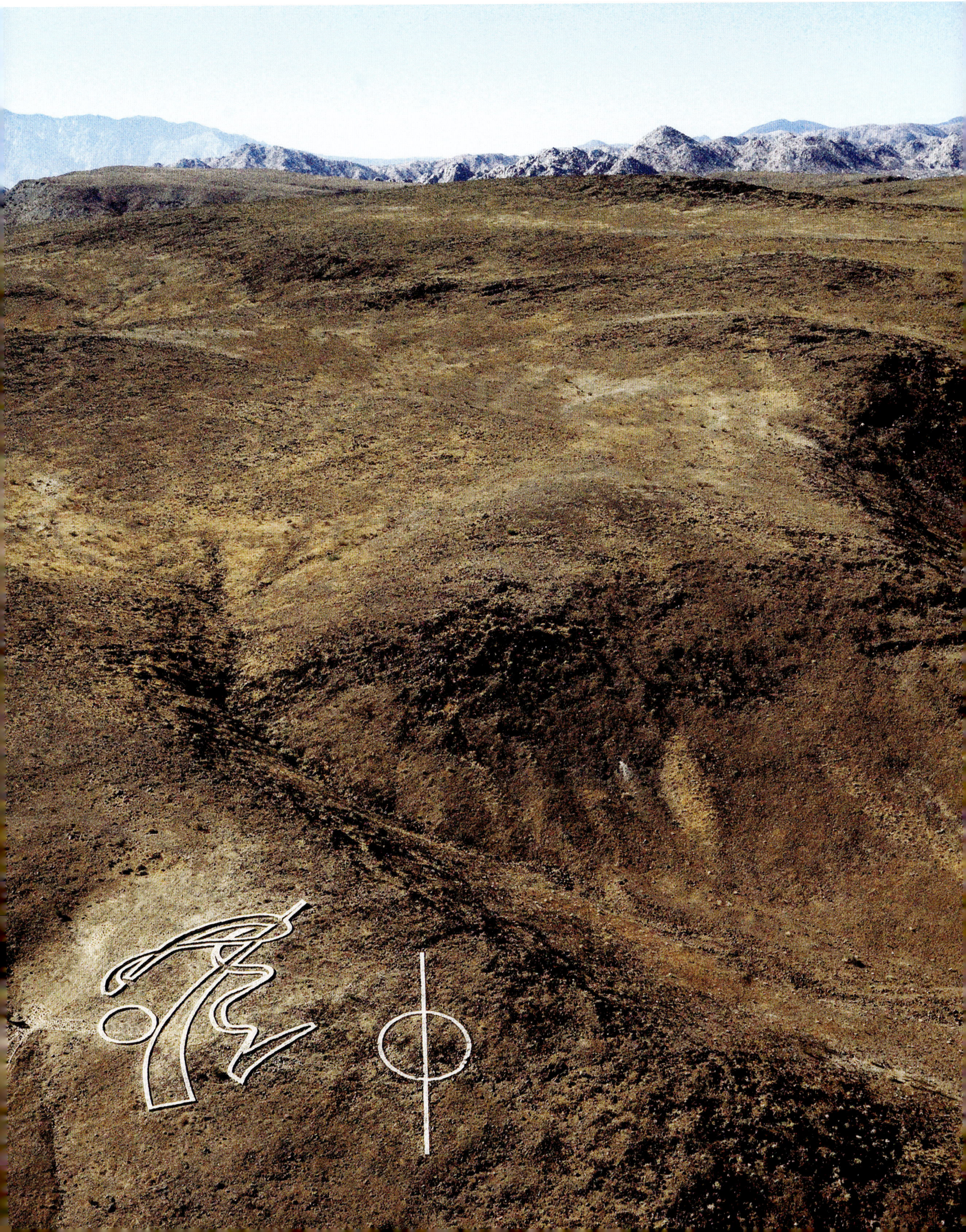

COURAGE AND STRENGTH
CHYULU HILLS, KENYA

In the national language of Swahili, *safari* means "journey." Andrew Rogers's safari in Kenya not only took him to spectacular landscapes and breathtaking natural phenomena, he also met the Maasai, one of the seminomadic peoples of East Africa. They are warriors and herdsmen who live an archaic culture that is still largely cut off from the rest of the world; their living environment, however, is becoming more and more limited due to increasing urban sprawl. Ideal conditions for Andrew Rogers to organize a *Rhythms of Life* project with the Maasai—especially since these people have a strong connection to art. Both men and women wear imaginatively designed, opulent jewelry and strikingly colorful, painted fabrics. All of the colors have a meaning: red is the most important; it symbolizes blood and courage. Blue stands for the sky, green for the land, and orange for hospitality and warmth.

The artist decided in favor of a plateau in the Chyulu Hills, a 100-kilometer-long mountain range at the foot of Kilimanjaro, as the site for three geoglyphs: *Lion's Paw*, *Shield*, and *Rhythms of Life*. The sandy plateau is surrounded by a wide lava belt, whose dark, sharp-edged rocks, the remains from the surrounding small volcanoes, provided the artist with an abundance of building material for his land art installations.

A total of 1,300 Maasai, some from very far away, helped Rogers with his art project. None were familiar with bricklaying or stone masonry; the walls of Maasai huts consist of a mixture of earth and straw. They were otherwise only familiar with the *enkang*, or stockades, made of thorny acacia branches or other bramble that they build around their villages in order to protect themselves and their animals from unwelcome intruders. For a people who normally work in small groups, it was utterly unusual to suddenly work with large groups of people. It was foreign to wear gloves in order to work with the rocks to build these gigantic works of art, which they could also not imagine. For Rogers as well as for the Maasai,

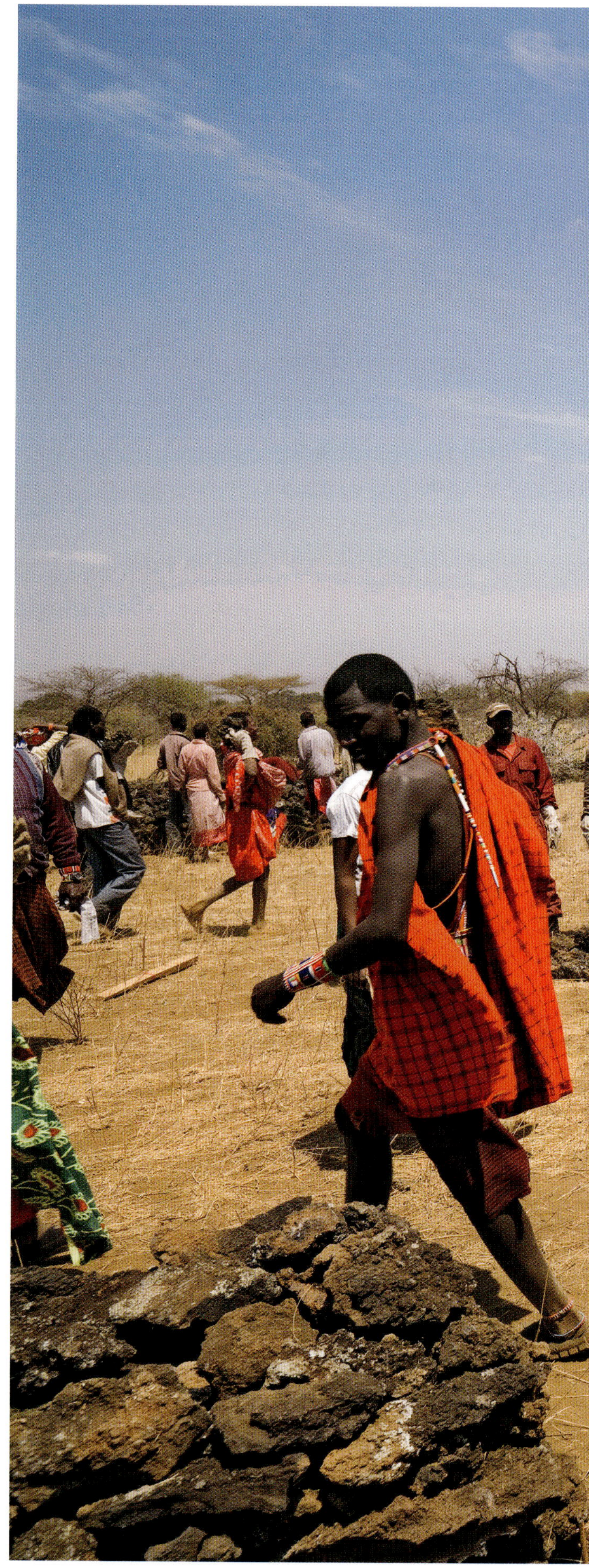

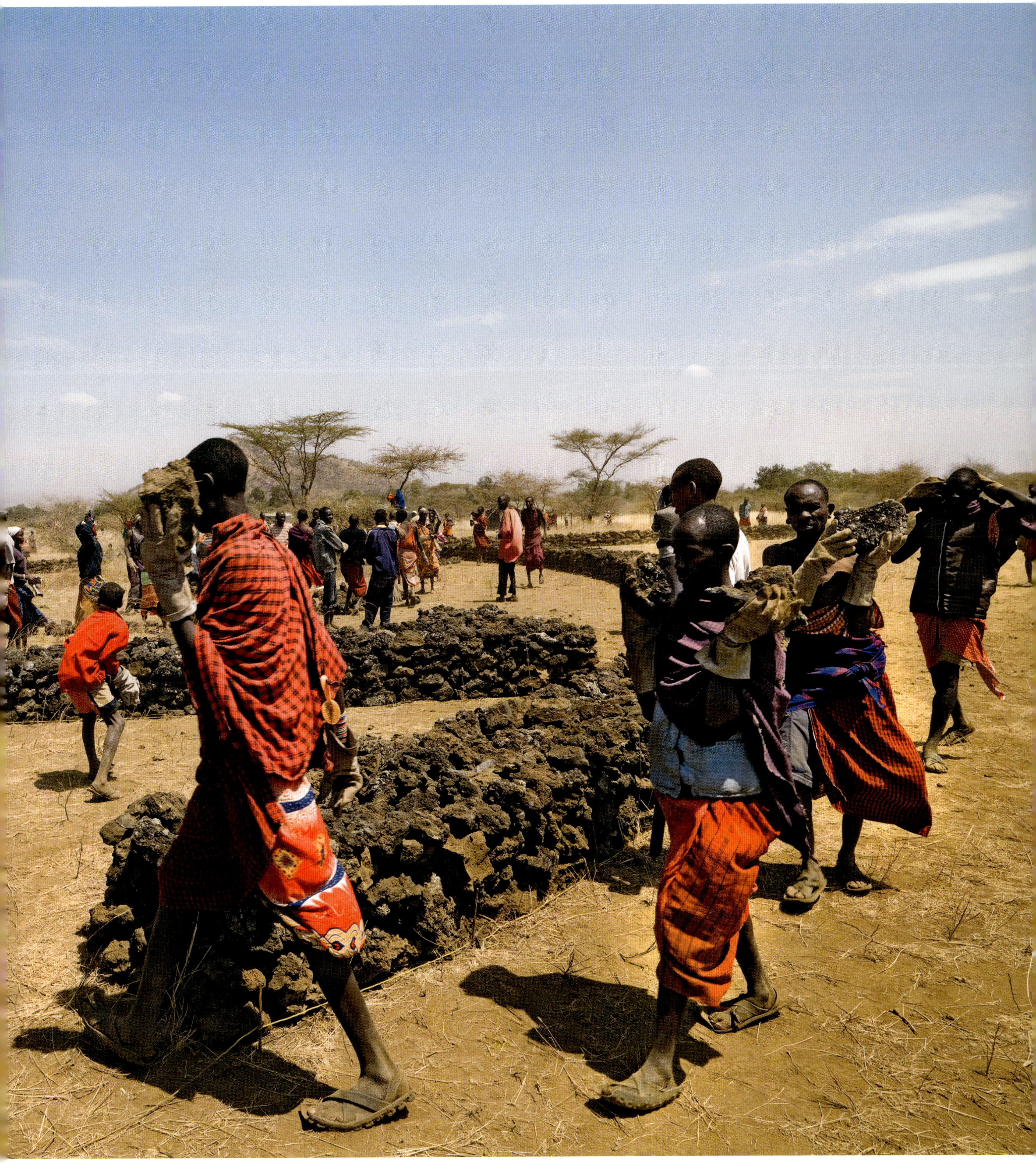

a people famous for their courage and pride, the large-scale collaborative act was a genuine challenge. But increasingly, as they shifted rocks together, the Maasai laughed a great deal, sang, and struck up friendships. Many of the women and young warriors put on additional amounts of jewelry and dressed in elaborately painted fabrics for this uncustomary work. Building the geoglyphs became an activity that filled everyone with pride. Sunday Mass even took place next to the half-finished artworks and was celebrated with singing and dancing. "My work in Kenya was all about life. I'll never forget that experience of addressing a crowd of 1,300 people, that sense of teeming humanity," recalled Rogers.

Besides *Rhythms of Life*, the recurring, life-affirming symbol in all of the artist's projects, there were two other forms: the depiction of a lion's paw and of a warrior's shield. These motifs, with which all Maasai could easily identify, were selected by tribal elders.

The Maasai are renowned warriors who have always been connected with the lion, which—as in many other cultures—symbolizes strength and courage. But for the Maasai the lion is also a symbol of manhood; killing a lion used to be a precondition for being allowed to have a wife.

While the form of *Lion's Paw*, with its five circular stone walls at a height of 2 meters (6.6 feet), were completed relatively quickly, the intricate lines of *Rhythms of Life* and *Shield* were more difficult for the participants to build. The shape and internal elements of the *Shield* geoglyph are based on the last warrior's shield in the village, and it was the pride and joy of the local inhabitants. The dark eye in the painted pattern indicates that the shield was passed down only to the bravest of the warriors. It was no small task to reproduce the shield's complex pattern enlarged to 100 × 70 meters (328 × 230 feet) and with shoulder-high walls. "They just could not imagine

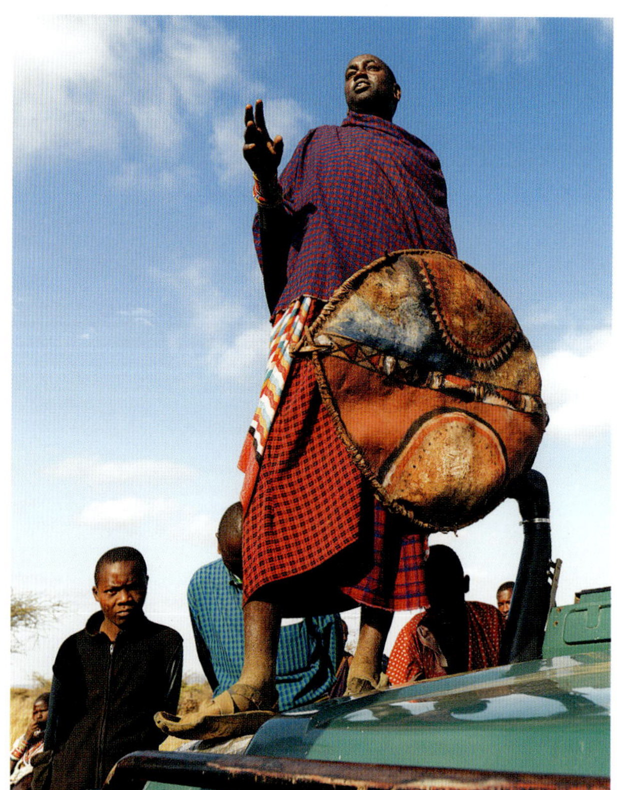
1

1 The shield maker: This shield was made from the hide of the buffalo that killed his brother.

2 RHYTHMS OF LIFE, SHIELD and LION'S PAW, satellite image taken 770 km (480 miles) above the earth.

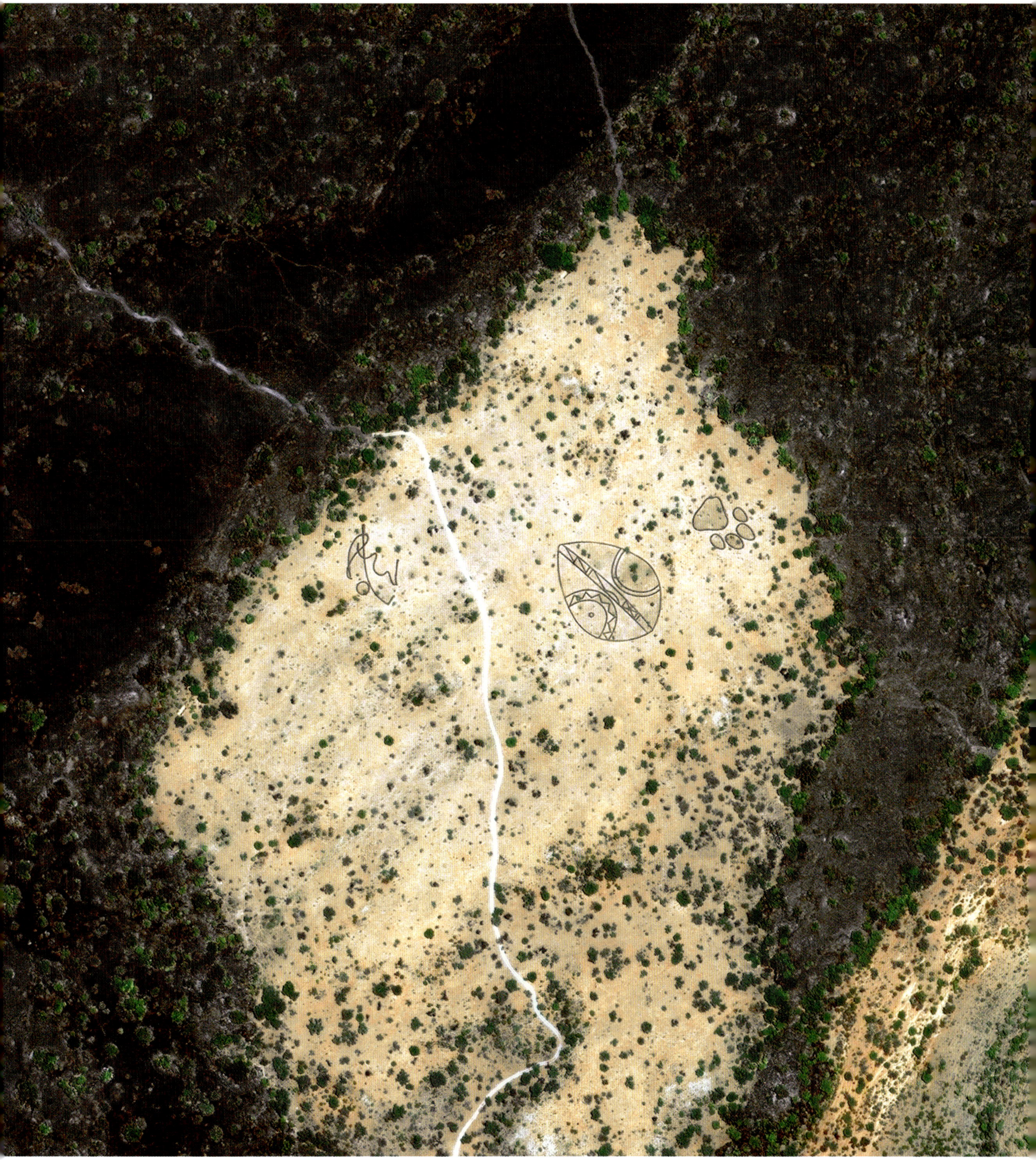

2

the final result," commented Rogers. Supplies became a persistent problem, since the Maasai preferred to walk to the lava field individually rather than form lines for the purpose of getting stones for the walls. Rogers's customary methods did not work with the Maasai. There was no alternative but to accept their determination. He took it with humor: "I'd call it *wandering*—where everyone wanders around and picks up stone and brings it to the site. But they don't like working in lines like we did the first couple of days. So they wanted to change the system, which is what we've done."

When the helicopter for Rogers's aerial photographs arrived early, the crowd scattered and assembled in front of the aircraft, wanting to fly in it. It required a lot of encouragement to get the workers to finally return to the construction site and concentrate on smoothing out the top of the walls of the geoglyphs. In the end, as an important symbol the shield's eye was visually raised by means of a heightened wall. Even before the geoglyphs were finished men were selected to gather cows and slaughter them for the final ceremony. It was a grand ceremony, as the Maasai have meat only on very special occasions. The fresh blood is drunk immediately as a coveted health drink. The male members of the tribe surprised Rogers by presenting him with a warrior's shield. This ancient warrior people could have not given him greater acknowledgment for his achievement and their own identification with this unusual art project than by presenting him with such an honor.

After nightfall, the final ceremony began with torches, rhythmic singing, and the famous jumping dances by the men. The young Maasai, the Morani, jump in place as high as possible and by doing so once again prove their strength.

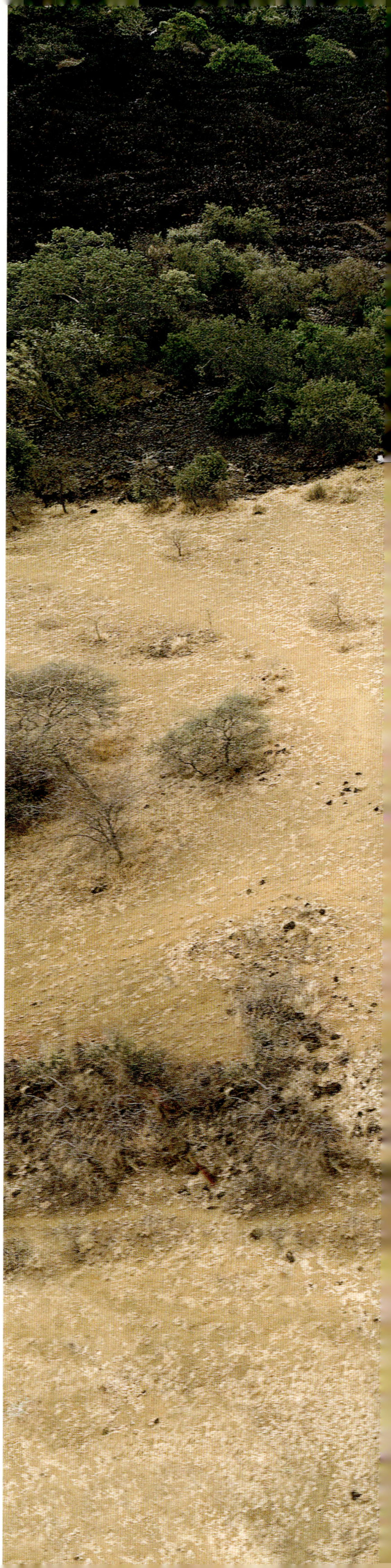

RHYTHMS OF LIFE 2010 / Volcanic rock / 69 x 69 m (226 x 226 ft.)

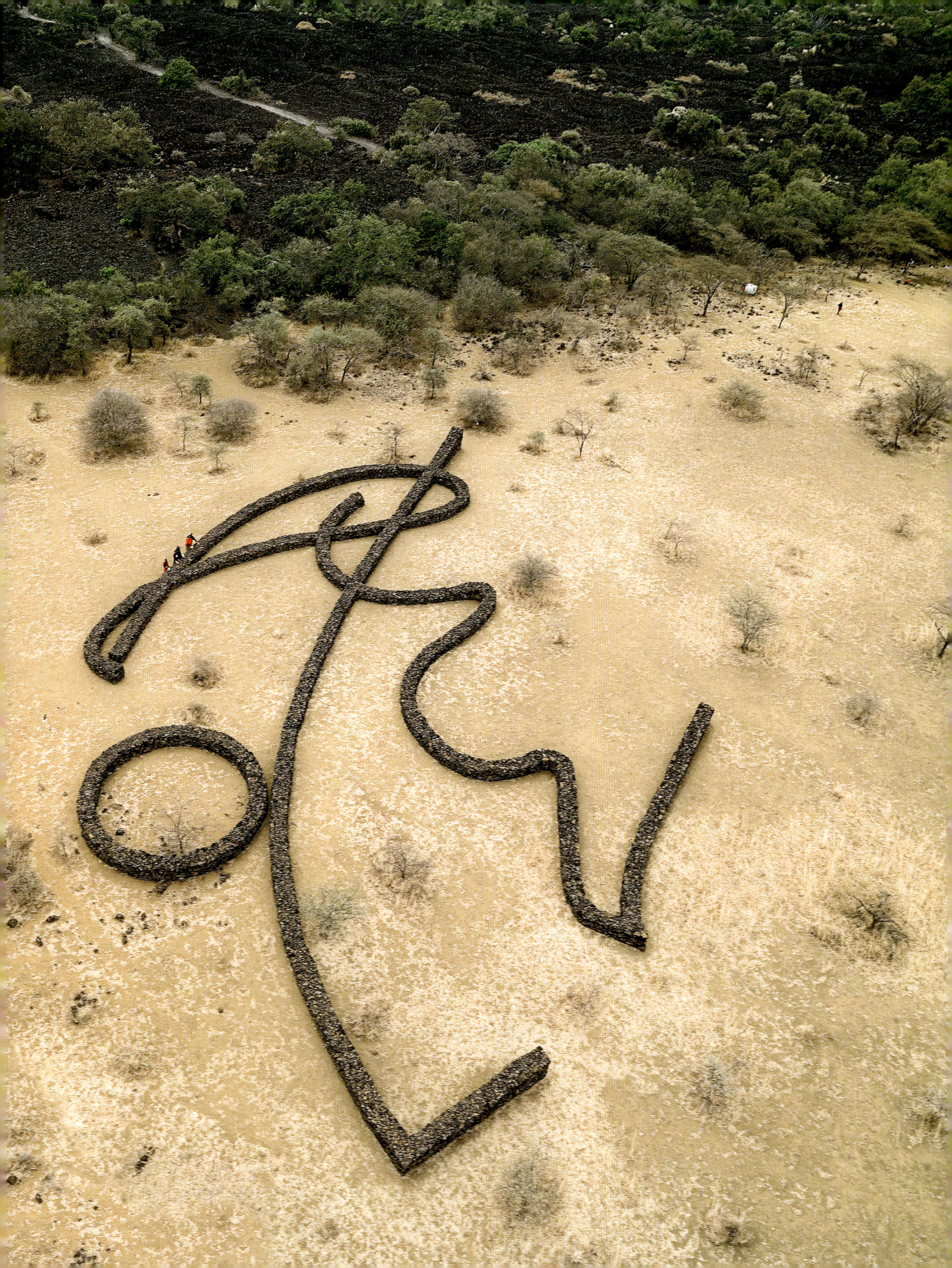

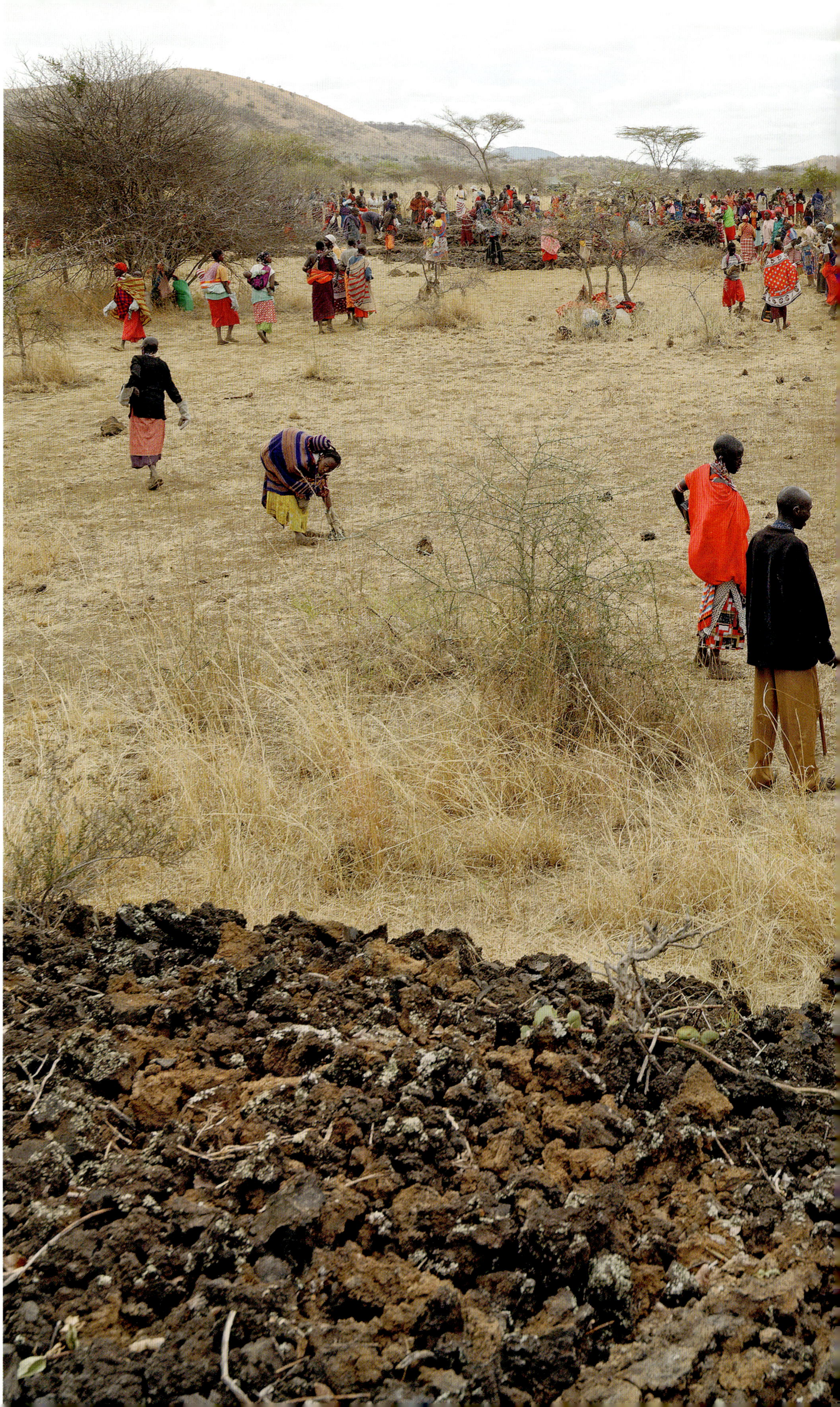

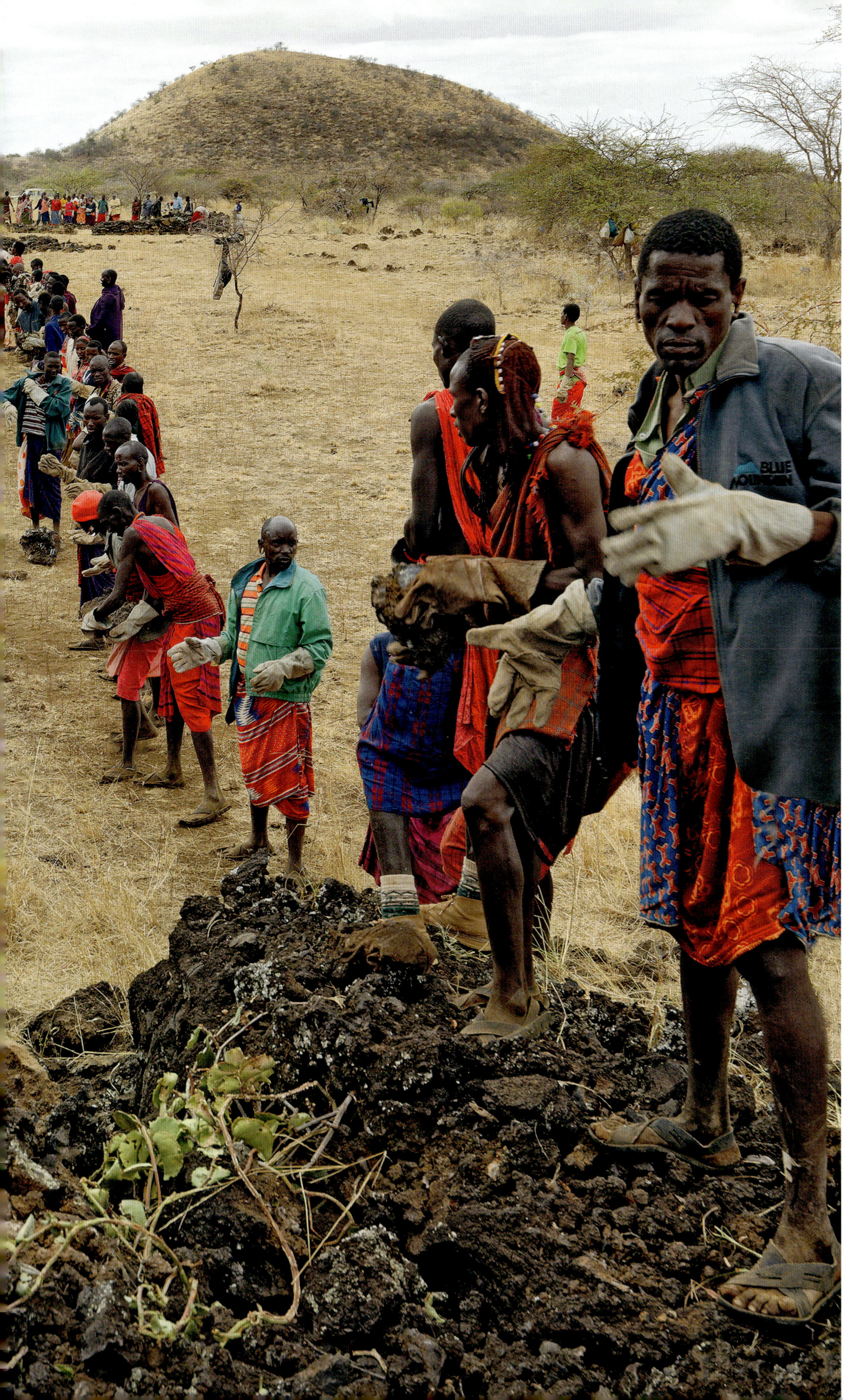
BLUE

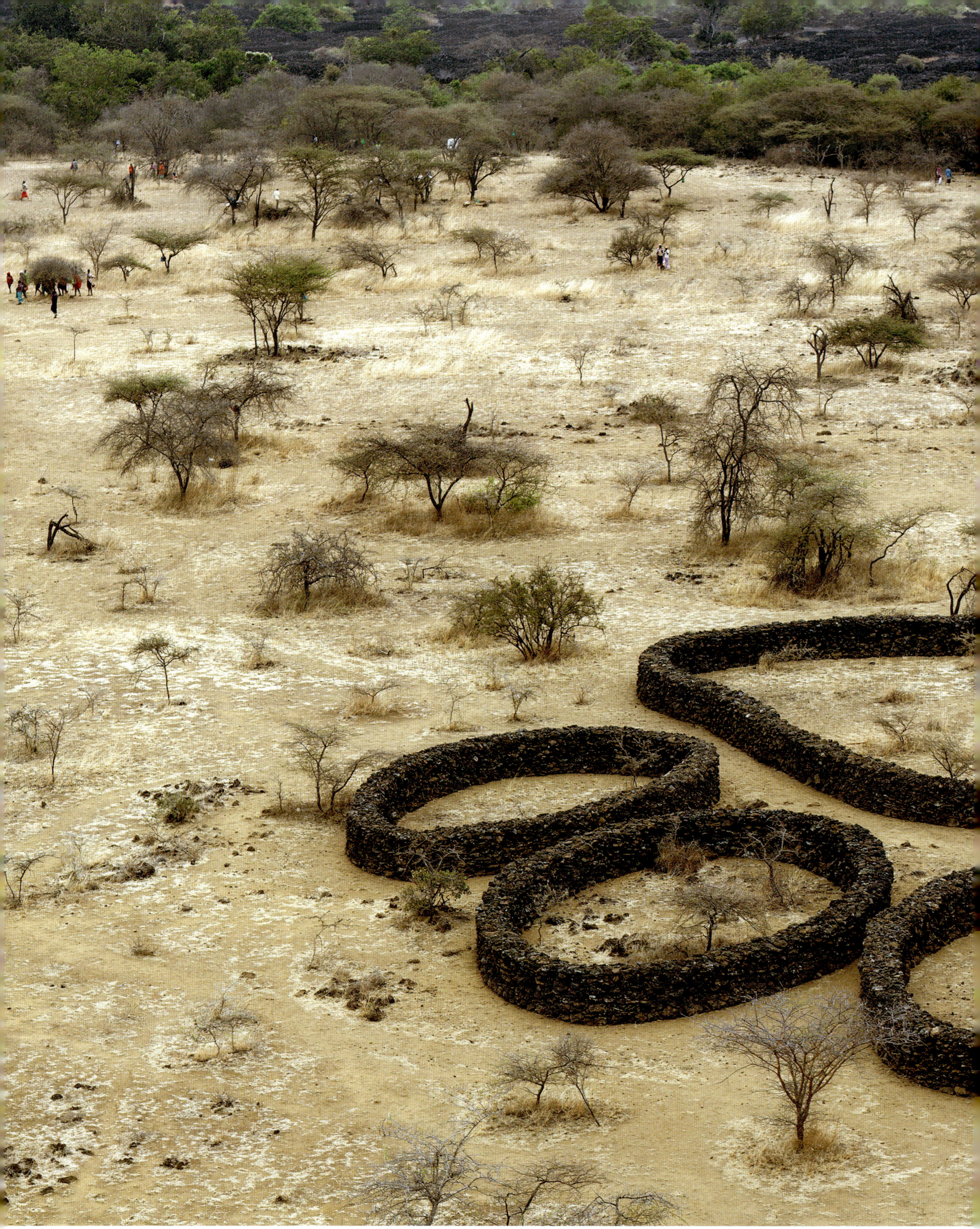

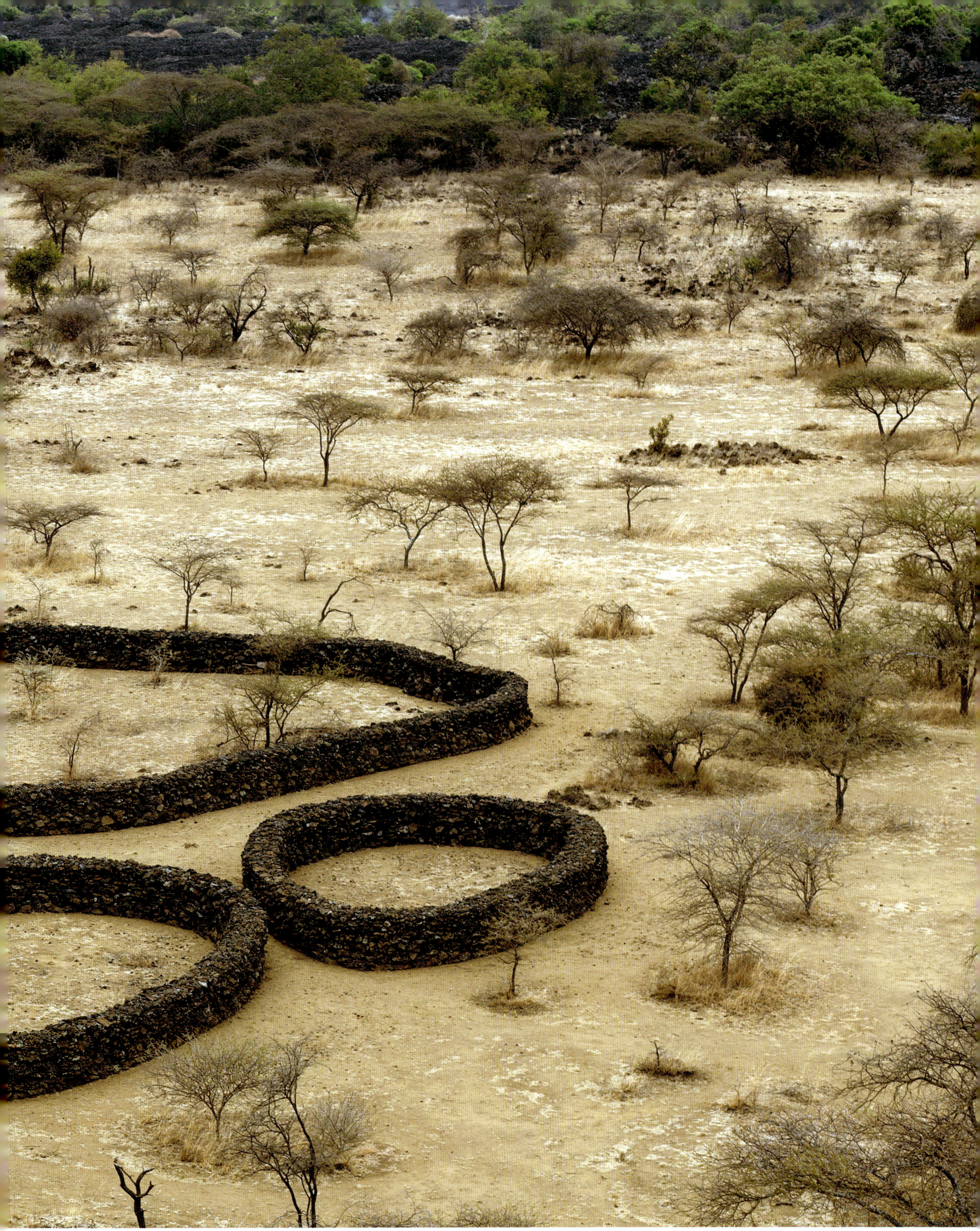

LION'S PAW 2010 / Volcanic rock / 2 × 40 × 40 m (6.6 × 131 × 131 ft.)

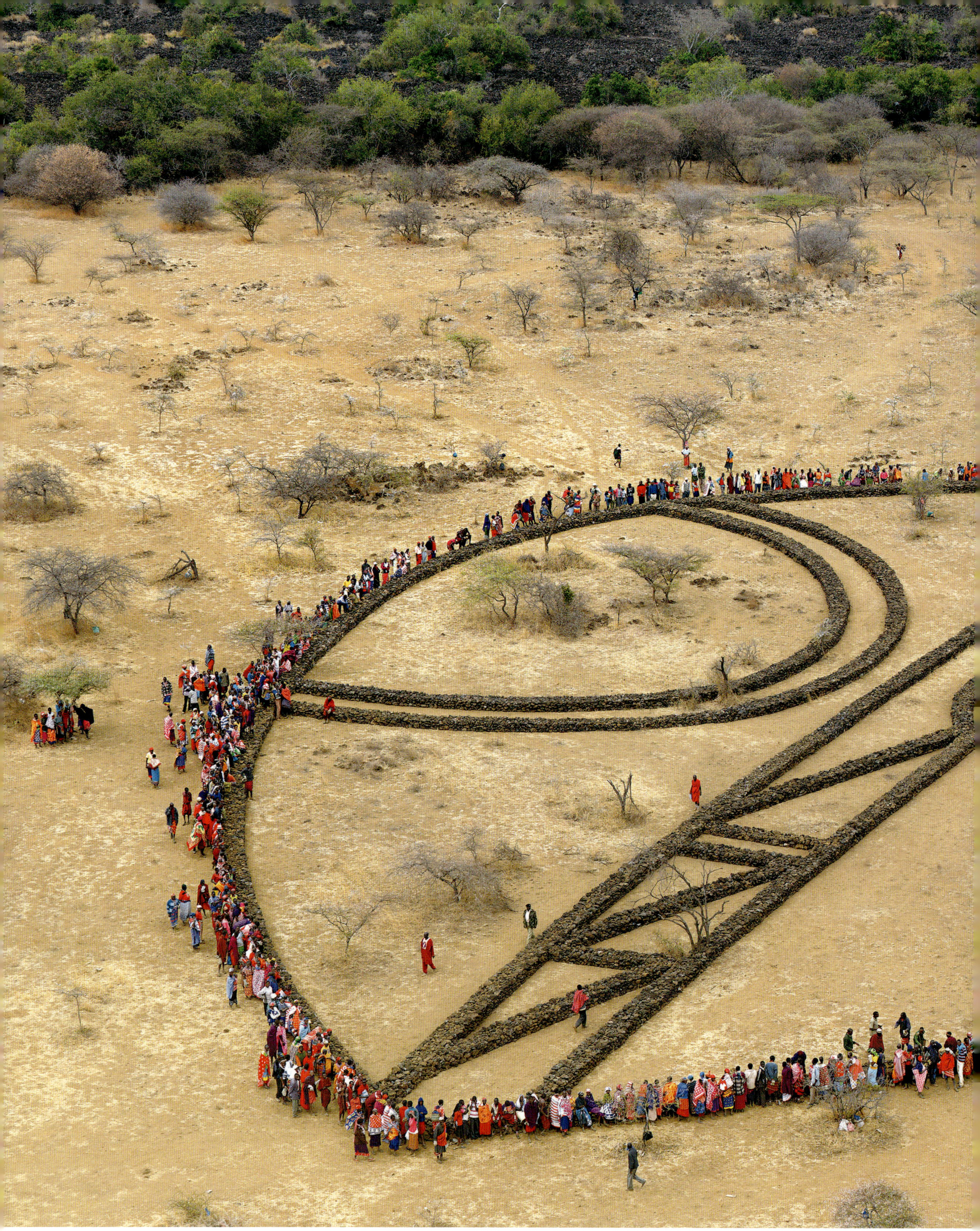

SHIELD 2010 / Volcanic rock / 1.5 × 100 × 70 m (5 × 328 × 230 ft.)

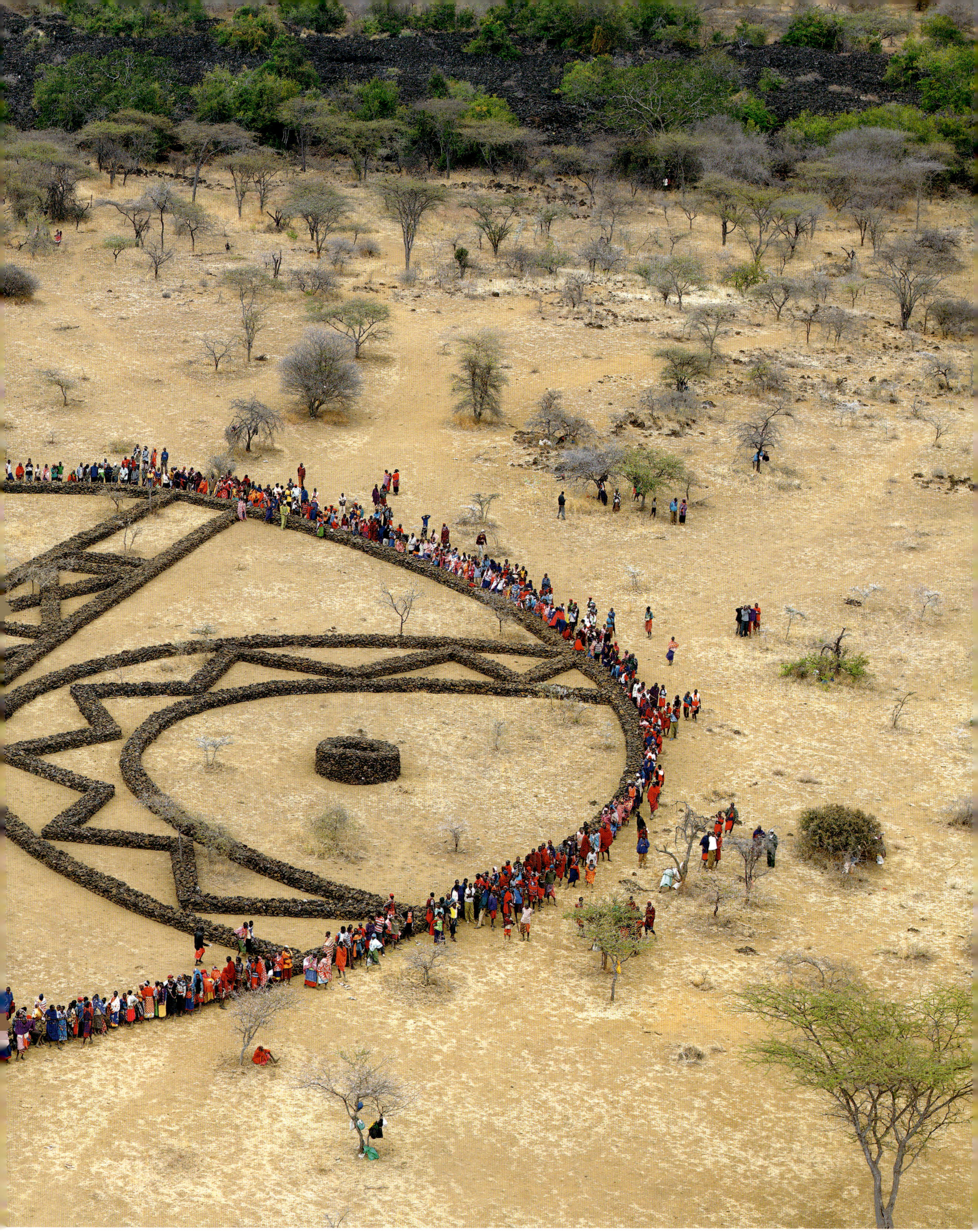

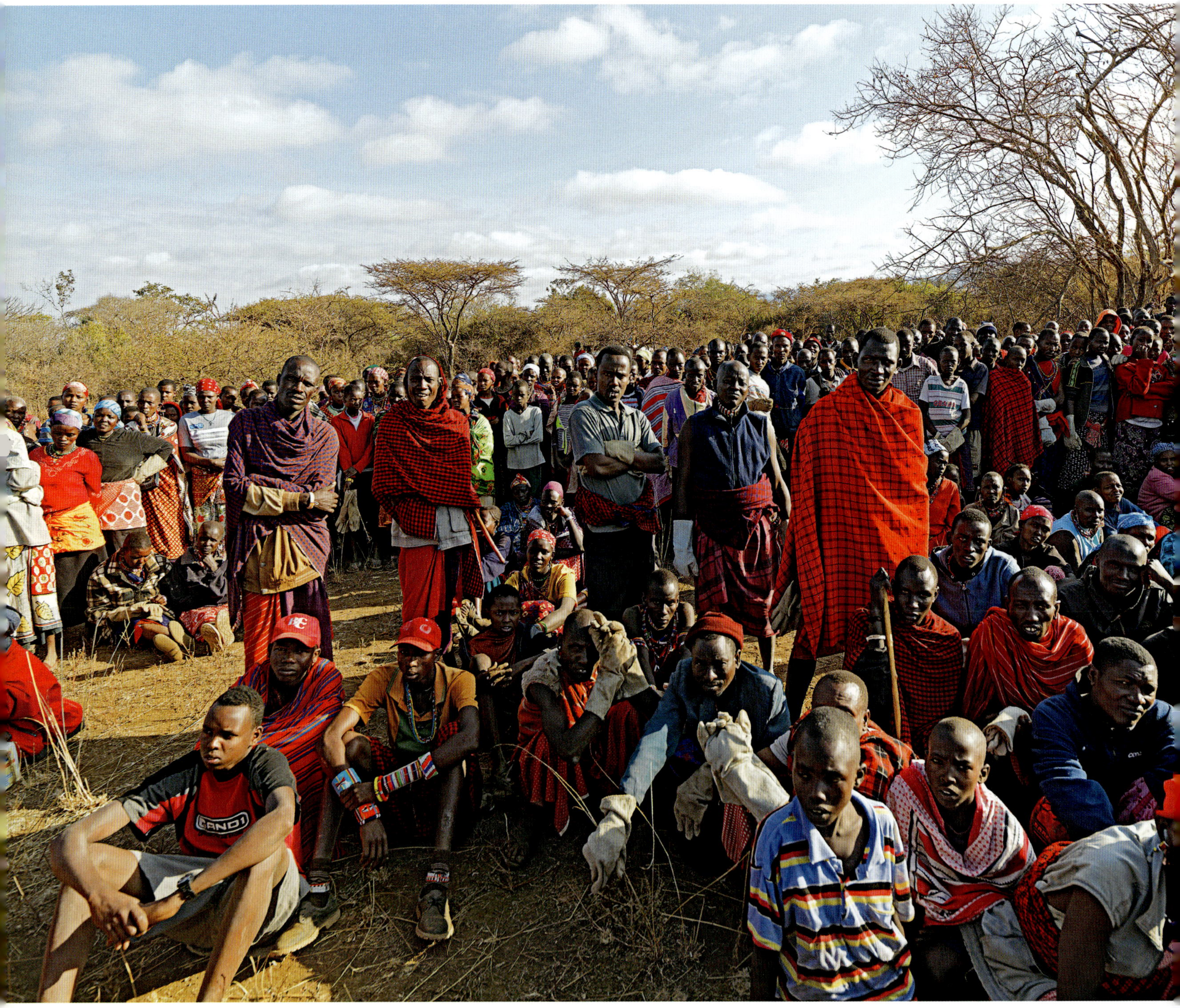

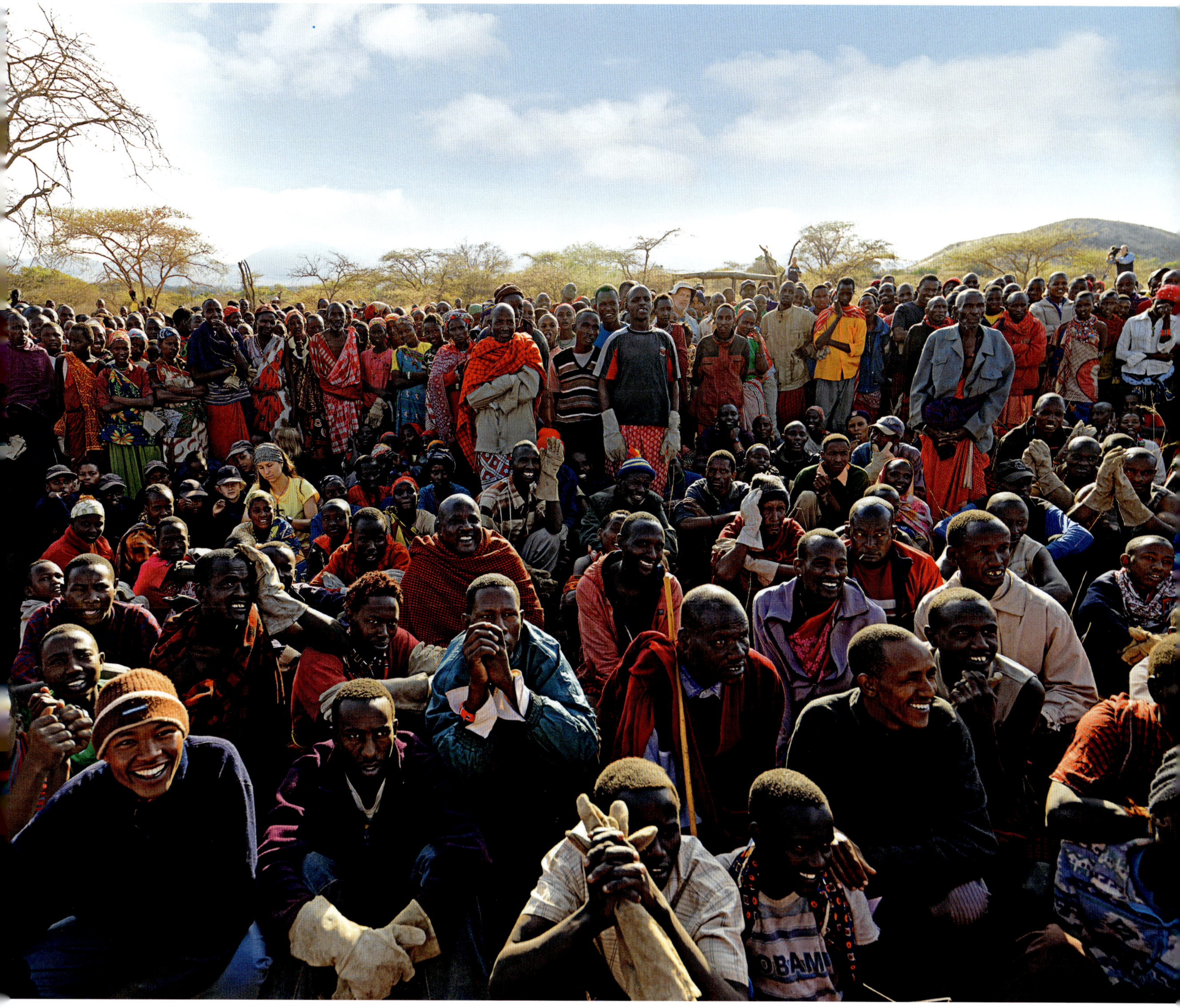

IN THE WHITE DESERT
DAKSHIN GANGOTRI GLACIER, ANTARCTICA

Antarctica's icy landscape is the high point for any adventurer who longs for the ultimate nature experience. Those who forget to put on sunglasses when the airplane begins its final descent quickly learn how brutal the forces of nature, in this case the reflection of sunlight, can be: one becomes snow-blind. Unparalleled degrees of cold prevail here in the "white desert," and the notorious katabatic winds hit without warning and with unknown force; snow drifts turn many crevasses in the ice into deadly traps.

Earth's south polar cap is a continent with a unique ecosystem, for whose preservation the rest of the world has joined forces with great commitment. In the Antarctic Treaty of 1959, the twelve nations active in Antarctica at the time also pledged to exempt Antarctica from any type of economic exploitation or military use. "It's a place that is special in terms of the ideals with which it has been inhabited—which are peaceful and not for exploitation in terms of commerce or industrialization," Andrew Rogers explained. "So it can be a beacon for values for the future."

Andrew Rogers's inspiration for his *Rhythms of Life* projects around the world had previously always been the rhythm of human life. In Antarctica he discovered it exclusively in nature, incomparable in its color reduction and simultaneous wealth of forms, "with ancient ice waves where you can see what a wonderful sculptor nature is, with undulations of the ice and all the fracturing and the aeration—and with contrasts in the colors, the white through to the deep blue," noted the artist.

Rhythms of Life in Antarctica was the only work of the project created without the participation of local inhabitants, for while the southernmost continent in the world may be comparable to the United States in terms of size, it is practically unpopulated. Rogers therefore dispensed with building a culturally connoted symbol and only built his iconic *Rhythms of Life* geoglyph. In another departure from the custom

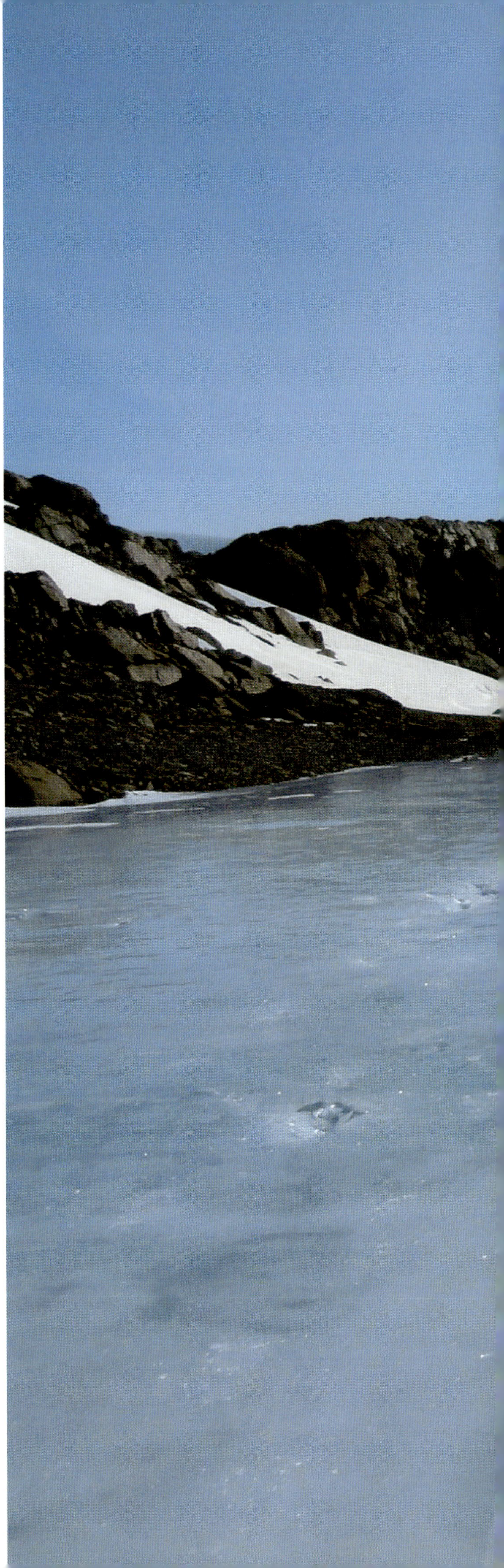

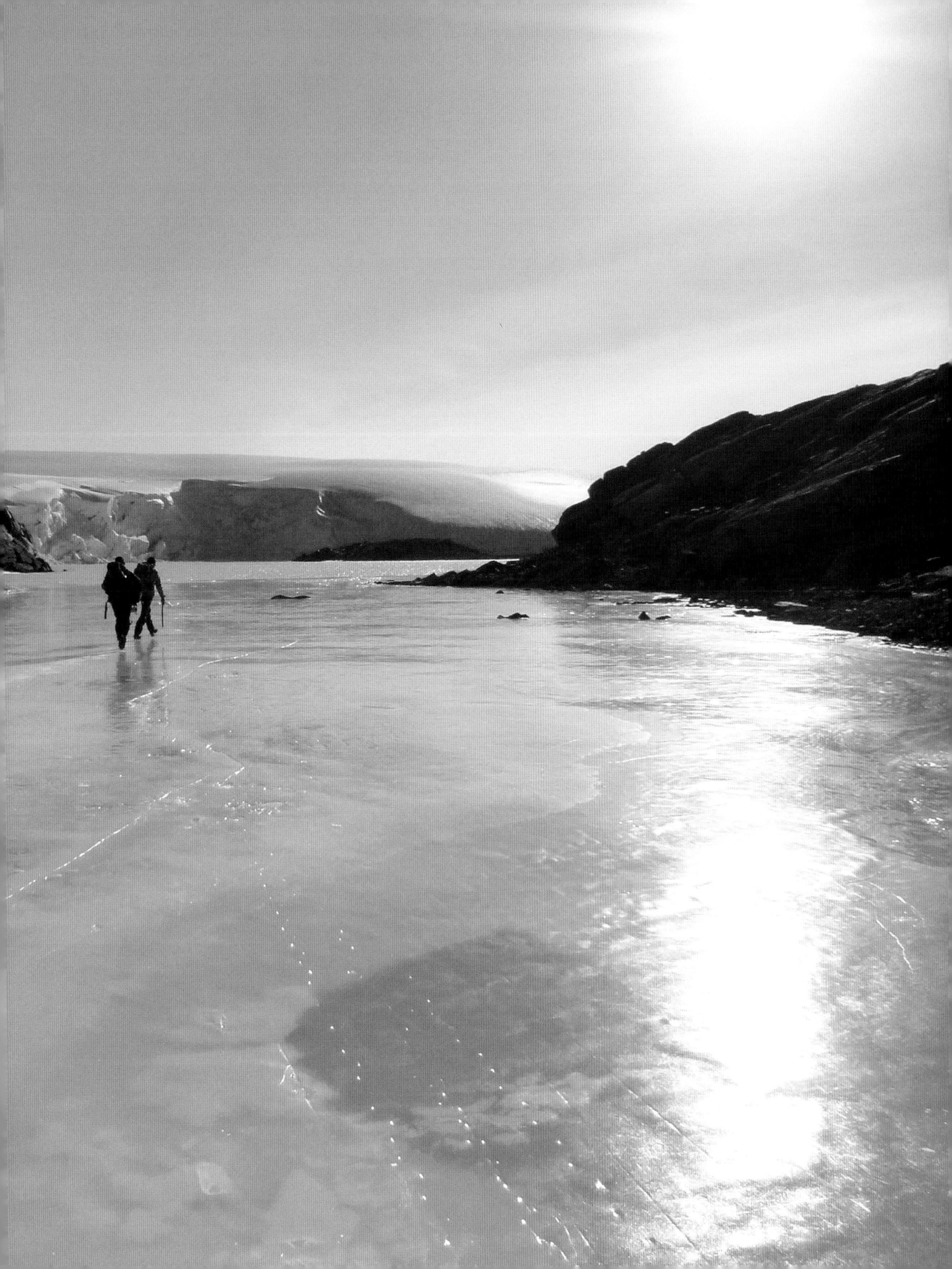

of the project, this work was not permanently set into the landscape as a built drawing but out of respect for nature and the Antarctic Treaty, was created as an ephemeral work which after several hours was swept up leaving behind no trace whatsoever. "I know this work's not going to be here in another few hours, and I know that the only evidence of what I've created will be generated by the satellites that are flying over me now, because it is totally ephemeral. It is not about the structure in the future. It is about the idea of creating it and its not being there. And what is left over is just the idea for people to consider. So this work is probably the purest form of my message," said the artist.

For this artistic message, Rogers had a 60 × 60-meter (197 × 197 feet) fabric template sewn out of thin parachute silk that was marked with 100 rectangular, precisely cut-out holes that were later filled with moraine gravel outlining the form of *Rhythms of Life*. "We started off just looking at ordinary fabric. But then I had to think about the logistics of getting the template there. This would be a huge piece of fabric and it would be so heavy we wouldn't have been able to carry it. Everything we took there we would have to physically carry," he recalled. The enormous fabric tarpaulin itself became a global work of art: the fabric came from Taiwan, was sewn in China, sent to Australia, and taken by Rogers via South Africa to Antarctica.

Rogers flew from Cape Town in South Africa and after a five-and-a-half-hour flight landed on the endless ice shelf in Dronning Maud Land. After a short period of acclimatization in the icy cold, he set out with his guides to seek a suitable site for *Rhythms of Life*. The search led them to the end of the Dakshin Gangotri Glacier to a hidden ice lake from which the dark rocks of moraine shone forth—deposits of

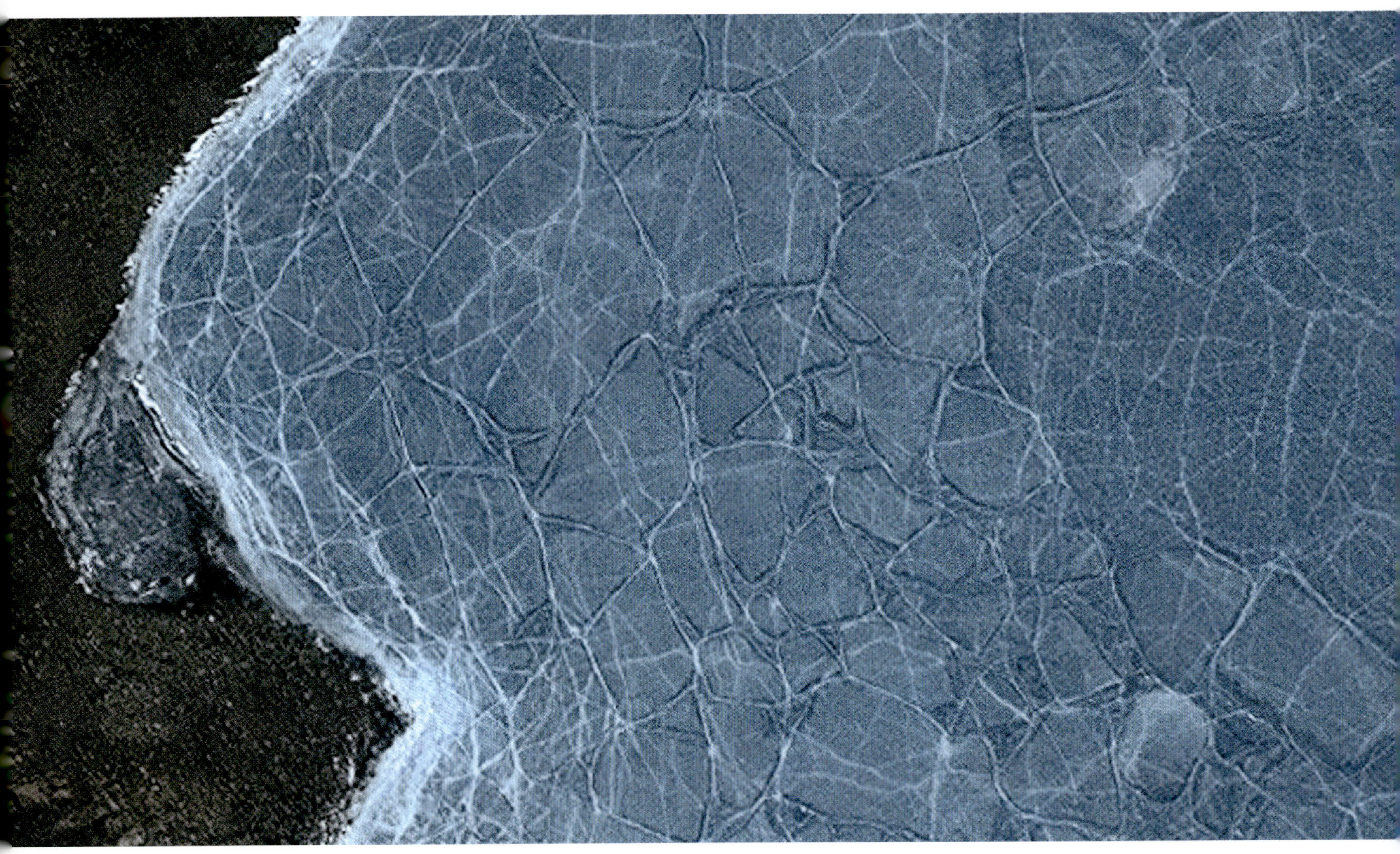

rock material at the edges of the ice that had once been taken up by the glacier and then left behind as it continued on its path. Adélie penguins live in the area and were in the process of building their nests. So as not to disturb them, the team collected the fine, dark gravel for marking the *Rhythm of Life* symbol on the surface of the ice at a somewhat more remote moraine cliff. Just as the first cutouts in the fabric tarpaulin had been carefully filled with gravel poured from a pitcher and gently tapped down, an ice storm set in, interrupting the work. Only the next day could the sculpture be completed. And then came the grand moment of revealing it: the tarpaulin was carefully removed, and *Rhythms of Life* stood out majestically from the deep blue of the glistening ice as a precisely defined sculpture.

It was a work of art with a brief lifespan: After being captured in photos, on film, and in satellite images, the moraine gravel used to create the sculpture was swept up and returned to its source.

Without intervening in Antarctica's fragile ecosystem, Rogers succeeded in completing the chain of his global art project with a very special *Rhythms of Life* geoglyph on the seventh and last continent, once again clearly communicating his message: "What's special about Antarctica isn't its physical terrain. It isn't the minus five degrees. It isn't the isolation. What's special about Antarctica is what is in your mind that has been put there, why we have to have regard for the planet and each other."

RHYTHMS OF LIFE, satellite image taken 680 km (422.5 miles) above the earth. An ephemeral land art installation on the surface of a frozen glacial lake.

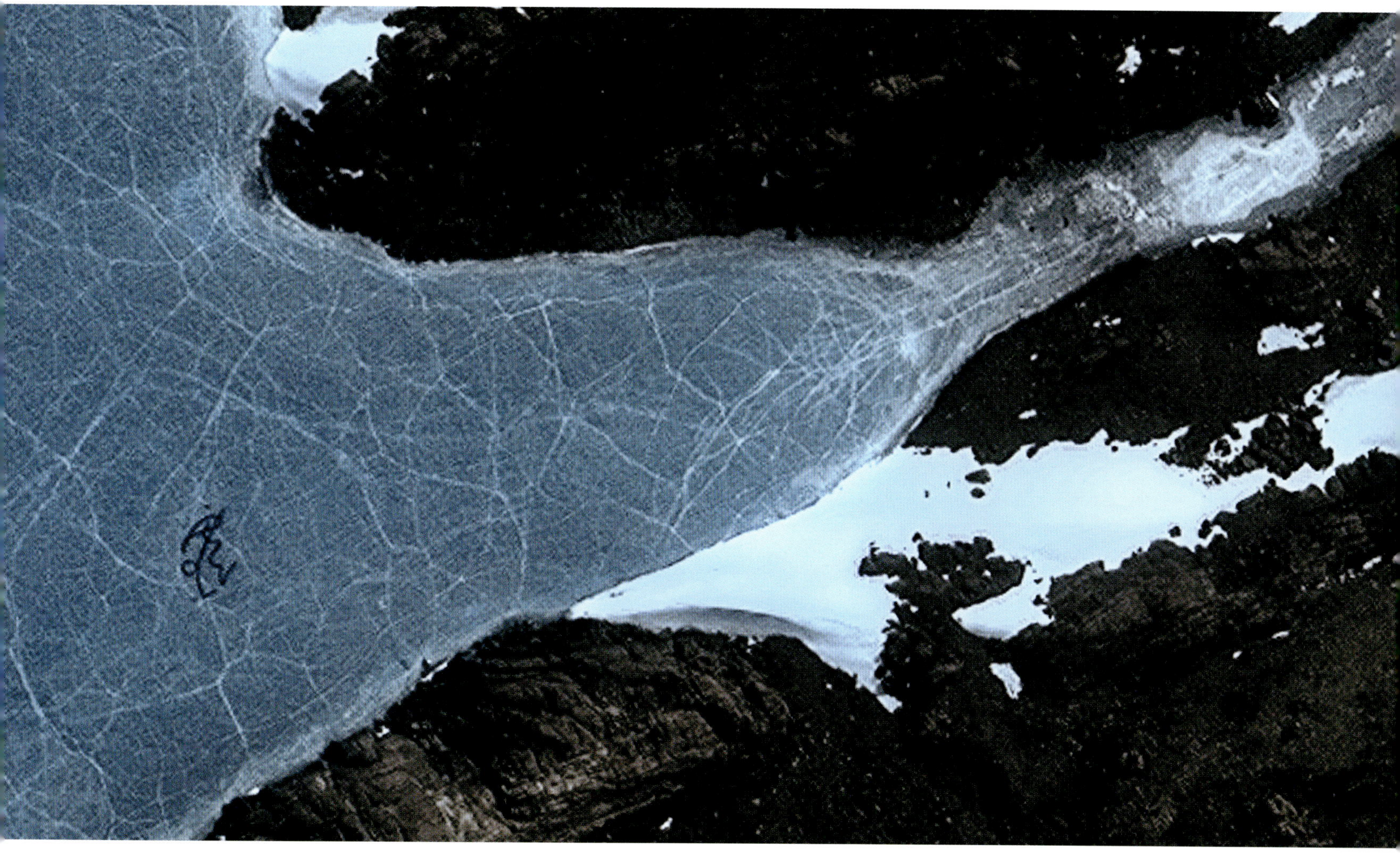

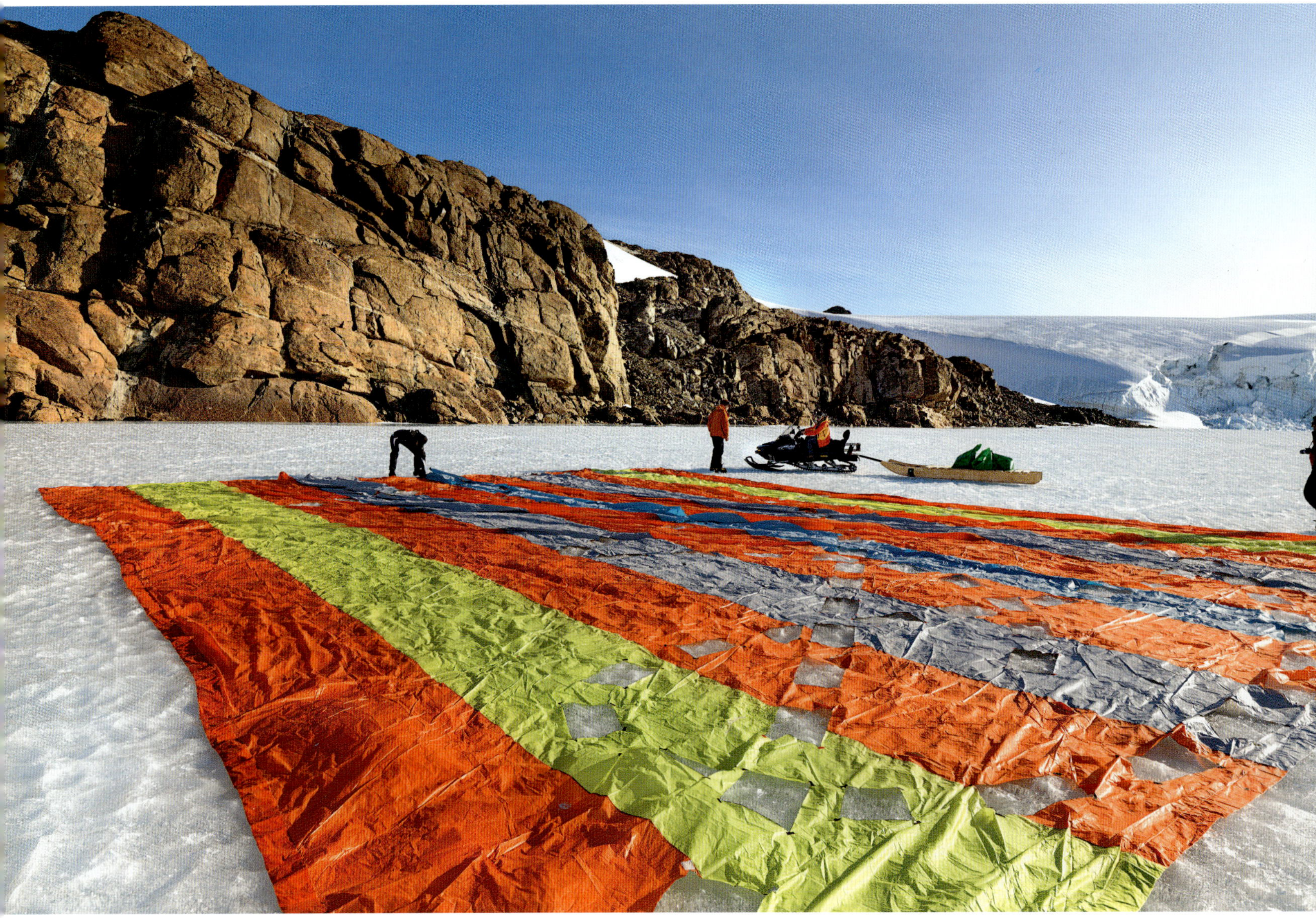

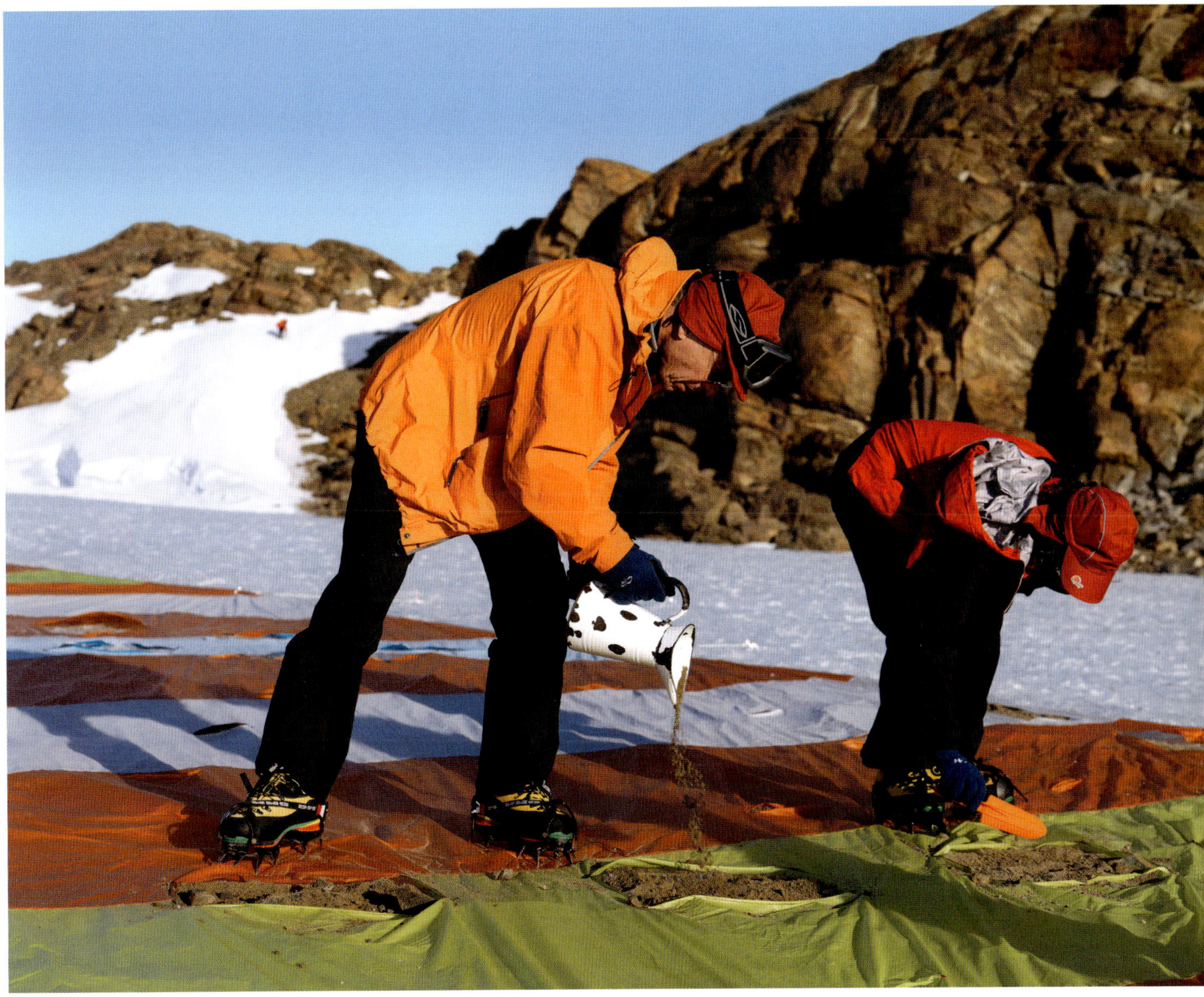

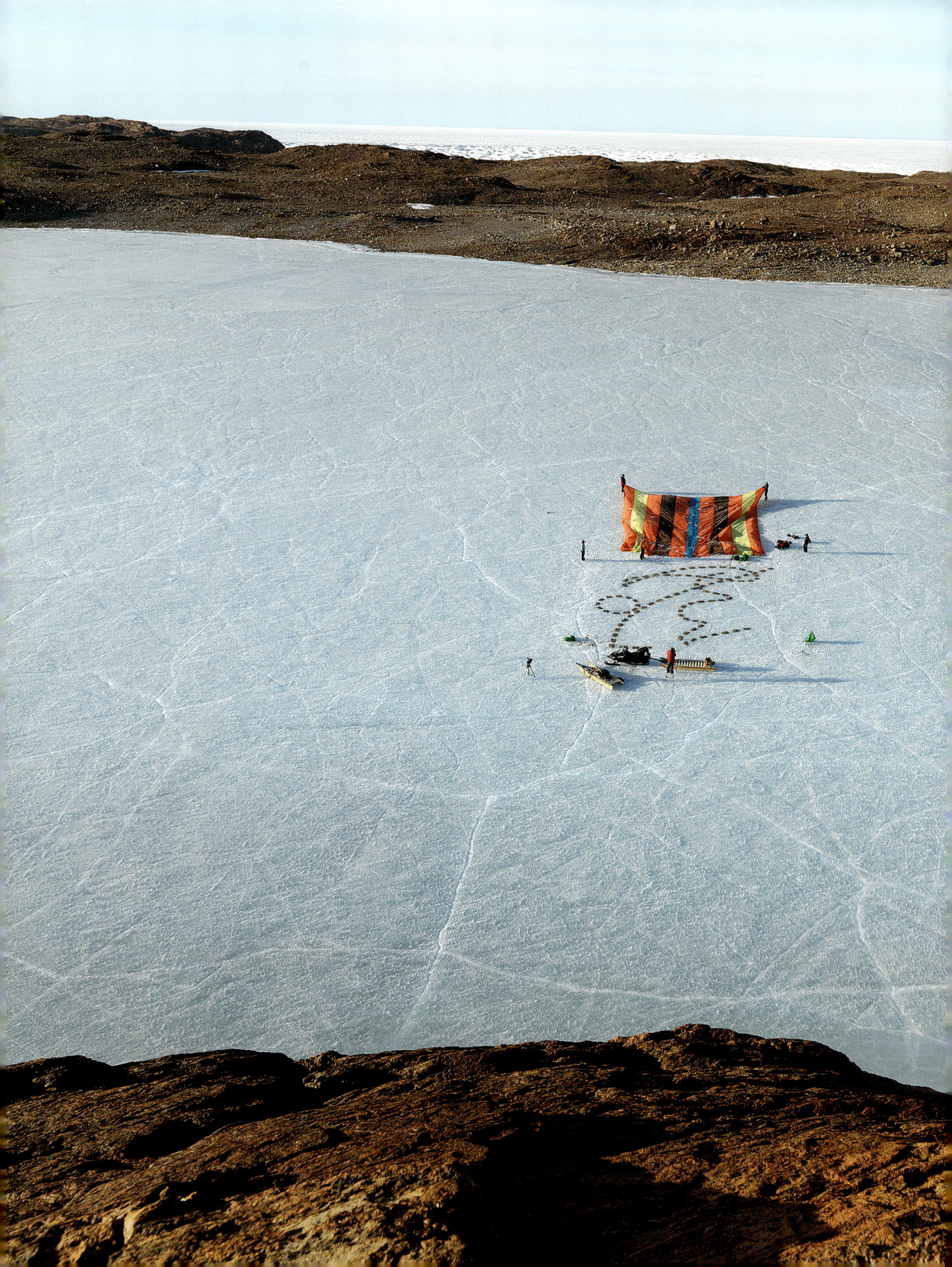

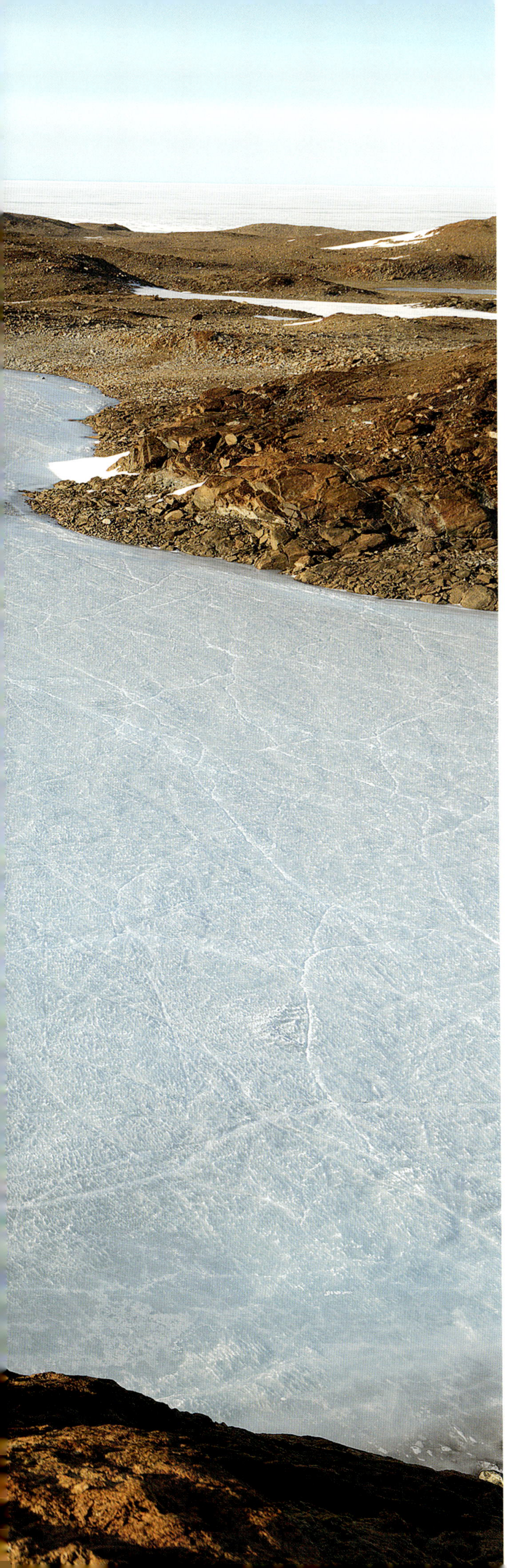

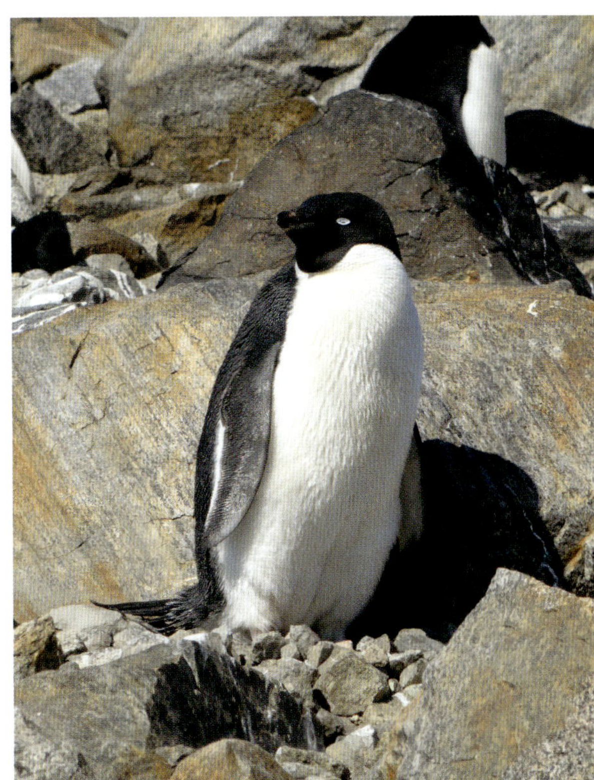

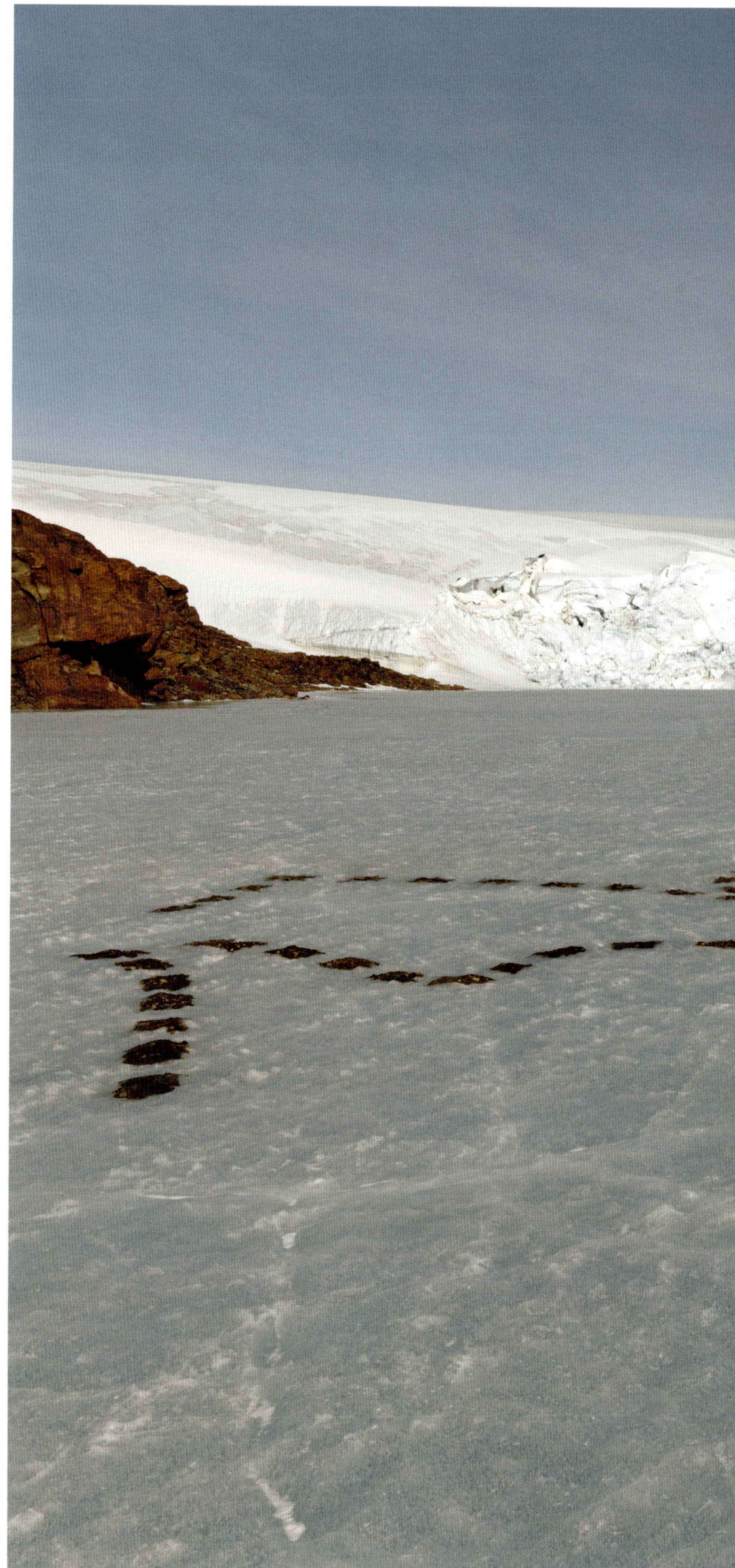

RHYTHMS OF LIFE 2010 / Moraine gravel / 60 × 60 m (197 × 197 ft.)

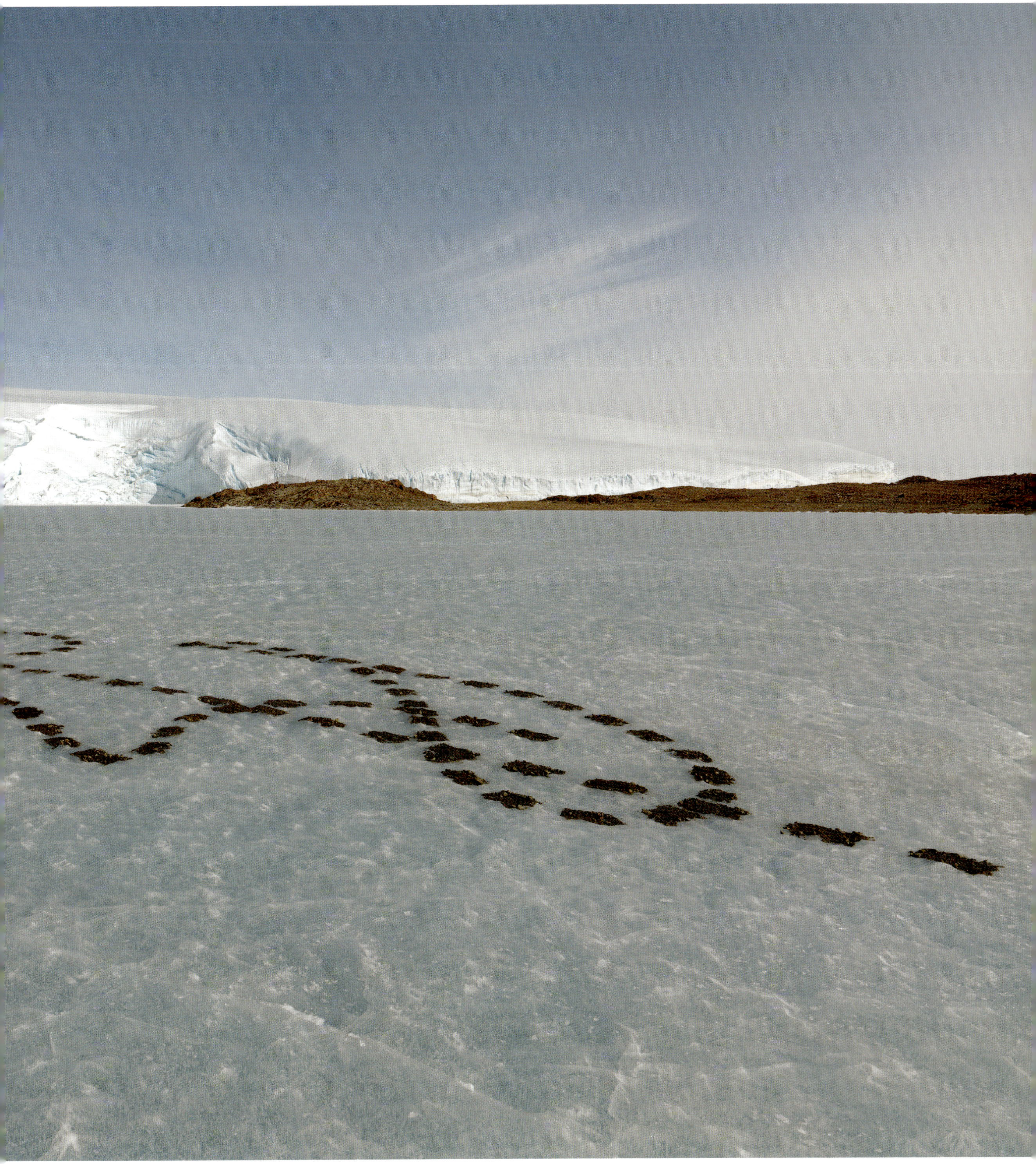

TIME AND SPACE
CAPPADOCIA, TURKEY

The eight basalt steles situated on the top of a hill high above the rugged landscape of Cappadocia in Central Anatolia are like signposts from ancient times: *Sentinels*, one of thirteen monumental installations that Andrew Rogers built between 2007 and 2011 in the enormous, isolated high valley between Avanos and Nevşehir—a new dimension within his global *Rhythms of Life* project.

The installations and geoglyphs are located near the tourist destination of Göreme, in the immediate vicinity of an extraordinary volcanic landscape where bizarre rock formations rise up into the sky like gigantic stone mushrooms, chimneys, and pointed caps. Fifty million years ago, two active volcanoes covered the region with a thick layer of lava, and when the mixture of basalt, ash, and sand solidified, it formed tuff, a soft rock that was shaped into this bizarre magical world by wind, water, and large fluctuations in temperature.

People started carving homes in the caves and later built multistory, subterranean cities into the soft rock of this special landscape as early as the Bronze Age. A wide variety of sophisticated cultures lived here—from the Assyrians, Hittites, Mongolians, Persians, Seljuk, and Greeks to the Armenians, Romans, and Ottomans. The underground churches in the truncated cave system provided refuge to Christians and later to Muslims fleeing persecution. This rich history with traces of all cultures at the interface between Europe and the Middle East as well as one of the world's most spectacular landscapes caused the artist to rise above himself: he calls the gigantic art landscape of thirteen monumental installations *Time and Space*. They are distributed over a distance of 2.5 kilometers (1.5 miles) in the expansive Karadag Mountain Valley, 1,210 meters (3,970 feet) above sea level. With *Time and Space*, Rogers created the largest contemporary land art park in the world. Stone weighing 10,500 metric tons was formed into stone walls totaling 7 kilometers (4.3 miles) in length. Rogers seeks to invite people who visit the legendary cave cities to also see this unique *Time and Space* sculpture park and to reflect on the impermanence of all earthly things. Rogers

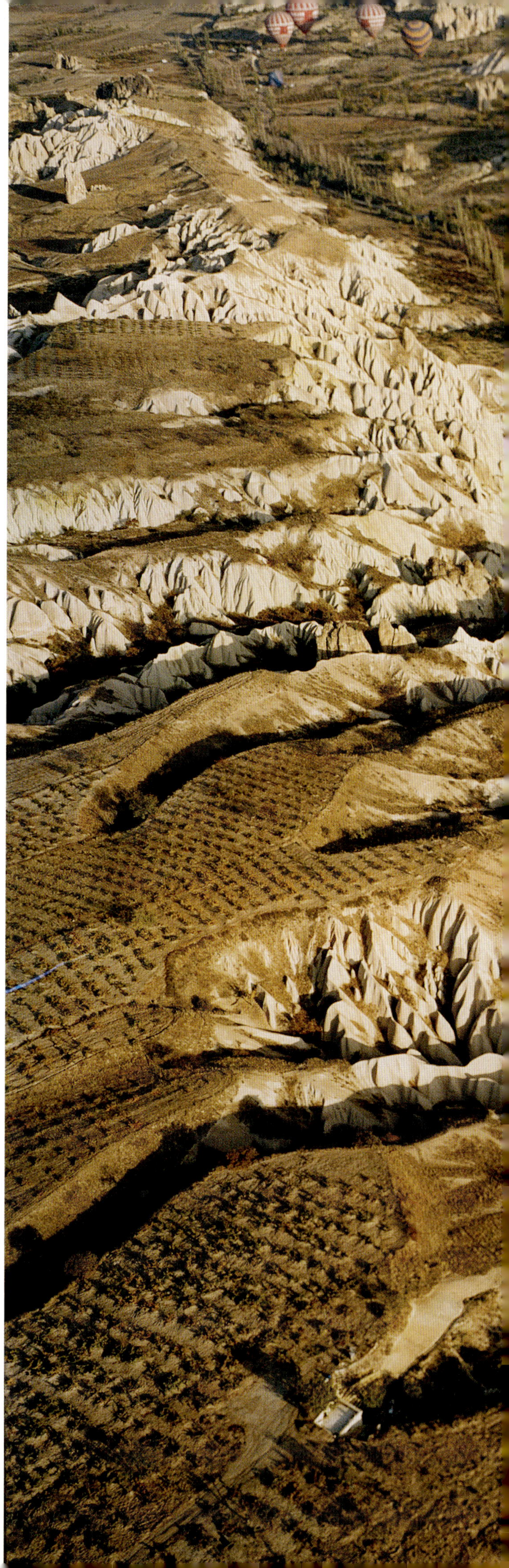

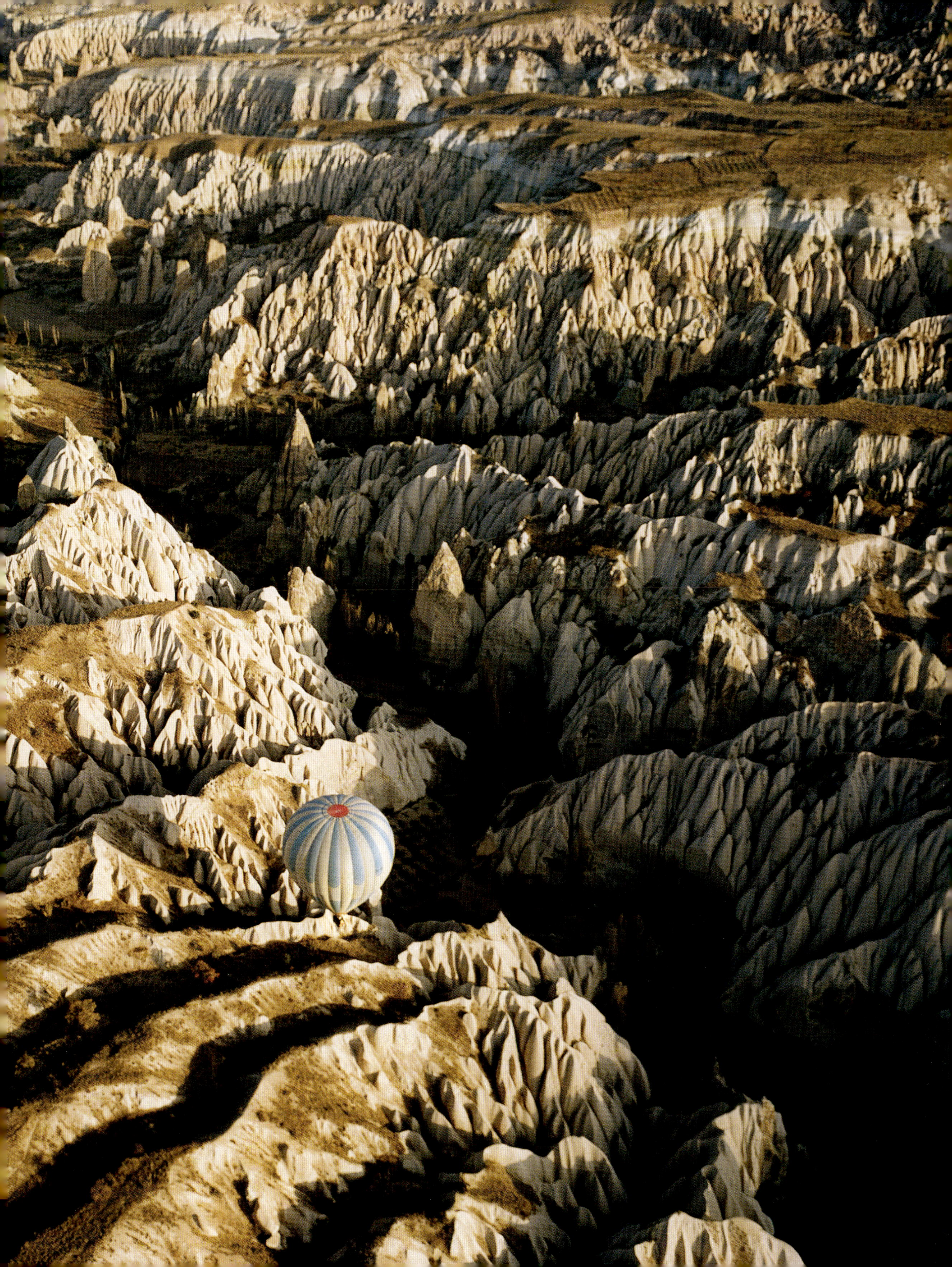

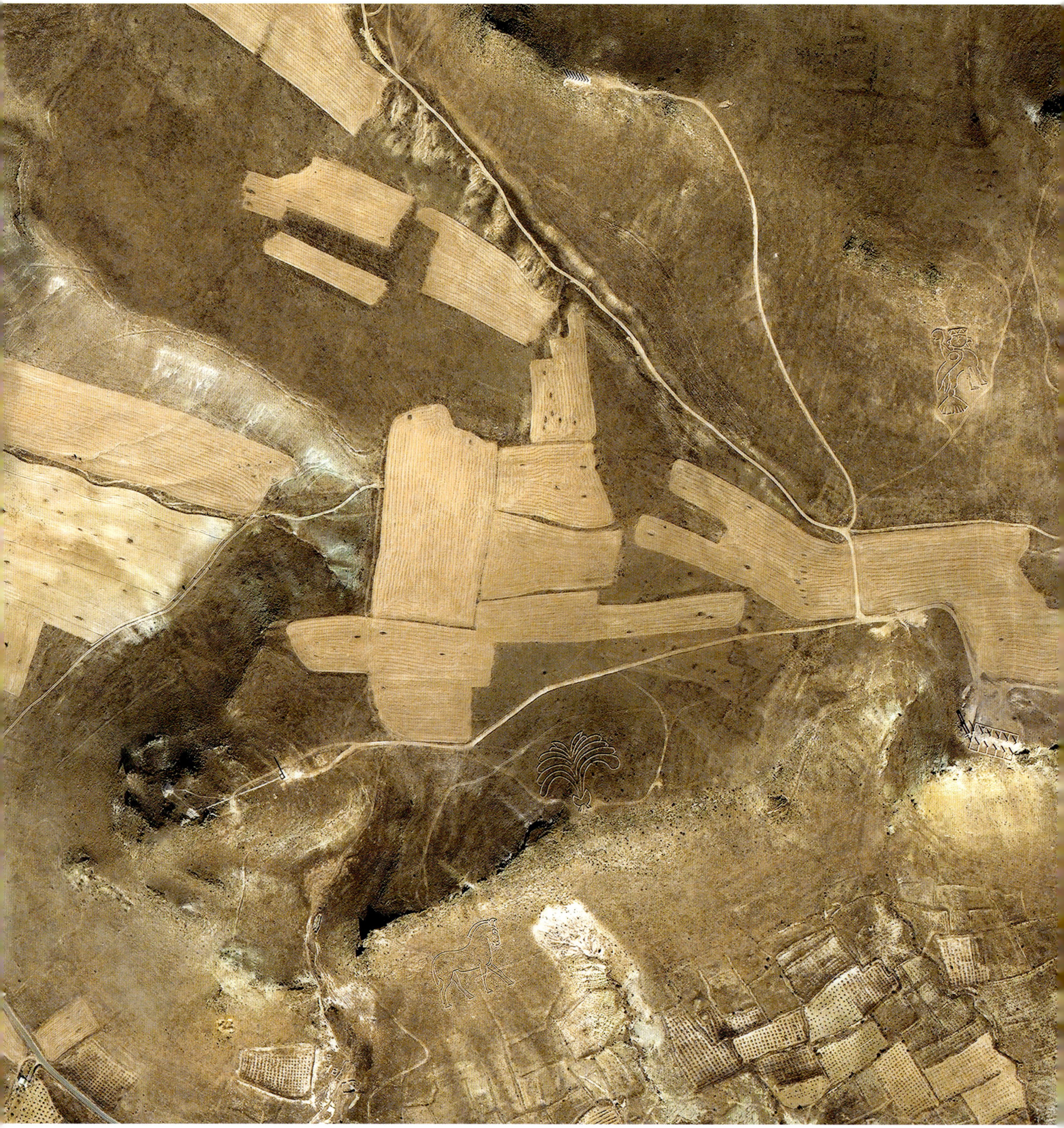

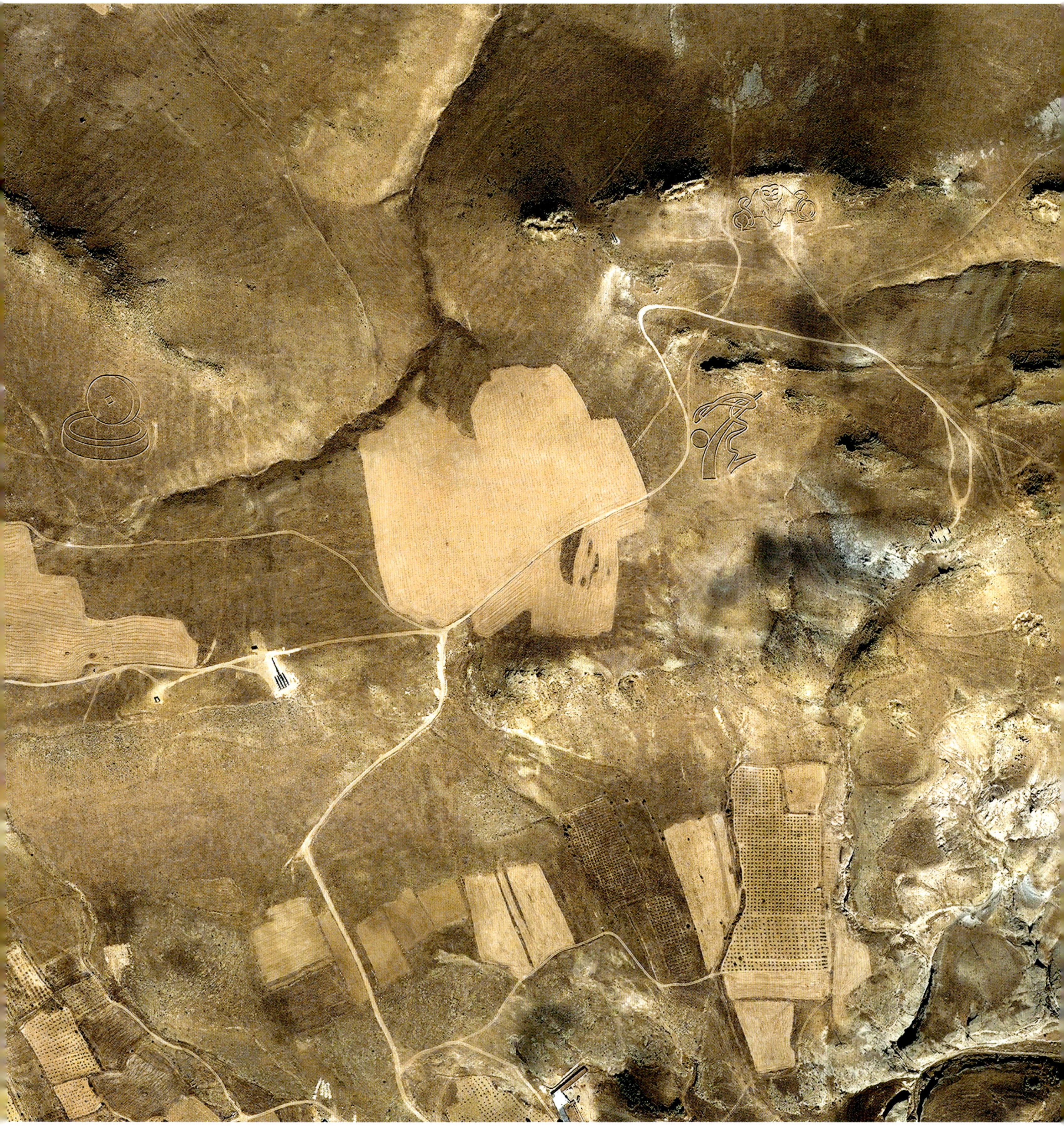

TIME AND SPACE sculpture park, satellite image: 13 major stone structures along a 2.5-kilometer (1.5-mile) expanse of the Karadag Mountain Valley. This image was taken 770 km (480 miles) above the earth.

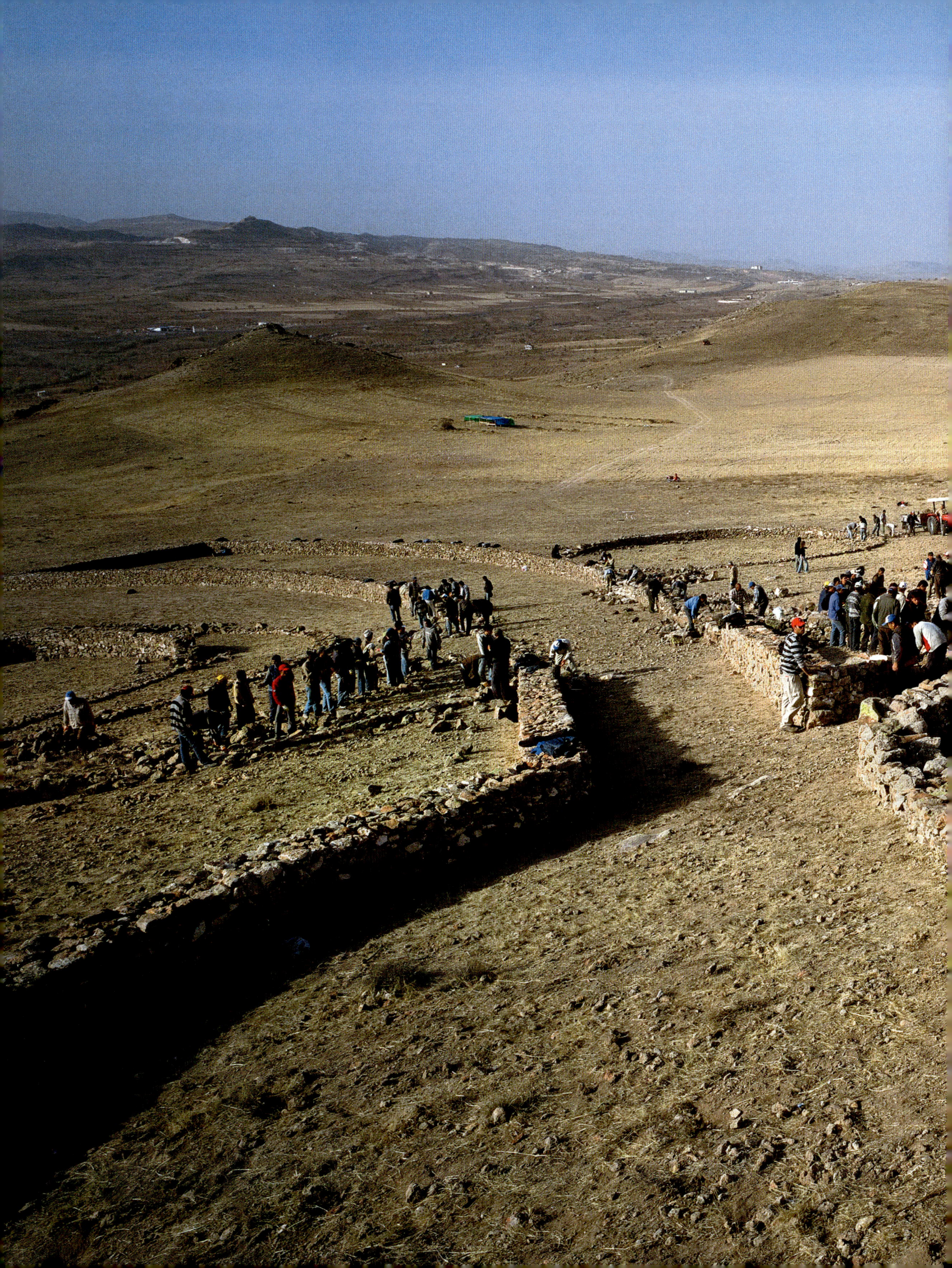

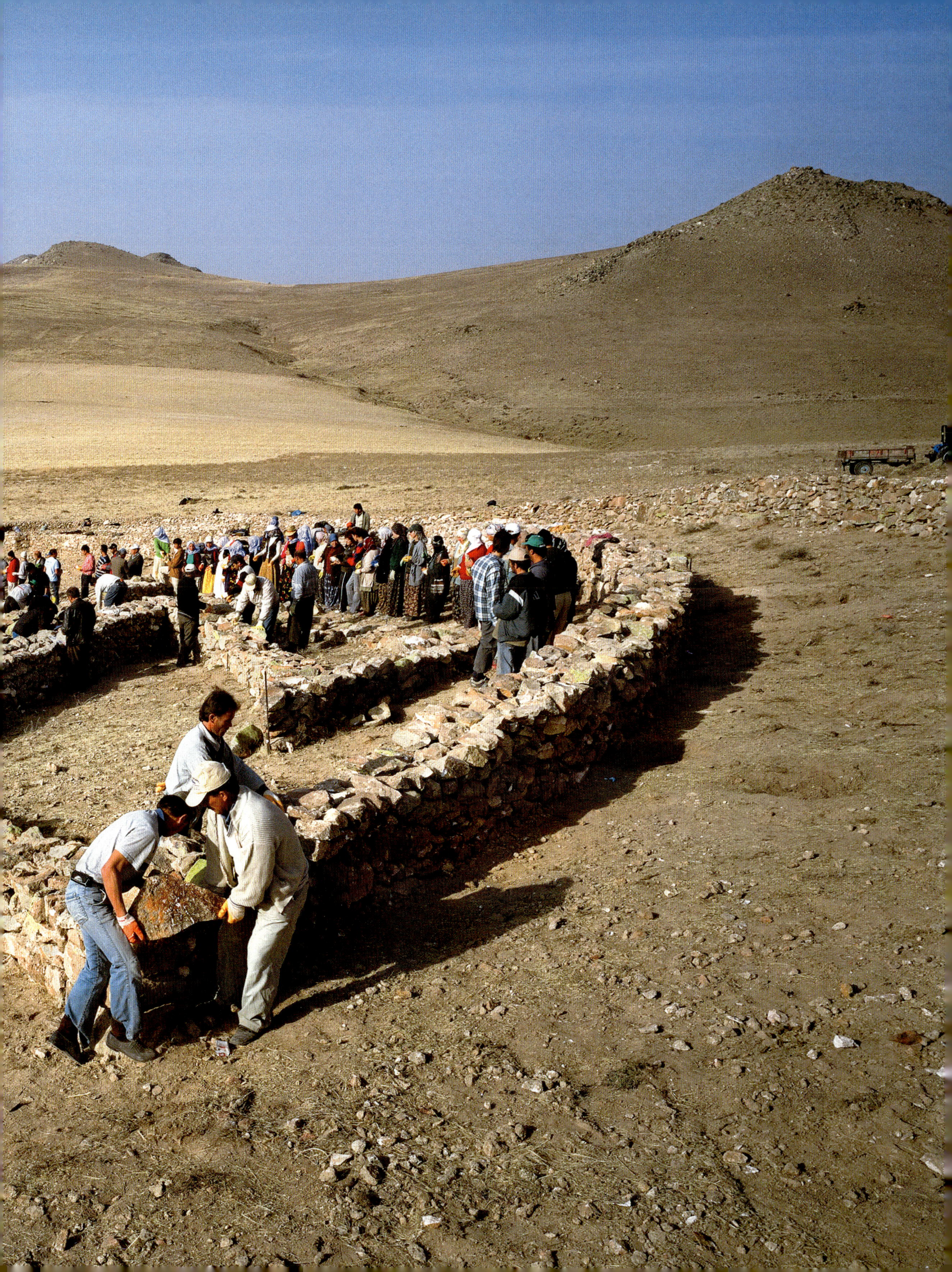

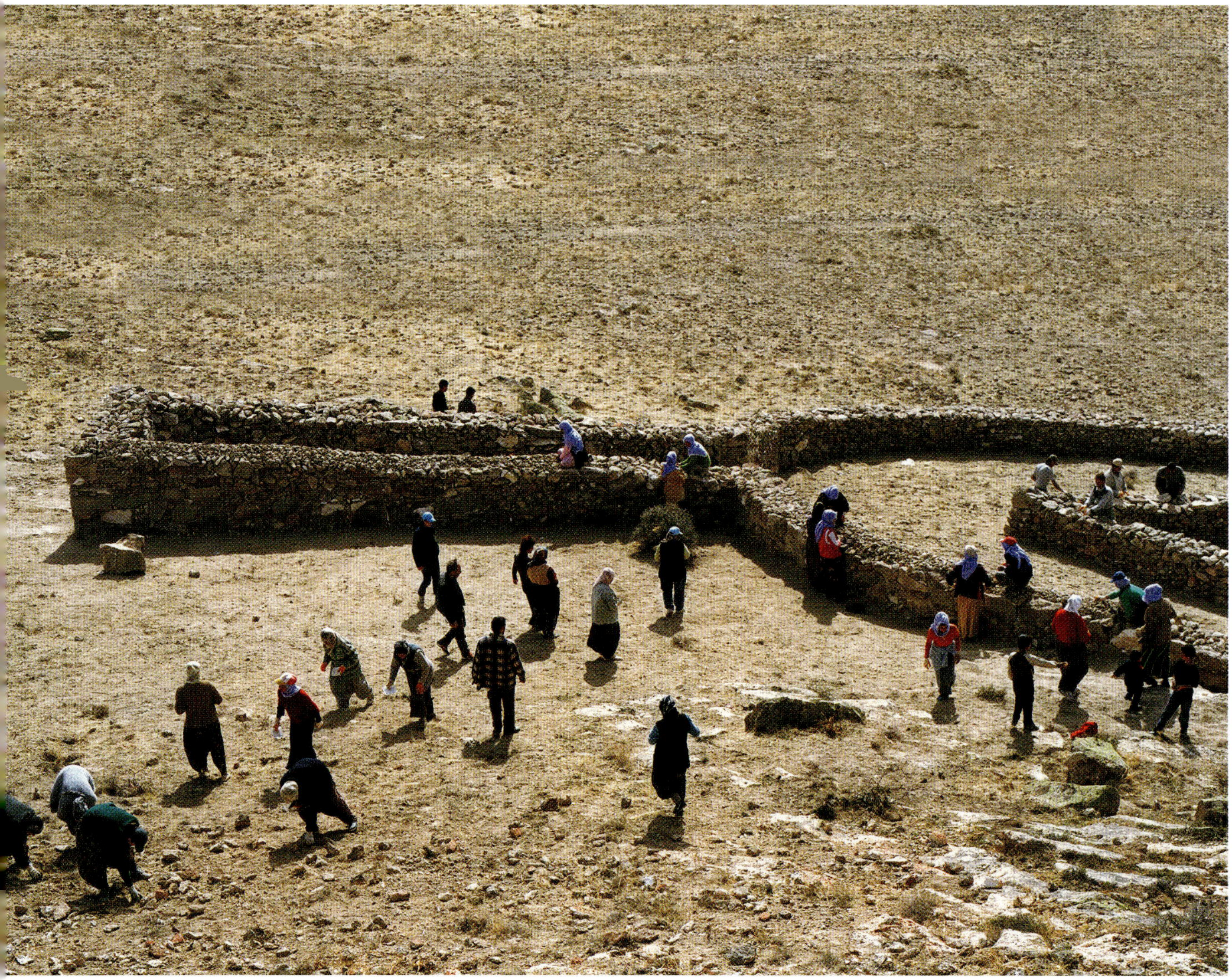
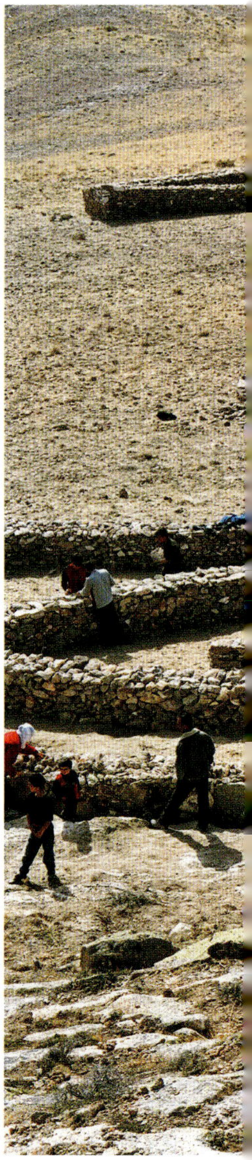

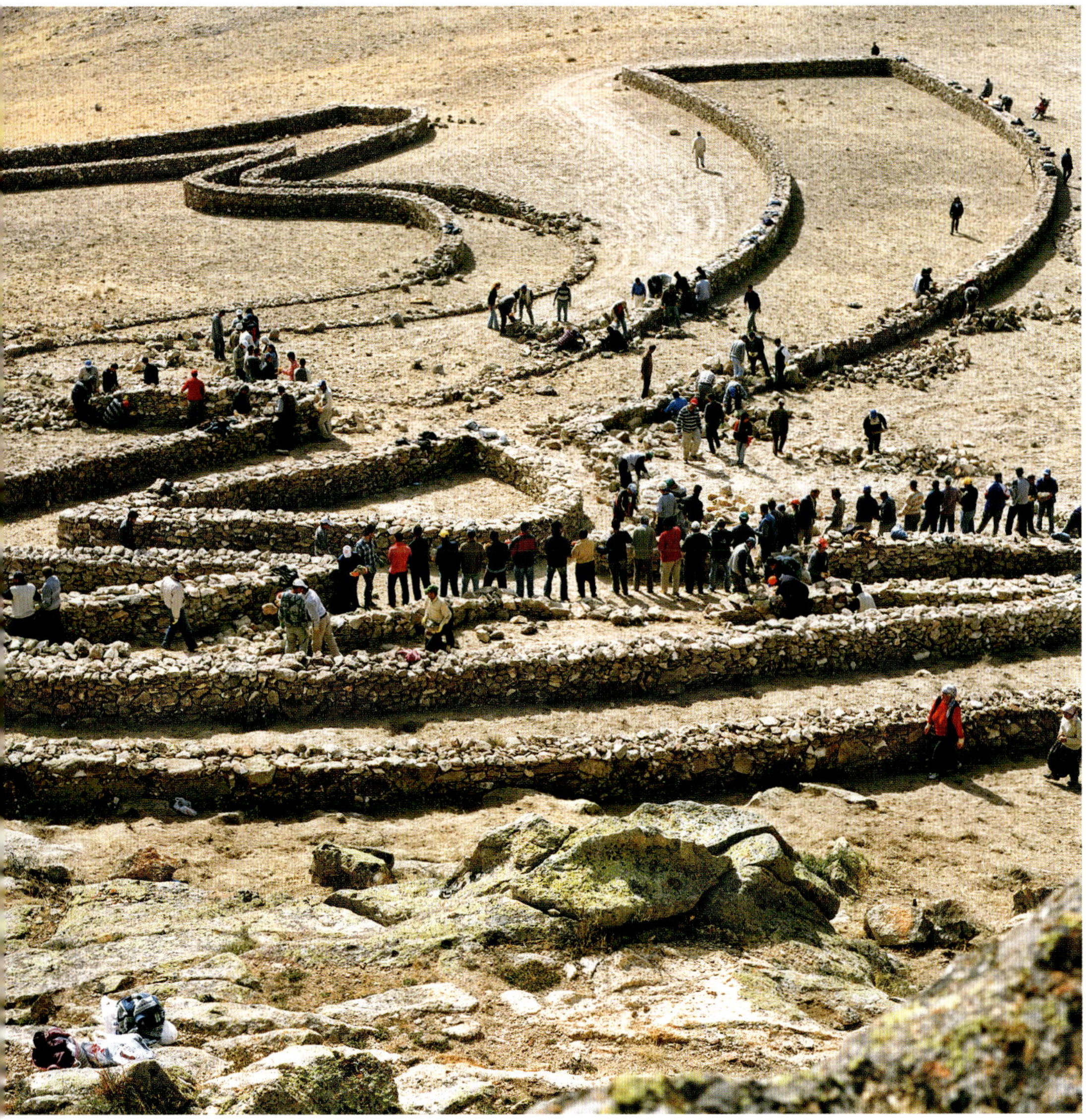

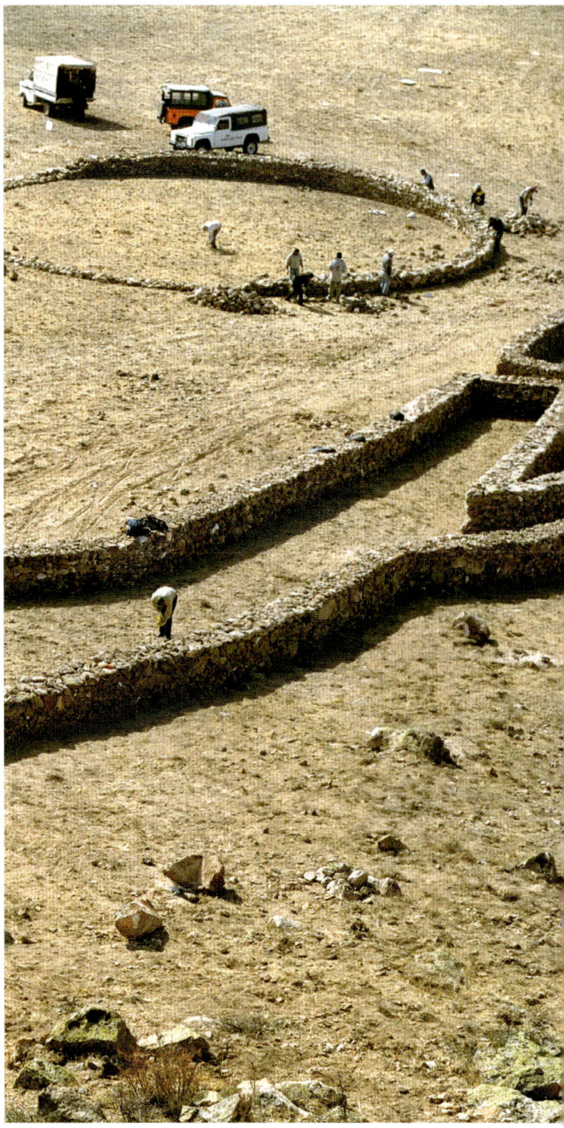

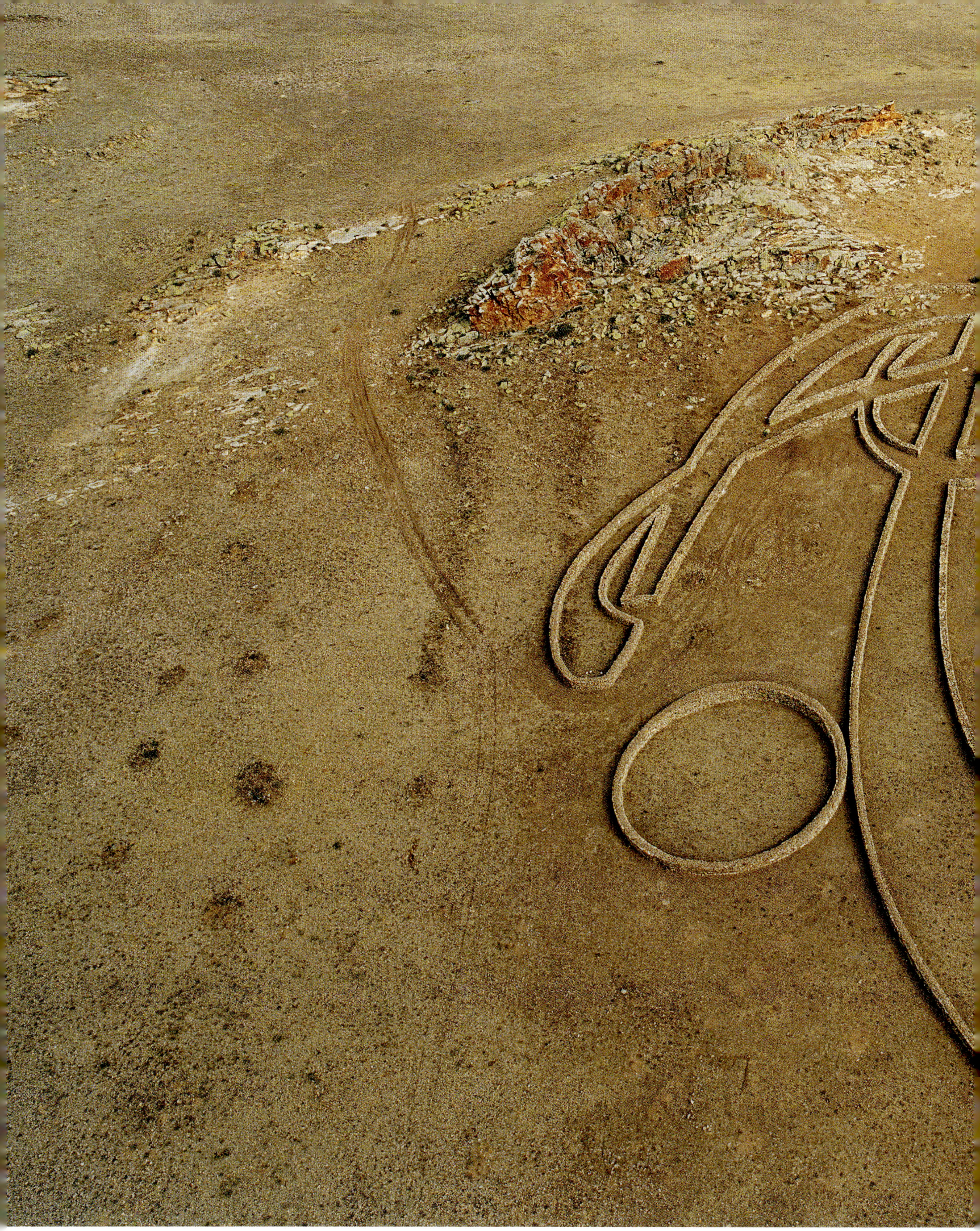

RHYTHMS OF LIFE 2007 / Volcanic rock / 100 x 90 m (330 x 295 ft.)

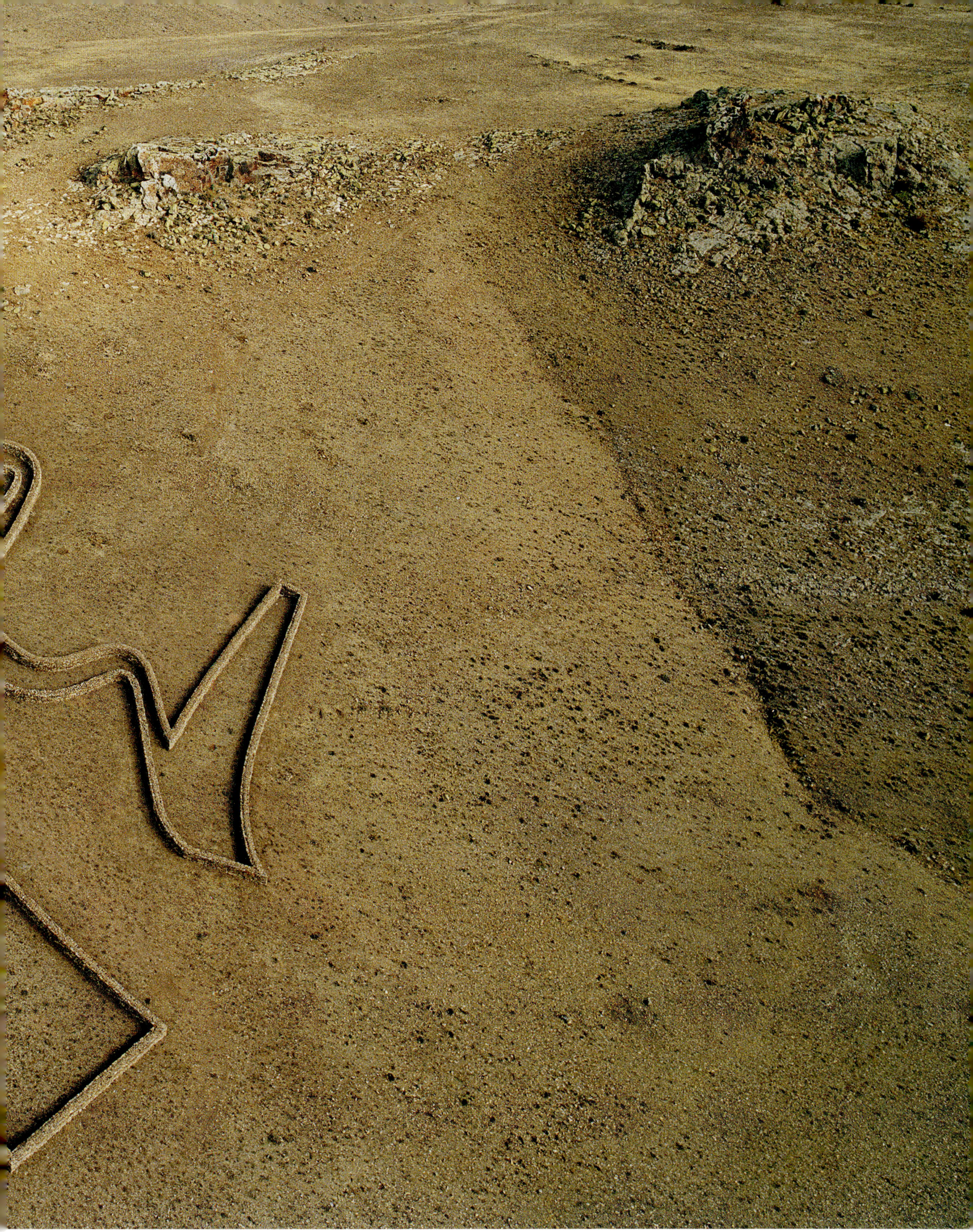

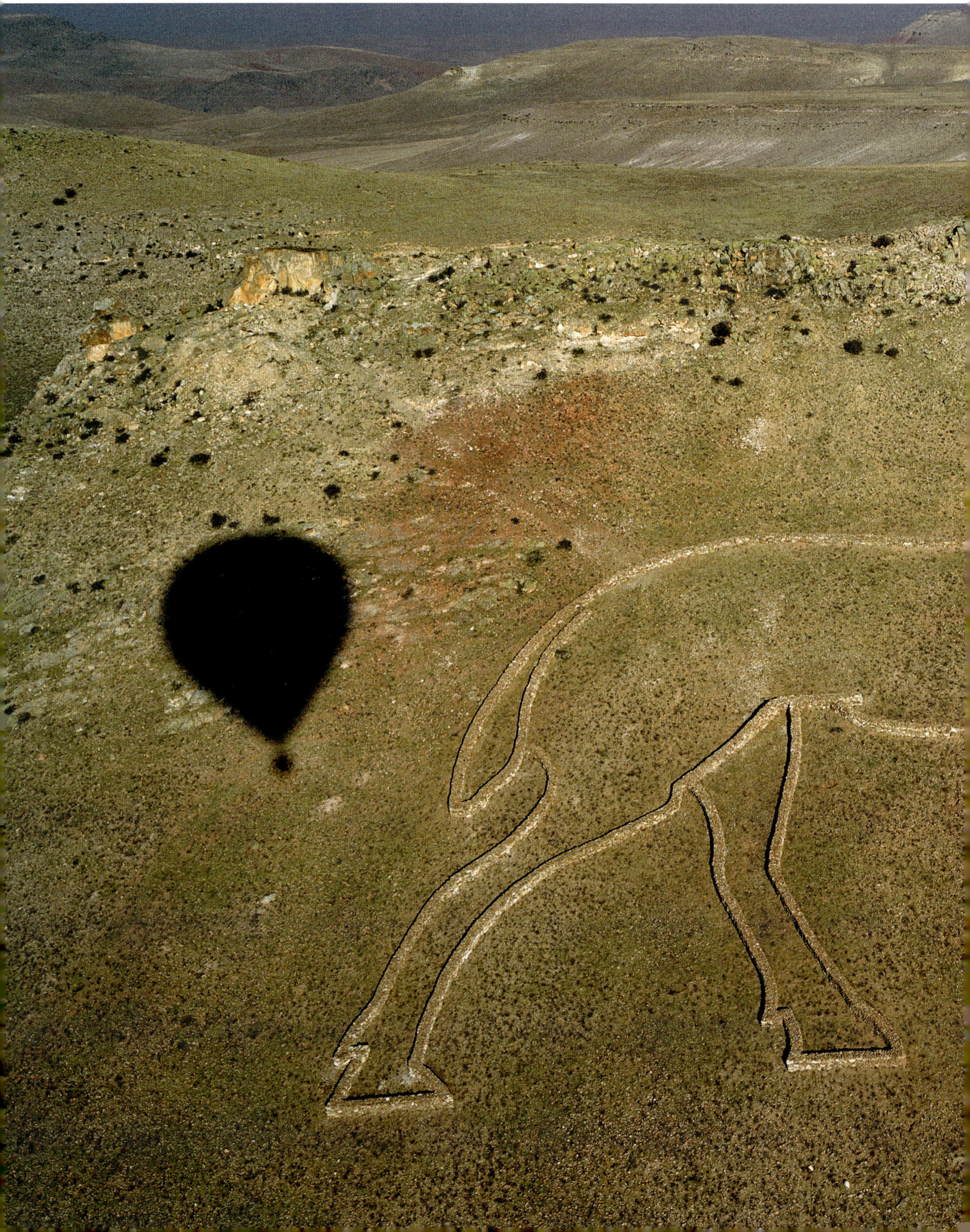

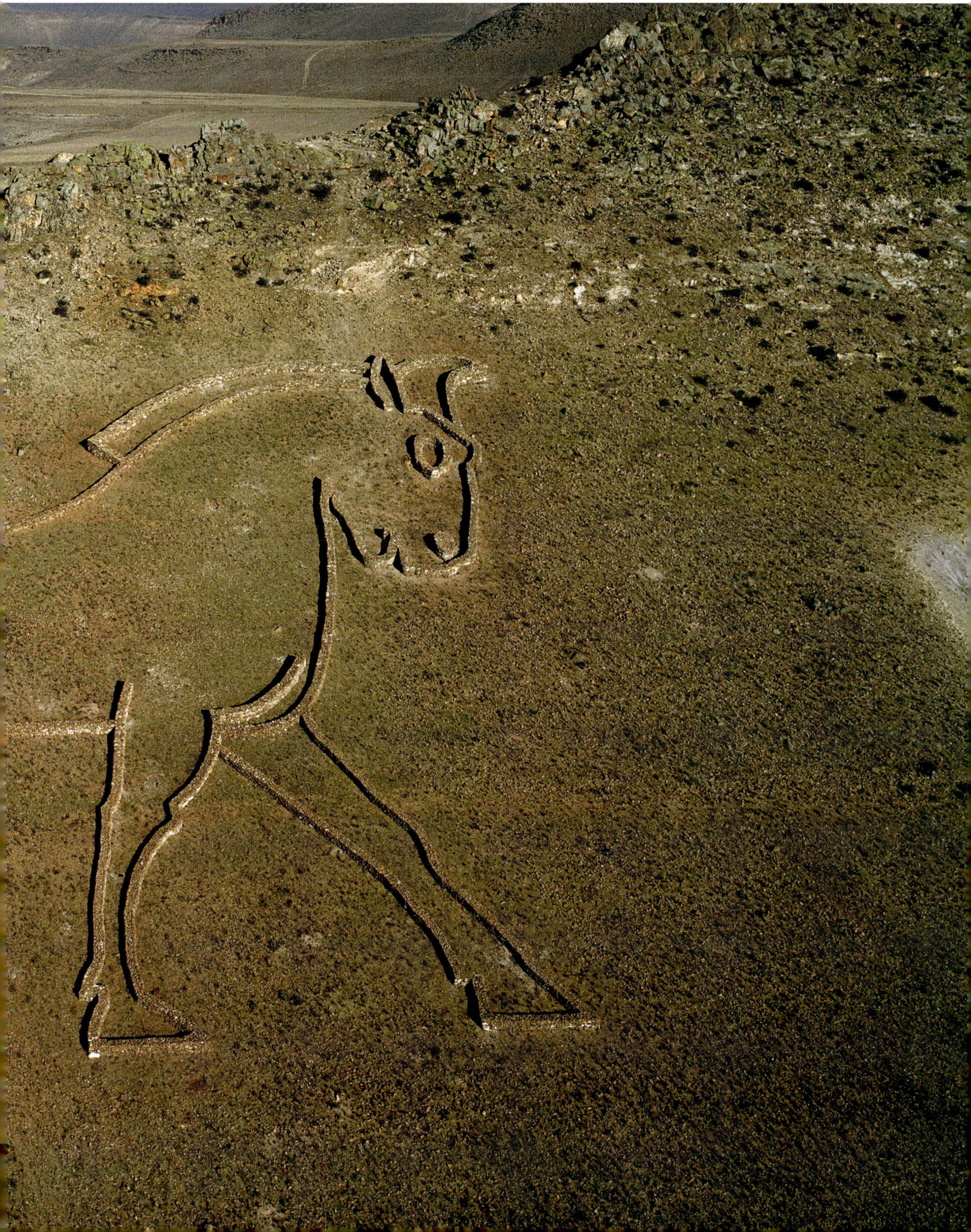

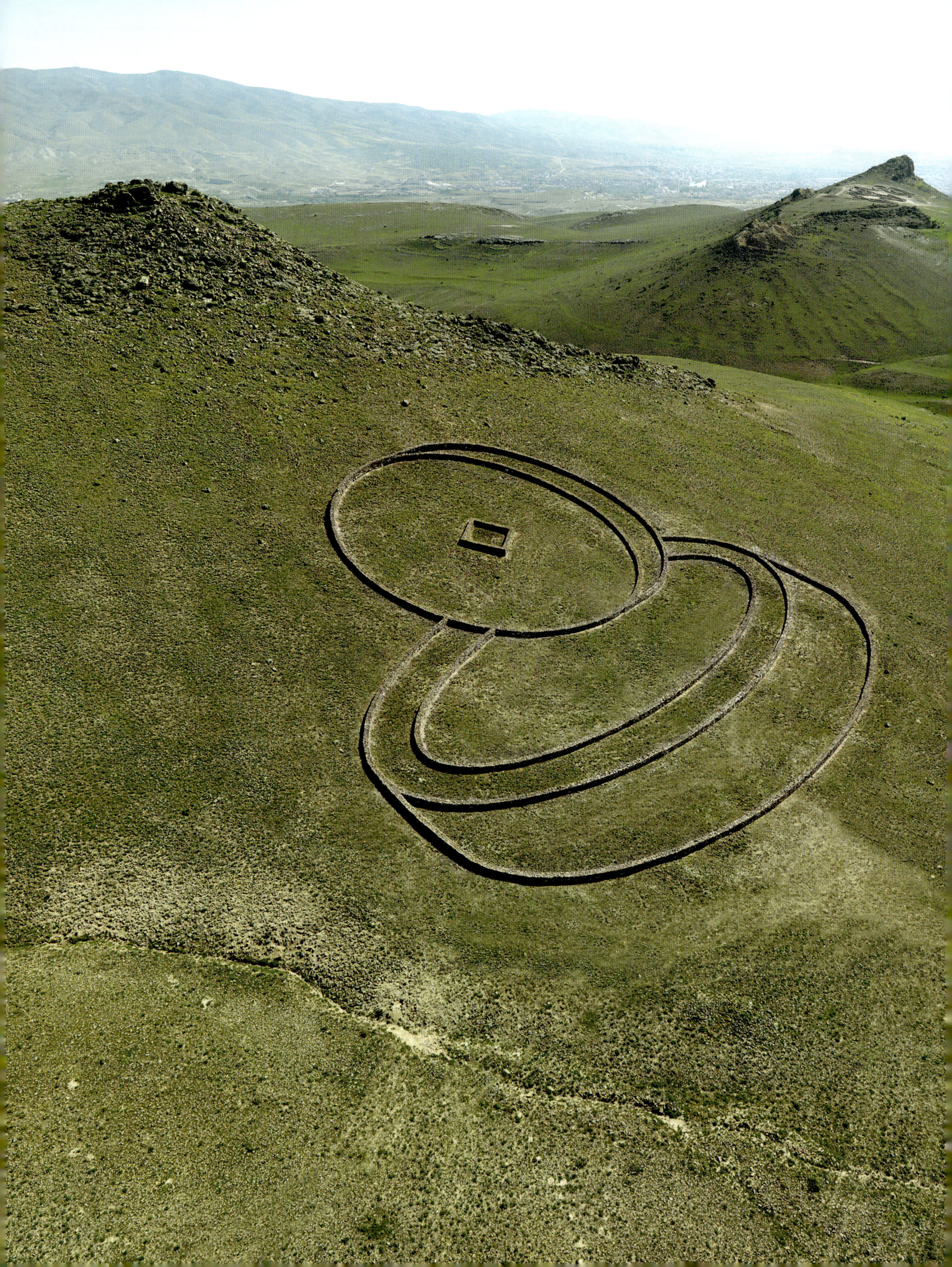

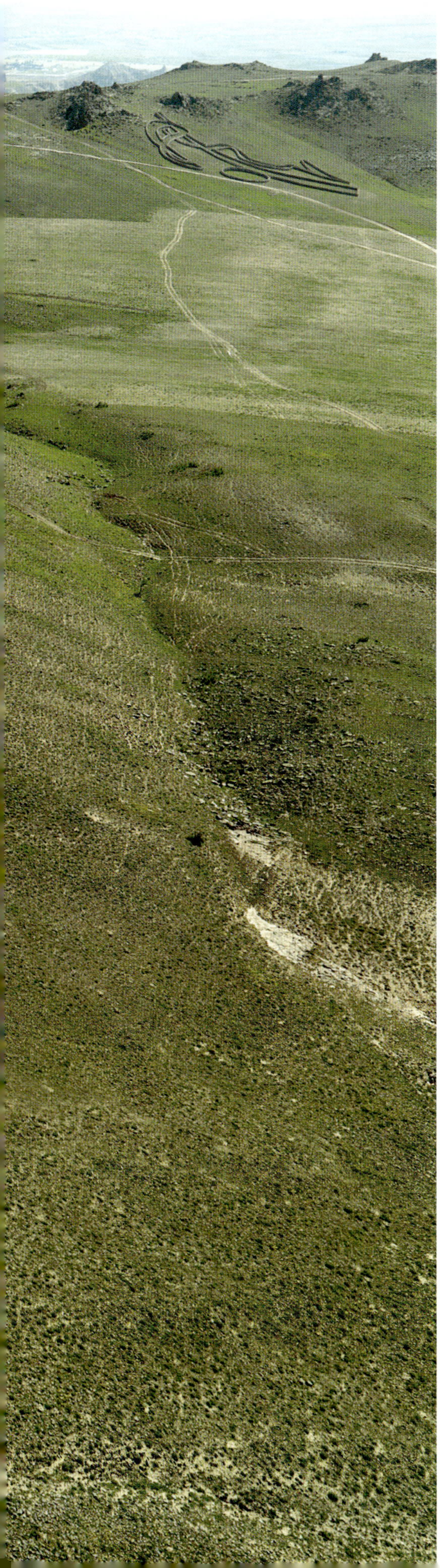

GRIND 2009 / Volcanic rock / 100 × 100 m (330 × 330 ft.)

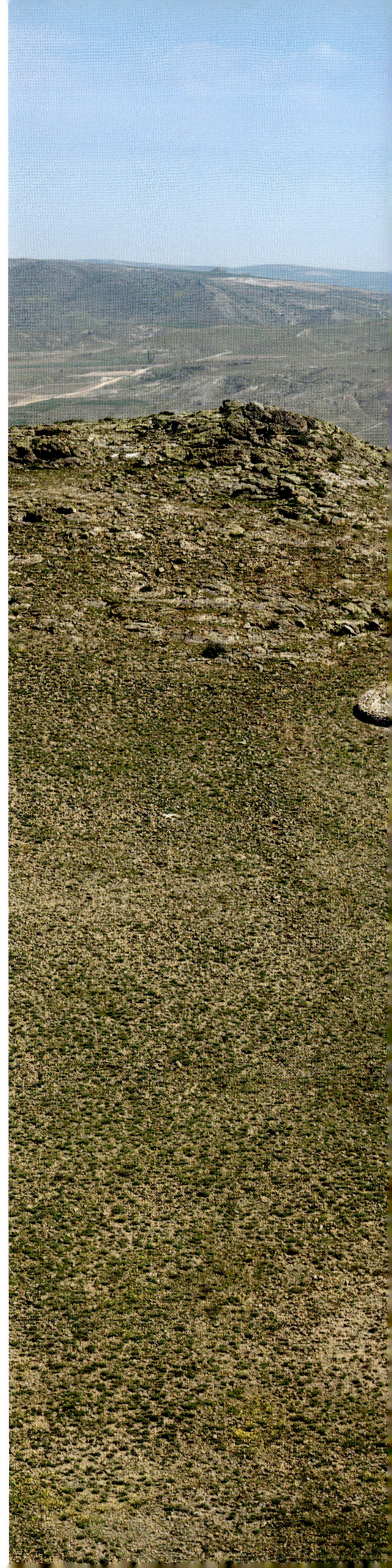

SIREN 2009 / Volcanic rock / 69 × 100 m (213 × 330 ft.)

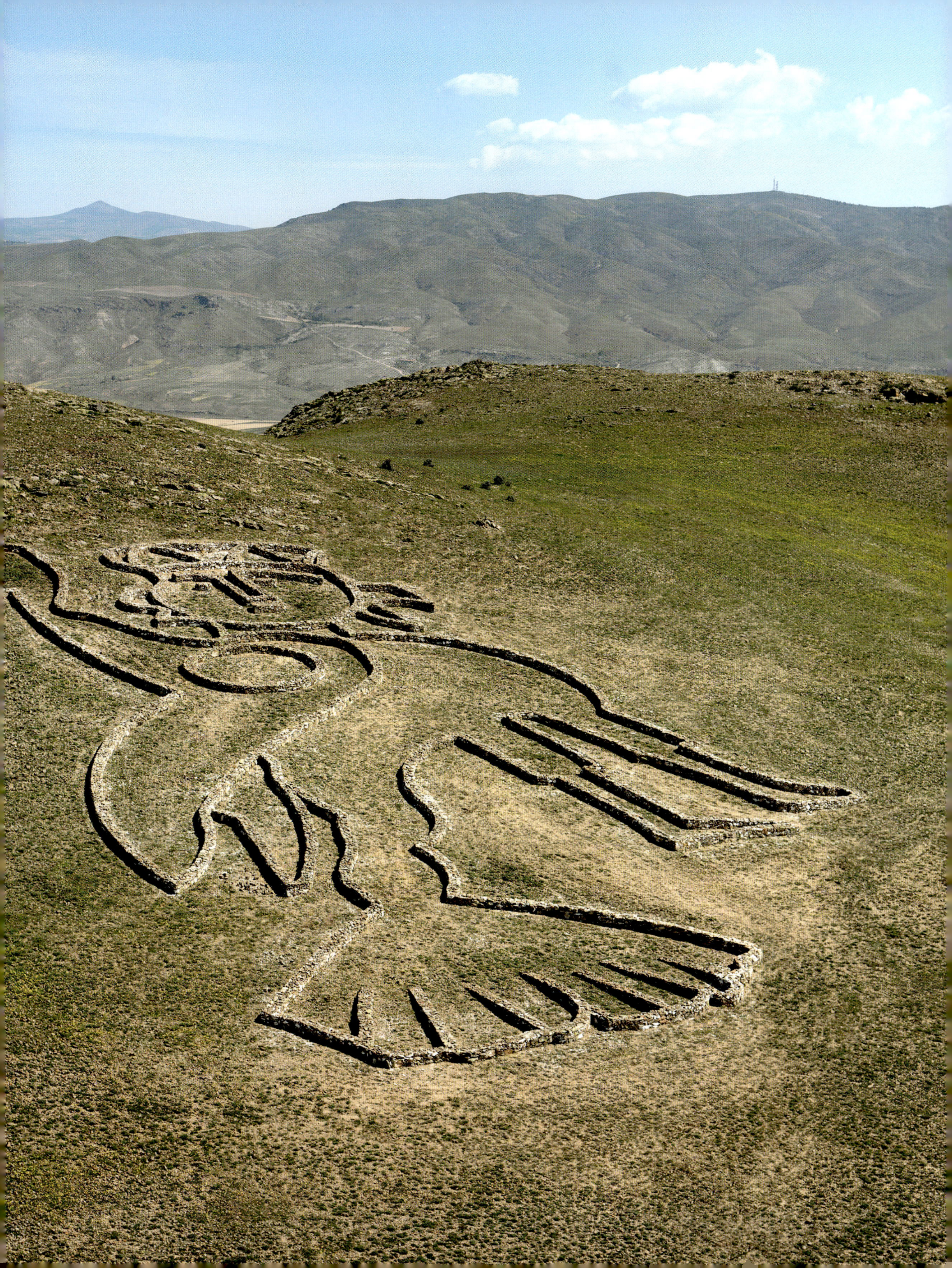

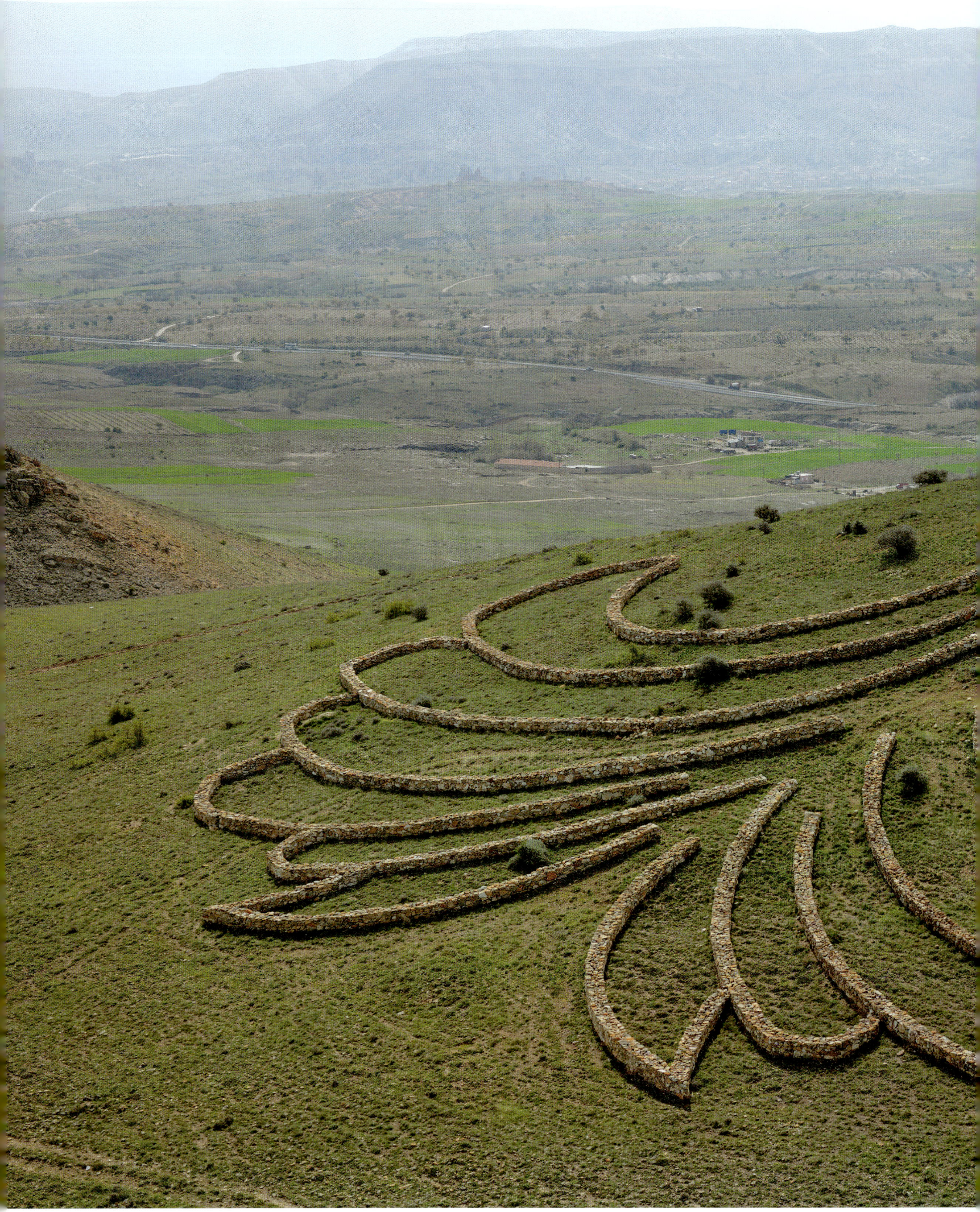

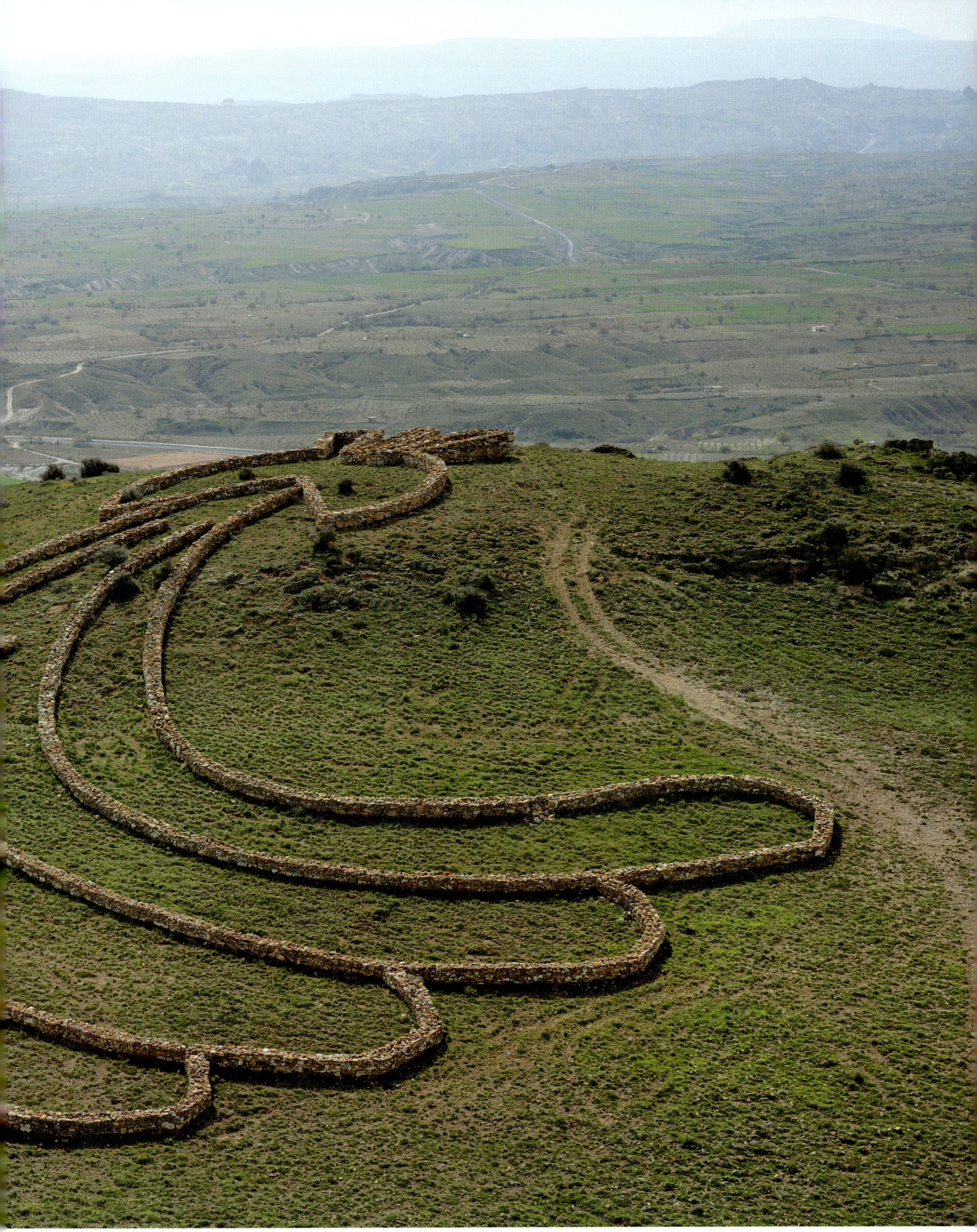

SUSTENANCE 2009 / Volcanic rock / 100 × 100 m (330 × 330 ft.)

STRENGTH 2009 / Volcanic rock / 100 × 50 m (330 × 164 ft.)

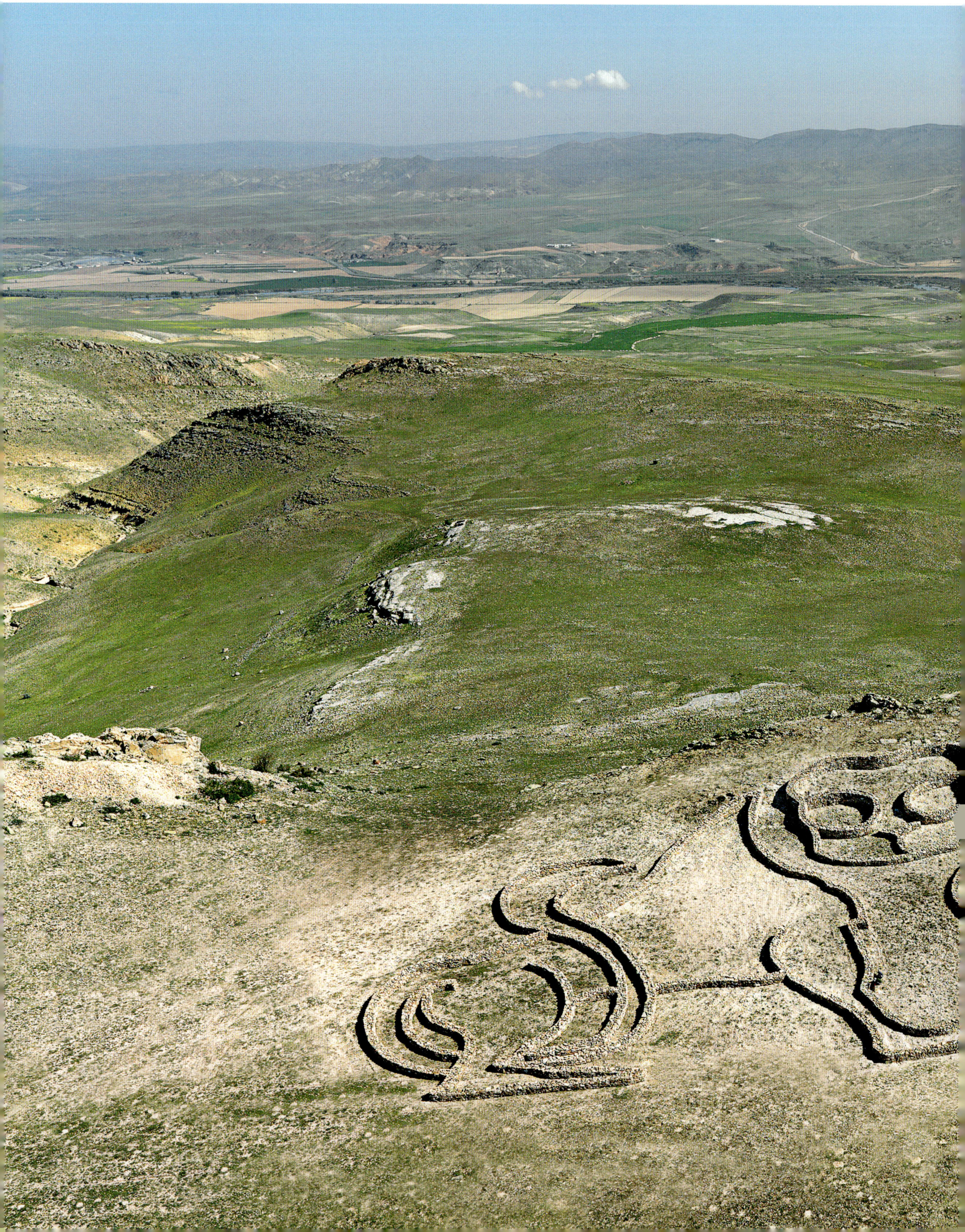

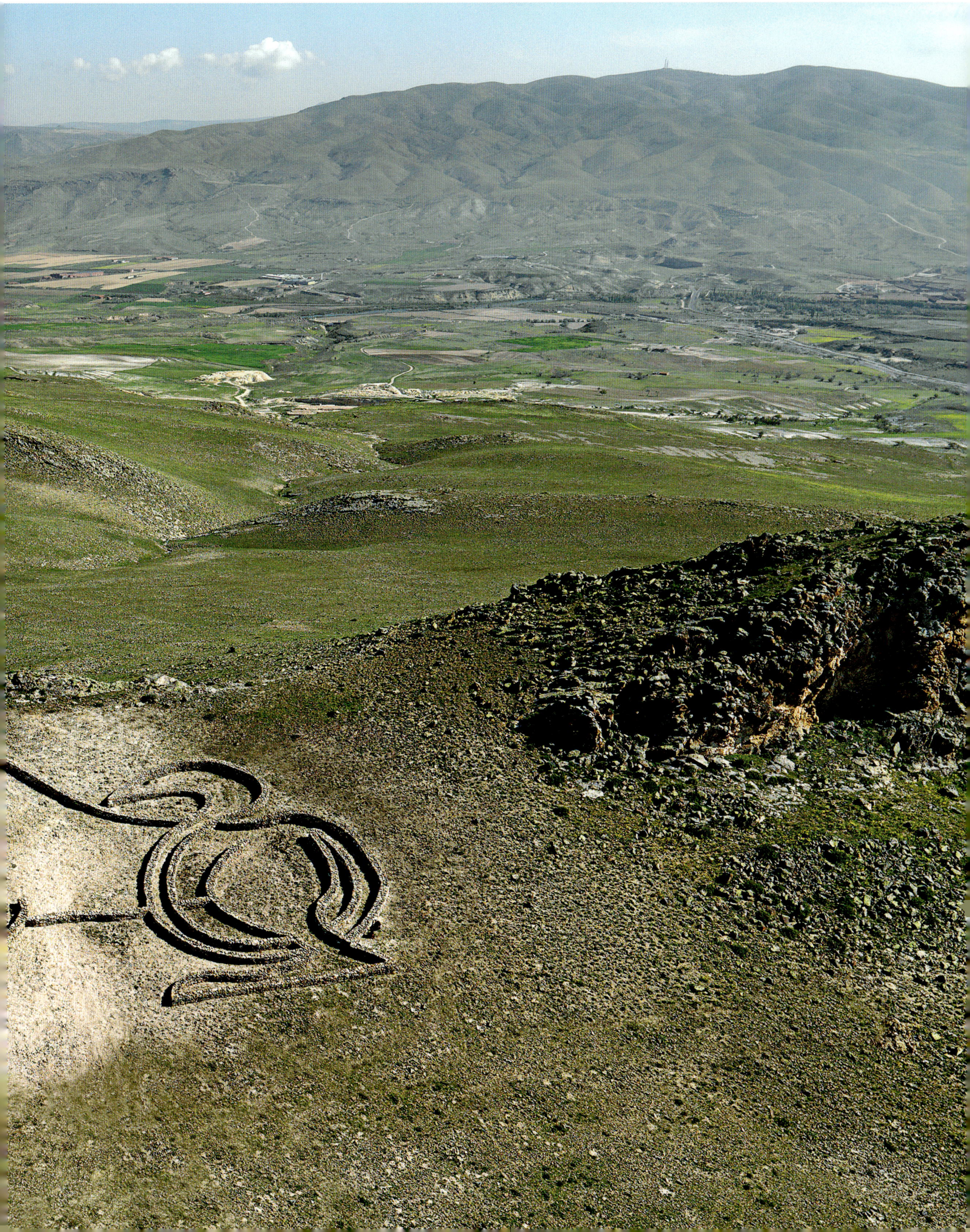

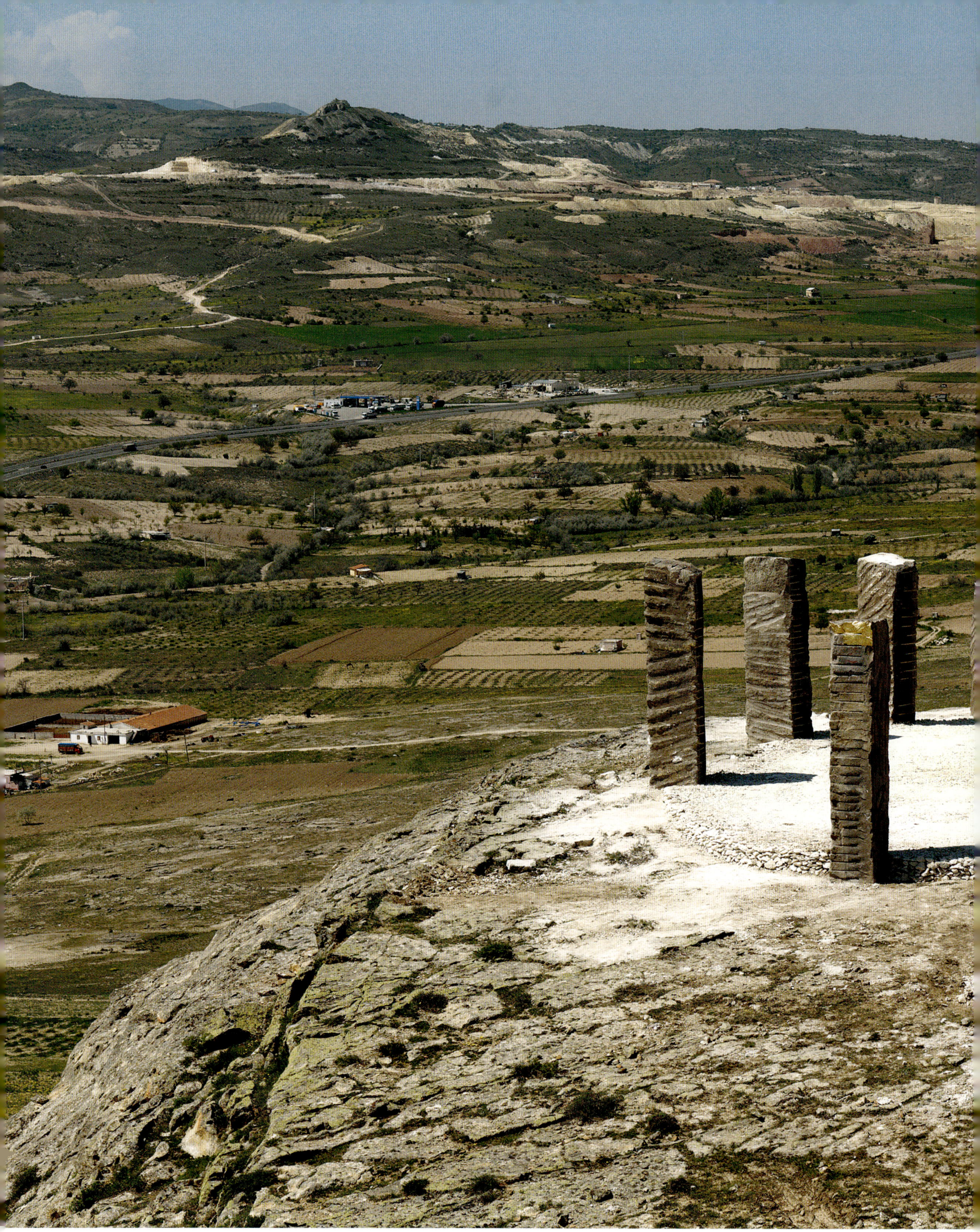

TIME AND SPACE 2009 / Basalt / 5.3 × 16 × 24 m (18 × 53 × 79 ft.)

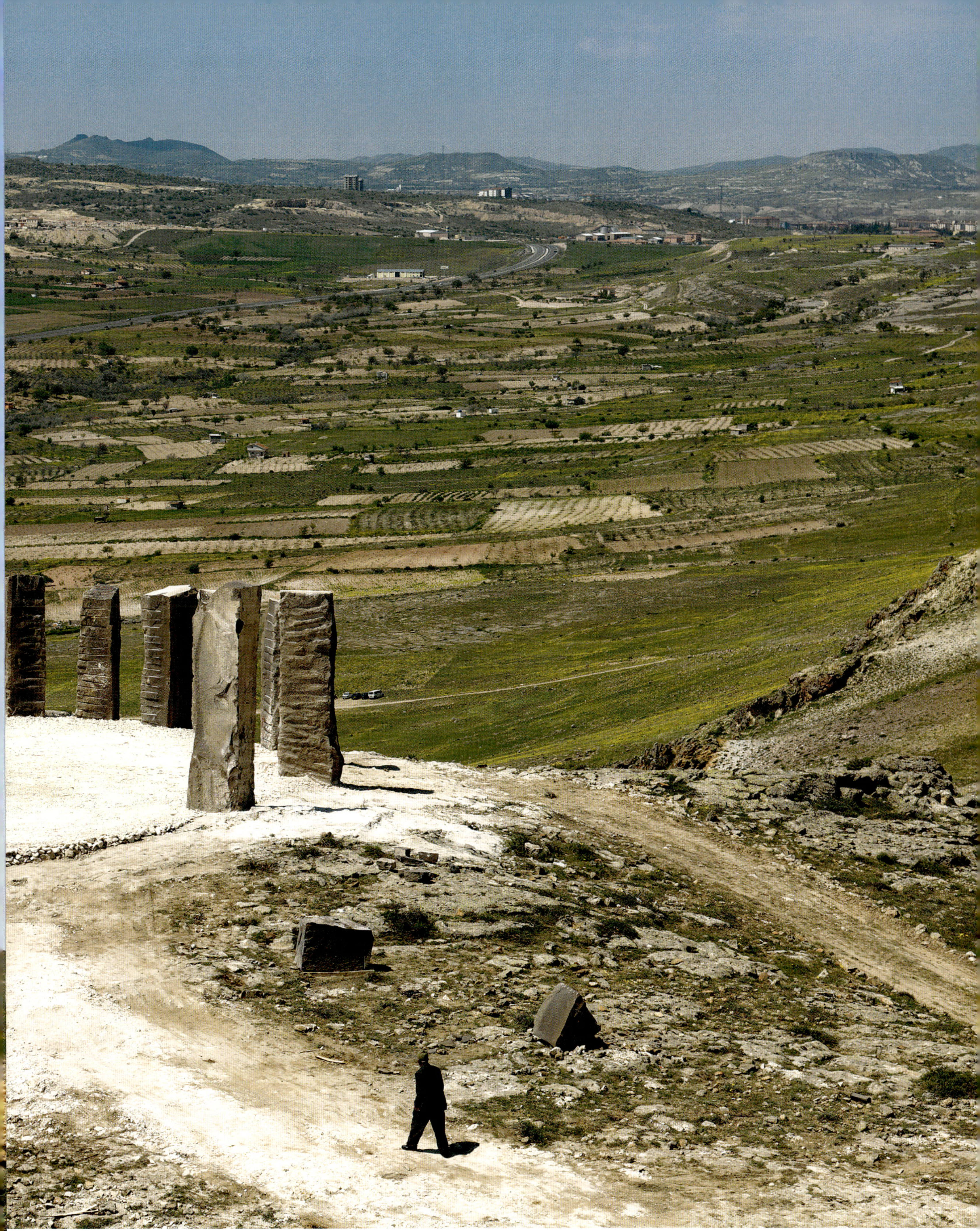

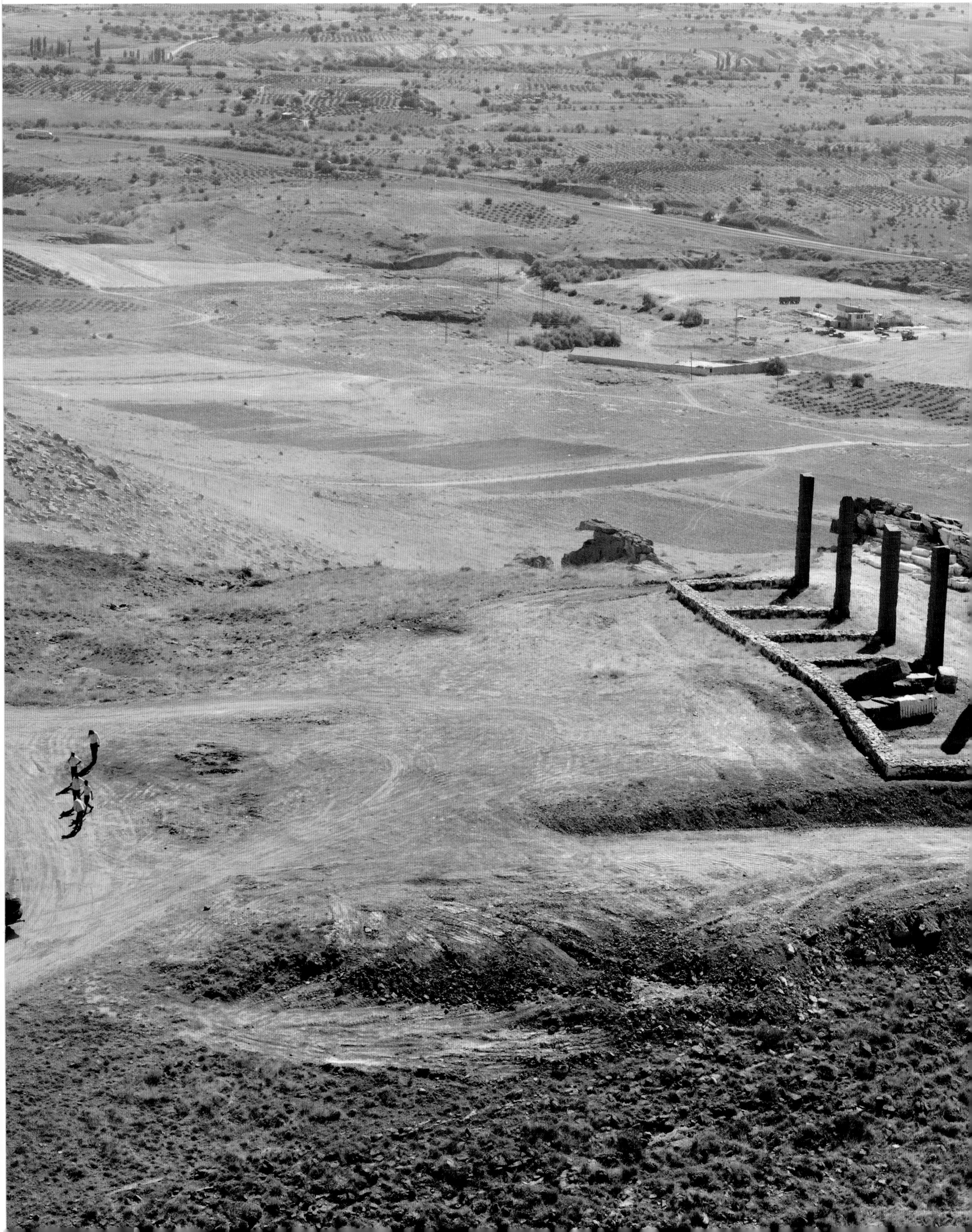

A DAY ON EARTH 2011 / Basalt and volcanic rock / 19.5 × 31.5 × 51 m (64 × 103 × 167 ft.)

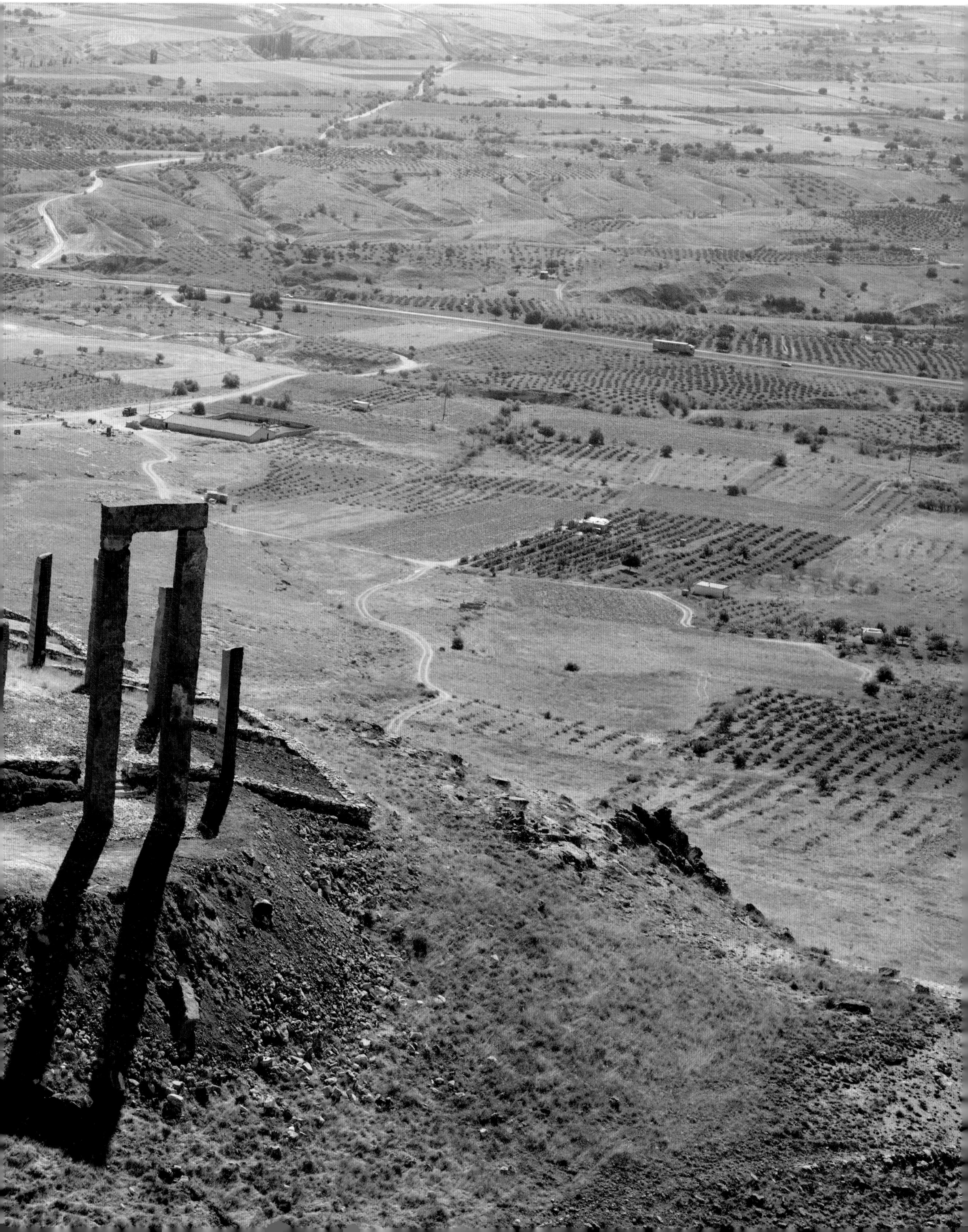

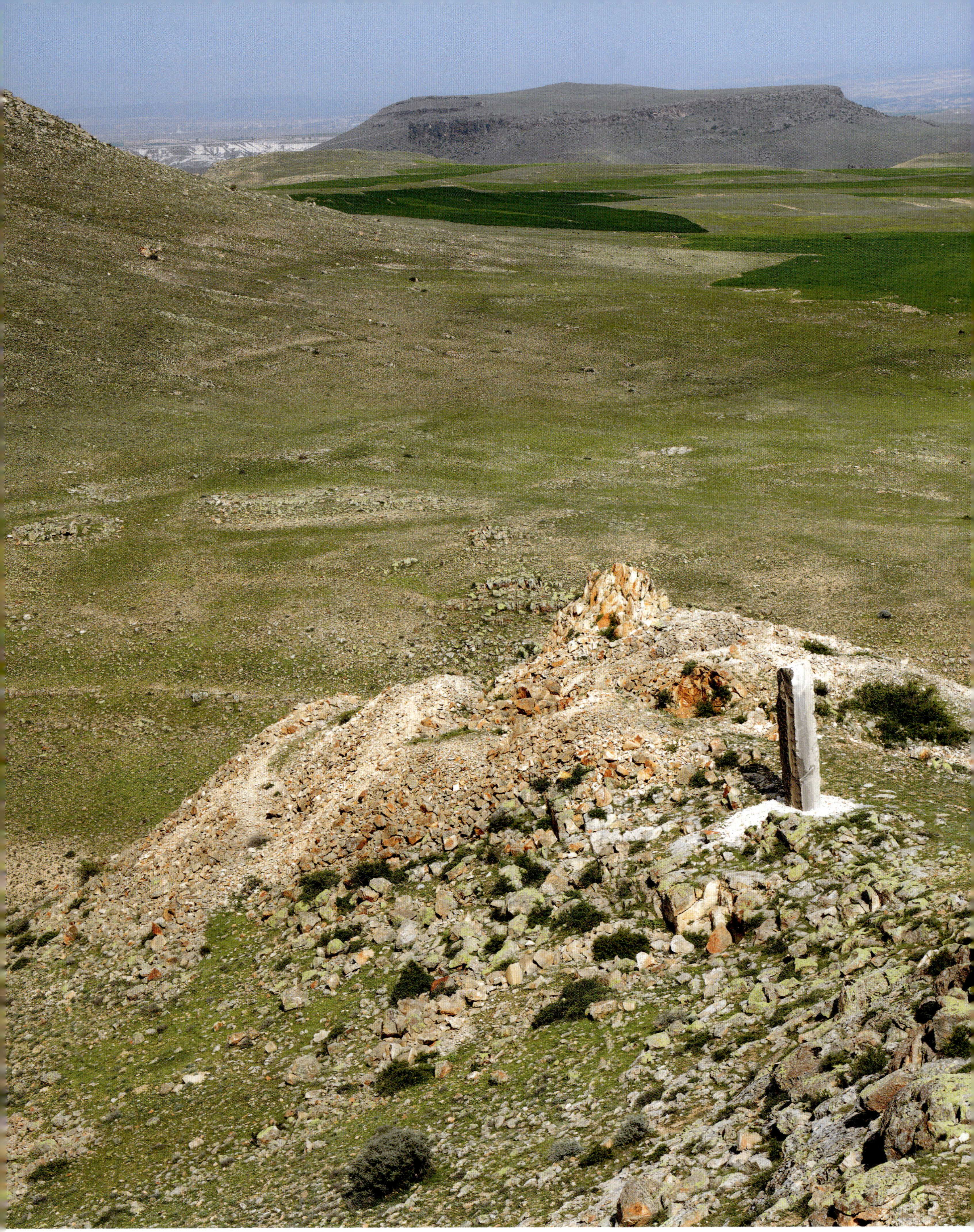

YESTERDAY TODAY TOMORROW 2009 / Basalt / 6 m (20 ft.)

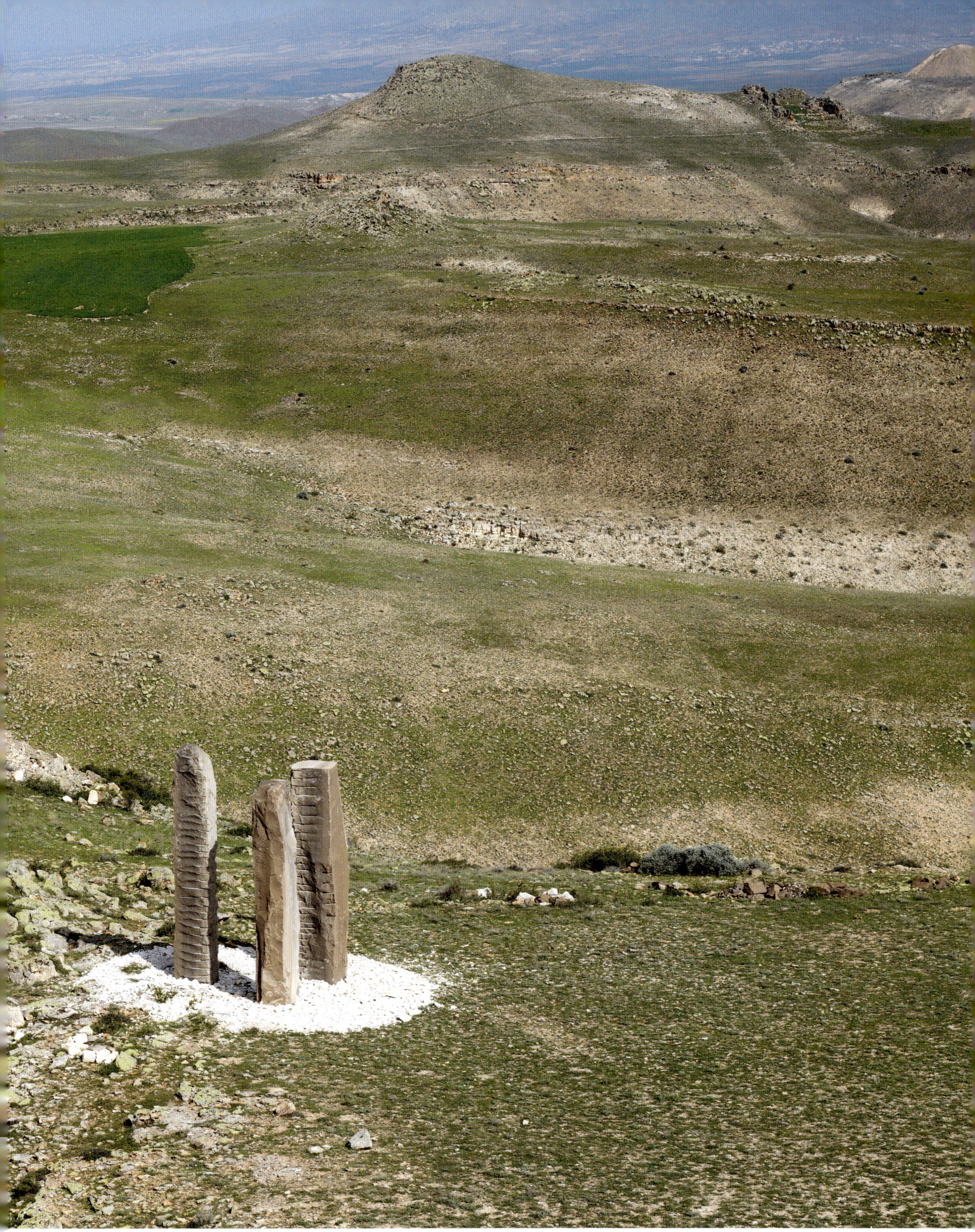

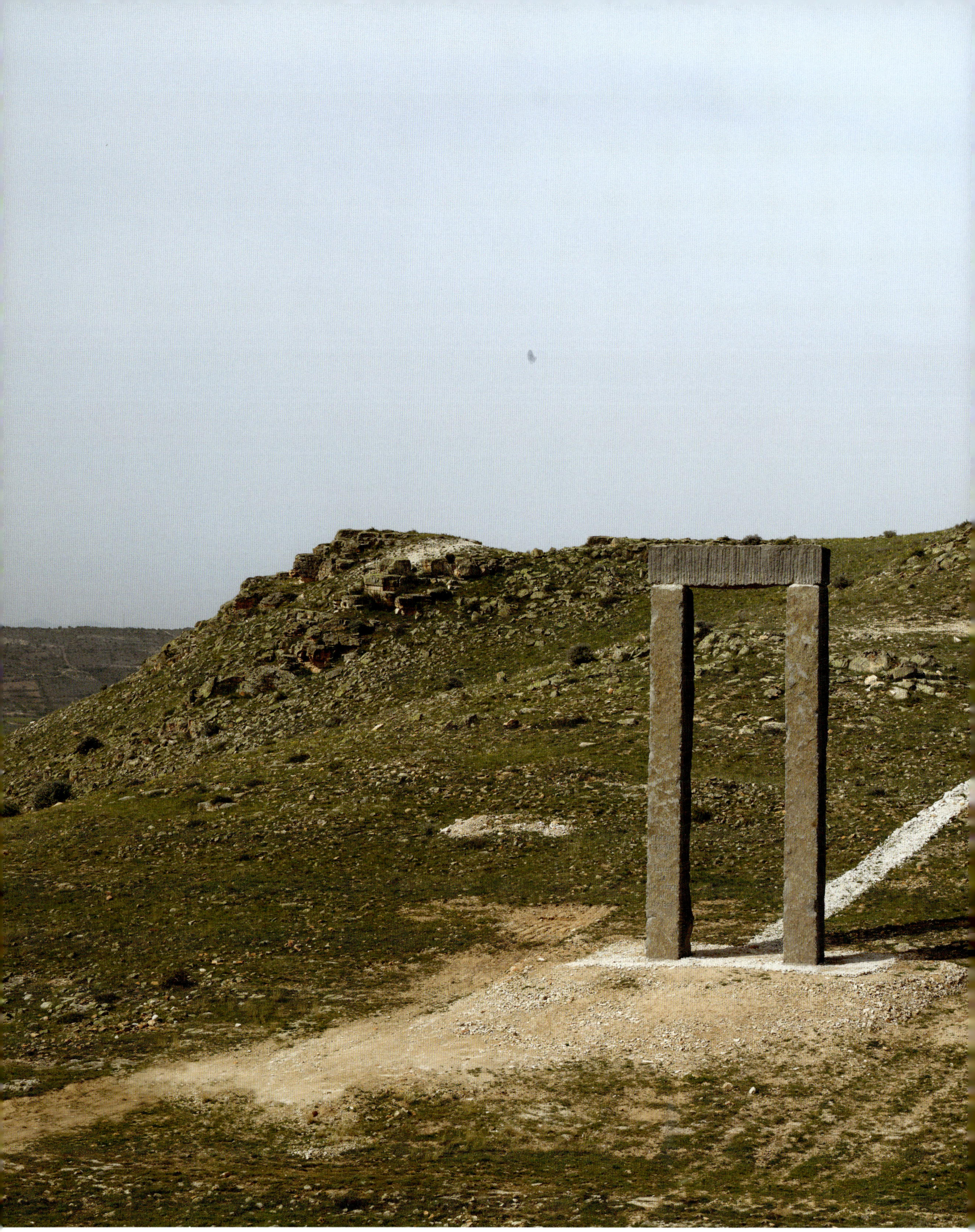

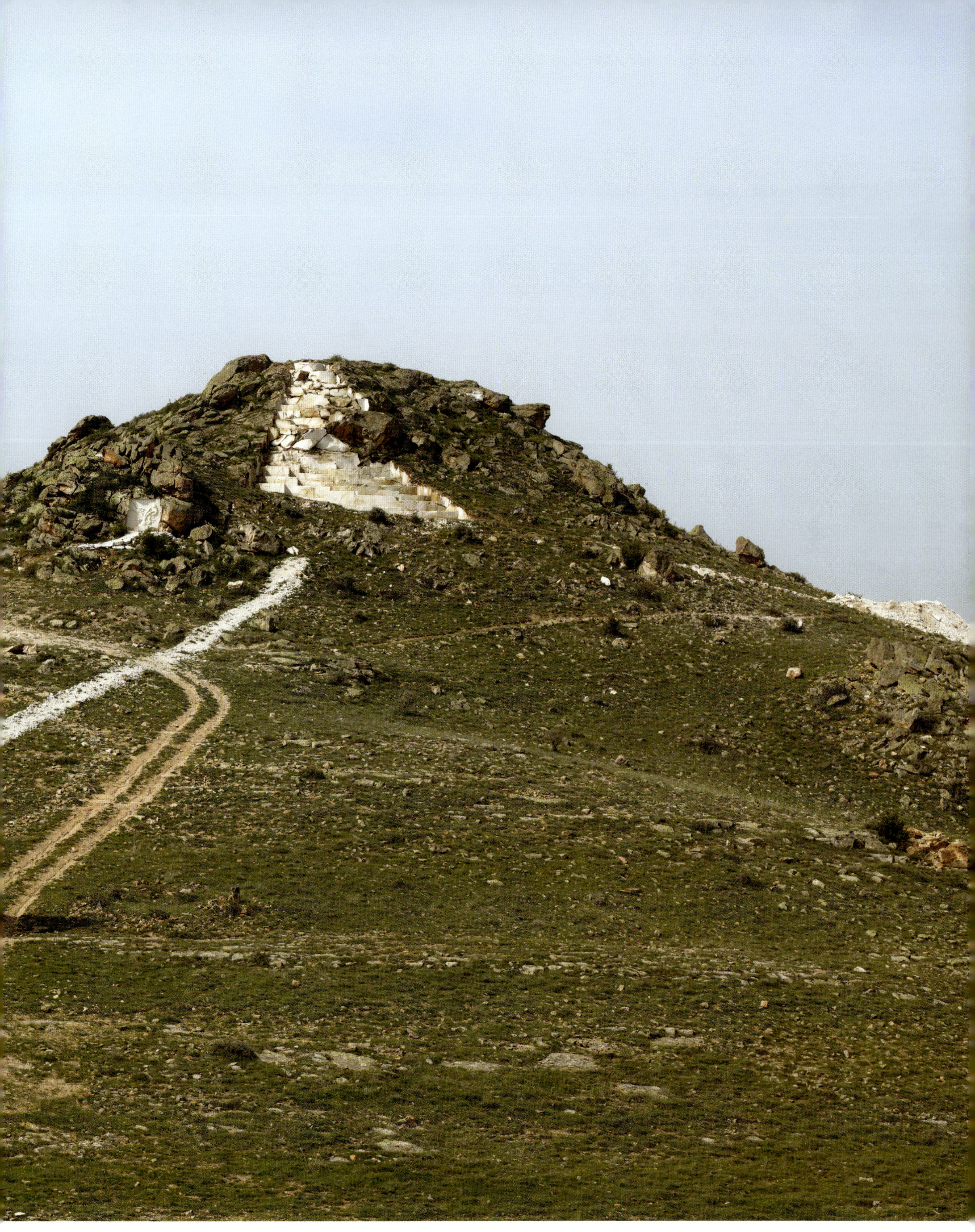

LISTEN 2010 / Basalt arch and amphitheater / 15 m (52 ft.)

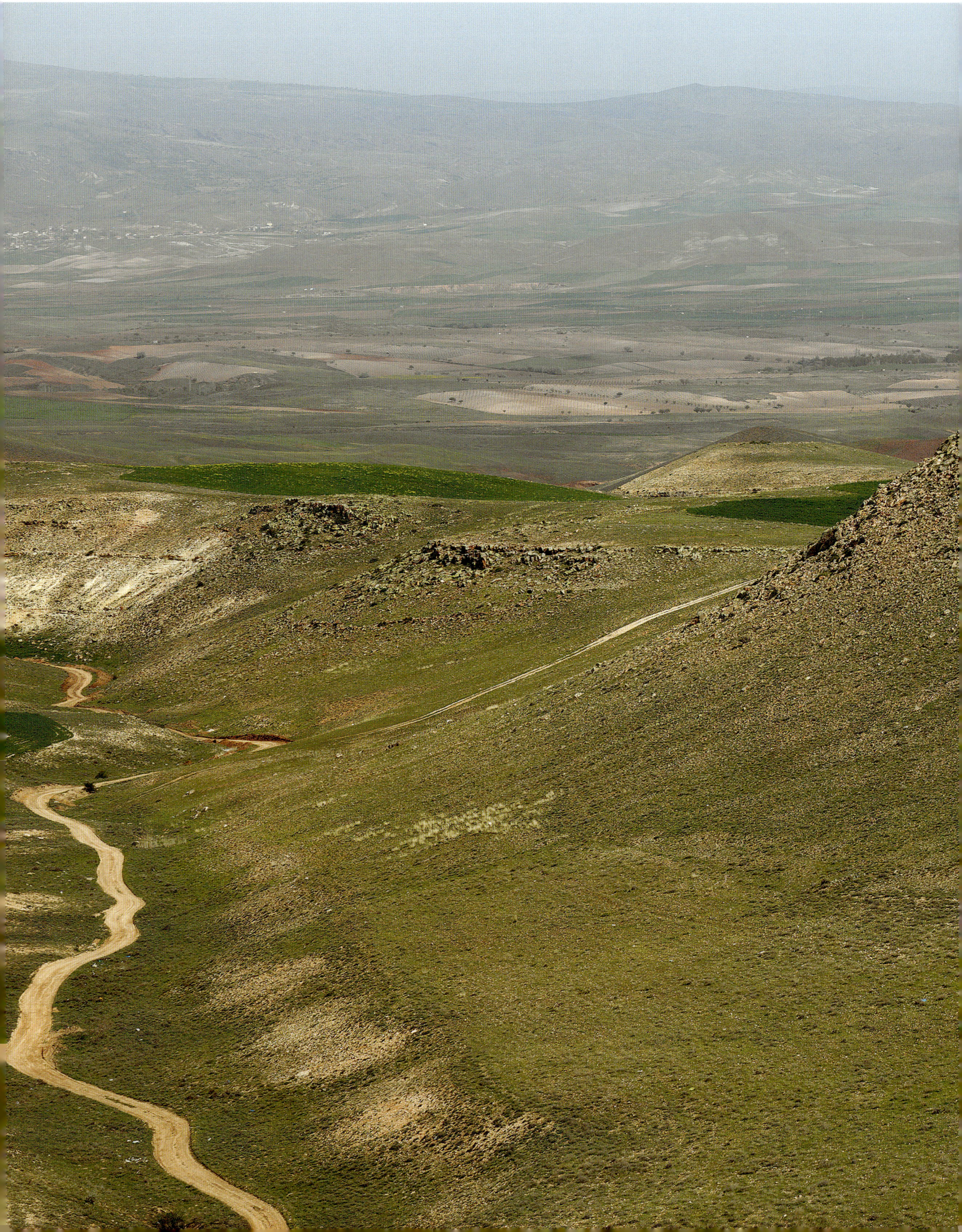

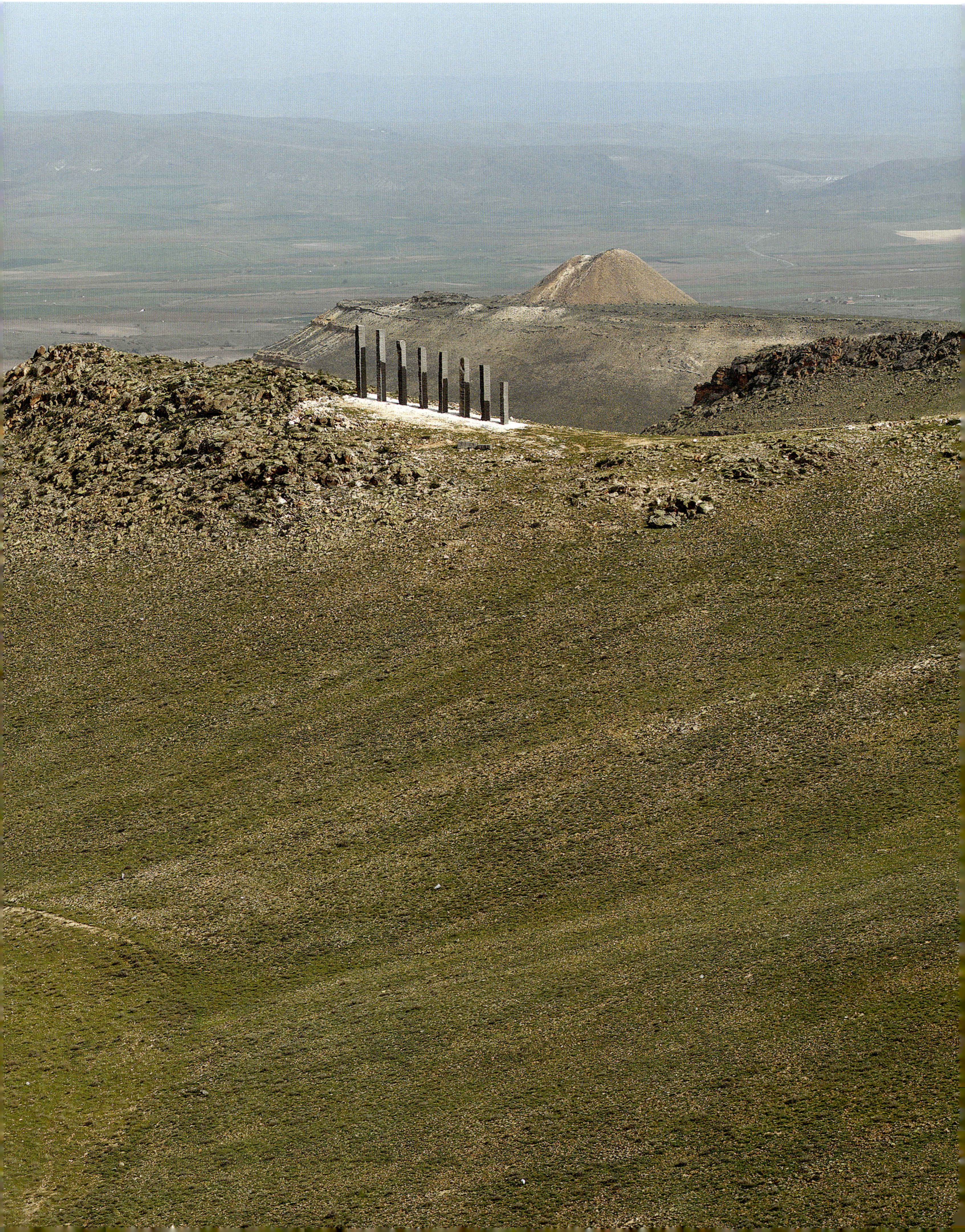

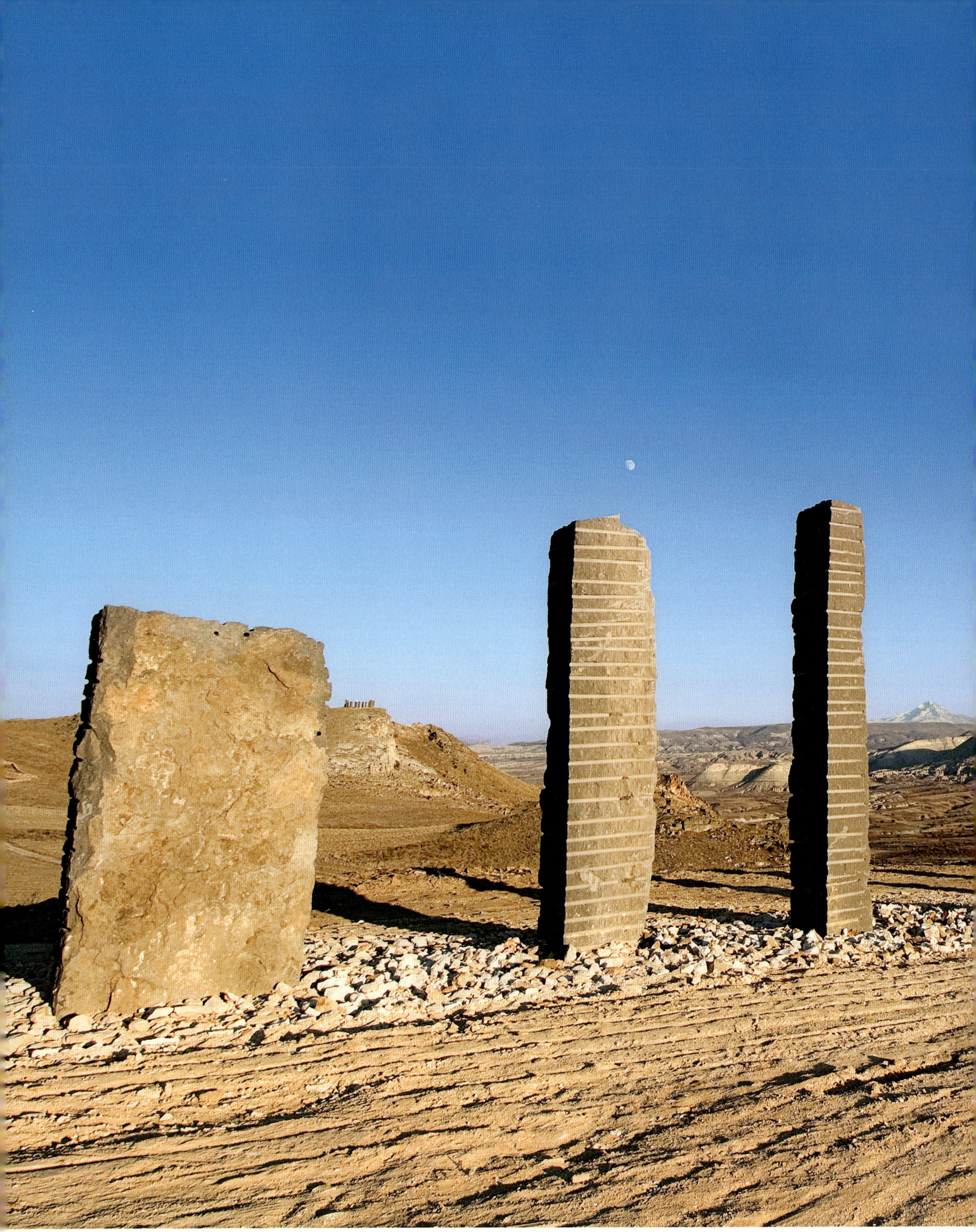

PRESENCE 2011 / Basalt / 9 × 22 × 38 m (30 × 72 × 125 ft.)

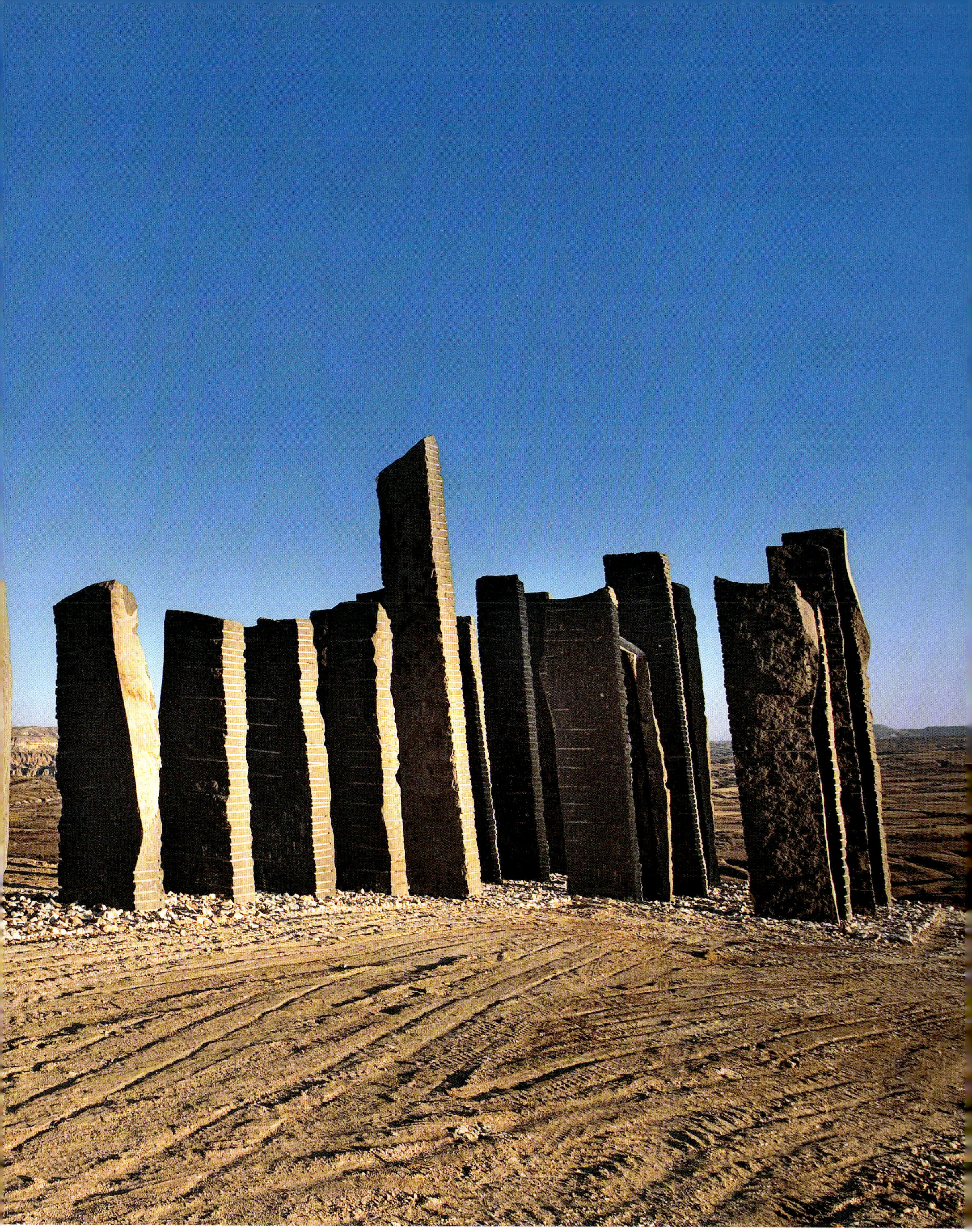

SACRED FIRE
NAMIB DESERT, NAMIBIA

The Himba in Namibia number as many as 50,000 and live virtually untouched by civilization in the Kaokoveld Desert, a nearly 50,000-square-kilometer (19,306-square-mile) inhospitable and rugged desert region in the north of the country. This nomadic people have no electricity, no technical equipment, and no running water. Their pride and joy is their cattle, their livelihood. They still wear scant loin-cloths and great quantities of jewelry which, like their complicated hairstyles, defines the status of each individual member of the tribe. They are known as the "red people" due to the women's use of *otjize*, a mixture of bright red ocher and butterfat from goat's milk that they rub on their bodies and hair several times a day. It serves both as beauty makeup as well as protection against insects, dryness, and heat.

In Himba culture, fire has major importance: it means life. An eternal sacred fire burns in front of the chief's hut. At night, the glowing ash is taken into the hut and used the next morning to rekindle the fire. The Himba use this sacred fire to communicate with their ancestors and with their god, Mukuru.

The vibrant culture of the Himba people inspired Andrew Rogers to build a geoglyph using the sacred fire as the symbol of the cycle of life. The design of the artwork, to be built by village inhabitants, was selected by the tribal elders. As Rogers explained: "It is a traditional shape that we are creating a fire in. It is a fire that you see in every village. It is a sacred fire and a lot of community activity is centered around this fire—like rituals related to birth, death, circumcision, marriage. So it's a very central focus and it's seen as a connection with two generations of ancestors."

Rogers selected an abandoned Himba village, a kraal in Kunene in the northwestern-most region of the country, as the site for *Sacred Fire*. The region is famous for its desolate desert landscapes with impressive mountain ranges such as the Giraffenberge or the Hartmannberge. "The reason we chose this area is so we don't cause any disturbance to the land that

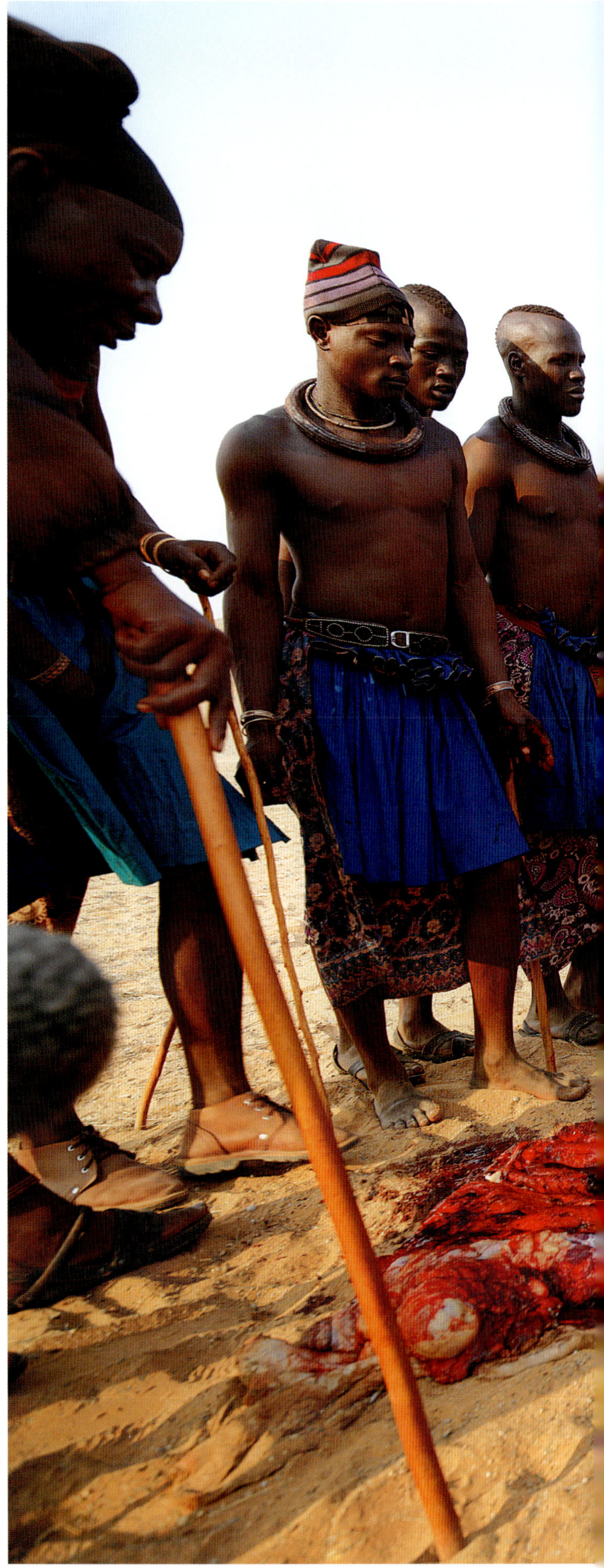

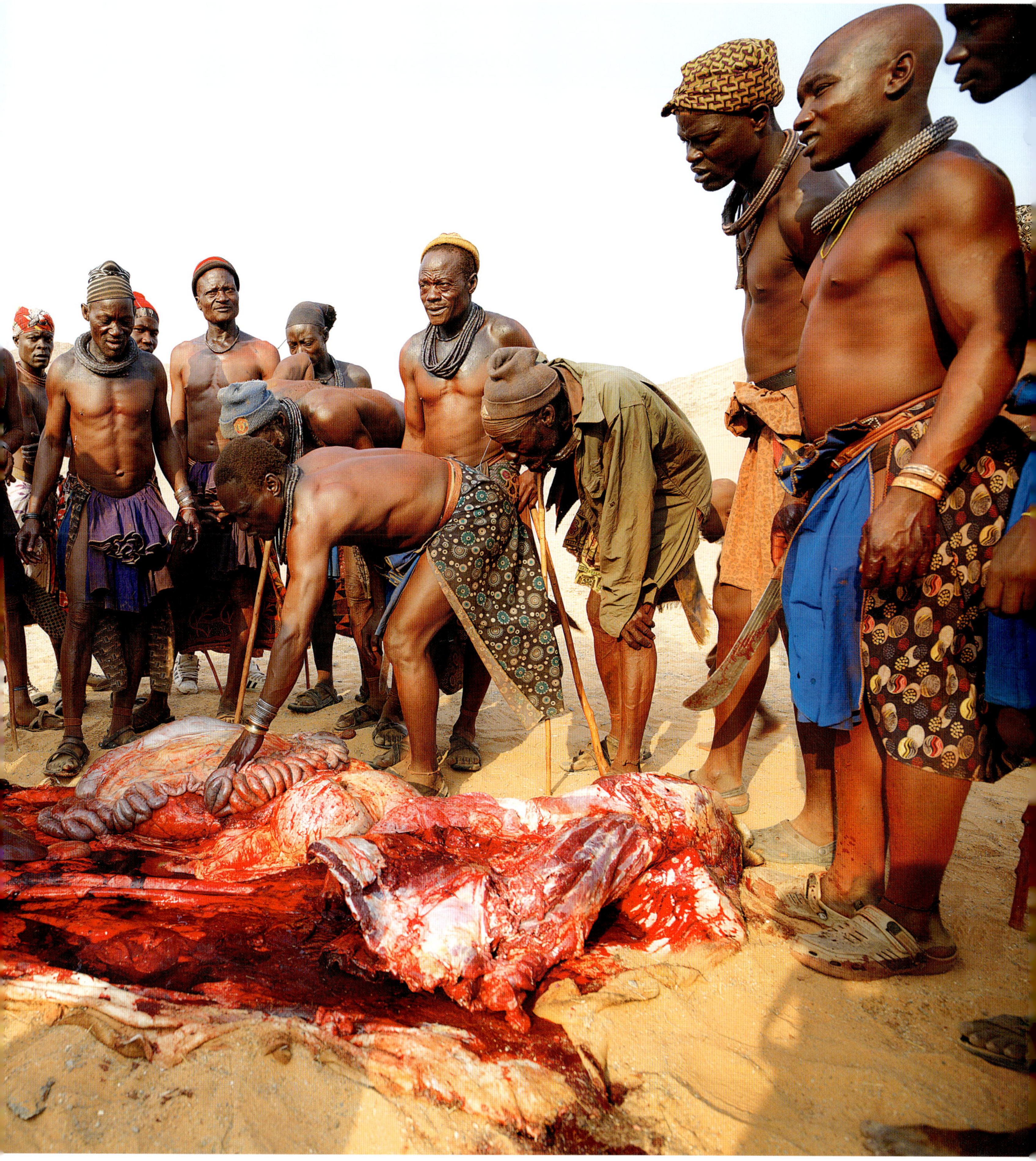

hasn't already been disturbed," recalled Rogers. It was against this backdrop that he laid out the work of art on flat sands—a large circle of stones comprised of eight smaller, filled circles with an overall diameter of 14 meters (46 feet). *Sacred Fire,* the symbol of the sacred fire of the Himba, the symbol of life. Each circle represents a stone in the sacred fire.

The art project was unusual in every respect, for the building team consisted of eighty-five Himba from the neighboring areas. The nomadic people had never before built anything with stones. The walls of their huts are made from a mixture of cow dung, earth, and water; the roof is made of straw. This was also the first time that men and women worked together, including representatives of all generations—from grandson to grandfather, and even pregnant women. For Rogers, the women and the children who accompanied their mothers during work became more and more important as vital "sparks of life" in many of his *Rhythms of Life* projects.

Sacred Fire also posed new challenges to the artist. It was difficult at first to find enough Himba to build the geoglyphs. He had to gain the approval of the tribal elders for his project, and he insisted on uniform wages for men and women. It was repeatedly necessary to explain every step of the work to them, and the work would slow down in the battle against heat and dryness. When the stone circles were nearly finished and the Himba recognized the symbol of the sacred fire, a serious discussion began over the entrance to the structure. Ritual required that it be arranged in such a way that it captures the sunlight in the morning. Rogers again consulted the elders. The solution consisted of reducing the diameter of one of the circles of stone and raising its height. This resulted in the necessary intermediate space for the incidence of light at sunrise. Finally, in keeping with tradition, the Himba placed branches in front of the entrance as a ready source of fuel and referencing the sacred fire symbol and the fire's symbolic awakening.

Thus for the Himba, what was initially a mysterious and abstract undertaking became a clearly identifiable, meaningful structure that made them proud. The most important tribal elders performed a consecration ceremony with fresh leaves and water for the purpose of connecting with their ancestors. As part of the ceremony the chief then asked the ancestors questions which were answered in chorus by the elders as their ancestors' representatives. Following this ritual, a final question was posed to the world of ancestors. Because the Himba are connected with the past by way of their herds of cattle, which they acquire from their ancestors, a cow was chased through the desert and slaughtered; bad veins had to be searched for in the entrails as signs of possible hardship in connection with the artwork. It was not until everything was declared all right that everyone—from the very old to children—could dance and celebrate to the vibrant and rhythmic clapping of the festive congregation.

SACRED FIRE, satellite image taken 770 km (480 miles) above the earth

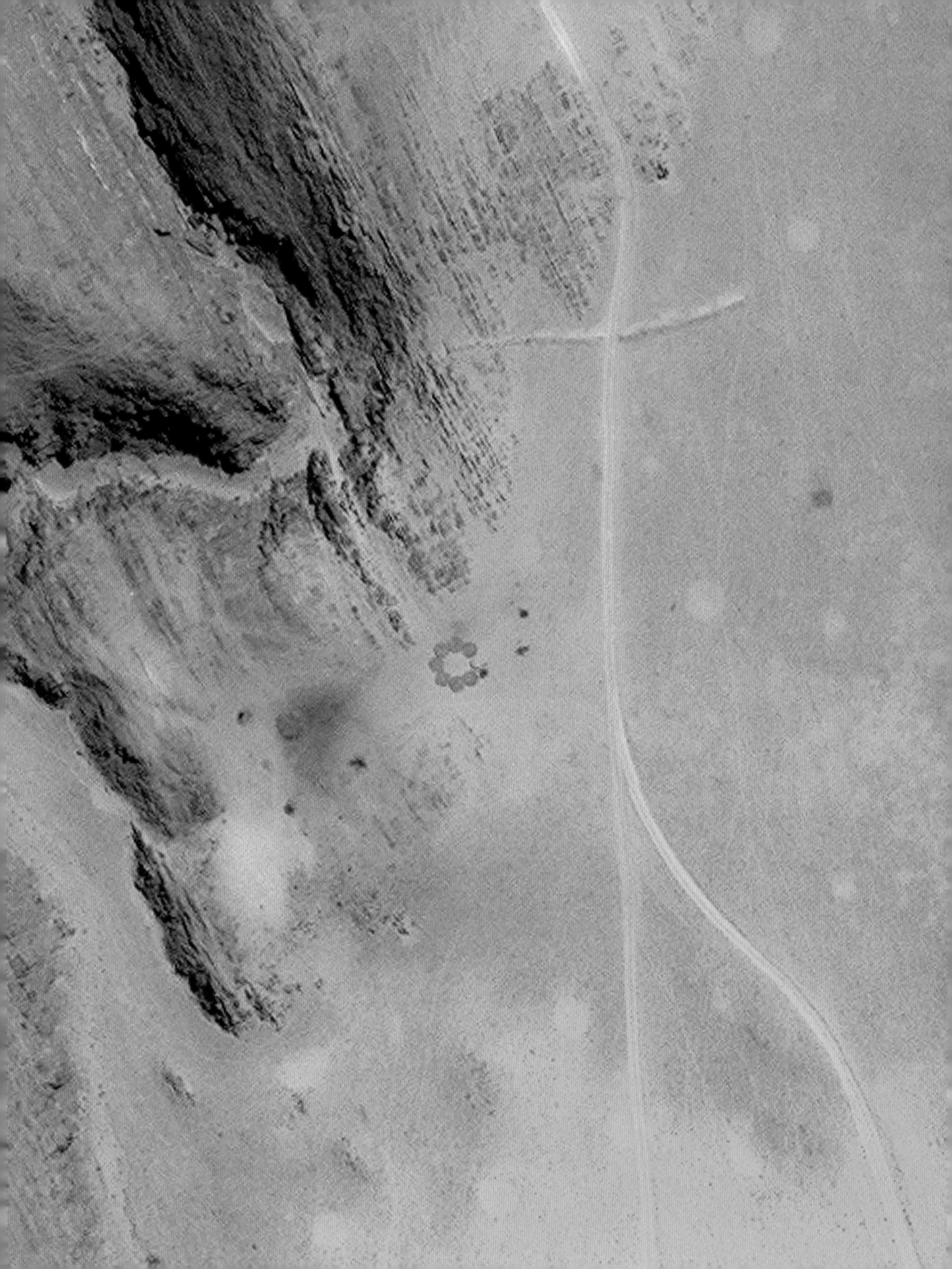

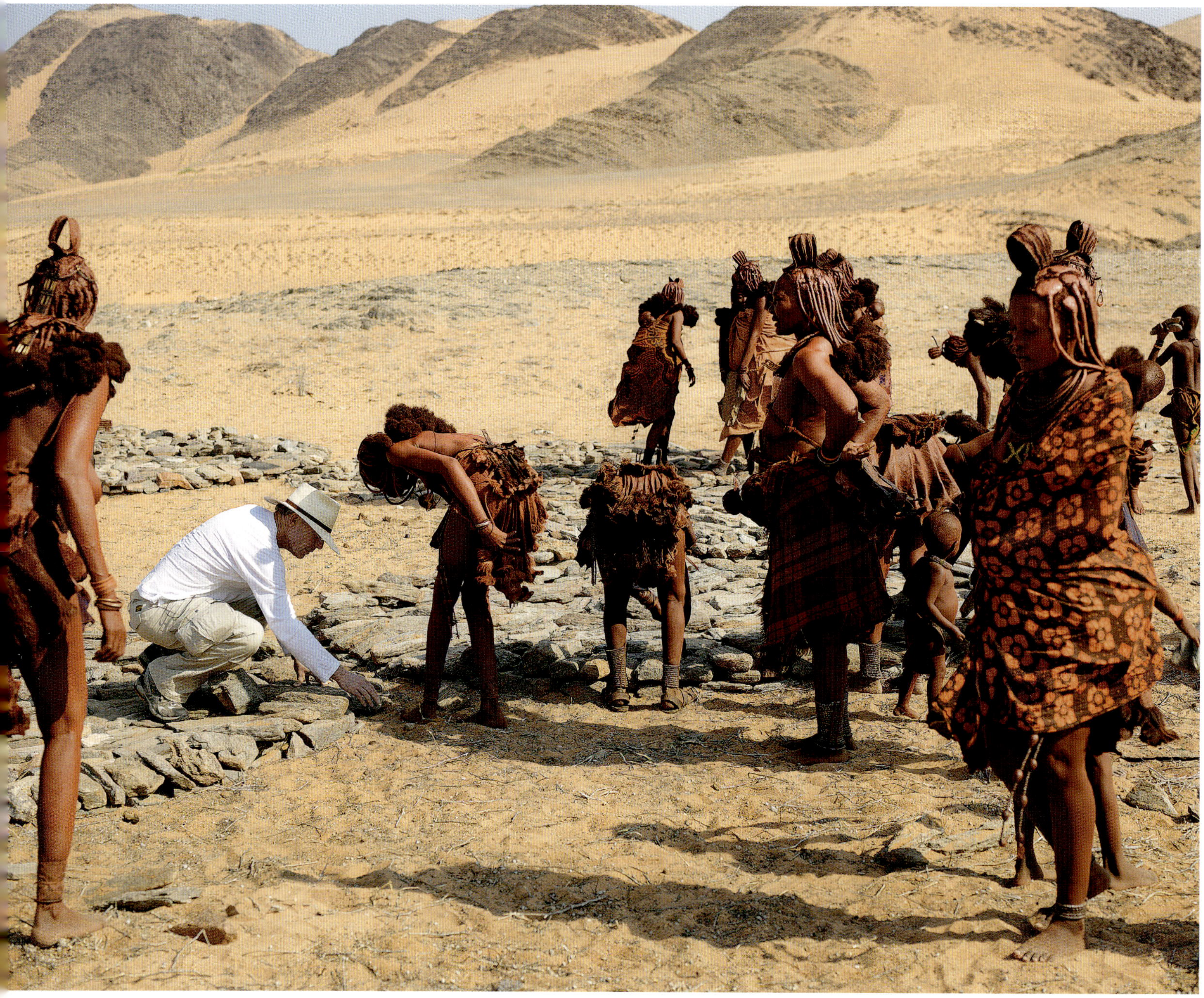

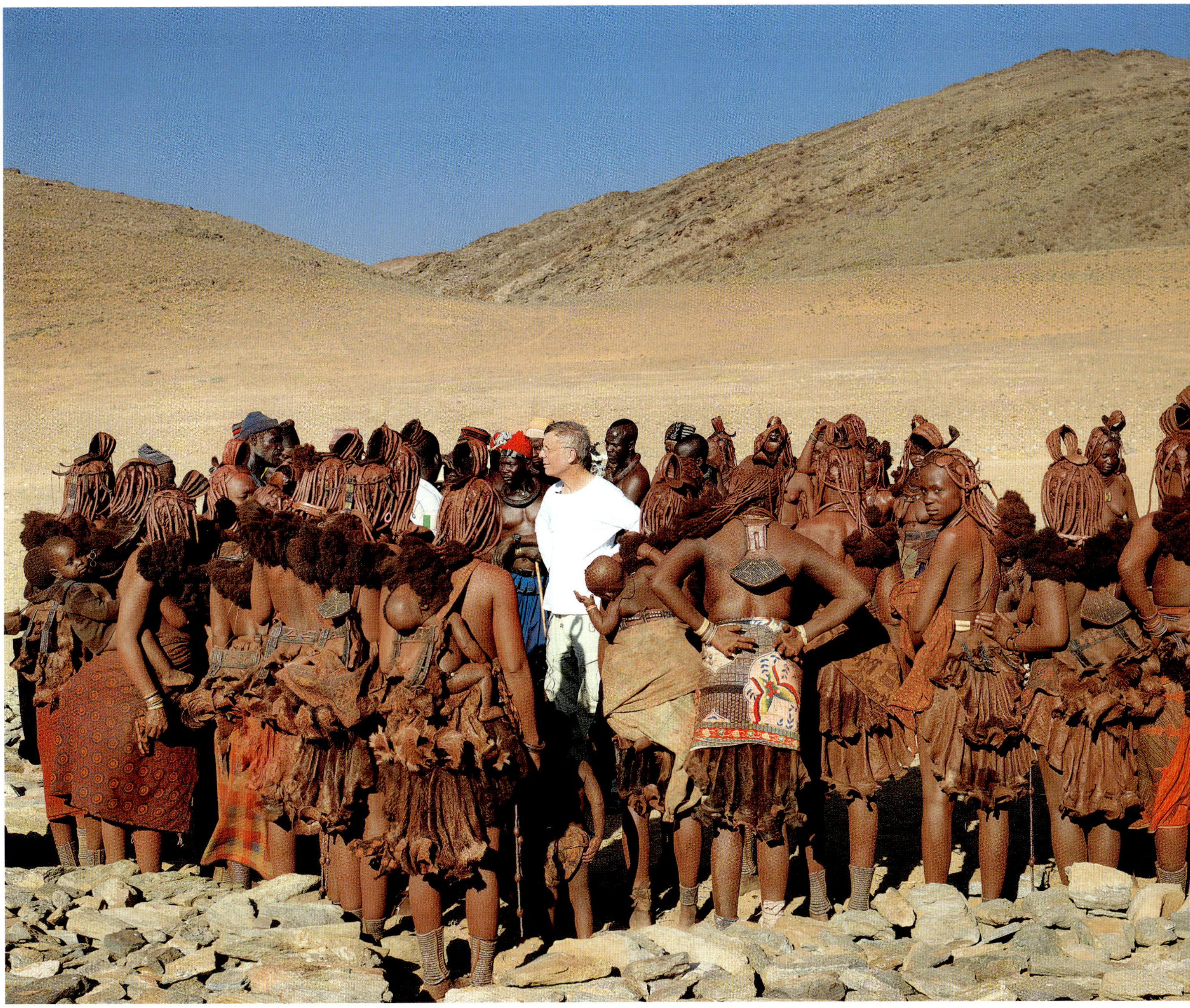

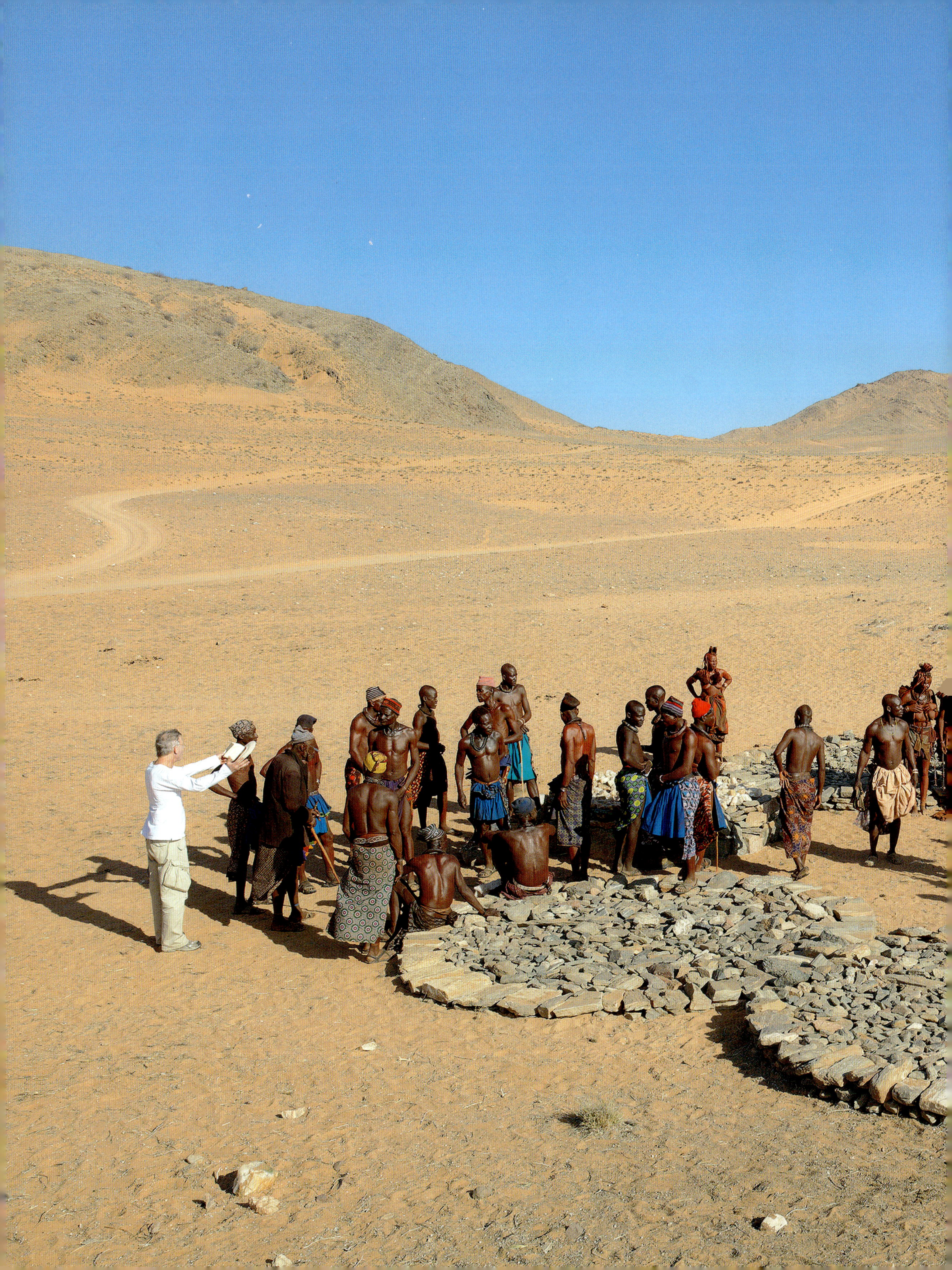

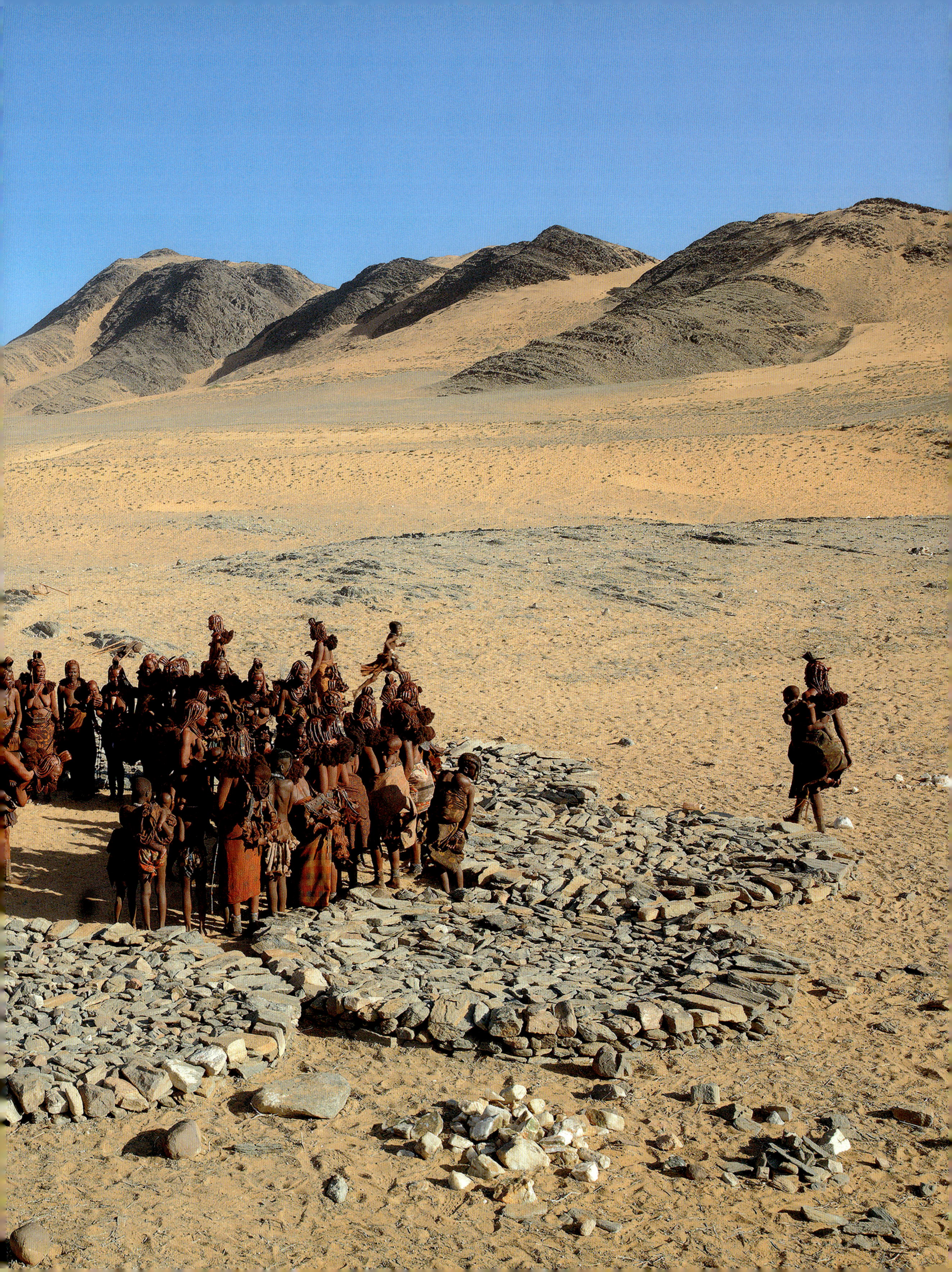

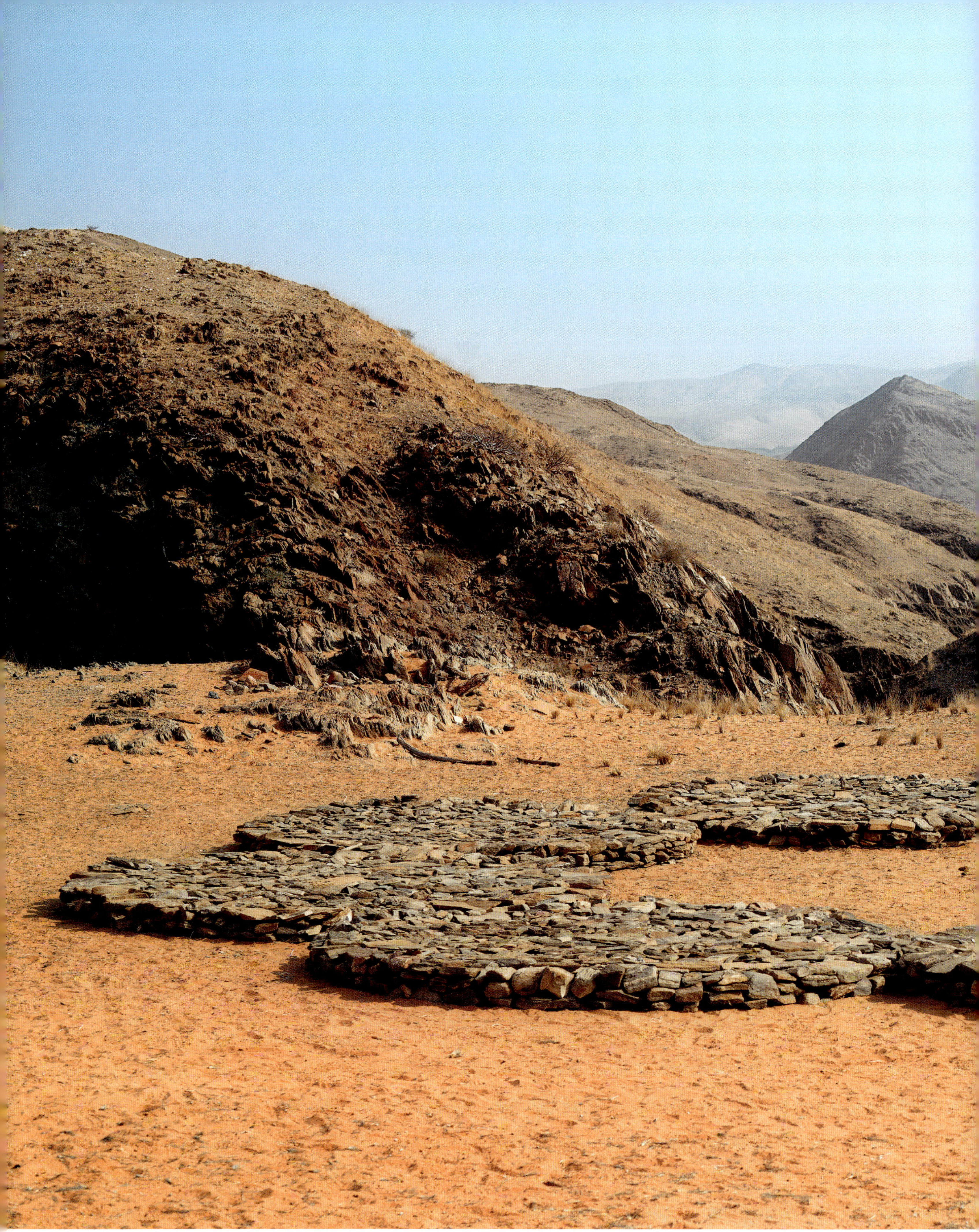

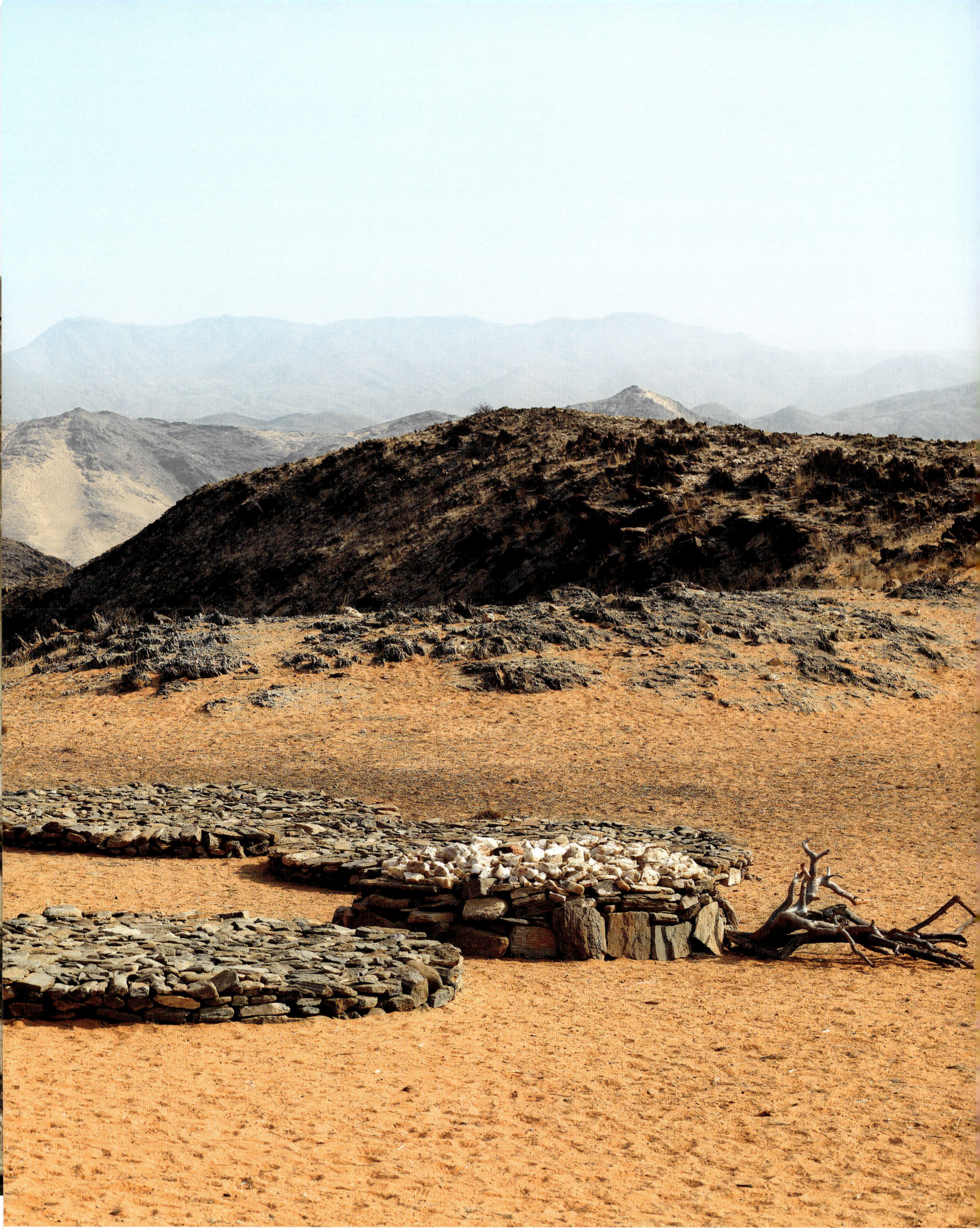

SACRED FIRE 2012 / Stone / 14 m (46 ft.) diameter

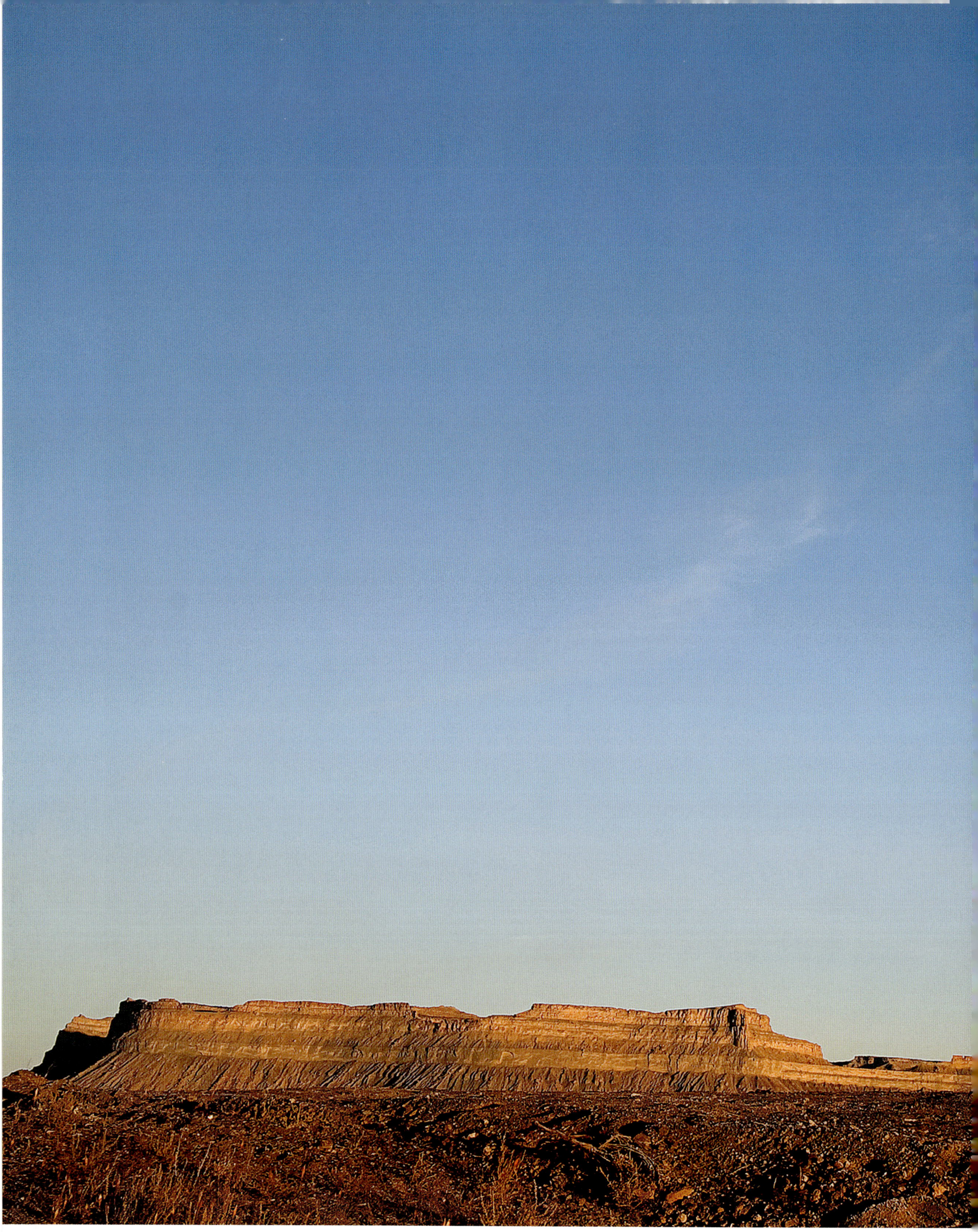

RATIO 2010 / Concrete / 13.5 × 13 × 2m (44 × 42 × 6.6 ft.), commissioned by Herbert Steiner

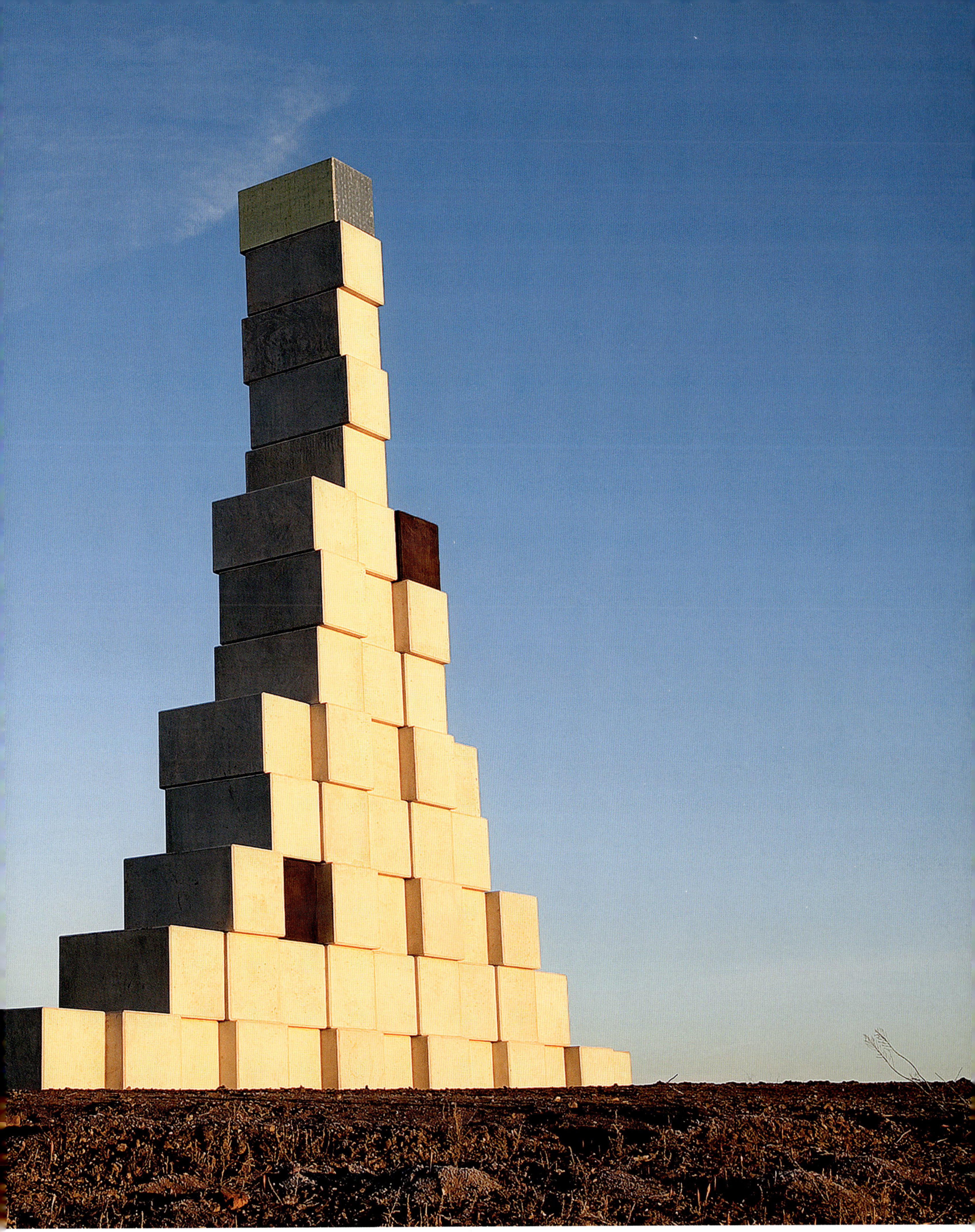

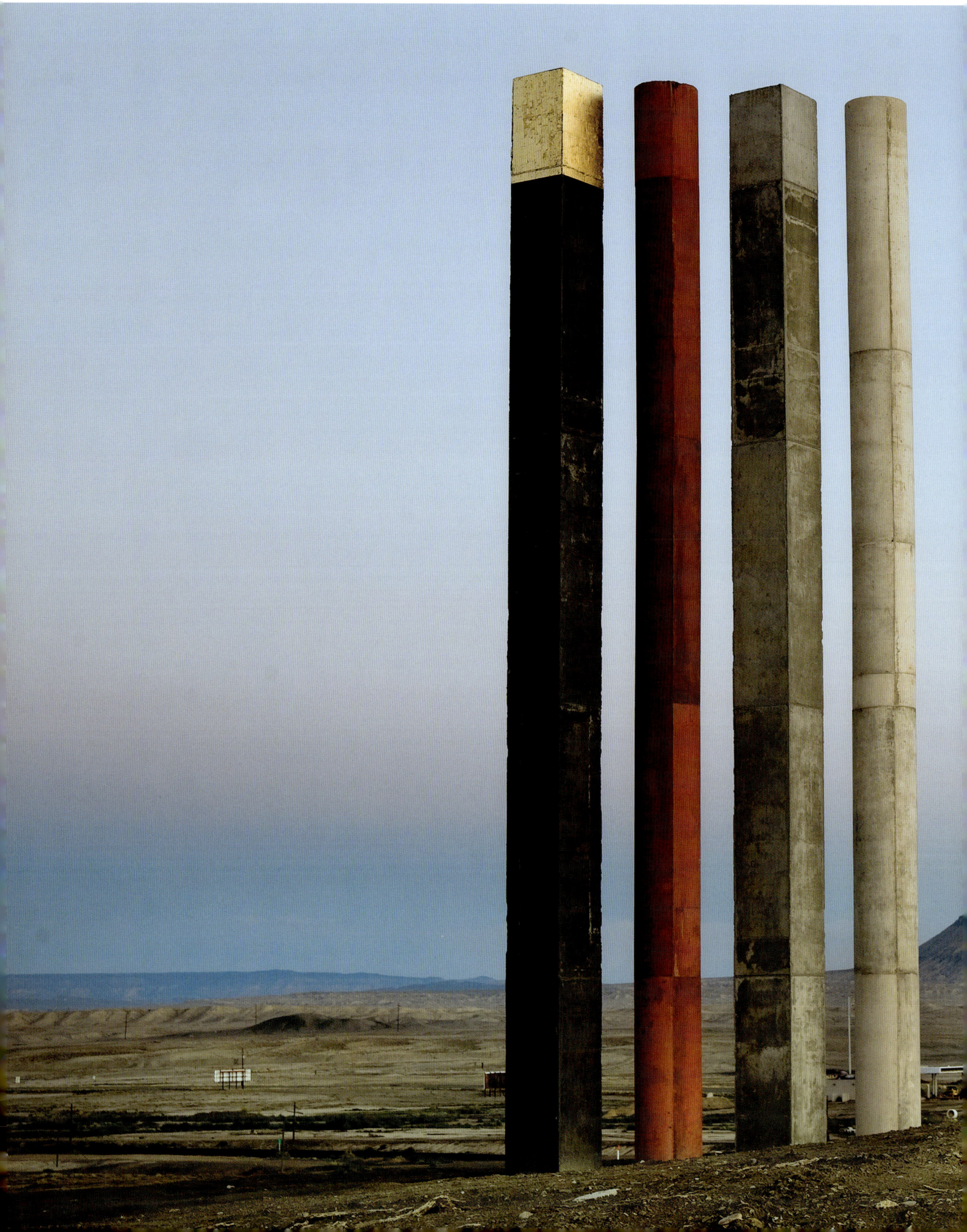

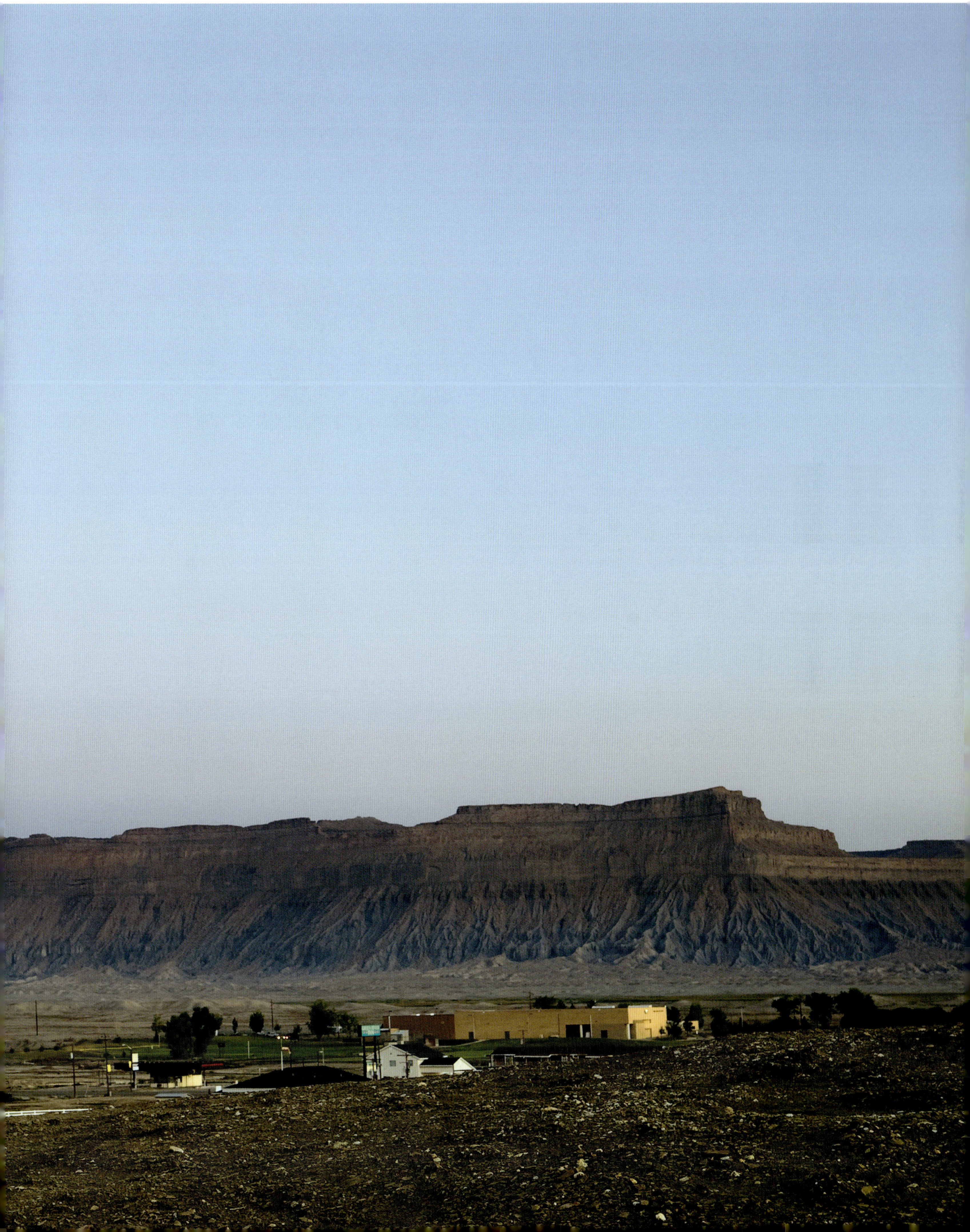

WEST COAST, IBIZA, SPAIN
(FURTHER PROJECT)

***TIME AND SPACE THE SPEED OF LIGHT* (2014)**

This installation of thirteen tall basalt columns is situated on a sheer cliff with a spectacular view of the open sea on the western side of the Balearic island of Ibiza. The monumental work of art is laid out similar to an installation that Rogers had built on the barren hills in Cappadocia, Turkey, entitled *Time and Space*. There the installation is one of thirteen gigantic land art sculptures that comprise an entire sculpture park which is part of his global *Rhythms of Life* project. The project in Spain also began in Cappadocia. The effort required to create this connection between Cappadocia and Ibiza in terms of both form and content was enormous. The basalt columns weighing several metric tons that Rogers used in Ibiza came from the same quarry as the columns in the Turkish installation. Together with their equally massive bases, each weighing up to 12.5 metric tons, they had to be finely honed in line with the artist's precisely defined dimensions. Sophisticated logistics were required for the packing and transportation of this 420-metric-ton load in giant containers. Following a 4,400-kilometer (2,700-mile) journey via truck and a dedicated cargo ship, the columns finally arrived on Ibiza. The transportation and above all the erection of the columns were accompanied by the constant worry that they might break. "The skill and great care displayed by the crane operators whilst erecting each of the columns and mounting them into the carved bases was a wondrous sight," recalled the artist, obviously relieved.

As was the case with *Time and Space* in Cappadocia, the columns were arranged according to the Fibonacci sequence. The basalt steles are organized in an ellipse. "It is a vision of time and space and the interconnectedness of humanity," explains Rogers. The Fibonacci sequence is again demonstrated in both the spacing between the columns and the respective column heights. However, in Ibiza the diameter of the ellipse on which the columns are arranged is larger than in Turkey. The tallest column is in the middle of the oval. It is a massive 10 meters (32.8 feet) in height and weighs 19.5 metric tons. The sides of the top of the column were covered with 23-karat gold leaf. The installation is specifically arranged in such a way that on the winter solstice the light of the setting sun aligns with the center column. The gold leaf reflects the sun's rays, radiating them almost magically over the land and the sea all the way to the magnetic fields of the island of Es Vedra. There is no better place to watch this special spectacle of nature than from beside the Ceremonial Bowl and the sign of the Speed of Light; a large basalt form comprised of five hewn parts that when combined constitute the letter C—the mathematical symbol for the speed of light (C = wavelength × frequency). Rogers deliberately placed this C-shaped rock bench formation between the columns, the Ceremonial Bowl and the edge of the cliff so that viewers can take a seat there. This is an ideal site to marvel, contemplate, and reflect on the connection between the path of the sun and the cycle of life, the necessary elements of our existence.

TIME AND SPACE THE SPEED OF LIGHT, satellite image taken 770 km (480 miles) above the earth

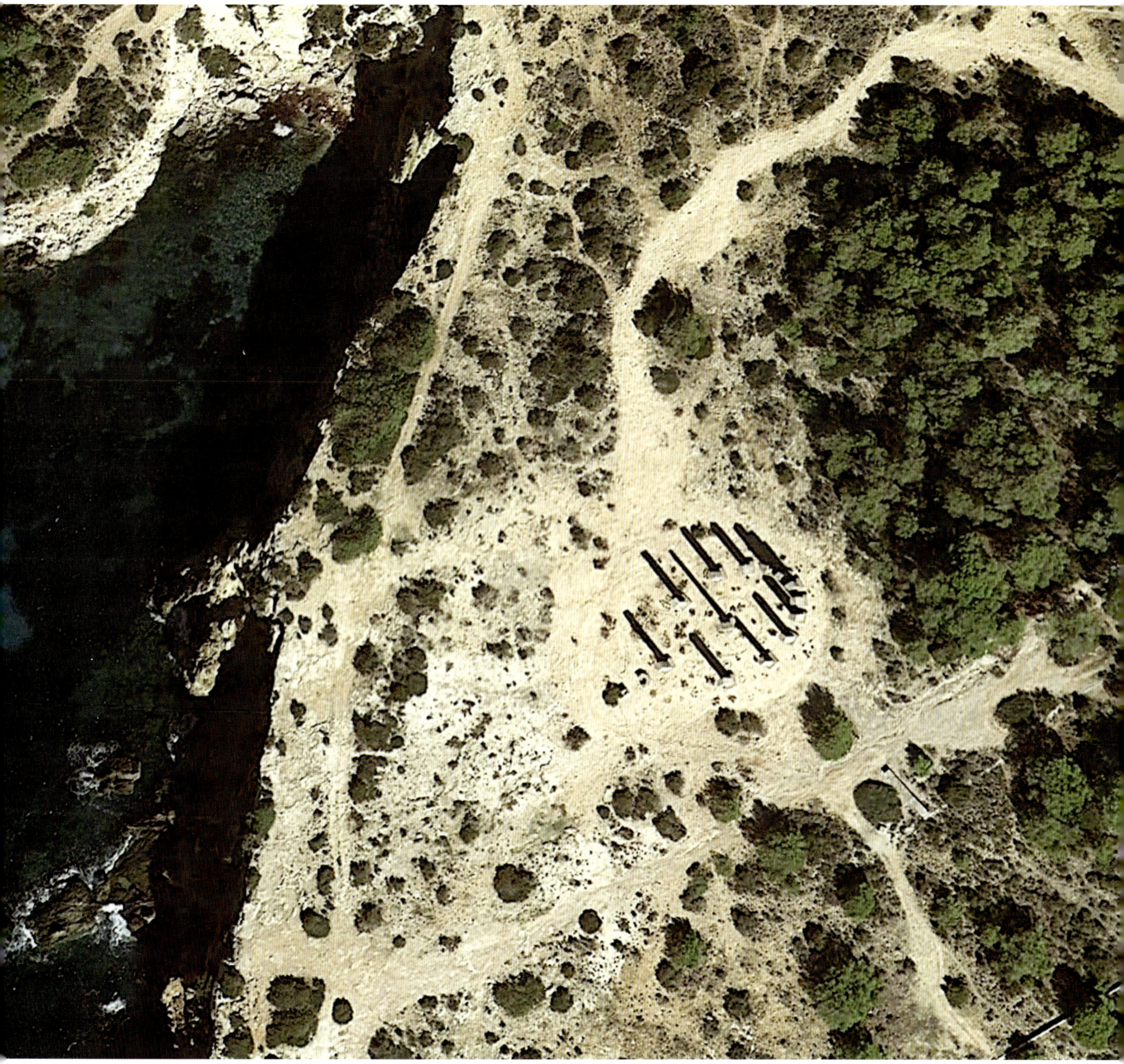

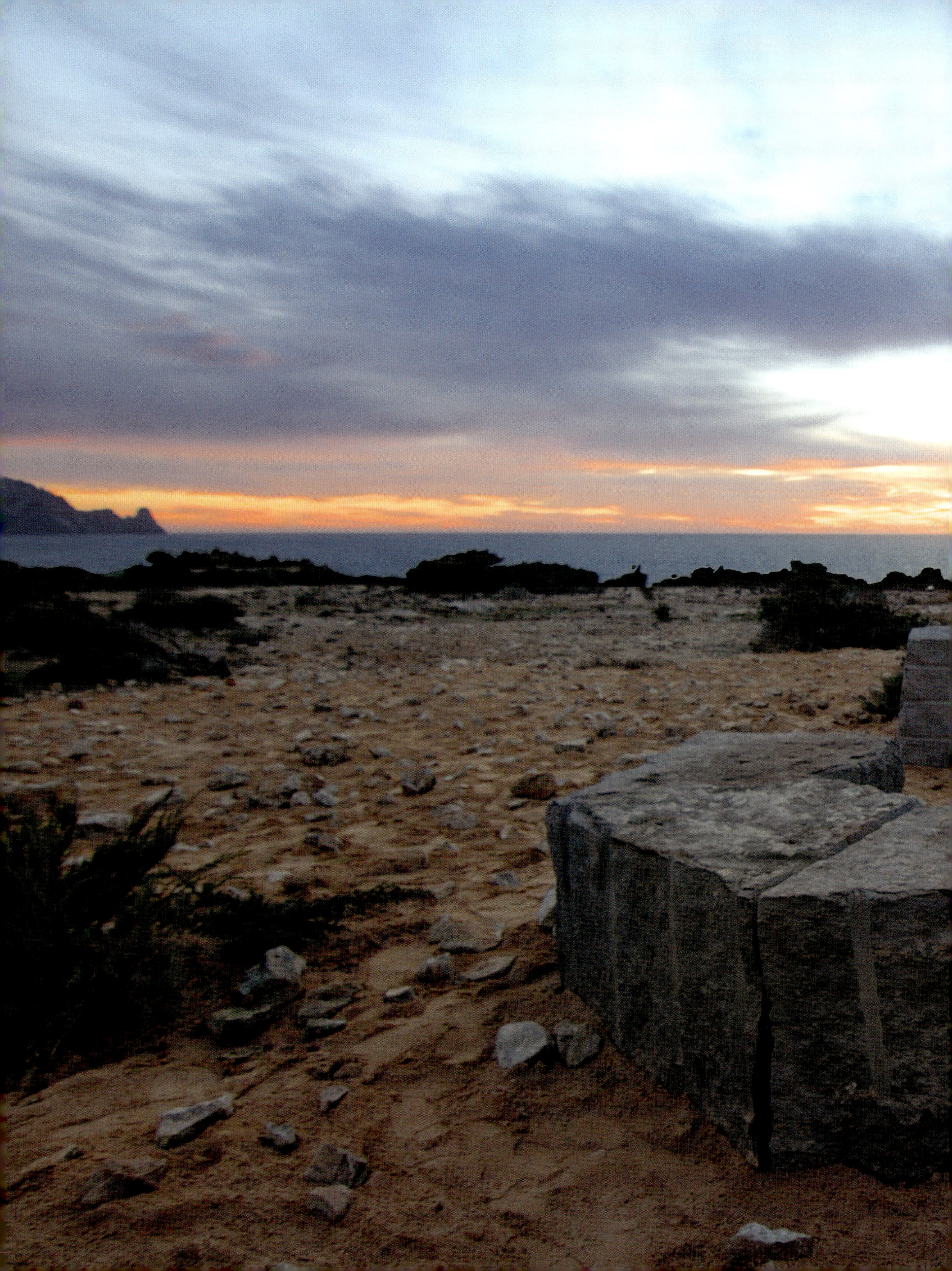

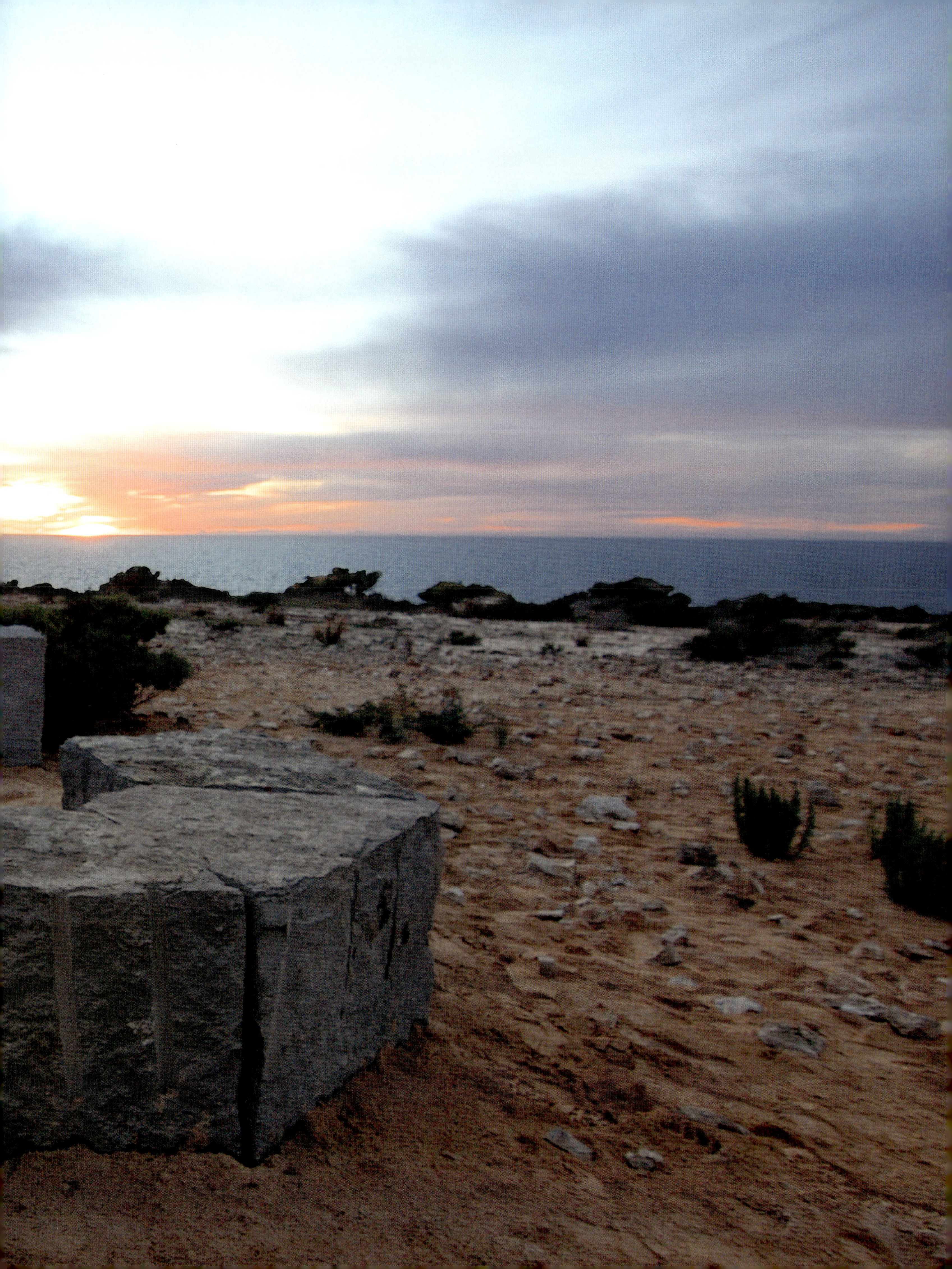

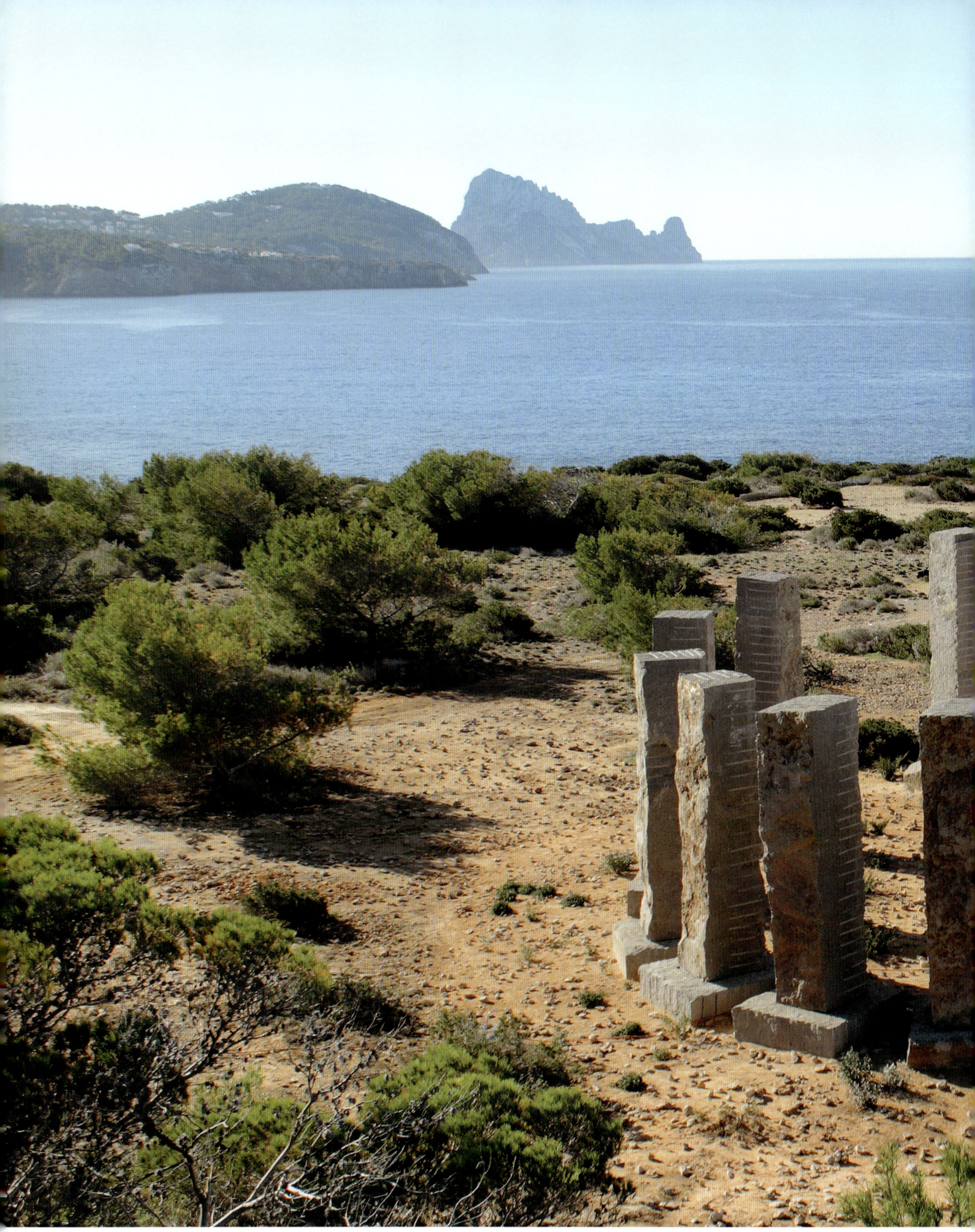

TIME AND SPACE THE SPEED OF LIGHT 2014 / Basalt / 10 × 16 × 29 m (32.8 × 52.5 × 95.14 ft.); commissioned by Guy Laliberté, founder of Cirque du Soleil

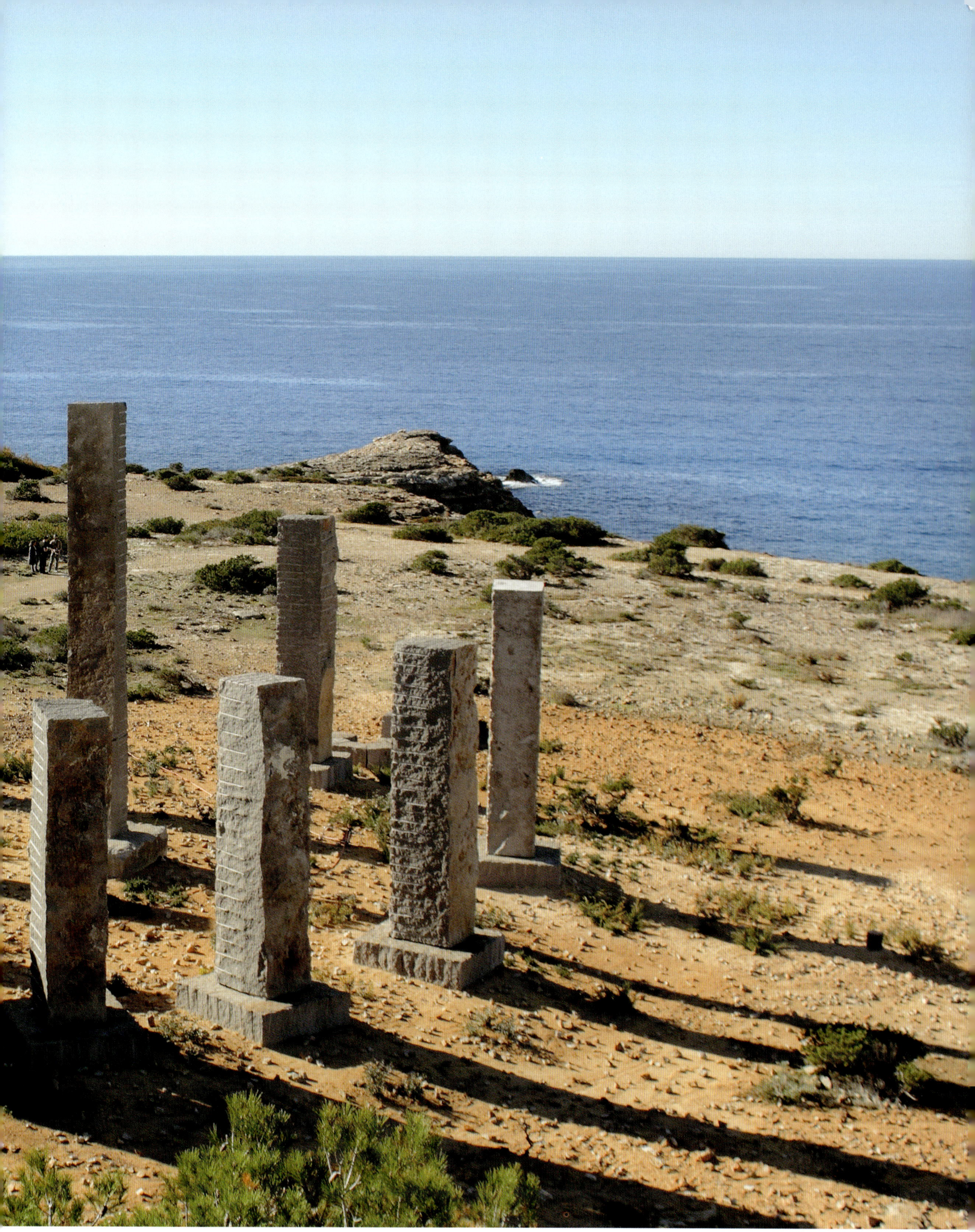

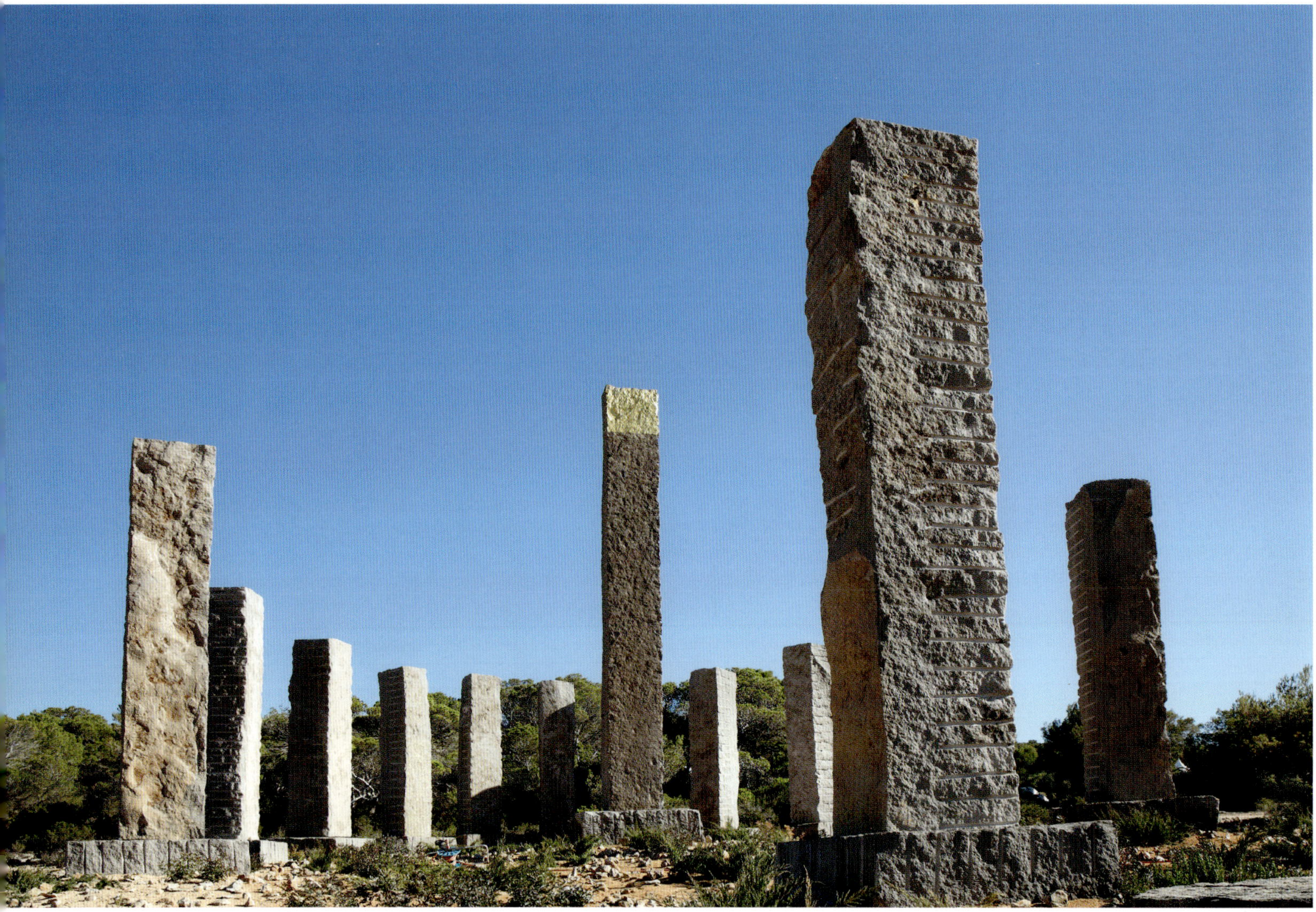

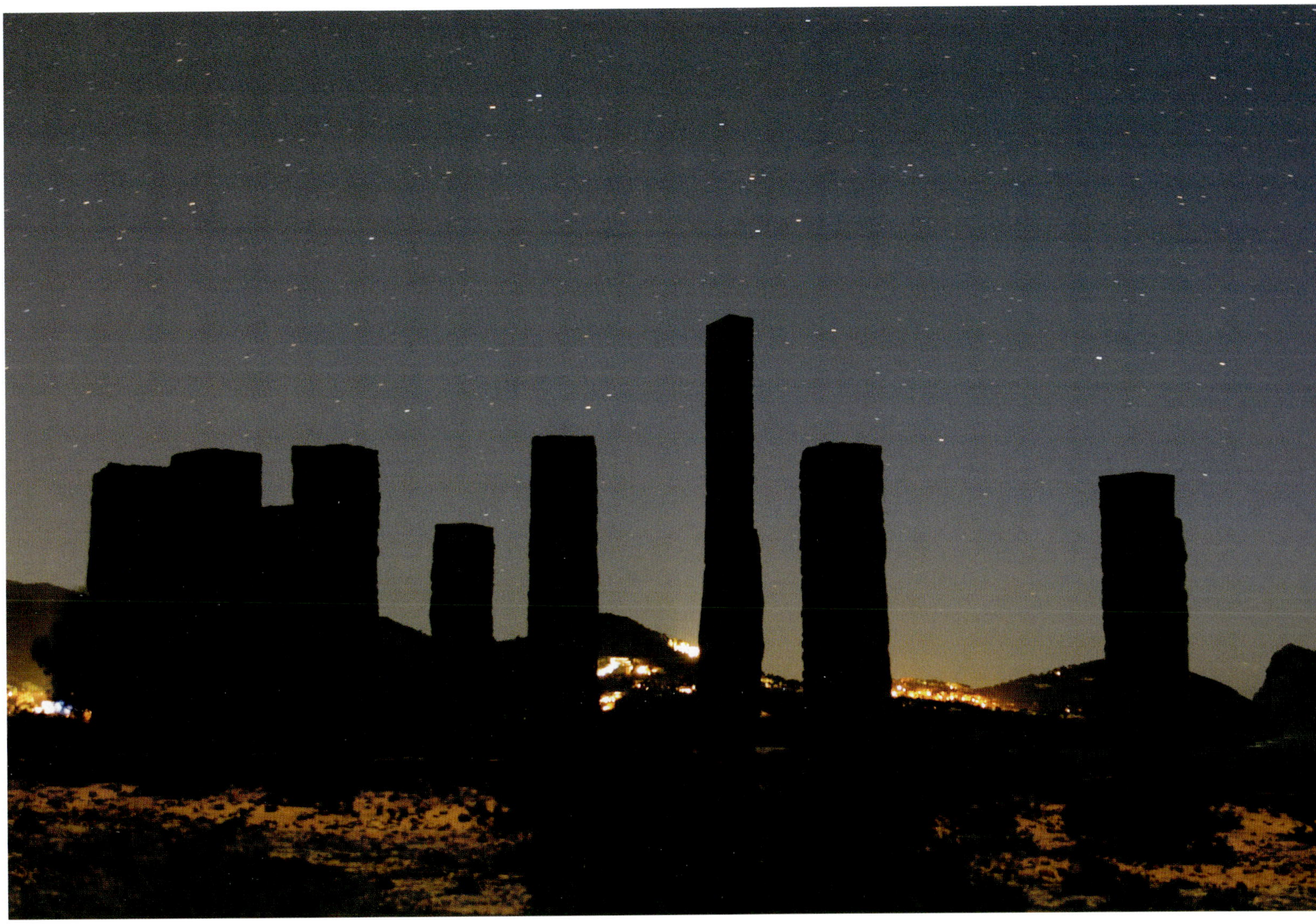

RHYTHMS OF LIFE - LIST OF WORKS

IBIZA, SPAIN, 2014

TIME AND SPACE THE SPEED OF LIGHT

Basalt
10 × 16 × 29 m (32.8 × 52.5 × 95.14 ft.)
N 38°56'50.13", E 1°13'42.19"
pp. 218–19

GREEN RIVER, UTAH, USA, 2013

ELEMENTS

4 columns
Concrete
10.7 × 3.4 × 0.6 m (35 × 11 × 2 ft.)
N 38°59'29.18", W 110°10'2.54"
pp. 212–13

NAMIB DESERT, NAMIBIA, 2012

SACRED FIRE

Stone
14 m (46 ft.) diameter
S 17°14'4.70", E 12°13'23"
pp. 206–7

CAPPADOCIA, TURKEY, 2007–2011

Time and Space Land Art Park: 13 structures, the tallest of which is a basalt arch that weighs 200 metric tons (220.5 tons) and rises to a height of 19.5 m (64 ft.)

A DAY ON EARTH

Basalt, volcanic rock
19.5 × 31.5 × 51 m (64 × 103 × 167 ft.)
N 38°41'22.43", E 34°47'8.52"
pp. 188–89

THE GIFT

Volcanic rock
60 × 60 m (197 × 197 ft.)
N 38°41'14.56", E 34°46'42.76"
pp. 174–75

GRIND

Volcanic rock
100 × 100 m (330 × 330 ft.)
N 38°41'33.50", E 34°47'21.02"
pp. 176–77

LISTEN

Basalt
15 m (52 ft.) arch and amphitheater
N 38°41'21.52", E 34°46'34.58"
pp. 192–93

PREDICTING THE PAST

Basalt
4.2 × 4.7 × 1.1 m (14 × 15.5 × 3.6 ft.)
N 38°41'23.44", E 34°47'23.53"
pp. 186–87

PRESENCE

24 columns abating from 9 m (30 ft.) in height
Basalt
9 × 22 × 38 m (30 × 72 × 125 ft.)
N 38°41'24.04", E 34°47'29.14"
pp. 196–97

RHYTHMS OF LIFE

Volcanic rock
100 × 90 m (330 × 295 ft.)
N 38°41'32.90", E 34°47'50.39"
pp. 172–73

SENTINELS

8 columns
Basalt
6 m (20 ft.)
N 38°41'47.17", E 34°46'49.54"
pp. 194–95

SIREN

Volcanic rock
69 × 100 m (213 × 330 ft.)
N 38°41'36.15", E 34°47'7.49"
pp. 178–79

STRENGTH

Volcanic rock
100 × 50 m (330 × 164 ft.)
N 38°41'41.03", E 34°47'53.31"
pp. 182–83

SUSTENANCE

Volcanic rock
100 × 100 m (330 × 330 ft.)
N 38°41'21.73", E 34°46'48.91"
pp. 180–81

TIME AND SPACE

Basalt
5.3 × 16 × 24 m (18 × 53 × 79 ft.)
N 38°41'29.12", E 34°48'1.34"
pp. 184–85

YESTERDAY TODAY TOMORROW

3 columns
Basalt
6 m (20 ft.)
N 38°41'39.95", E 34°47'46.11"
pp. 190–91

CHYULU HILLS, KENYA, 2010

LION'S PAW

Volcanic rock
2 × 40 × 40 m (6.6 × 131 × 131 ft.)
S 2°50'26.52", E 37°54'38.69"
pp. 146–47

RHYTHMS OF LIFE

Volcanic rock
69 × 69 m (226 × 226 ft.)
S 2°50'27.55", E 37°54'29.64"
pp. 142–43

SHIELD

Volcanic rock
1.5 × 100 × 70 m (5 × 328 × 230 ft.)
S 2°50'28.26", E 37° 54' 35.87"
pp. 148–49

DAKSHIN GANGOTRI GLACIER, ANTARCTICA, 2010

RHYTHMS OF LIFE

Moraine gravel
60 × 60 m (197 × 197 ft.)
S 70°45'58.23", E 11°36'53.28"
pp. 160–61

GREEN RIVER, UTAH, USA, 2010

RATIO
Concrete
13.5 x 13.0 x 2 m (44 x 42 x 6.6 ft.)
N 38°59'28.70", W 110°10'10.83"
pp. 210–11

HIGH TATRAS, SLOVAKIA, 2008

RHYTHMS OF LIFE
Granite
35 x 45 m (115 x 148 ft.)
N 49°08'29.38", E 20°13'52.26"
pp. 130–31

SPIŠSKÝ HRAD, SLOVAKIA, 2008

SACRED
Travertine
100 x 100 m (330 x 330 ft.)
N 49°00'10.28", E 20°46'13.82"
pp. 128–29

JOMSOM, NEPAL, 2008

LABYRINTH
Granite
60 x 60 m (197 x 197 ft.)
N 28°47'26.21", E 83°44'15.77"
pp. 118–19

RHYTHMS OF LIFE
Granite
100 x 100 m (330 x 330 ft.)
N 28°47'27.14", E 83°44'21.49"
pp. 111

POKHARA, NEPAL, 2008

KNOT
Granite
60 x 60 m (197 x 197 ft.)
N 28°10'50.89", E 83°59'47.55"
pp. 120–21

YUCCA VALLEY, CALIFORNIA, USA, 2008

ATLATL
Slate, quartzite
0.75 x 61 m (2.5 x 200 ft.) long
N 34°11'11.57", W 116°26'16.20"
pp. 136–37

RHYTHMS OF LIFE
Slate, quartzite
50 x 50 m (164 x 164 ft.)
N 34°11'09.59", W 116°26'15.61"
pp. 136–37

RAJASTHAN, INDIA, 2007

RATIO
Sandstone
6.5 x 8.5 m (21 x 28 ft.)
N 26°58'01.75", E 75°23'17.08"
pp. 106–7

RHYTHMS OF LIFE
Sandstone
90 x 75 m (295 x 246 ft.)
N 21°34'12.43", E 78°35'51.14"
pp. 104–5

AKUREYRI, ICELAND, 2006

EAGLE
Volcanic rock
100 x 100 m (330 x 330 ft.)
N 65°39'12.68", W 18°08'35.55"
pp. 80–81

RHYTHMS OF LIFE
Volcanic rock
100 x 100 m (330 x 330 ft.)
N 65°39'17.88", W 18°10'10.80"
pp. 76–77

RUNE
Volcanic rock
100 x 100 m (330 x 330 ft.)
N 65°40'20.70", W 18°01'38.07"
pp. 82–83

GOBI DESERT, CHINA, 2006

CAVEMAN
Sandstone
150 x 150 m (492 x 492 ft.)
N 39°42'49.75", E 98°13'34.38"
pp. 98–99

THE MESSENGER
Sandstone
150 x 150 m (492 x 492 ft.)
N 39°43'12.13", E 98°12'49.36"
pp. 90–91, 92–93

RHYTHMS OF LIFE
Sandstone
200 x 200 m (656 x 656 ft.)
N 39°44'03.55", E 98°13'54.84"
pp. 94–95

VICTORIA, AUSTRALIA

In association with the 2006 Commonwealth Games

EASTERN PARK, GEELONG, VICTORIA, 2006

RHYTHMS OF LIFE
Limestone
100 x 90m (330 x 295 ft.)
S 38°08'42.02", E 144°22'57.72"
pp. 72–73

YOU YANGS, VICTORIA, 2006

BUNJIL
Granite
100 x 80 m (330 x 263 ft.)
S 38°07'11.89", E 144°20'20.07"
pp. 74–75

KURUNEGALA, SRI LANKA, 2005

ASCEND
Granite
6.5 x 6.5 m (21 x 21 ft.)
N 7°30'16.77", E 80°22'26.05"
pp. 66–67

PRIDE
Granite
60 × 60 m (197 × 197 ft.)
N 7°29'32.35", E 80°21'34.26"
pp. 60–61

RHYTHMS OF LIFE
Granite
60 × 60 m (197 × 197 ft.)
N 7°29'36.40", E 80°21'23.65"
pp. 56–57

CERRO RICO, BOLIVIA, 2005

CIRCLES
Volcanic rock
100 m (330 ft.) diameter
S 19°34'21.44", W 65°46'28.03"
pp. 50–51

PRESENCE
Volcanic rock
100 × 100 m (330 × 330 ft.)
S 19°33'31.71", W 65°47'23.29"
pp. 50–51

RHYTHMS OF LIFE
Volcanic rock
100 × 100 m (330 × 330 ft.)
S 19°38'49.86", W 65°43'24.02"
pp. 46–47

ATACAMA DESERT, CHILE, 2004

ANCIENT LANGUAGE
Volcanic rock, clay, guano
3 × 80 m (10 × 263 ft.)
S 22°52'20.60", W 68°18'30.48"
pp. 38–39

THE ANCIENTS
Volcanic rock, clay, guano
90 × 90 m (295 × 295 ft.)
S 22°53'20.00", W 68°17'35"
pp. 40–41

RHYTHMS OF LIFE
Volcanic rock, clay, guano
40 × 30 m (131 × 98 ft.)
S 22°54'05.35", W 68°17'42.39"
pp. 36–37

ARAVA DESERT, ISRAEL, 2004

RATIO
Limestone
8 × 32 × 2 m (26 × 105 × 6.5 ft.)
N 30°36'14.08", E 35°11'46.02"
pp. 26–27, 28–29

ARAVA DESERT, ISRAEL, 2003

SLICE
Sandstone
80 × 38 m (263 × 125 ft.)
N 30°36'17.69", E 35°11'39.43"
pp. 22–23

ARAVA DESERT, ISRAEL, 2001

RHYTHMS OF LIFE
Sandstone
4.5 × 29 × 24 m (15 × 95 × 79 ft.)
N 30°36'39.23", E 35°12'20.57"
pp. 20–21

ARAVA DESERT, ISRAEL, 1999

TO LIFE
Sandstone
3.7 × 38 × 33 m (12 × 125 × 108 ft.)
N 30°36'18.96", E 35°11'45.73"
pp. 24–25

ABOUT THE ARTIST

Andrew Rogers is a distinguished and internationally recognized artist. International exhibits are frequent and his critically acclaimed sculptures and photographs are in numerous private and prominent public collections around the world. He receives many international commissions and has created *Rhythms of Life*, the largest contemporary land art undertaking in the world, forming a chain of 51 massive stone sculptures, or geoglyphs, around the globe. The project has involved more than 7,500 people in 16 countries across 7 continents.

SOLO EXHIBITIONS

2015

Andrew Rogers A Retrospective: Maquettes 1996–2015, McClelland Sculpture Park+ Gallery, Langwarrin, VIC, AUS

Come to the Edge, Mossgreen, Melbourne, VIC, AUS

Geoglyphs: The Land Art Projects of Andrew Rogers, Geelong Gallery, Geelong, VIC, AUS

2013

Individuals, Dag Hammarskjöld Plaza, City of New York, NY, USA

Time and Space: Rhythms of Life, Proje4L Elgiz Museum of Contemporary Art, Istanbul, TUR

Winding Path, City of Basel, CHE

A Winding Path: A Search for Truth, Proje4L Elgiz Museum of Contemporary Art, Istanbul, TUR

2012

Andrew Rogers Contemporary Geoglyphs, Nevada Museum of Art, Reno, NV, USA

Andrew Rogers: Rhythms of Life, Wriston Art Galleries, Lawrence University, Appleton, WI, USA

Fire and Understanding, City of Linzhou, Henan Province, CHN

Global Land Art: Projects by Andrew Rogers, Aidekman Arts Center, Tufts University Art Gallery, Medford, MA, USA

Molten Concepts, Mossgreen Gallery, Melbourne, VIC, AUS

Rhythms of Life, Center for Contemporary Arts Santa Fe, NM, USA

Rhythms of Life, Hammer Gallery, Zurich, CHE

2011

Andrew Rogers Time and Space, Art Gallery, Istanbul, TUR

Time and Space: Drawing on the Earth, Momentum, Berlin, DEU

Time and Space, 18th Street Arts Center, Santa Monica, CA, USA

2009

Andrew Rogers: Odysseys and Sitings (1998–2008), White Box Gallery, New York, NY, USA

2008

William Mora Galleries, Richmond, VIC, AUS

2007

Rhythms of Life I–VII, Poprad, SVK

Rhythms of Life I–VII, Akureyri Art Museum, Akureyri, ISL

James Gray Gallery, Santa Monica, CA, USA

William Mora Galleries, Richmond, VIC, AUS

2005

Victorian Arts Centre, Melbourne, VIC, AUS

2004

Grounds for Sculpture, Hamilton, NJ, USA

Gomboc Sculpture Park, Middle Swan, WA, AUS

2003

Deakin University, Geelong, VIC, AUS

2002

Comune di Auronzo di Cadore, Auronzo di Cadore, ITA

Centro per la Cultura e le Arti Visive, Le Venezie, Treviso, ITA

Mudima Foundation, Milan, ITA

1999

Rhythms of Life, Boritzer Gray Hamano, Santa Monica, CA, USA

1998

Rhythms of Life, Embassy of Australia, Washington, DC, USA

1997

Rhythms of Life, Lauraine Diggins Fine Art, Caulfield North, VIC, AUS

1995

Of Freedom and Will, Meridian Gallery, Melbourne, VIC, AUS

1993

Mankind in the Gesture of an Individual, Meridian Gallery, Melbourne, VIC, AUS

SELECTED GROUP EXHIBITIONS

2016

Sculpture Inside, Sculpture by the Sea, Cottesloe, Perth, WA, AUS

2015

From Nature, Gasworks, Albert Park, VIC, AUS

Sculpture by the Sea, Bondi, Sydney, NSW, AUS

2014

Lorne Sculpture Biennale, Lorne, VIC, AUS

McClelland Contemporary Sculpture Survey & Award, Langwarrin, VIC, AUS

Sculpture by the Sea, Cottesloe, Perth, WA, AUS

2013

Art Miami, FL, USA

Art Stage Singapore, SGP

PULSE New York, NY, USA

Sculpture by the Sea, Bondi, Sydney, NSW, AUS

Sydney Contemporary, Sydney, NSW, AUS

2012

McClelland Contemporary Sculpture Survey & Award, Langwarrin, VIC, AUS

Mount Buller Sculpture Award, National Alpine Museum, Mount Buller, VIC, AUS

SCOPE Basel, CHE

The Wynne Prize Exhibition, Art Gallery of New South Wales, Sydney, NSW, AUS

2011

Rassegna Internazionale di Scultura di Roma, Rome, ITA

SCOPE Basel, CHE

Sculpture by the Sea, Bondi, Sydney, NSW, AUS

Sculpture by the Sea, Aarhus, DNK

Elemental, The Sculpture Foundation and the City of West Hollywood, CA USA

2010

Art Basel, Miami, USA

Art Karlsruhe, DEU

SCOPE Basel, CHE

Sculpture by the Sea, Bondi, Sydney, NSW, AUS

2009

In the Beginning: Artists Respond to Genesis, Yeshiva University Museum, New York, NY, USA

Season of Sculpture, Sarasota, FL, USA

2008

Soho Galleries, Sydney, NSW, AUS

2007

Contempora2, Docklands, Melbourne, VIC, AUS

Cornice Art Fair, Venice, ITA

Sculpture by the Sea, Cottesloe, Perth, WA, AUS

Soho Galleries, Sydney, NSW, AUS

2006

Sculpture by the Sea, Sydney, NSW, AUS

Soho Galleries, Sydney, NSW, AUS

2005

McClelland Contemporary Sculpture Survey & Award, Langwarrin, VIC, AUS

Soho Galleries, Sydney, NSW, AUS

2004

Navy Pier Walk, Chicago, IL, USA

Geelong Art Gallery, Geelong, VIC, AUS

Helen Lempriere National Sculpture Award, VIC, AUS

Soho Galleries, Sydney, NSW, AUS

2003

McClelland Survey and Sculpture Park, VIC, AUS

Sculpture by the Sea, Bondi, Sydney, NSW, AUS

Soho Galleries, Sydney, NSW, AUS

2002

Art Singapore: Contemporary Asian Art, SGP

Soho Galleries, Sydney, NSW, AUS

2001

Sofa, Chicago, USA

1998

Grounds for Sculpture, New Jersey, USA

Latrobe University, VIC, AUS

1997

Sculpture at Heidelberg Medical Centre, VIC, AUS

1994

4th Australian Contemporary Art Fair

COLLECTIONS: INTERNATIONAL

SELECTED MUSEUMS, PUBLIC, CORPORATE & PRIVATE

* denotes multiple collections

AUSTRIA

City of Vienna, Nussdorferstrasse, presented on behalf of State of the World Forum by the United States Ambassador to Austria

Estate of Dr. Simon Wiesenthal through the State of the World Forum

BHUTAN

Jigme Lynpo, Minister for Culture, Thimphu

BRAZIL

Curitiba

CANADA

Cirque du Soleil, Montreal

Private Collection, Montreal*

FRANCE

Private Collection, Paris

GERMANY

Private Collection, Berlin*

Private Collection, Cologne

GREECE

Maroussi Multiplex, Athens

ICELAND

Akureyri Museum, Akureyri

Private Collection, Reykjavik

ISRAEL

City of Jerusalem

Ephraim Katzir, Former President of Israel, Jerusalem

Hebrew University of Jerusalem, Jerusalem

International Conference Center, Jerusalem

Israel Museum, Jerusalem

Private Collection, Jerusalem*

Sapir, Arava

Technion – Institute of Technology, Haifa (Artist in Residence)

JAPAN

Australian Consul General's Residence, Kobe

Hokoku Construction, Kobe

MALAYSIA

Private Collection, Kuala Lumpur

MEXICO

Vincente Fox, Former President of Mexico

NEW ZEALAND

Private Collection, Wellington

NIGERIA

Hasfat Abiola, Founder, Kuridat Institute for Nigerian Democracy

PERU

Machu Picchu Municipality, Cusco

RUSSIA

Private Collection, Moscow

SINGAPORE

Golden Village, Marine Square South Multiplex, Singapore

SPAIN

Private Collection

SWITZERLAND

Balexert Cinemas, Geneva
Private Collection, Basel*
Private Collection, Gstaad

TAHITI

Private Collection, Papeete

TAIWAN

Warner Brothers Complex, Taipei

TURKEY

Bank Garanti, Istanbul
Borusan Holdings, Istanbul

UNITED KINGDOM

Private Collection, Kettering
Private Collection, London*
Warner Village Cinemas, Berkshire

UNITED STATES OF AMERICA

California

Google Headquarters, Mountain View
Hall Vineyard Inc., Napa Valley
Private Collection*
State of the World Forum

Colorado

Private Collection, Aspen

Connecticut

Yale University, New Haven

Florida

Private Collection*

Hawaii

Private Collection

Maryland

Private Collection*

Massachusetts

Private Collection
Tufts University Arts Center, Medford

Nevada

Nevada Museum of Art, Reno, Archives

New Jersey

Grounds for Sculpture, Hamilton

New York

Australian Consul General's Residence, New York
Private Collection, New York*
United Jewish Federation, New York

Tennessee

Private Collection

Texas

Hall Arts, Dallas
Hall Park, Frisco
Harwood Center, Dallas
Starplex Cinemas, Dallas, Texas
TLC Development, The Tower, Fort Worth

COLLECTIONS: AUSTRALIA

SELECTED MUSEUMS, PUBLIC, CORPORATE

Art Gallery of New South Wales, Sydney, NSW
The Arts Centre, Melbourne, VIC
Becton Corporation, Port Melbourne, VIC
Bendigo Art Gallery, Bendigo, VIC
Bristol-Myers Squibb, Melbourne, VIC
Canberra International Airport, Canberra, ACT
Castlemaine Art Gallery, Castlemaine, VIC
Central Equity, Melbourne, VIC
Citibank Building, Melbourne, VIC
City of Geelong, Geelong, VIC
City of Melbourne, Jolimont Terrace, East Melbourne, VIC
City of Melbourne, corner of King and Jeffcott Streets, Melbourne, VIC
City Recital Hall, Sydney, NSW
Copelen, South Yarra, VIC
Crown Casino and Entertainment Complex, Southbank, VIC
Elgee Park, Red Hill, VIC
Flinders, VIC
Friends of the Hebrew University of Jerusalem, Melbourne, VIC
Gippsland Art Gallery, Sale, VIC
Heide Museum of Modern Art, Bulleen, VIC
High Court Building, Melbourne, VIC
Horwath Pty Ltd, Melbourne, VIC
Jam Factory, Prahran, VIC
Jewish Museum of Victoria, St Kilda, VIC
Jewish Holocaust Centre, Elsternwick, VIC
King David School, Armadale, VIC
Macquarie University, Sydney, NSW
McClelland Sculpture Sculpture Park+ Gallery, Langwarrin, VIC
Mildura Art Centre, Mildura, VIC
Montalto Vineyard, Mornington Peninsula, VIC
Mornington Peninsula Regional Gallery, Mornington Peninsula, VIC
Mount Scopus Memorial College, Melbourne, VIC
National Alpine Museum of Australia, Mount Buller, VIC
National Foods Headquarters, Docklands, VIC
National Gallery of Australia, Canberra, ACT
National Gallery of Victoria, Melbourne, VIC
Novotel Melbourne Glen Waverley, VIC
Office of the Prime Minister, Parliament House, Canberra, ACT
One East, East Melbourne, VIC
Peter MacCallum Cancer Centre, East Melbourne, VIC
Point Leo Sculpture Park, Merricks, VIC
Springvale Cemetery, Springvale, VIC
Office of the Prime Minister, Commonwealth Parliamentary Offices, Melbourne, VIC
Temple Beth Israel, St Kilda, VIC
University of Melbourne, Parkville, VIC
University of New South Wales, Sydney, NSW
University of Sydney, Sydney, NSW
Village Roadshow Theatres Presentation for the 1998, 1999, and 2002 Melbourne Cup, Australia
Wesley College, Prahran, VIC
Westfield Corporate Ltd., Sydney, NSW
Westpac Banking Corporation, Melbourne VIC
World Square, Sydney, NSW
Yabby Lake Vineyard, Mornington Peninsula, VIC

INVITED LECTURES & WORKSHOPS

International Sculpture Centre Symposium, Auckland, NZL

Art Gallery of New South Wales, Sydney, NSW, AUS

agIdeas, Melbourne, VIC, AUS

Art Month Sydney Creative Collaborations, Sydney, NSW, AUS

Symposium at Sculpture by the Sea, Bondi, Sydney, NSW, AUS

State of the World Forum, San Francisco, CA, USA

Artist in Residence, Institute of Technology at Technion University, Haifa, ISR

The Young Presidents' Organization, Auckland, NZE

SELECTED BIBLIOGRAPHY

PRESS

Daniel Danielson, "Andrew Rogers: Global Awareness," in: *ArtLA* (January 2015): 13–18.

Gareth Harris, "The Ibiza Art Circus," in: *Financial Times* (London), July 31, 2015; http://www.ft.com/cms/s/2/31b24714-2974-11e5-acfb-cbd2e1c81cca.html#slide0.

Bhakthi Puvanenthiran, "Body of Work is All About Thinking Big," in: *The Age* (Melbourne), February 21, 2014, 30.

Umut Eroğlu, "Kader bir seçim mi yoksa bir şans mı?" (Is destiny a choice or luck?), in: *Radikal* (Istanbul), May 6, 2013; http://www.radikal.com.tr/hayat/kader-bir-secim-mi-yoksa-bir-sans-mi-1132304/.

Anthony Haden-Guest, "Think Local, Act Global," in: *The Art Newspaper* 23, no. 251 (November 2013), 64.

Alexandra Ivanoff, "Sculptor Andrew Rogers' Monuments to Truth at Elgiz," in: *Today's Zaman*, April 22, 2013; http://www.todayszaman.com/arts-culture_sculptor-andrew-rogers-monuments-to-truth-at-elgiz_313375.html.

Troy McMullen, "Art Invades the United Nations," in: ABC News (USA), May 8, 2013; http://abcnews.go.com/blogs/headlines/2013/05/art-invades-the-united-nations/.

Elizabeth Fortescue, "Sculptures, Satellites and What It Means to Be Human," in: *The Art Newspaper*, UK, May 21, 2012; http://old.theartnewspaper.com/articles/Sculptures,%20satellites%20and%20what%20it%20means%20to%20be%20human/26482.

Diana Streak, "Striking Pose to Alter Perception of Airport," in: *Canberra Times*, April 3, 2012; http://www.canberratimes.com.au/act-news/striking-pose-to-alter-perception-of-airport-20120402-1w931.html.

James Grayson Trulove, "Seen from Afar," in: *Landscape Architecture Magazine* 102, no. 1 (January 2012), 102–115.

Anna Waldmann, "Reclaimed by the Land: Andrew Rogers's *Time and Space*," in: *Art & Australia* 46, no. 3 (March 2012), 412–413.

Lilly Wei, "Rome Biennale: International Exhibition of Sculpture," in: *Sculpture* 31, no. 2 (March 2012), 75–76.

"'Andrew Rogers: Time and Space' on View at the 18th Street Arts Center," in: *Art Knowledge News*, April 27, 2011.

"Australian Artist Andrew Rogers Completes the Arch of Memory, the World's Largest Basalt Arch," in: *Art Daily*, July 29, 2011; http://artdaily.com/news/49437/Australian-Artist-Andrew-Rogers-Completes-the-Arch-of-Memory--the-World-s-Largest-Basalt-Arch-#.VrUCZGg4GUk.

Viviana Bucarelli, "Rogers, il Ritmo della Vitain tonnellate di pietra," in: *La Stampa* (Turin), November 8, 2011; http://www.lastampa.it/2011/11/08/cultura/arte/rogers-il-ritmo-della-vitain-tonnellate-di-pietra-HTatkpLyoQnORm6L5J150K/pagina.html.

Shana Nys Dambrot, "Andrew Rogers, Land Artist: Now Playing on a Continent Near You," in: *LA Weekly*, May 13, 2011; http://www.laweekly.com/arts/andrew-rogers-land-artist-now-playing-on-a-continent-near-you-2372542.

David Ebony, "Roman Holiday: The Sculpture Biennial That Might Have Been, and More," in: *Art in America*, July 7, 2011; http://www.artinamericamagazine.com/news-features/news/rome-suplture-biennial-macro/.

Gareth Harris, "Land Art Writ Large: Art Park in Cappadocia Set to Open," in: *The Art Newspaper* 20, no. 224 (May 2011), 9.

Jeremy Hunt, "Andrew Rogers: Time and Space—A Land Art Park in Cappadocia, Turkey," in: *Art and Architecture Journal*, July 26, 2011; https://aajpress.wordpress.com/2011/07/26/andrew-rogers-time-and-space-a-land-art-park-in-cappadocia-turkey/.

Tom Wharton, "In Green River, a Touch of the Divine," in: *Salt Lake Tribune*, May 23, 2011, 1.

Leonard Janiszewski, "Sculpture Park," in: *Macquarie Matters* (Winter 2011), 23.

"Jongleur der Superlative," in: *Monopol*, August 2011; http://www.monopol-magazin.de/jongleur-der-superlative.

Melanie Magruder, "Andrew Rogers' Monumental *Rhythms of Life* at 18th Street Art Center," in: *The LookOut*, May 18, 2011; http://www.surfsantamonica.com/ssm_site/the_lookout/news/News-2011/May-2011/05_18_2011_Andrew_Rogers_Monumental%20Rhythm_of_Life.htm.

Susan Moore, "Out of the Ordinary," in: *The Spectator*, June 4, 2011; http://www.spectator.co.uk/2011/06/out-of-the-ordinary-3/.

Liza Power, "Sculpture on a Grand Scale," in: *The Age* (Melbourne), January 22, 2011; http://www.theage.com.au/entertainment/art-and-design/sculpture-on-a-grand-scale-20110121-1a024.html.

Claudia Steinberg, "Rekordverdächtig" (Record-breaking), in: *Kunstzeitung* October 31, 2011, 16.

Karin Tuxen-Bettman, "Explore Land Art with Google Earth," in: *Google Maps*, August 2, 2011; http://google-latlong.blogspot.com/2011/08/explore-land-art-with-google-earth.html.

Hatice Utkan, "Discovering the Rhythms of Life in Cappadocia's Stones," in: *Hurriyet Daily News* (Istanbul), September 20, 2011.

Andrea R. Vaucher, "Andrew Rogers: Rhythms of Life on Seven Continents," in: *Huffington Post*, October 5, 2011; http://www.huffingtonpost.com/andrea-r-vaucher/andrew-rogers-rhythms-of-_b_994975.html.

Richard Warren, "SCOPE for the Best," in: *Identity*, no. 96 (September 2011), 22–26.

Lilly Wei, "Andrew Rogers's Turkish Earthworks," in: *Art in America*, December 5, 2011; http://www.artinamericamagazine.com/news-features/news/andrew-rogers/.

"Andrew Rogers: Rhythms of Life," in: *Istanbul Contemporary Etc*, March–May 2010, 4.

Jenny Brown, "You Yangs Link to a World of Sculpture," in: *The Age Newspaper*, April 17, 2010, 12.

"Land Art in Cappadocia," in: *Skylife* (May 2010); http://www.skylife.com/en/2010-05/land-art-in-cappadocia.

Penny Modra, "The Winding Path," in: *The Age Newspaper*, September 8, 2010, 16.

Chris Wright, "Boulder and the Beautiful," in: *Qantas, The Australian Way* Magazine, August 2010, 74–76.

Natalia Nevskaya, "Рисунки На Континентах" (Figures on the continent), in: *Luxury Magazine* (Russia) 4 (July–August, 2010), 114.

Ximena Jordan "Rhythms of Life in Chile," in: *Chile Magazine*, November 2010, 26–27.

Ivan Watson, "The Sculpture Park You Can See from Space," in: *CNN*, July 7, 2010; http://www.cnn.com/2010/WORLD/meast/07/07/turkey.cappadocia.sculpture.park/.

Chris Wright, "Giants over Time and Space," in: *Asian Geographic* (October 2010); http://www.chriswrightmedia.com/asian-geographic-giants-over-time-and-space/.

David Ebony, "Earthly Homage," in: *Art in America* (October 2009), 108–111.

"Australian Sculptor in Cappadocia Once Again," in: *Hurriyet Daily News* (Istanbul), May 19, 2009; http://www.hurriyet.com.tr/australian-sculptor-in-cappadocia-once-again-11680942.

Raquel Laneri, "Carving Up the Land," in: *Forbes*, May 13, 2009; http://www.forbes.com/2009/05/13/andrew-rogers-geoglyphs-opinions-book-review-land-art.html.

Ximena Jordan, "Ritmos de Vida," in: *Tell Magazine* (June 2009), 26–30.

Ken Scarlett, "Geoglyphs Spanning the Globe," in: *Sculpture* 28, no. 10 (December 2009), 56–61.

Carol Strickland, "The 'Land Art' of Andrew Rogers," in: *Christian Science Monitor*, May 12, 2009; http://www.csmonitor.com/The-Culture/Arts/2009/0512/p17s01-algn.html.

Peter Webster, "Sculptor as Alchemist," in: *Interior Design* 80, no. 10 (August 2009), 48.

"Australian sculptor Andrew Rogers laid the geoglyph foundation stone which will be located under the Spissky Hrad," in: *Podtatranské Noviny* (Poprad), May 27, 2008, 1.

Evrim Altuğ, "Kâinata taşlarla fisildayan adam" (The man who whispers to the universe with stones), in: *Sabah* (Istanbul), September 28, 2007; http://arsiv.kultur.sabah.com.tr/2007/09/28/ser112-10320-20070928-103.html.

"Potosi has Stone Sculptures Visible only from the Air" "Land Art Potosi, Bolivia," in: *La Prensa* (La Paz), December 13, 2006.

Wei Ming, "Andrew Rogers and the Rhythms of Life," in: *Sculpture Magazine of China Sculptors Association* (2006), 61–63.

Ian Findlay, "Pushing Limits: Andrew Rogers," in: *World Sculpture News* 11, no. 2 (Spring 2005), 38–43.

Jonathan Goodman, "Andrew Rogers at Ground for Sculpture," in: *Art in America* 93, no. 6 (June/July 2005), 190.

Andrew Rogers, "Life's Rhythms: Andrew Rogers," in: *World Sculpture News* 10, no. 4 (Autumn 2004), 59-61.

Ken Scarlett, "Andrew Rogers and the Rhythms of Life," in: *Sculpture* 23, no. 3 (April 2004), 54–59.

Books, "Rhythms of Life: The Art of Andrew Rogers by Ken Scarlett," in: *World Sculpture News* 9, no. 4 (Autumn 2003), 53–54.

"On Record," in: *Sculpture* 22, no. 1 (January/February 2003).

Daniela Palazoli, "Australia," in: *Kult* (March 2002).

Meir Ronnen, "Another Geoglyph in the Arava," in: *Jerusalem Post*, February 1 and February 8, 2002, B14.

MULTIMEDIA

Google Cultural Institute Art Project Partnership, 2016

Monumental Vision, ten 30-minute episodes, Producer, Guiding Light Productions. National Geographic Television Channels, 2015

Mega Art, three 60-minute episodes, Producer, Guiding Light Productions, National Geographic Television Channels, 2015

Sacred Fire, 30-minute documentary, Producer, CM Film Productions, National Geographic Television Channels, 2015

First alignment of the setting sun on the winter solstice with the sculpture *Time and Space the Speed of Light*, Ibiza, ESP, 2014; https://www.youtube.com/watch?v=pdf5Ts1GkdU&feature=youtu.be

Mega Art, television series Producer, Guiding Light Productions, Sky Arts, three 60-minute episodes, 2014

Monumental Vision, Gem Television Series, Middle East and United Kingdom, ten 30-minute episodes, 2013

Mega Art, Sky TV, United Kingdom and Ireland: Television series, three 60-minute episodes, 2012

Arte TV, Germany, *Earth Art*, 2011

CNN *Inside the Middle East*, "The Sculpture Park You Can See from Space," reporter Ivan Watson, July 2010

CBS *Sunday Morning*, "The Big Picture," producer Anthony Laudato, April 2009

PBS *Sunday Arts Profile*, "Andrew Rogers," producer Bob Morris, October 2009

Reuters News, "The World's Largest Land Art Project," reporter Sarah Toms, April 2009

USA Ovation TV Series, *Monumental Vision*, ten 30-minute episodes, 2009

Monumental Vision, ABC Television Series, eight 30-minute episodes, 2008

Monumental Vision, Canadian Television Series: three 30-minute episodes, 2008

Monumental Vision, Discovery International: television series, three 30-minute episodes, 2008

Monumental Vision, ABC Television Series: five 30-minute episodes, 2007

Monumental Vision, Discovery International: Television series, three 30-minute episodes, 2007

CNN *Inside the Middle East*, "Geoglyphs in the Arava Desert, Israel," producer Michael Schwartz, 2005

BOOKS

Phoebe Hoban and Andrew Rogers, *White Desert*. Dandenong South, VIC: Courtney Colour Graphics, 2016 (ISBN 978-0-9943685-3-9)

Phoebe Hoban and Andrew Rogers, *Sacred Fire*. Dandenong South, VIC: Courtney Colour Graphics, 2016 (ISBN 978-0-9943685-1-5).

Phoebe Hoban, "Portal to another dimension," in *Time and Space*. Dandenong South, VIC: Courtney Colour Graphics, 2015 (ISBN 978-0-9943685-4-6).

Frances Lindsay, "Andrew Rogers: Breaking the Mold," in *FORMS III*. Dandenong South, VIC: Courtney Colour Graphics, 2015 (ISBN 978-0-9943685-2-2).

Phoebe Hoban and Andrew Rogers, *Shield: Rhythms of Life, Chyulu Hills, Kenya 2010*. Melbourne: Bond Colour, 2015 (ISBN 978-0-9943685-0-8).

Silvia Langen, *Outdoor Art: Extraordinary Sculpture Parks and Art in Nature*. Munich: Prestel, 2015 (ISBN 978-3-7913-8118-3).

Helen Lee, ed., *Urban Landscape Sculpture I*. Hong Kong: Hi Design International Publishing, 2014.

Andrew Rogers and David Elliott, *Time and Space: Cappadocia, Turkey, 2007–2011*. Melbourne: Bond Colour, 2013 (ISBN 978-0-9577671-5-7).

Andrew Rogers and Robert Lindsay, *Forms II*. Melbourne: Bond Colour, 2012 (ISBN 978-0-9577671-6-4).

Chris van Uffelen, *500× Art in Public*. Salenstein: Braun Publishing, 2012 (ISBN 978-3-03768-098-8).

Eleanor Heartney and Andrew Rogers, *Andrew Rogers Geoglyphs, Rhythms of Life*. Milan: Edizioni Charta, 2009 (ISBN 978-88-8158-712-4).

Kate Armstrong, Maric Vesna, and Andy Symington, *Bolivia*, 6th ed. Footscray, VIC: Lonely Planet Publications, 2007, 262.

Andrew Rogers and Chris McAuliffe, *Forms*. 2005 (ISBN 0-9577671-3-7).

Ken Scarlett, *Elgee Park: Sculpture in Landscape*. Melbourne: Macmillan Art Publishing, 2004 (ISBN 1-875-832-32-0).

Ken Scarlett, *Rhythms of Life: The Art of Andrew Rogers*. Melbourne: Macmillan Art Publishing, 2003 (ISBN: 1-876-832-61-4).

CATALOGUES

Andrew Rogers and Robert Lindsay. *Andrew Rogers: A Retrospective: Maquettes 1996–2015*. Langwarrin, VIC: McClelland Sculpture Park+Gallery, 2015 (ISBN 978-0-9874010-6-9).

Andrew Rogers and Frances Lindsay. *Come to the Edge*. Armadale, VIC: Victoria Mossgreen Gallery, 2015 (ISBN 978-0-9577671-8-8).

Andrew Rogers and Callum Reid. *Andrew Rogers: Molten Concepts*. South Yarra: Mossgreen Gallery, 2012.

Andrew Rogers and Lilly Wei. *Weightless*. Richmond, VIC: William Mora Galleries, 2007 (ISBN 0-9577671-4-5).

Andrew Rogers, Hannes Sigurđsson, and Listasafnið á Akureyri. *Rhythms of Life I–VII*. Akureyri, ISL: Akureyri Art Museum, 2007 (ISBN 978-9979-9632-7-1).

Daniel Thomas, Simon Turner, and Ken Scarlett. *Rhythms of Life II*. Milan: Mudima Foundazione, 2002.

Andrew Rogers, *Rhythms of Life II*. North Caulfield, VIC: Lauraine Diggins Fine Art Pty. Ltd., 2000.

Andrew Rogers, *Pillars of Witness*. Elsternwick, VIC: Hadasa & Szymon Rosenbaum Holocaust Research Centre, 1999 (ISBN 0-646-38229-2).

Andrew, Rogers, *Rhythms of Life*. North Caulfield, VIC: Lauraine Diggins Fine Art, 1997.

Of Freedom and Will. Fitzroy, VIC: Meridian Gallery, 1995.

Deidre O'Driscoll, *Andrew Rogers: Mankind in the Gesture of an Individual*. Fitzroy, VIC: Meridian Gallery, 1993.

www.andrewrogers.org

ACKNOWLEDGMENTS

I was already fascinated by Andrew Rogers's global art project *Rhythms of Life* within the context of my book *Outdoor Art: Outstanding Sculpture Parks and Art in Nature* (Prestel, June 2015). It was the first book to focus on sculpture parks that pursue a distinct theme. I was all the more delighted to have the opportunity to present Andrew Rogers's unique land art project in a separate book and to immerse myself even deeper into his complex concept for *Rhythms of Life*. My gratitude goes to the artist for his trust in me as an author as well as for his profound assistance, without which I could not have documented his *Rhythms of Life*. Katharina Haderer from Prestel Verlag was immediately enthusiastic about my undertaking, as was Iris Forster, who tended to the coordination of the publication down to the last detail and always had good advice on hand for dealing with any problems that came up. Copy editor Keonaona Peterson and Debbie Chang also provided important suggestions for the book. Readers can dip into my world of thought thanks to Rebecca van Dyck's sensitive translation of the texts. Finally, Katrin Kleinschrot ensured that the book was not only a pleasure to read, but to leaf through and marvel at, and Andrea Cobré prudently supervised the production of the same. I would like to extend my wholehearted thanks to all of you for your wonderful cooperation and your personal and always highly professional commitment, which cannot necessarily be taken for granted.

SILVIA LANGEN

A member of Verlagsgruppe Random House GmbH
Neumarkter Strasse 28 · 81673 Munich

Prestel Publishing Ltd.
14-17 Wells Street
London W1T 3PD

Prestel Publishing
900 Broadway, Suite 603
New York, NY 10003

Library of Congress Control Number: 2016938557
A CIP catalogue record for this book is available from the British Library.

EDITORIAL DIRECTION Iris Forster
COPYEDITING Keonaona Peterson
DESIGN AND LAYOUT Karin Hauptmann, Katrin Kleinschrot, Marion Köster
PRODUCTION MANAGEMENT Andrea Cobré
SEPARATIONS Repro-Ludwig, Zell am See
PRINTING AND BINDING DZS Grafik, Slovenija
TYPEFACE Granjon and Neutraface
PAPER 170 g Profisilk

MIX
Paper from responsible sources
FSC® C106600

Verlagsgruppe Random House FSC® N001967

Printed in Slovenija

ISBN 978-3-7913-5540-5

www.prestel.com